COLORBLIND
SHAKESPEARE

The Droeshout engraving of Denzel Washington.

COLORBLIND SHAKESPEARE

New Perspectives on Race and Performance

EDITED BY

AYANNA THOMPSON

Routledge
Taylor & Francis Group
New York   London

Routledge is an imprint of the
Taylor & Francis Group, an informa business

Routledge
Taylor & Francis Group
270 Madison Avenue
New York, NY 10016

Routledge
Taylor & Francis Group
2 Park Square
Milton Park, Abingdon
Oxon OX14 4RN

© 2006 by Taylor & Francis Group, LLC
Routledge is an imprint of Taylor & Francis Group, an Informa business

Printed in the United States of America on acid-free paper
10 9 8 7 6 5 4 3 2 1

International Standard Book Number-10: 0-415-97802-5 (Softcover) 0-415-97801-7 (Hardcover)
International Standard Book Number-13: 978-0-415-97802-6 (Softcover) 978-0-415-97801-9 (Hardcover)

Library of Congress Cataloging-in-Publication Data

Colorblind Shakespeare : new perspectives on race and performance / edited by
Ayanna Thompson.
    p. cm.
Includes bibliographical references and index.
ISBN 0-415-97801-7 -- ISBN 0-415-97802-5 (pbk.)
    1. Shakespeare, William, 1564-1616--Dramatic production. 2. Shakespeare, William, 1564-1616--Stage history. 3. Theater--Casting. 4. Race in literature. I. Thompson, Ayanna, 1972-

PR3091.C63 2006
792.9'5--dc22   2006005526

Visit the Taylor & Francis Web site at
http://www.taylorandfrancis.com

and the Routledge Web site at
http://www.routledge-ny.com

This book is dedicated to my mother,
Nina Parish,
who first taught me the value of colorblindness.

Contents

Part III: Future Possibilities/Future Directions

Illustrations

Acknowledgments

This project began with a comment made over the Routledge book stall at the 2004 Shakespeare Association of America Conference in New Orleans. As I was thumbing through the books, I said to a friend that there should be a collection about the use of colorblind casting in Shakespearean productions. Luckily, Matthew Byrnie, an editor at Routledge, was eavesdropping and encouraged me to put such a collection together. So, the first person who needs to be acknowledged is Matt for being the perfect sounding board and editor. Without his encouragement, this collection literally would not exist. Since the collection's inception, there have been many people who have also encouraged, challenged, and inspired me. The first and foremost are my fabulously gifted and incredibly generous Renaissance colleagues here at Arizona State University: Curtis Perry, Cora Fox, and Ian Moulton. Curtis, Cora, and Ian both heard and read early versions of the volume's introduction, and they offered salient comments and critiques. Their intellectual generosity has been overwhelming, and I will be forever grateful. I would also like to thank my colleague James Blasingame, Jr. for arranging for me to give a lecture on the topic in the English Department's Faculty Lecture Series. I am still humbled thinking about the amazing turn out for that lecture, and I know that a large part of its success stemmed from Jim's support. At that lecture, Neal Lester and Maureen Daly Goggin both asked questions about the constructed nature of notions of "talent" that really challenged my theoretical approach. Their insights helped me reconceptualize the direction for the collection. I also want to thank Bryan Reynolds for putting me in touch with one of the contributors. He and I have always had fruitful conversations at conferences, and I am grateful for his friendship. In the final stages of the project, my graduate research assistant, Carol Mejia-LaPerle, was invaluable. She helped me make these wonderful essays hang together as a collection, and I am ever so grateful for her attention to detail. Maria Goveas in Film and Media Studies helped me technically by capturing and improving film stills. Many of the fascinating images in this collection would not have appeared without her good-natured guidance and support. Bruce Matsunaga in the English Department helped create the "Droeshout engraving of Denzel." I simply described what I wanted, and he brought it to "life." I appreciate the time and effort he put into making that image look both natural and strange. That, I think, is the heart of *Colorblind Shakespeare*. My family, Derek and Dashiell Thompson, deserves the lion's share of thanks and gratitude, however. They kept the home fires burning when I had to put in extra hours to complete this project, and they rarely complained. Derek's intellectual and spiritual energy is inspiring, and his love and warmth always keep me going. And little Dashiell's sense of humor keeps me smiling! So much of what I do stems from a desire to make the world a better place for him. I love you both!

N.B.: All citations from Shakespeare in this collection are taken from the Norton anthology. *The Norton Shakespeare: Based on the Oxford Edition*, ed. Stephen Greenblatt, et. al. (New York: W. W. Norton & Company, 1997).

Foreword

ANIA LOOMBA

Everyone has a story or two about "colorblindness." In 1991, I moved from New Delhi to Tulsa, Oklahoma. The move was a traumatic experience for my eleven-year-old son: nothing in his relatively sheltered middle-class existence in India had prepared him for entering the Tulsa public school system, where he was rejected by both white and black students as being neither one nor the other. He was also regularly harassed for not believing in Jesus, accused of having body odor, and baited for preferring India to the United States. The one bright spot was his friend Sam, who also happened to live in our neighborhood. Sam seemed to take effortlessly to our household; he enjoyed a variety of Indian foods, which he often ate in the customary manner, as we did, with our fingers, squatting on the floor as he ate (not because that is an Indian custom, but because we took a while to acquire furniture!), and he did all this without remarking on its novelty. I told his father that I was impressed by Sam's easy cosmopolitanism, unusual in any eleven-year-old, but especially in one who had led a fairly circumscribed existence. His father then narrated an extraordinary story. Some time earlier, Sam had overheard him say that he wished someone like Jesse Jackson could become the president of the United States. "Why is that?" inquired young Sam. "Because," his father replied, "I think it would be great for this country to have a black president." "But," asked his son, "how will people *know* he's black?" The father looked at his son, wondering if he was pulling his leg, and realized that, in this magic moment, his son was colorblind.

At least this is the way the story was told. Through the years, it has come back a hundred times to me and my family, if only as a somewhat utopian counterpoint to other iterations of colorblindness. Last semester, for example, a student told me that she had worked with a professor who insisted that he was colorblind and simply could not see any difference between people of different ethnicities or nationalities. It was hardly surprising that this conversation happened after a particularly lively but difficult session on contemporary race relations, during which the participants had also acknowledged that it is not easy to create the space for such discussions in the classroom. Of course, such a session, and in fact many of the classes I offer in early modern race studies or postcolonial studies, would simply be unnecessary if we all insisted on our colorblindness — or if we believed that to focus on racial difference is necessarily to entrench it further, or that to discuss it is to perpetuate it; or, as some critics allege, that to study its histories, its formations, and its complicated workings out in our lives is to essentialize it.[1] As Lisa Anderson trenchantly asks in this volume: "What, exactly, does it mean for race not to matter?"

Colorblind Shakespeare forces us to think about this question in all its complexity. This timely (actually, long overdue) collection makes it clear that to discuss colorblind casting in Shakespeare is necessarily to tread the difficult places where questions of representation and theatrical practice intersect with the politics of multiculturalism and antiracism. The theatre is a place that allows — indeed, demands — the transformation of identities, but in actual practice such transformations have been carefully policed, especially with regard to Shakespeare's plays. In their original context, Shakespearean performances sanctioned one particular kind of racial transformation — blackface — which was, of course, not colorblind at all, although at least one critic has argued that precisely because black characters were played by white actors, blackness could sometimes be imagined in a *more* positive way than if real black people were representing themselves (see Callaghan). Traditions of blacking up in Renaissance England (not only on the public stages but in private performances, masques, mayoral shows, and morris dancing) are often unyoked from the traditions of blackface minstrelsy in the United States, both by scholars and by the popular press. Thus, for example, a recent CNN report that the British Royal Opera House has discontinued the practice of blackface does not mention the early modern history of this practice, noting simply, "'Blacking up' was common in the United States for about 100 years, from the first minstrel shows in the 1840s until the National Association for the Advancement of Colored People, a leading rights group in the United States, began criticizing the practice in the 1940s. In Britain, 'The Black and White Minstrel Show,' a popular musical variety show featuring blackface actors, was on TV until 1978" (CNN). However, in the British press, several actors who had once blacked up in Shakespearean roles were interviewed, and they defended blackface on the grounds of the necessary *difference* between the actor's identity and those of the character being played — in short, on the grounds of the necessity of colorblind casting:

> Sir Michael Gambon, who blacked up to play Othello in the eighties, said:
> "It was borderline then and I wouldn't be allowed to now, although I had
> letters from a lot of black actors who said, 'Go ahead'. It's all nonsense: it's
> a bit like saying to play Macbeth you have to be a murderer." (Smith)

Of course, such philosophies were never evoked to allow black actors to expand their repertoire.[2] Because black actors, then and for many centuries afterward, were not allowed to play major Shakespearean roles of *any* color, seemingly contradictory demands — that only blacks should play black characters in Shakespeare, and that black and other nonwhite actors should be allowed to play *all* Shakespearean characters — could *both* be voiced in the interest of wrenching open the closed and elite world of Shakespearean performance. In many non-Western societies, by contrast, a species of colorblind casting of Shakespearean plays is more in evidence, but casting practices are still shaped by social hierarchies. In India, for example, all Shakespearean characters can be and are played by nonwhites, but directors discriminate on the basis of caste, class, and/or region. This point was recently made via an adaptation of *Othello* in New Delhi, which exposed dominant prejudices against people who cannot speak the mainstream languages or those who come from the marginalized tribal areas of India (see Loomba).

Because of the global cultural capital of Shakespeare, people disenfranchised on varied grounds have felt empowered by laying claim to his plays. At the same time, of course, such claims reinforce the authority of dominant culture in all sorts of ways, suggesting that Shakespeare and other Western works are indeed of universal relevance or value and making difficult a critique of their ideologies and prejudices. This doubleness is most poignantly explored in this volume by Antonio Ocampo-Guzman, who writes of ways in which he felt both enabled and disabled by performing Shakespeare. It is hardly surprising that while many black actors have demanded the right to play the lead character in *Othello* and have used the role to advance antiracist struggles, some have argued that blacks should *not* play a role that can be seen as the product of a white imagination. As Hugh Quarshie has famously argued, "When a black actor plays a role written for a white actor in black make-up and for a predominantly white audience, does he not encourage the white way, or rather the wrong way, of looking at black men. ... Of all the parts in the canon, perhaps Othello is the one which should not be played by a black actor" (Quarshie, 5). It is equally telling to note how establishment responses to nontraditional casting have changed in the past couple of decades. The anger such casting once aroused in certain quarters speaks for itself. When, twenty years ago, Hugh Quarshie himself had celebrated the idea of a black actor playing Enobarbus as a "coup," one British commentator retorted: "Too true, Hugh. It will also be a coup when played by a Chinese midget, nude on rollerskates" (Editorial). More recent celebrations of "colorblindness" are equally revealing. A *New York Times* review of the National Asian-American Theater Company's 2000 production of *Othello* praised it for casting Asian-Americans of various ethnicities in all the roles: "Remove the appearance of sharp racial differences from *Othello* and the difference in the play is so striking that it makes you wonder how many other stories have been distorted in our imaginations by our historical obsession with race. ... [One] leaves this performance thinking mostly about how clear the plot is and how swift its development if all the baggage of race we tend to bring to it is simply left at the door" (Bruckner).

Not surprisingly, it is precisely those who do not feel that race can be simply "left at the door" who have challenged the idea that colorblind casting necessarily erodes racial difference, including, most famously, the playwright

August Wilson. Blindness to difference is often blindness to inequality, just as "inclusion" can often be on terms that reinforce existing hierarchies, a point that has often been made in debates about secularism, multiculturalism, and antiracism in various contexts. Most recently, questions about the terms of social and cultural inclusion have flared up the controversy over Muslim schoolgirls wearing head-scarves in France, as well as in discussions following the rioting in Paris suburbs in 2005. Various contributors to this volume explore the shifting and complex politics of colorblindness, both theoretically and in relation to specific theatrical spaces, revealing striking patterns; for example, even when they appear to practice nontraditional casting, directors rarely cast blacks and whites as belonging to the same family, or in sexual relationships with each other; equally, they may maintain existing assumptions about class. Thus, nontraditional casting need not break with established attitudes toward the family, sexuality, or class. However, several essays also urge us to reconsider the possibilities of challenging social privilege and theatrical hierarchies via nontraditional casting.

But no matter what approach they take, these essays remind us that casting cannot by itself change the meaning of "color" or identity on the stage. The contexts of performance, the audiences, and the dynamics between actors, the place of the stage in that particular society, and the place of individual actors are crucial to the social significance of color in theatre. Nor are the meanings of race, color, or indeed colorblindness the same across different contexts, and as one reads this volume, each essay offers a different vantage point from which to view the question. By the end, we have an extended meditation on the contours of identity and theatrical transformation. A key question that the volume raises is the one highlighted by Ayanna Thompson's introduction: What constitutes an actor's merit? For if we claim that merit, not color, should be the basis for casting, the term itself is not self-explanatory. In debates over affirmative action, both merit and identity have become especially contentious terms. This volume shows how theatrical practices, especially in relation to Shakespeare, can uncover new dimensions of these large and difficult questions.

As it scrutinizes both the possibilities and the pitfalls of colorblind casting in staging Shakespeare, *Colorblind Shakespeare* also opens up the question of race in Shakespeare studies in new and exciting ways. It is indeed striking that while there is a vital body of scholarship on racial ideologies and practices in early modern England, and their intersection with Shakespearean drama, as well as on the subsequent histories of performance, including performance in different global contexts, there has been no sustained attention so far to colorblind casting. Is this because to address this question is necessarily to engage with a politics beyond the text and beyond the past, and to step into the controversial terrain of race and representation? Although some essays range further, most engage with Shakespearean performances in the United States.

Here, color *has* become the privileged marker of racial identity, although these essays show the myriad ways in which color is shaped by other factors, including sexuality, gender, language, gesture, nationality, and ethnicity. In addition, I suggest, we need to consider the new forms taken by neo-racism today and to think about how religious difference and contemporary geopolitics, for example, may inflect the ideas of both race and colorblind casting. But beyond its discussion of specific situations, this book forces us to examine what it might mean to interrogate the perceived boundaries of social identities. It makes clear that to pay attention to colorblind casting of Shakespeare is to do nothing less than to engage in the most vital discussions about identity, performance, and the politics of contemporary multiculturalism.

Notes

1. For a claim of this nature see Richard Burt's essay in this volume.
2. Some notable black actors, such as Ira Aldridge, did whiten up to play some Shakespearean roles, as several essays in this volume discuss.

References

Bruckner, D. J. R. "New Clarity from a Colorblind *Othello*." *New York Times*, February 7, 2000.

Callaghan, Dympna. *Shakespeare without Women: Representing Gender and Race on the Renaissance Stage*. London and New York: Routledge, 2000.

CNN. "No More Blackface at the Royal Opera House." http://edition.cnn.com/SPECIALS/, November 21, 2005.

Editorial. *Plays and Players*, July 1986.

Loomba, Ania. "Shakespeare and the Possibilities of Postcolonial Performance." In *A Companion to Shakespeare and Performance*, edited by Barbara Bodgdon and William Worthen. London: Blackwell, 2006.

Quarshie, Hugh. "Second Thoughts about *Othello*." *International Shakespeare Association Occasional Papers* 7 (1999): 1-25.

Smith, David. "So Long Mammy: Opera Says Farewell to Blacking Up." *The Guardian*, November 20, 2005.

1

Practicing a Theory/Theorizing a Practice: An Introduction to Shakespearean Colorblind Casting

AYANNA THOMPSON

The systematic practice of nontraditional or colorblind casting began with Joseph Papp's New York Shakespeare Festival in the 1950s. Although colorblind casting has been practiced for half a century now, it still inspires vehement controversy and debate. The black playwright August Wilson famously decried: "Colorblind casting is an aberrant idea that has never had any validity other than as a tool of the Cultural Imperialists. ... It is inconceivable to them that life could be lived and even enriched without knowing Shakespeare" (Wilson, 29). Wilson's focus on Shakespeare within his argument against colorblind casting relies on several important but unmentioned suppositions about the relationship between England's most famous playwright and this twentieth-century casting practice. First, the practice of colorblind casting is inextricably enmeshed in the contemporary history of Shakespearean production. Second, the immense and enduring weight of Shakespeare's cultural legacy has helped to create the perceived need for colorblind casting. And finally, the popular notion that Shakespeare's plays are "universal" lends itself to the theory that casting agents, directors, actors, and audiences can be "blind" to race, color, and/or ethnicity. These fascinating suppositions, which have been critically neglected, are the focus of *Colorblind Shakespeare*. This collection explores both the production history of colorblind casting in cultural terms and the theoretical implications of this practice for performing Shakespeare in a contemporary context.

Back in the Day: The History of Colorblind Casting

When the African Theatre in New York, a company comprised of and for ex-slaves and the sons of ex-slaves, put on a production of *Richard III* in 1821, white critics ridiculed the black actors: "People of colour generally are very imitative, quick in their conceptions and rapid in execution ... [and are better suited for] the lighter pursuits requiring no intensity of thought or depth of reflection" (Noah 1821a). Theatre, and in particular the performance

1

of Shakespeare's language, was deemed too difficult for these uneducated ex-slaves. Transposing his rendition of the black Richard's first lines, one critic wrote: "Now is de vinter of our discontent made glorus summer by de son of New-York." The critic then derisively noted, "It was evident that the actor had not followed strictly the text of the author" (Noah 1821b). Another white visitor to the African Theatre intoned that it was "too much for frail flesh and blood to see an absolute negro strut in with much dignity, bellowing forth." He added that seeing blacks perform in *Richard III* forced one "to hear the King's English murdered" (Nielson, 20). Close to 150 years later, in 1963, the same type of criticism could be heard about a multiracial casting of *Antony and Cleopatra*: "Negro actors often lack even the rudiments of Standard American speech ... . It is not only aurally that Negro actors present a problem; they do not look right in parts that historically demand white performers" (John Simon in the *Hudson Review*, quoted in Epstein, 291). In a fascinating displacement, these critics voiced their objection to the sight of black actors performing Shakespeare through a critique of the actors' inappropriate mastery of Shakespeare's language. These passages exemplify how Shakespeare's language began to represent a powerful cultural capital that these critics felt should be withheld from people of color.

Although Shakespeare is often described as having created "universal" plays with "timeless" themes, the universality and timelessness of the Bard's works are often tested when actors of color are involved. What is revealed in the quotations above is the fact that Shakespeare has historically been held as a litmus test for civility and culture.[1] For example, there are stories of black Americans being denied the right to vote because they could not recite specific lines from Shakespeare. Of course, their poor and illiterate white American counterparts did not have to endure the same literacy tests at the voting booth. The historian Shane White, writing about the early nineteenth century in the United States, argues that "the body of [Shakespeare's] work became an important part of the linguistic barrier that whites used to hem in the recently freed blacks in northern cities [in America] and thus to continue their subjugation. The great dramatist had rapidly become, for blacks, a suffocating presence" (White, 69). Shakespeare, far from being described as the father of "the human," as he has been called by one recent critic, was instead the test to limit the freedoms of certain humans.[2] The practice of colorblind and nontraditional casting sought to address and redress the appropriation of Shakespeare's works as a "suffocating presence" for people of color.

Although there were all black troupes (like the African Theatre in New York) and black actors (like James Hewlett and Ira Aldridge) who performed in various Shakespearean productions and Shakespearean monologue performances in the nineteenth century, these performances were never conceived of or advertised as colorblind or nontraditional. Instead, these actors primarily performed Shakespeare's "black" roles: Aaron the Moor in *Titus Andronicus*, the Prince of

Morocco in *The Merchant of Venice*, and Othello. If they did take on the popular Shakespearean roles of the nineteenth century — Richard III, Shylock, and King Lear — then they performed in "whiteface." Far from performing Shakespearean characters as if they represented universal types in which race had no bearing, these nineteenth-century black actors were extremely attentive to their own color.[3] For example, Ira Aldridge, the famous black American actor who toured England and Europe throughout the mid-nineteenth century, first made a name for himself in 1825 playing the African prince Oroonoko in *The Revolt of Surinam, or a Slave's Revenge*. He eventually became famous for his portrayals of Othello and Aaron the Moor. Although the portraits and daguerreotypes of him performing as Othello and Aaron are widely reprinted and therefore more familiar to twenty-first-century scholars and performers, his fame in the nineteenth century came as much from his whitefaced roles, such as Shylock, Macbeth, and Lear, as from his "black" ones.

Figure 1.1 Ira Aldridge as King Lear. Photo owned by Bakhrushin State Central Theatrical Museum, Moscow.

It was not until the 1940s that black actors began to appear in nonblack roles without the aid of whiteface. For example, the black actor Canada Lee performed as Caliban in Margaret Webster's 1945 production of *The Tempest* in New York. Lee is thought to be the first black actor to portray Caliban, and it is believed that his portrayal represents one of the first nonblack Shakespearean roles assigned to a black actor in a mixed cast.[4] But not even Lee can be considered a visionary in the forefront of colorblind casting, since one year later, in 1946, he performed as Bosola in *The Duchess of Malfi* in whiteface. Clearly, then, historically it has been difficult to balance the supposed universality of Shakespeare's plays and characters with notions of the actual significance of race and color. Universality was not understood as being raceless in the nineteenth and early twentieth centuries.

It was not until the 1940s, as Actor's Equity and the Dramatist's Guild were fighting against the segregation of the theatres, that colorblind casting came to the forefront. The desegregation of the theatres forced a discussion about the significance of race in performance. Joseph Papp, who eventually pioneered the systematic practice of colorblind casting in his New York Shakespeare Festival, spoke frankly about the problems of segregated theatres of the 1940s. As a member of the Actor's Lab in Los Angeles in the 1940s, Papp wrote a letter to the *Los Angeles Daily News* protesting the columnist Hedda Hopper's invective against the Lab's racially mixed social events: "In the best tradition of theatre and democracy, there was no discrimination against fellow human beings. We, as a theatre, are part of the tremendous struggles being waged by Equity and the Dramatist's Guild against the segregation of the theatres" (quoted in Epstein, 69). A truly integrated theatre that practiced colorblind casting, Papp argued, would necessarily challenge the overdetermined nature of color and thus deconstruct the need for whitefaced performances. Papp envisioned a theatre in which race would have no reliable signification in performance.

Unlike Papp, however, the leaders of the Lab perceived that there were significant impediments facing the desegregation of the theatres. They couched their argument in terms of the quality of the black actors available, attempting to disavow the notion that the problems might stem from the actual integration of black and white actors. In 1945 members of the Actor's Lab met with Paul Robeson, the most famous black actor of the time, to discuss "the problems of the Negro actor." The problems were clearly pinpointed: (1) there were not enough classically trained actors of color, so the language of the classics posed a challenge; (2) there was not a sufficient audience base among populations of color, so aspiring actors of color were not exposed to enough classical theatre; and (3) the trend of presenting classic plays by authors like Shakespeare "historically" often meant that actors of color were limited to the few "black" roles written.

It is interesting to note how many of these perceived problems were about classical theatre pieces, despite the fact that the Lab did not focus on the classics. Just as had happened in the nineteenth century, the idea of Shakespeare and classical theatre was appropriated as a litmus test for authority, civility, and culture that actors of color were set up to fail. The myth of Shakespeare's universality was sacrificed for the myth of Shakespeare's historicity when the Lab frequently rejected proposals for colorblind casting as "historically inappropriate." Papp recalled, "They talked about a problem with minorities, a lot of these people. But they *did* nothing" (quoted in Epstein, 69). Papp vowed to do something instead of just talking about it. The use of colorblind casting in Shakespearean productions became one of his signature practices, and his insistence on employing the practice for Shakespeare's plays marks an important counter-appropriation of the Bard's cultural capital.

Proving the old maxim that life imitates art, Papp's first introduction to Shakespeare in performance came from the only black teacher in his Brooklyn high school. Eulalie Spence, Papp's speech coach and mentor, arranged for him to see two productions of *Hamlet* that were playing on Broadway in 1936. Seeing both John Gielgud and Leslie Howard in the competing title roles, Papp decided at that young age that he did not like a declamatory style of acting. He preferred a more naturalistic Shakespeare, and when he opened his New York Shakespeare Festival twenty years later in 1955, colorblind casting was part of his naturalistic approach. The language and the actors would sound and look more like the world around them. Papp said, "If you try to reproduce a play the way it was done originally ... it becomes a museum piece. You have to draw from what exists. What exists in New York, and all throughout the world are different colored people" (quoted in Gaffney, 39–40). Turning the racist focus on Shakespeare's language on its head, Papp appropriated the perceived aural problems: he promoted the idea that Shakespeare's language became natural and living in the mouths of people of color. From the 1950s to the 1970s, famous actors such as Gloria Foster, Ruby Dee, James Earl Jones, Roscoe Lee Browne, Raul Julia, Morgan Freeman, Denzel Washington, and Michelle Shay actually received their start in Papp's colorblind castings of Shakespeare. One must wonder how many of these actors would be living in obscurity without having benefited from the cultural capital of William Shakespeare in Papp's wildly popular and populist colorblind productions.

Talking the Talk: Defining the Practice

Ellen Holly, a black actress who joined Joseph Papp's New York Shakespeare Festival in 1957, gives voice to the conundrum black actors faced in the midtwentieth century. She had trouble finding work because she was considered both "inappropriate for white roles because [she] was black and inappropriate for black roles because [she] was light." Holly states:

> Given this mind-bending scenario in which your own personhood has to be constantly obliterated for you to be deemed acceptable, the

Festival fell into my lap as something of a miracle — not only the sole venue where I could work with some kind of consistency, but the sole venue in which it was okay to work with my own face. (quoted in Epstein, 169)

Colorblind casting sought to create an environment in which actors were judged not on their "personhood" or their "own face" but on their talent. Colorblind casting, therefore, was based on a meritocratic model in which talent trumped all other aspects of an actor's "personhood." This was the original idea behind colorblind casting, but the practice has created complex theoretical disputes. In some ways, it is difficult to write about colorblind casting because its theoretical underpinnings are so unstable that they make the practice itself not one practice but a set of practices that not only are in competition with one another but also are deconstructing one another. Before delving into a more closely focused theoretical analysis of colorblind casting, I would like to describe the three main ways in which the practice of colorblind casting manifests itself. The disparate nature of these practices speaks volumes about the challenges facing this particular formation of nontraditional casting.

The initial idea behind colorblind casting was that neither the race nor the ethnicity of an actor should prevent her or him from playing a role as long as she or he was the best actor available. In other words, the best actor, regardless of race, should be cast for the best part. In this approach the audience is expected to make a distinction between the actor's appearance and the character's position, just as the audience would differentiate between a mask and a face, or even more fundamentally between the sign and the signified. Denzel Washington's portrayal of Don Pedro in Kenneth Branagh's film version of *Much Ado About Nothing* (1993) is a good example of this approach to colorblind casting. The audience is expected to ignore or forget Washington's race and only *see* Don Pedro as the "Prince of Aragon." His bastard brother, Don John, is played by Keanu Reeves in the film, and once again the audience is expected to differentiate between the fact that the actors, Washington and Reeves, are of different races and the fact that the characters, Pedro and John, are not supposed to be.[5] In this version of colorblind casting, the onus of being "blind" to race is completely on the audience. In other words, the casting agents, directors, and producers who employ this approach assume that blindness to an actor's race is not only desirable but also possible.

Almost from the beginning, however, another very different practice for colorblind casting emerged. Some actors and directors began to complain that this "blind" approach was not always appropriate, especially for roles in which the race of the character was central to the plot. Thus, a practice emerged in which the best actor was hired for the best role, except when the race of the character was identified and significant within the corpus of the text. Under this practice, for instance, it became unacceptable for white actors to play

Othello in blackface, even if a white actor were in fact the best actor available. The Royal Shakespeare Company, for example, halted productions of *Othello* for twenty years because they did not want to darken up a white actor. Despite the fact that the RSC had a long tradition of white actors playing Othello in blackface, including, in the mid-twentieth century, Anthony Quayle (1953), John Gielgud (1961), and Donald Sinden (1979), the company halted productions of the play until 1999, when the black actor Ray Fearon was cast in the title role.[6] There were three main perceived problems that led to this permutation of the practice. First, because there were roles that were designated as "black" ones in the nineteenth century, it was thought unfair to take these few "black" roles away from black actors. Second, the complex history of blackface minstrel shows from the nineteenth century in the United States made "darkening up" an actor a culturally dangerous endeavor. Many white actors were reluctant to apply blackface lest they be linked with horribly racist minstrel shows. And third, the casting agents, directors, and producers who employed this version of colorblind casting implicitly argued that the audience was not always able to be "blind" to race. Inherent in this approach to colorblind casting is an admission that socio-political and cultural-historical factors influence an audience's viewing abilities.

Almost as if it were resisting the limits of definition, colorblind casting has recently undergone yet another permutation. Actors of color have been cast in roles not traditionally associated with race, color, or ethnicity in order to make a socio-political statement about the character's subjection, outsider status, untraditional knowledge, and so on. Although this casting or directing decision is more appropriately designated as nontraditional casting, nontraditional casting is often collapsed together with colorblind casting. Directors and producers who engage in this practice do not assume that the audience can or will be "blind" to an actor's color, race, or ethnicity. Actors and directors, then, exploit this lack of "blindness" by drawing attention to the actor's race. An example of this type of casting occurred in the 1992–1993 production of *The Winter's Tale* at the Guthrie Theater in Minneapolis. Hermione was played by a black actress, and she came out dressed in a burlap sack and shackles when Leontes accused her of adultery. The director, Douglas Hughes, was employing this black actress and the traditional symbols of American slavery to call attention to the subjected status of married women in Elizabethan England. Because it was not assumed that the audience could be "blind" to the actress's race, the director capitalized on this lack of colorblindness in order to make a statement about the nature of subjection in general.

As these protean descriptions demonstrate, colorblind casting has never had one stable definition. As a practice it changes quite fluidly, almost as if it is resisting the rigidity of definition. The deep anxieties that pervade contemporary American and English cultures about the (in)significance of race, color, and ethnicity are made manifest in the slipperiness of the definitions for and practices of colorblind casting. The exact significance of an actor's race is perpetually in flux within colorblind casting because we as a society have not been able to pinpoint a stable signification for race. The practice(s) of colorblind casting cannot resolve the larger societal tensions in which they are enmeshed. Instead, the various and often contradictory practices of colorblind casting merely replicate the anxieties our society has about defining race.

Walking the Walk: Manifestations of the Practice

If the conflicting definitions of colorblind casting reveal tensions about the significance of race, then the actual practice(s) of colorblind casting demonstrate that it is never quite free from the specter of racism. Like the ghost of Hamlet's father, racism looms large in the background of productions, forever calling, "Remember me!" Despite the fact that the rubric "colorblind" suggests that the practice makes color and/or race invisible, the specter of racism will not let race be forgotten or erased.

The practice of colorblind casting tells us a lot about what actors and directors believe a "blindness" to race looks like. Although the records from Joseph Papp's New York Shakespeare Festival are dated — they are primarily from the 1950s through 1970s — they represent the casting practice in its most idealized form. Nevertheless, these records reveal that the practice of colorblind casting could still result in bizarre typecasting.[7] For example, the black actor Roscoe Lee Browne, who was regularly employed by the Festival in the 1950s and 1960s, was never cast as a romantic lead despite what the film critic Leonard Maltin describes as "his cultured voice and bearing" (Maltin, 110). Instead, Browne was consistently cast as the more earthy sidekick. He played Balthasar in *Romeo and Juliet* in 1957, the Soothsayer in *Julius Caesar* in 1959, the Fool in *King Lear* in 1962, Autolycus in *The Winter's Tale* in 1963, and Ulysses in *Troilus and Cressida* in 1965. This black actor who was known for his strength, wit, and cultured appeal could not ascend into the rank of Shakespeare's romantically involved lead characters. Despite the festival's colorblind approach, there were still roles that were not open to this black actor: the use of colorblind casting did not eradicate the glass ceiling for Browne. What makes this example even more disturbing is the realization that colorblind casting can still traffic in race-based stereotypes. The casting of Roscoe Lee Browne in these various supporting roles, instead of leading ones, unwittingly replicates the stereotype that black men are less threatening when they are presented as sidekicks. And in turn, this practice implicitly "races" leading men and lovers, like Romeo, Julius Caesar, Lear, Leontes, and Troilus, as white.

When black actors were allowed to perform in Shakespearean roles with romantic counterparts, interracial casting still proved a strange barrier. Again, it becomes clear that colorblind casting was never as blind as Papp and other proponents of the practice imagined it to be. There are many examples of Festival productions in which actors of color were cast to play opposite each other so that interracial unions were avoided. For instance, Robert Hooks and Ellen Holly performed opposite each other as Henry and Catherine in the 1965 production of *Henry V.* James Earl Jones and Ellen Holly were the Macbeths in the 1966 production of *Macbeth.* Jonelle Allen and Clifton Davis were Silvia and Valentine in the 1971 and 1972 productions of *Two Gentlemen of Verona.* Coupling, more often than not, was not an interracial affair in the Festival's colorblind casting. Likewise, Shakespearean families were often constructed in a monochromatic fashion when colorblind casting was employed. When playing King Lear in a 1973 production, James Earl Jones was provided with black daughters. In other words, the practice of colorblind casting continued to demonstrate instead of ameliorate the problems with performance and race. Shakespearean theatre critics have grappled with precisely this issue. Lest they be accused of not being "blind" enough to race, critics have struggled with whether or not it is appropriate to write about specific casting practices in their reviews.[8]

While these examples may seem like ancient history to proponents of colorblind casting (after all, these examples come primarily from the 1960s and 1970s), it is worthwhile noting that when interracial families are the result of colorblind casting, critics often fault Shakespearean productions for being

Figure 1.2 1965 New York Shakespeare Festival production of *Henry V.* Photo owned by Friedman-Abels.

Figure 1.3 The 1973 New York Shakespeare Festival production of King Lear. Photo owned by Friedman-Abels.

unrealistic. When in 2000 David Oyelowo was cast as King Henry in the three parts of *Henry VI*, some critics faulted the productions because he did not have black children (see Daileader's excellent essay, "Casting Black Actors"). The practice of colorblind casting in this production could not make these critics blind to Oyelowo's race. A slightly different production issue reveals a similar type of problem. When in a 1977 production of *Macbeth* Lady Macbeth was staged as hypersexualized, the blackness of the actress playing Lady Macbeth unwittingly came into blinding light. Ellen Montgomery's Lady Macbeth was faulted because she inadvertently played upon the stereotype of the Hottentot Venus — the stereotype of black female sexual wantonness (Hill, 162–163). If the onus of being "blind" to race is completely upon the audience, then how can a director or an actor be sure that this will occur? Errol Hill and James Hatch in their *History of African American Theatre* suggest that talent is all that is needed to ensure blindness to race. Writing about the Actor's Equity Association's Nontraditional Casting Project Festival in 1986, they argue: "Those performances at the Shubert Theatre in New York demonstrated that good acting decreases awareness of race, while poor acting intensifies it" (Hill and Hatch, 460). What this argument unconsciously reveals, however, is the fact that implicit trust in the audience's ability to "decrease [their] awareness of race" is not always tenable. In fact, this argument quietly admits the uncontrollable and uncontainable aspects of racism: it can creep up to the surface at any moment, rendering an actor of color suddenly too visible in spite of the colorblind approach.

Another example of how the practice of colorblind casting deconstructs the notion of its own belief in blindness occurs when Shakespearean productions are altered to accommodate actors of color. In an extraordinary example, the San Francisco Shakespeare Festival mounted a production of *A Midsummer Night's Dream* in which an Asian American performed as Tom Snout. Snout plays the role of Wall in the "rude mechanicals" version of *Pyramus and Thisbe*. Because this Asian American was playing the part of Wall, it was thought inappropriate for him to say the lines, "And such a wall as I would have you think / That had in it a crannied hole or chink" (5.1.156–157), and so they were excised. Like the other examples listed above, this demonstrates how often racism, or in this instance the fear of appearing racist, floats to the surface. Of course, the implication is that the audience's "blindness" to race can only be accomplished when there are no other challenges present (even misinterpreted ones). Challenges, however, are part and parcel of the history of defining what race signifies in the modern world. The practices of colorblind casting, far from ameliorating the tensions about the significance of race, often reveal precisely this "crannied hole or chink" in them. The practice reveals the hauntingly unspoken question that hovers behind the arras of every Shakespearean production in which colorblind casting is employed: What constitutes a blindness to race? If old fears and stereotypes continue to be perpetuated in productions that employ colorblind casting, how "blind" is the approach? The specter of racism in these instances whispers in the ear that blindness may never be possible.

Signifying the Blind: Theorizing the Practice

If the practices for colorblind casting are varied and often contradictory, then theorizing these contradictions complicates the practices even more. In an interview about colorblind casting in school productions, one high school drama teacher notes:

> I think there's a difference between Shakespeare in an educational context and in a professional production. In a school play anyone can do a role … . But I can see that if Henry VI is played by a black actor and his son is played by a white boy then my class will be asking, "Does this mean he didn't father his children?" (quoted in Moser)

It is instructive to analyze the way this teacher frames his discussion of colorblind casting because this commentary reveals the complex negotiations that occur among directors, actors, and audience members when colorblind casting is employed. While almost everyone supports colorblind casting in the most abstract theoretical sense, the actual practice of it often challenges these ideals. The teacher quoted above exemplifies the problem of audience reception: he receives school productions differently from professional ones. Because so much of the success of colorblind casting is based on the audience's willingness to suspend disbelief, the effectiveness of the practice lies in the audience's color-sensitive or colorblind eyes. As is evident from the teacher's comments, however, analyzing audience reception is a complex matter.

William H. Sun, theorizing an alternative approach to colorblind casting, has argued that "classical plays," like those by Shakespeare, "have less of a problem [incorporating colorblind casting] because their plots are already so familiar that audiences do not have to decipher the character's ethnicity through the actor's physical features" (Sun, 91). In modern plays with an unfamiliar plot, Sun goes on to argue, "the ethnicity of a stage image will always register in spectators' minds until they are told otherwise by a conflicting and stronger impression" (91). For Sun, then, the audience members' familiarity with the plot, story, and events enacted helps to alleviate their anxiety about how to interpret the significance of racial differences. Papp, the harbinger of the practice in the United States, clearly seems to have tapped into this belief as well. The familiarity of Shakespeare's plays, he implicitly argued, could make the visible differences between actors insignificant: the familiarity of Shakespeare's plays could teach the audience to see the character instead of the actor. Papp also implied that the familiarity of Shakespeare's plays could train the audience not to see race at all. Many critics, actors, producers, and directors have found it difficult to accept this theory, however, because it erases and whitewashes the historical and personal significance of racial differences. In addition, it disavows the complexities of both the sociology of viewing and the mimetic nature of performance. In this section, I address various reception/performance theories in order to demonstrate (1) how the employment of colorblind casting highlights the intricacies of the production-reception contract, and (2) how theorizing the mimetic nature of performance both exemplifies the difficulties of a colorblind approach and potentially provides a remedy for these difficulties.

Most critics engaged in reception theory for performance have examined the sociology of viewing, but few have addressed how multicultural and/or colorblind performances affect viewing (e.g., Blau and Carlson). Building on reception theories established by critics like Herbert Blau and Marvin Carlson, Susan Bennett has written about how race affects the sociology of viewing. In fact, for the second edition of her influential book *Theatre Audiences* she included a new chapter titled "Spectators across Culture." Although she begins with an argument that resembles Sun's with her attention to familiarity, Bennett complicates the relationship between reception and familiarity by considering what she labels the "production-reception contract." For example, Bennett writes, "A crucial aspect of audience involvement, then, is the degree to which a performance is accessible through the codes audiences are accustomed to utilizing, the connections they are used to recognizing, at a theatrical event" (Bennett, 104). One code that makes a performance "accessible" is the familiarity of the text. The contract between production and reception, however, complicates the notion of what is "accessible" to audiences. It is never simply familiarity with the text itself. Instead, it involves "multiple horizons of expectations ... [that] are, always, open to renegotiation before, during, and after the theatrical performance" (106). While Bennett focuses primarily on the factors that affect the idea of theatre/theatrical events, one horizon that she highlights is the audience's "obsession" with viewing "their Other(s)" (166). For Bennett, this obsession complicates "what [the audience] sees and how they see" it (167). Quoting de Certeau's discussion of the relationship between seeing and believing, Bennett asks, "Should an audience see — and therefore believe (in the name of artistic freedom) — that Jonathan Price *is*, or even appears as, an Asian man [in *Miss Saigon*]" (175). Even when productions attempt to complicate the relationship between seeing and believing, Bennett argues, the "obsession" of viewing the other cannot fully be ameliorated. She writes:

> It is as if ... what will extend to its reception is the affirmation of the power of the one who sees and the necessary subjection of those who make themselves, willingly or otherwise, there to be seen. This suggests that even when the condition of spectatorship is by some strategy made a subject of the work itself ... the power of the gaze can exert itself so as to repeat and thus instate the normative values of that white Eurocentric gaze. (190–191)

For Bennett, then, reception is never simply determined by the production itself. Instead, reception is complicated not only by the immediate effects of the production (what is being staged, where it is being staged, when it is being staged, etc.), but also by a larger, multilayered history of viewing (which bodies have historically been made objects, which bodies have historically been made subjects, which bodies have historically been allowed to be spectators, etc.). In other words, Bennett's account of the production-reception contract necessarily complicates a simplistic view that the choice of text would alleviate the tensions about the employment of colorblind casting. Seeing race onstage, Bennett suggests, applies pressure to the multiple and often conflicting "horizons of expectations."

Ethel Pitts-Walker, writing about the larger issue of "multiculturalism" in theatre, offers a slightly different angle for a theoretical analysis of colorblind casting. While Bennett focuses on the difficulties involved in the reception of colorblind casting, Pitts-Walker addresses the difficulties involved in producing these plays. Discussing the lack of critical engagement with the topic among producers, directors, and actors, she writes, "It is important to admit that most theatricians have little knowledge of what multiculturalism entails or how to effectively implement the concept" (Pitts-Walker, 9). In other words, it is not enough to employ a colorblind approach by simply placing actors of color in roles that were not originally intended for them. A true engagement with multicultural theatre, Pitts-Walker argues, would involve a "painful" process. "The most effective remedy," she writes, "is to insist on a more seri-ous, honest interchange that allows individuals to present criticisms — both positive and negative — about new artistic visions. This dialog, if honest, will often be painful as artists examine not only attitudes towards each other, but attitudes towards artistic values and a culture of diversity" (9). If one applies this idea to productions employing colorblind casting, it becomes clear that the theatricians involved should be encouraged to discuss the larger implications of these casting decisions. One must analyze how talent in theatrical produc-tions is judged, for instance. Theatre, unlike professional orchestras, cannot employ a color- and/or gender-blind assessment of talent, even if a colorblind approach is desired. The qualities that producers, casting agents, directors, and audiences value are not assessed in colorblind terms. In fact, it would be naïve to assume that talent could be judged without thinking about "attitudes towards artistic values and a culture of diversity." The honest dialogue that Pitts-Walker calls for would be painful indeed if the theatricians were forced to acknowledge the venues into which bias creeps, perhaps unaware.

Of course, by encouraging such honest dialogues, one also invites even larger theoretical discussions about the performative or essentialist nature of identity. Although not addressing issues of race per se, Elin Diamond's work on the politicization of identity raises an important point about the violent nature of mimesis. She argues that "identification never loses the horrific aspect of introjection — the primitive incorporation of the rivalrous other" (Diamond, 391). Performing roles that were not intended for actors of color, these actors are asked to perform and perhaps incorporate what is potentially the "rivalrous other." Diamond argues that, despite the fact that "identifica-tion seems to promote the annihilation of difference — and thus violence to the other — it may also suggest the problematizing of models that support such violence. Rather than upholding a strong unitary subject that constrains others to become copies of ourselves, identification might be understood as a psychic activity that destabilizes the subject" (390–391). In other words, the very "painful" nature of the discussions that Pitts-Walker urges should occur in any multicultural production, including colorblind casting ones, could stem from the fact that the mimetic nature of performance destabilizes iden-tity. When identity is racialized, this destabilization could be even more pain-ful: painful for both the actors performing and the viewing audience. Thus, these performances should raise questions about the very nature of identity. They should accomplish this not by claiming that race is insignificant, but rather by asking how significance is achieved and perceived.

These productions bring to the fore the usually silenced (except in academic circles) debates about the constructions and perceptions of racial identity. Once again, Diamond's words, although not specifically about race or color-blind casting, offer salient and relevant rejoinders about the painful nature of performance. Through the mimetic nature of identification:

The subject takes on, takes in, features of the other and is "transformed," wholly or partially, in conformity to that model. This implies that the subject has no prior identity; rather, identity is formed in the crucible of identifications; the subject is "specified," distinguished from all other subjects not by his immortal soul but by his identifications. (392)

Thus, the performance of the other is painful not only because the potential exists to be "transformed" into the other through the erasure of one's own identity, but also because the mimetic nature of performance highlights the performative nature of all identities. Judith Butler has championed the notion that identities are performative (i.e., gender and race are not material). She has famously argued that perceptions/understandings of the materiality of bodily differences stem from an "effect of power" and not from a fact of nature (Butler, 2). While Butler has admitted that her original conception of performance theory did not take into account race, only gender, she has found that "the unanticipated reappropriations of ... [the] work in areas for which it was never consciously intended are some of the most useful" (19). She analyzed the "racialization of sexuality" by asking what it would mean "to consider the assumption of sexual positions ... as taking place not only through a heterosexualizing symbolic ... but through a complex set of racial injunctions" (167). Taboos of miscegenation, she argues, indicate the performative nature of race because "race itself is figured as a contagion transmissable through proximity" (171). In other words, fears of miscegenation signal that race is never defined solely by a physical materiality and is, instead, defined by a cultural, discursive construction. Thinking about Butler's notion of performance theory with regard to colorblind casting, then, one must realize that productions employing colorblind casting should highlight the performative nature of the racialization of certain individuals.

Although Butler attempted to eschew the "narrowness" of the gender-focused origins of performance theory, many black scholars have been loath to think about race as solely a cultural and discursive construction. As the black performance artist and scholar E. Patrick Johnson has argued, there is a "gap between those who view race as biological essence and those who view race as a discursive category" (Johnson, 12). Arguments by scholars like Butler have failed to convince those in the "essence" camp, Johnson argues, because they "eclipse" the "corporeality and materiality" of the black body (20). As Johnson explains, "the black body has historically been the site of violence and trauma. It is these consequential aspects of bodily harm that I believe racial performativity fails to account for" (40). If performance in general, and multicultural performance in particular, raises the question of the instability of identity, as both Pitts-Walker and Diamond suggest, then colorblind performances often raise the question of the stability of racial identity without acknowledging what Johnson refers to as the history of "violence and trauma" on racialized bodies. Eclipsing the "corporeality and materiality" of racialized performers, Benny Ambush has argued, is problematic because "theatre is a dangerous illusion that whitewashes aesthetically different people into invisible men and women" (Ambush, 5). This "whitewashing" could result in the negation of the "consequences of bodily harm" that Johnson highlights. Thus, performances that employ colorblind casting inevitably raise the specter of performance theory debates. Far from ameliorating the debates about the nature of racial identity, performances end up replicating the exact tensions about the performative nature of identity.

Applying these scholars' theoretical terms about performance to colorblind casting, one is left with the sense that the practice can be "painful," "destabilizing," and "dangerous." The late ethnographer of performance Dwight Conquergood, however, strongly urged against this kind of skepticism. Writing about the ethical dimensions of the ethnography of performance, Conquergood describes "four ethical pitfalls ... that are morally problematic" (Conquergood, 4). Although he was framing this theoretical discussion for ethnographers who perform oral narratives from "minority peoples and disenfranchised subcultures" (e.g., Conquergood made a name for himself by studying and then performing the narratives from Lao and Hmong refugees in Chicago; he then turned his attention to street gangs in Chicago), Conquergood's outline for the ethical pitfalls seems relevant and applicable to colorblind casting as well (2). He labels the ethical pitfalls "performative stances": "The Custodian's Rip-Off," "The Enthusiast's Infatuation," "The Curator's Exhibitionism," and "The Skeptic's Cop-Out" (4). Conquergood describes the "tensive counterpull" among these four performative stances as being between "Identity and Difference" and "Detachment and Commitment" (5). In theorizing the potential dangers for the application of colorblind casting, I think the Skeptic's Cop-Out is the most relevant for this discussion. The Skeptic's Cop-Out is aligned with both detachment and difference. Conquergood describes the Skeptic's Cop-Out: "Instead of facing up to and struggling with the ethical tensions and moral ambiguities of performing culturally sensitive materials, the skeptic, with chilling aloofness, flatly declares, 'I am neither black nor female: I will not perform from *The Color Purple.*'"[9] Conquergood continues, "When this strange coupling of naïve empiricism and sociobiology ... is deconstructed to expose the absurdity of the major premise, then the 'No Trespassing' disclaimer is unmasked as cowardice or imperialism of the most arrogant kind" (8). Finishing his discussion of this ethical pitfall, Conquergood declares, "The Skeptic's Cop-Out is the most morally reprehensible corner of the map because it forecloses dialogue" (8). Applying this notion to the practice and theorization of colorblind casting, one can see the "ethical pitfalls" that Conquergood describes: it is all too easy to foreclose the necessary dialogues about the relationship among identity, performance, and race when they are so painful, destabilizing, and potentially dangerous. Foreclosing the dialogue and discouraging the practice, however, is potentially more dangerous than exploring the problems in colorblind approaches.

Borrowing from Mikhail Bakhtin's notion of the dialogic imagination, Conquergood argues that dialogical *performances* are not only possible but also desirable. Dialogical performances, Conquergood writes, bring "self and other together so that they can question, debate, and challenge one another" (9). Applying the theory of the dialogical performance to colorblind casting, then, one would not want to be blind to the actor's race, ethnicity, and/or color. Instead, the performance would be "intensely committed to keeping the dialogue between performer and text open and ongoing" (9). Combating the notion of blindness in performance, Conquergood's theory aims to highlight precisely those moments when tensions exist between the performer and the text: "It brings self and other together even while it holds them apart ... [and] affirm[s] cross-cultural accessibility without glossing very real differences" (9). Echoing a similar sentiment about the importance of maintaining both plurality and unity in colorblind performances, Benny Ambush has warned directors and producers to "not be afraid of people being different from you" (5). Because the affirmation of cross-cultural accessibility should not be achieved by glossing over differences, productions that utilize colorblind casting may be in a unique position to achieve this dialogical performance. They offer the opportunity to initiate the potentially painful and destabilizing dialogues that Pitts-Walker and Diamond describe without the "dangerous" whitewashing against which Ambush warns. This open, honest, painful, and potentially destabilizing dialogue must occur on both the production and reception sides, which means that casting agents, producers, directors, and actors must discuss how the production can bring "self and other together" without "glossing very real differences." And critics and audience members must not be afraid to discuss moments in a production that make them uncomfortable. A true colorblind/dialogical performance would challenge the production-reception contract by forcing a more open conversation about constructions *and* perceptions of race.

Shakesploitation: Colorblind Casting and the Bard

If colorblind casting emerged as a way to combat systematic racism (Joseph Papp, the practice's most ardent supporter, clearly thought it was), then the mapping of colorblind casting onto Shakespearean performance has functioned as an appropriation of the Bard's continuing cultural capital. Addressing one of his detractors in 1824, James Hewlett, one of the first black Shakespearean actors, implicitly argued for the universalism of the Bard:

> Why these reflections on our color ...? Our immortal bard says, (and he is *our* bard as well as yours, for we are all descendents of the Plantagen-

ets, the white and red rose) our bard Shakespeare makes sweet Desdemona say,

"I saw Othello's *visage* in his mind."

Now when you were ridiculing the "chief black tragedian," and burlesquing the "real negro melody," was it my "mind," or my "visage," which should have made an impression on you? (Hewlett)

Hewlett attempts to legitimize his own position as an actor and as a black American by creating a new lineage for himself as a descendent of Shakespeare and Shakespeare's creations. The idea that Shakespeare is *"our* bard" promises a universality that must necessarily apply to all people, regardless of race. Appropriating the myth of the "immortal bard," Hewlett sought to free himself from the ridicule and derision of white critics. Capitalizing on the notion of universality, Hewlett's playbills in the early nineteenth century advertised him as "Shakespeare's proud representative" (quoted in White, 152). As I noted at the beginning of this essay, the practice of colorblind casting and the modern production history of Shakespeare are deeply entwined precisely because of the myth of Shakespeare's universalism. This appropriation, however, is not as straightforward as the proponents of colorblind casting would have one believe. In the case of James Hewlett, for instance, it is unclear what one's "visage," or race, should signify. If Hewlett calls himself a descendent of "our immortal bard," does his status as a free black American in a country still in the grip of slavery impart anything to his understanding of *Othello*, Shakespeare, or performance in general? It seems impossible to argue that it would not, but the current articulations of colorblind casting do not really take this into account.

If theorizing the actual casting practice often complicates the notion of colorblindness, then including a discussion of the Shakespeare effect into this analysis adds yet another layer of complexity. The essays in this collection examine how the mapping of colorblind casting onto Shakespearean performance problematizes issues of race as much as it turns a "blind" eye to, erases, and/or resolves them. These essays, however, analyze the significance of race in performance through intentionally disparate lenses. They analyze colorblind Shakespearean productions in theatre, film, and television, and they discuss plays from all of Shakespeare's genres — histories, comedies, tragedies, and romances. I have organized the collection into three sections. The essays in each section speak to each other most directly, but they also speak (and often debate) with essays in other sections. As will become clear, even though many of the contributors disagree with one another, there are threads that tie the collection together in ways that one might not anticipate: the personal nature of many of the articles makes the idea of color-conscious Shakespeareans an important back story; the conflicted nature of many of the responses reveals how often theoretical opinions bump up against personal beliefs; and the ghostly presence of August Wilson throughout the collection emphasizes how powerful and important his arguments about colorblind casting were and continue to be.

In the first section, "The Semiotics of (Not) Viewing Race," essays by Angela Pao, Sujata Iyengar, Courtney Lehmann, Lisa Anderson, and Krystyna Kujawinska Courtney work together to apply pressure to the semiotics of theatre, the semiotics of race in the theatre, and the protocols that help establish those semiotics. Angela Pao examines nontraditional casting approaches to *Othello* in her chapter "Ocular Revisions: Re-casting *Othello* in Text and Performance" and interrogates the importance of viewing protocols. Through an analysis of the recent trend to cast black actors in the roles of Iago and Emilia, Pao argues that the success of nontraditional approaches (as evidenced by favorable reviews) often depends on the clear establishment of the protocol for theatre semiotics with regard to race. Nontraditional casting, Pao writes, poses new challenges for semiotic interpretation that must be addressed for, and not by, the viewer.

Like Pao, Sujata Iyengar places heavy emphasis on theatre reviews as evidence of the new challenges facing theatre semiotics. In "Colorblind Casting in Single-Sex Shakespeare," however, Iyengar adds the additional components of sex and sexuality. Examining the "original practices" emphasis employed by the Globe Theatre's single-sex productions, Iyengar asks if it is true that the more precisely observers are aware of a character's sex, the less precisely they are aware of the character's race. She suggests that reading race and sex together presents a particular challenge to interpretation and has done so ever since women and minorities began to appear on the English stage.

While Pao and Iyengar examine nontraditional casting methods, Courtney Lehmann and Lisa Anderson turn their attention to productions that employ traditional colorblind casting techniques. Lehmann's "Faux Show: Falling into History in Kenneth Branagh's *Love's Labour's Lost*" analyzes Branagh's utopian vision of colorblind casting. Through an analysis of Branagh's casting practices in his Shakespearean films, with special attention to his musical adaptation of *Love's Labour's Lost*, Lehmann argues that Branagh's unwillingness to address race and color as meaningful and/or meaning-packed signifiers shadows an ascending scale of the importance of whiteness in his films. In the end, Lehmann suggests that Branagh's simplistic conception and employment of colorblind casting produces a myopic vision of the world.

Lisa Anderson's "When Race Matters: Reading Race in *Richard III* and *Macbeth*" also examines two productions that employ the original approach to colorblind casting. Like Lehmann, Anderson suggests that this approach is dangerous because it requires that viewers ignore 300 years of cultural, social, and political history. Her analysis, however, focuses on how the semiotics of theatre viewing — learning *what* to read onstage and *how* to read it — sets the audience up to fail when racialized bodies are denied significance. Focusing on reviews of a 2001 London production of *Richard III* and a 1996 Chicago production of *Macbeth*, Anderson argues that the semiotics of viewing the black male body as the stereotypical Tom, Coon, or Buck float to the surface too easily when viewing protocols are not fully established ahead of time.

Concluding the section on the semiotics of race, Krystyna Kujawinska Courtney's essay "Ira Aldridge, Shakespeare, and Color-Conscious Performances in Nineteenth-Century Europe" provides an important global and historical dimension. Through an analysis of Aldridge's performances and receptions in central and eastern Europe, Courtney argues that Aldridge's black and whiteface performances became moments to discuss national and ethnic concerns. Like most of the other contributors in this section, Courtney delves into theatre reviews to gauge how the semiotics of race were understood.

In Section Two, "Practicing Colorblindness: The Players Speak," two important actors and directors discuss their own employment in and employment of colorblind and nontraditional Shakespeare. Antonio Ocampo-Guzman's "My Own Private Shakespeare; or, Am I Deluding Myself?" examines his relationship with Shakespeare's work and cultural capital in an extremely frank and personal way. A Colombian actor and director who trained and worked with Shakespeare & Company for several years, Ocampo-Guzman analyzes the cultural politics of socially defined minorities participating in Shakespearean productions.

Likewise, my interview with Timothy Douglas, "In the Blood: William Shakespeare, August Wilson, and a Black Director," probes the cultural and political decisions made by a black director whose resume consists of "50% dead white playwrights and 50% living black playwrights." Like Ocampo-Guzman's contribution, the Douglas interview not only adds anecdotal material about how actors and directors handle colorblind productions but also shows how actors and directors struggle with the theoretical and philosophical underpinnings of the practice. These essays address how often nontraditional productions present unforeseen challenges for the actors and directors involved.

Section Three, "Future Possibilities/Future Directions," pushes the collection into areas for research *and* practice in the future. Richard Burt's essay, "Civic ShakesPR: Middlebrow Multiculturalism, White Television, and the Color Bind," challenges critics of Shakespeare and race to examine a largely neglected area: televisual references to Shakespeare. Burt argues that Shakespeare has been so thoroughly penetrated by capitalism that the consequent televisual citations call attention to commonalities between Shakespeare and multiculturalism on the political left and right. Analyzing how Shakespearean blackness is constructed in conflicting ways in three television shows, *The Lone Ranger, Have Gun — Will Travel*, and *The West Wing*, Burt complicates not only the materials used to analyze Shakespearean colorblind casting but also the lenses to approach those materials.

Margo Hendricks's essay, "Gestures of Performance: Rethinking Race in Contemporary Shakespeare," seeks to challenge the ways that race is understood phenomenally. Attending to gesture in Julie Taymor's *Titus*, Baz Luhrmann's *William Shakespeare's Romeo + Juliet,* and Andrzej Bartkowiak's *Romeo Must Die*, Hendricks argues that specific gestural moments serve both to construct and to deconstruct the notion of the phenomenology of race. Almost as if responding to Burt's call to attend to the ways digital media allow audiences to read films and television shows in minute fashion, Hendricks's attention to gestural details implicitly highlights the power of these new media.

Celia Daileader's "The Cleopatra Complex: White Actresses on the Interracial 'Classic' Stage" addresses the white monopoly on playing Cleopatra and argues that this casting history poses as many problems on feminist as on antiracist grounds. Daileader suggests that it may be time to denaturalize this unnatural coupling by having actresses of color perform Cleopatra in whiteface. As challenging as viewing such a performance would be, Daileader argues, it would force conversations about the racist constructions of white femininity and power.

Finally, Francesca Royster's essay "The Chicago Shakespeare Theater's *Rose Rage*: Whiteness, Terror, and the Fleshwork of Theatre in a Post-Colorblind Age" reads *Rose Rage* as an exemplary nontraditional production. Royster elucidates and analyzes a number of ways that this 2003 production (an amalgamation of the *Henry VI* plays) denaturalized the ways bodies are constructed in socially disparate ways. In particular, Royster argues, it asked the audience to think about whiteness as an unmarked privileged location. Attending to what she identifies as the "fleshwork" of this production, Royster examines the way the audience was made to think about the civilizing process that constructs some as bodies and others as flesh, without identity or history.

Taken as a whole, these essays examine how the multiple, and at times contradictory, definitions and practices of colorblindness speak to the difficulties one faces when deconstructing structures of power. As an African American Shakespeare scholar, I have extremely mixed views about the practice of colorblind casting. Although I did not know it at the time, I benefited from colorblind casting practices in high school and college: I played everything from an Angel in *Anything Goes* to Marty Maraschino in *Grease*. Thinking back to my teenage years, I know it would have been a bitter pill to swallow if I had been told that I could not play a "white" character. I did not see race in acting roles; I only saw the roles themselves. In addition, I was and still am deeply committed to the idea that black actors and actresses should have as many opportunities as their white counterparts. Why should talented thespians like Denzel Washington, Halle Berry, and Samuel L. Jackson have to wait around for specifically designated "black roles"? They are talented enough to make any role their own, regardless of the race for which it was initially conceived. On the other hand, like many African Americans, I consider Othello to be a black role; I cringe when watching Laurence Olivier and other white actors play Othello in blackface. In a similar vein, I wonder if being "blind" to race and ethnicity is even desirable. Being black is so much a part of my identity that I am offended when people say they do not notice race, color, or ethnicity. My race informs the way I experience the world in so many complex ways that I do not want it whited out or e-raced by others.

Naturally, my conflicted responses to colorblind casting stem from my conflicted responses to the significance of race; and, of course, these conflicted responses are not uniquely my own. Whenever a topic engages with contemporary notions of the (in)significance of race, the history of racism, and our current attempts to rectify inequities and injustices perpetrated on the basis of race, conversations tend to be emotionally tense and theoretically dense. Taken as a whole, *Colorblind Shakespeare* does not present one evaluation or even one evaluative approach to the practice. Instead, this collection seeks to apply pressure to both the cultural capital of the Bard and the attempted appropriation of that capital by the "colorblind." The essays in *Colorblind Shakespeare* seek not only to initiate a discussion among academics, students, performers, and directors/producers in terms that we can all understand, but also to invite the creation of new terms to analyze these complex issues.

Because this is the first collection to address colorblind casting, there are areas that were simply beyond its scope. I think, for example, that there needs to be more attention to the differences among casting for film, television, and theatre. Although a few of the essays touch on this fascinating area of research, I think more attention should be paid to the subtle differences between Shakespearean productions, Shakespearean spin-offs, and Shakespearean citations in these various venues. I also think that the effects of star power should be analyzed with respect to colorblind casting. Whenever I teach *Much Ado About Nothing* and show the 1993 Branagh film, my students always refer to Don Pedro as "Denzel." They do not, however, call Benedick "Branagh" or Beatrice "Emma Thompson." There is something about Denzel Washington's star power that affects my student's viewing and their desire to collapse Don Pedro with Denzel. A thoughtful piece that analyzes if and how star power, race, and Shakespeare work together or against one another would be a fruitful addition to this conversation.[10] I also think that more attention should be paid to the global aspects of colorblind casting. Many of the essays in the collection focus on U.S. and U.K. obsessions with black and white, which is an important starting place, but a more international focus might reveal different issues. And finally, I think it is revealing how often the contributors in this collection cite one another. Here is just one train of references: I cite Celia Daileader, who cites Francesca Royster, who cites Sujata Iyengar, who cites Margo Hendricks, who cites Richard Burt, who cites almost everyone included in this collection! This is not to suggest that we are self-congratulating scholars — in fact, many times our references are to disagree — but it does reveal just how few of us are investigating this field. We need more voices included in this important work. This is all to suggest that I hope *Colorblind Shakespeare* will inspire the creation and publication of other collections. This is a topic that deserves an inclusive debate articulated in rigorous theoretical *and* practical discourses.

Notes

1. See Bristol for an excellent account of the history of Shakespeare's cultural capital.
2. Representative of an older style of "bardolatry" that claims Shakespeare's works are "universal," Harold Bloom writes: "Shakespeare, by inventing what has become of the most accepted mode for representing character and personality in language, thereby invented the human" (Bloom, 714).
3. William Sun chronicles a similar attentiveness to color in modern Chinese productions. He posits that the "modern Chinese theatre's decades-long tradition of realistic ethnic makeup" offers a challenging alternative approach to nontraditional casting (Sun, 91).
4. For a discussion of the problematic history of racial casting in *The Tempest*, see Reynolds and Thompson 2003.
5. For an excellent analysis of the complex presentation of race in Kenneth Branagh's 1993 film *Much Ado About Nothing*, see Lehmann.
6. The RSC's website has an interesting exhibition on "Shakespeare and Race" in which they discuss the company's history of colorblind casting. See www.rsc.org.uk for details.
7. All of the information I include about the actors and plays presented by the New York Shakespeare Festival comes from Horn.
8. Two critics included in the Non-Traditional Casting Project's "New Traditions Compendium Forums and Commentaries 1992–1996" express these anxieties. Jeremy Gerard, the New York theatre critic for Variety, and Dan Sullivan, the theatre critic for the Los Angeles Times, write about the critic's awkward position vis-à-vis race. See http://www.ntcp.org/compendium/JEREMY.html and http://www.ntcp.org/compendium/DAN.html for their respective commentaries.
9. Although Conquergood died before the opening of the Broadway musical *The Color Purple*, based on Alice Walker's novel, his words anticipate the lack of colorblind casting in that production.
10. I tried to obtain an interview with Denzel Washington for this collection during his Broadway run in *Julius Caesar* (at the Belasco Theatre, April 3–June 12, 2005), but his publicist informed me that Washington's schedule would not permit such an interview either in person or via e-mail (even if the questions were provided ahead of time).

References

Ambush, Benny. "Pluralism to the Bone." *American Theatre* 6 (1989): 5.
Bennett, Susan. *Theatre Audiences: A Theory of Production and Reception*. 2nd ed. London and New York: Routledge, 1997.
Blau, Herbert. *Audience*. Baltimore: Johns Hopkins University Press, 1990.
Bloom, Harold. *Shakespeare: The Invention of the Human*. New York: Riverhead, 1998.
Bristol, Michael. *Big-Time Shakespeare*. London and New York: Routledge, 1996.
Butler, Judith. *Bodies That Matter: On the Discursive Limits of "Sex."* London and New York: Routledge, 1993.
Carlson, Marvin, ed. *Theatre Semiotics: Signs of Life*. Bloomington: Indiana University Press, 1990.
Conquergood, Dwight. "Performing as a Moral Act: Ethical Dimensions of the Ethnography of Performance." *Literature in Performance* 5 (1985): 1–13.
Daileader, Celia. "Casting Black Actors: Beyond Othellophilia." In *Shakespeare and Race*, edited by Catherine Alexander and Stanley Wells. Cambridge: Cambridge University Press, 2000.
Diamond, Elin. "The Violence of 'We': Politicizing Identification." In *Critical Theory and Performance*, edited by Janelle Reinelt and Joseph Roach. Ann Arbor: University of Michigan Press, 1992.
Epstein, Helen. *Joe Papp: An American Life*. Boston: Little, Brown, 1994.
Gaffney, Floyd. "In the Dark: *King Henry V*." *Negro Digest* 18 (1969): 36–41.
Hewlett, James. *National Advocate*, May 8, 1824.

Hill, Errol. *Shakespeare in Sable: A History of Black Shakespearean Actors.* Amherst: University of Massachusetts Press, 1984.

Hill, Errol, and James Hatch. *History of African American Theatre.* Cambridge: Cambridge University Press, 2003.

Horn, Barbara Lee. *Joseph Papp: A Bio-Bibliography.* New York: Greenwood, 1992.

Johnson, E. Patrick. *Appropriating Blackness: Performance and the Politics of Authenticity.* Durham: Duke University Press, 2003.

Lehmann, Courtney. "*Much Ado About Nothing*? Shakespeare, Branagh, and the 'National-Popular' in the Age of Multicultural Capital." *Textual Practice* 12 (1998): 1–22.

Maltin, Leonard, ed. *Leonard Maltin's Movie Encyclopedia.* New York: Dutton, 1994.

Moser, David. "Playing the Race Card." *London Times Educational Supplement,* November 2, 2000.

Nielson, Peter. *Recollections of a Six Years Residence in the United States of America.* Glasgow: David Robertson, 1830.

Noah, Manuel. *National Advocate,* August 3, 1821a.

Noah, Manuel. *National Advocate,* September 21, 1821b.

Pitts-Walker, Ethel. "The Dilemma of Multiculturalism in the Theatre." *Drama Review* 38 (1994): 7–10.

Reynolds, Bryan, and Ayanna Thompson. "Inspriteful Ariels: Transversal Tempests." In Bryan Reynolds, *Performing Transversally: Reimagining Shakespeare and the Critical Future.* New York: Palgrave Macmillan, 2003.

Sun, William. "Power and the Problems of Performance across Ethnic Lines: An Alternative Approach to Nontraditional Casting." *Drama Review* 44 (2000): 86–95.

White, Shane. *Stories of Freedom in Black New York.* Cambridge, MA: Harvard University Press, 2002.

Wilson, August. *The Ground on Which I Stand.* Speech delivered 26 June 1996 to the 11th Biennial Theatre Communications Group National Conference, Princeton University. New York: Theatre Communications Group, 1996.

I

The Semiotics of (Not) Viewing Race

2

Ocular Revisions: Re-casting *Othello* in Text and Performance

ANGELA C. PAO

Colorblindness, as a visual deficiency, is located in the eye of the beholder. This is a matter of science, prescribed by biological and physical laws. In the realm of dramatic performance, the nature and origins of this alleged condition are not so readily located or characterized. Ideally, there is a happy complicity between the director who casts a production without regard to the race of the actors and the spectators who view it. The accord is founded on shared socio-cultural conditions, familiar theatrical protocols, and, most important, a common state of mind. Felicitous reception derives from a tacit agreement between practitioners and audience members to accept the exaggerated divergence between reality and its representation on stage that this particular form of nontraditional casting entails. If the protocols to be applied are not clearly indicated, even the most willing spectators can be confused about whether the matching of actors of one race with characters of another is incidental or central to the production concept. The same casting configuration can signal a major reinterpretation of core relationships in a play or simply be the accidental outcome of a casting decision made on the basis of qualities that have little or nothing to do with an actor's race or ethnicity.

In this essay, I will be using selected Anglo-American productions of *Othello* from the 1970s to the 1990s to consider how the same fundamental revision in casting encompassed radically different meanings. The change was to have Iago and Emilia (when she still appeared) played by black actors. In some cases, the change was incorporated into an adaptation of Shakespeare's text; in others, the alterations became evident only in performance. At whatever stage the modification was introduced, the impact was pervasive and new dimensions were added to the issues of race, which had moved from a supporting to a leading role over the course of five centuries.

Iago and Emilia, the Moors of Venice

In January 2004, the Calaveras Repertory Theatre presented a program of staged readings called "Asian Voices/Shakespearean Connections." The four one-act plays featured were written by emerging Asian American writers who had participated in a master class led by Tony Taccone, director of the Berkeley Repertory Theatre, and the playwright Philip Kan Gotanda. The exercise that spawned these works required the participants to use Shakespeare's *Othello* as the inspiration for new dramatic works exploring the themes of Shakespeare's play that continued to resonate for them. The connections with the original early-seventeenth-century play ranged from the fairly obvious in Lisa Kang's "Yi Hago," which focuses on an interracial couple, or Van Mai's tragedy of domestic abuse, "Who Shot Her," to the more tenuously connected exploration of the bond between two sisters, one lesbian and one heterosexual, in Nam Nguyen's "Ichiban," and the story of a book of poetry passed from a grandfather to his granddaughter in Samantha Chanse's "Subtext."

The choice of *Othello* as the core text for the Calaveras Repertory's workshops is hardly surprising; the most visibly racial of Shakespeare's plays, *Othello* has invited numerous professional adaptations designed specifically to offer comments on racial identity and race relations. This was a comparatively recent development. When Marvin Rosenberg wrote *The Masks of Othello: The Search for the Identity of Othello, Iago, and Desdemona by Three Centuries of Actors and Critics* (1961), there was only one production in which race figured prominently in the search for identity. In Rosenberg's opening chapter, he outlines the "problem of Othello" with a series of eighteen questions; "What is the meaning of his dark skin?" is the very last of these, and none of the other questions makes any reference to racial, ethnic, or cultural identity (Rosenberg, 6). In the eighteenth century, concerns over the play's "indelicacy" appeared to have had a more detrimental effect on reception than did its representation of miscegenation. This topic is just briefly raised in the section on nineteenth-century interpretations in the single paragraph on Ira Aldridge's performances. It is only in the discussion of Paul Robeson's appearances in the role that race emerges as a significant issue.

The extent to which questions of racial identity would be foregrounded in accounts of productions had as much to do with the degree of critical interest or awareness as with the content of the productions themselves. In an obscure 1954 tract called *Othello: Time Enigma and Color Problem*, published in Chicago with a run of 200 copies, Ernest Bloomfield Zeisler reviewed the debate as it stood in June 1953. The terms of the debate — traced back to Samuel Taylor Coleridge, A. C. Bradley, and Henry Reed — are confined to whether or not Othello was a black African (see Coleridge, Bradley, Reed). Zeisler describes his aims in revisiting the question:

> Until not many years ago Shakespearean scholars argued about whether or not Othello was a Negro, but for some time now all cognoscenti have agreed that he was. It may nevertheless be not without interest to cite the arguments of those who previously denied it. For this reason I have

followed the discussion of the time enigma with a brief resume of what
was formerly the color problem. (Zeisler, iv)

It would only be during and after the civil rights era in the United States, the
immigration of black Caribbeans to Great Britain in significant numbers, and
the emergence of postcolonial studies as a field of inquiry following decoloniza-
tion around the world that more complex investigations into the politics of identity would be brought to bear on performances and critical analyses of *Othello*.

In their comprehensive studies of the production history of *Othello* beginning with the first recorded performance on November 1, 1604, Virginia
Mason Vaughan and Lois Potter document the increasing prominence of productions in which race is no longer just a necessary though ancillary factor
in the tragic flow of events, but the defining element of Othello's character, a
core determinant of the interactions among characters, and a central theme
of the play (see Vaughan; Potter). As one would expect, the nature and timing
of these interpretive shifts are closely linked to contemporary socio-histori-
cal conditions. Nineteenth-century American performances were inevitably
affected by the conflict over slavery and the racial tensions that followed the
Civil War and emancipation. The institutionalized racism that attended British colonial enterprises and debates concerning slavery in the colonies similarly inflected the conception and reception of productions of *Othello*. In the
twentieth century, with developments that would culminate in the civil rights
movement in the United States and the breaking up of the European empires,
writers and directors began to take more aggressive approaches to exploring
the racial dimensions of *Othello* through rewriting and casting.

The most radical change in professional casting practices was to break
the centuries-old tradition of having Othello played by a white actor. Potter
underlines the significance of this move, noting that Paul Robeson's performance of the role "created a new dynamic in the history of the play [so that]
in the English-speaking world, it is now taken for granted that actor and role
should be racially identical" (Potter, 2). This assumption of racial identity
would entail a new sense of responsibility on the part of the black actors playing the part and arouse new antagonism from both conservative racists and
political activists — the former outraged by the interracial sexual contact and
the latter offended by the apparent legitimation of the portrayal of a black man
behaving irrationally and reprehensibly, duped by a white man and obsessed
with a white woman.

With Othello being routinely played by a black actor after the 1960s, in
subsequent decades new devices were needed to strike the audience's sensibilities sufficiently to generate new insights into the nature and functions of
racial identity. One of the most effective strategies has been to alter the racial
composition of the rest of the cast of characters. Since the 1970s, more than
one writer or director has had the idea of altering the racial dynamics of the

tragedy by having both Othello and Iago be black. In Charles Marowitz's one-act adaptation *An Othello* (1972), excerpts from Shakespeare's play are cut and pasted into an abbreviated text, with new dialogue for a black Iago whose speech is characterized by the idioms and obscenities of modern America. He denounces Othello as a "House Nigger who knows when to nod and when to keep mum; when to hold the door for Massa and when to stay in the pantry" (Marowitz, 265).[1] Pouring new poison into Othello's ear, Iago exposes Othello's obsession with Desdemona as a desire for revenge against white domination: "Did you tell her that it was Whitey who made the black woman the symbol of slavery and the white woman the symbol of freedom, and everytime [*sic*] you embraced a black woman you embraced slavery and everytime you put your arms around a white woman, you was huggin' freedom" (Marowitz, 266). In their introduction to the published play, Lionel and Virginia Tiger write:

> Of course, it's set in an American world, as so many disasters are these days. As an American — which is why he's presumably living in England — Marowitz uses the splenetic license of the exile to harass his elders and betters and now even youngers, because they (a) do not understand how historically reiterated the problem has been which so convulses the areas around the ghettos and (b) because underneath politics is a state-less style of lust and even underneath that is some ghastly community of humans so immune to subtlety as to be blinded by skin colour, even at night, even in the dark in their daughters' bedrooms. It is this unsub-tlety of racism which drives Marowitz's *An Othello*. (Marowitz, 256)

In a 1979 adaptation written by C. Bernard Jackson for the Inner City Cultural Center (Los Angeles), Othello, Iago, and Emilia are all conceived of as black. Titled *Iago*, this version incorporates a strong metatheatrical dimension, with a woman who turns out to be Emelia (Jackson's respelling) recounting the events of *Othello* with a new slant. Jackson imagined all three as Africans residing in Spain until the expulsion of Muslims forced their entire commu-nity to relocate to Venice, where they were granted asylum on the condition they support the Venetian forces in combating the Turks. Iago's machinations were designed not to destroy Othello but to bring him to his senses, and to forestall the military calamity that would ensue from promoting the inexpe-rienced Cassio to a position of authority. Iago's professed love for Othello is not the homosexual or homosocial love posited by several twentieth-century productions but the love for an inspiring leader and longtime friend. When Emelia proposes they abandon Othello, who refuses to lead the Moors back to Africa or to disrupt the burgeoning Portuguese slave trade, Iago reminds her that during the exodus from Spain, "It was Othello, who nourished our cour-age, who bolstered our spirits, who forced us on when each of us would eagerly have surrendered to Philip, to hunger, to cold wind" (Jackson, 67). As far as Iago is concerned: "It is politics we are involved in. Venetians must know that we will never abandon Othello to their tyranny. Before we would do that, we ourselves would take his life" (Jackson, 69).

The play was performed by a multiracial cast including black, Asian, and Latino Americans. The racial and ethnic diversity of the acting company was an important aspect of the Inner City Cultural Center, which was founded in 1965 immediately following the Watts riots. The Center's mission was "to explore the arts as a potential tool for bridging the communication gap existing between L.A.'s diverse communities ... and to increase public awareness of the rich pool of talent available within the American community" (Jackson, 49). With the focus being on the communities of twentieth-century Los Angeles, it is not surprising that the precise cultural identities and regional origins of Othello, Iago, and Emelia remained vague in Jackson's play. In positing a strong sense of solidarity between the Moors who were being driven from Spain and non-Muslim black West Africans who were being used as slave labor in the Western Hemisphere, Jackson seems to have been drawing on historical connections that reach back through the Berbers who moved north into the ancient kingdom of Mauritania (present-day Morocco and western Algeria) and south into modern Mauritania, in West Africa. Complete historical accuracy, however, is subordinated to contemporary relevance, and the emphasis is on the racial category of blackness, rather than on delineations along religious or tribal lines, which would be recognizable to American audiences. This was the category that had been made visible and meaningful through events, legislation, and representation.

Marowitz's and Jackson's aggressive modifications to the script leave no room for confusion on the part of audience members. The nature and function of the switches in the racial identity and the cultural origins of Iago and Emilia are overtly stated, and the connection between their new guises and the radically revised plots and arguments is obvious. Two later productions of *Othello*, in which Iago was played by an African American actor but Shakespeare's text was not adapted or revised, presented more subtle or ambiguous cases. Spectators could not rely on the dialogue to furnish them with the appropriate protocols of spectatorship. The first of these productions was directed in three versions by Harold Scott, and the second was the work of Penny Metropulos with the Acting Company.

The Shakespeare Theatre at the Folger[2]

Over the past two centuries, directors, actors, critics, and scholars have constantly returned to two central questions: What were Iago's motives for destroying Othello? And how could a man of Othello's stature and achievements be so easily manipulated? Satisfactory answers to these complementary questions form the foundation on which rest interpretations not just of the two roles but of the play as a whole. Director Harold Scott, a former Othello himself, says he always had trouble believing Iago — not because of the way the part was acted but because of the way it was written. He points out that even George Bernard Shaw "found it impossible to believe that a man as brilliant as Othello could be this stupid" (Henderson, 1). In his 1990 production of *Othello*, Scott solved the double problem of Iago's motives and Othello's trust through a radical application of nontraditional casting: he cast African American actors in the roles of Iago and Emilia. For Scott, the common racial identity of the principal actors made it possible to construct a shared past history that would have forged strong cultural and personal bonds between Othello (Avery Brooks) and Iago (Andre Braugher). Scott imagined Othello and Iago as having come to Venice together. Their common cultural origins and past experiences, combined with their shared status as partially assimilated outsiders, would place Iago in a special close relationship to Othello that could explain the latter's willingness to believe his innuendoes concerning Desdemona and Cassio. These same factors would magnify Iago's sense of betrayal and rejection when Othello promotes Cassio. His resentment would be compounded as he watches Othello solidify his position in Venetian society by marrying a highborn Venetian lady, but fail to use his power and influence to make sure that Iago advances with him.

Scott saw his casting decisions as "filling a void" by adding "a sociological rationale that makes what Shakespeare wrote more credible for a contemporary audience" (Henderson, 7). When asked if the casting of Othello, Iago, and Emilia as black would diminish Othello's isolation, thereby altering the dynamics of the play, Scott replied: "No, rather it heightens [his isolation] because three people can be isolated as one. If a culture locks you out, it doesn't lock you out just individually" (Henderson, 7). The new dynamics created by the casting were to be understood in cultural rather than racial terms. When asked if Iago's betrayal of Othello intensifies because it becomes a racial betrayal, he responded:

> No — I've had critics ask me if it's Black on Black crime. Well, yes, I suppose that's there, but what I meant was more of a cultural than a racial betrayal. If you and I come from similar circumstances, such as the same home town, I would think there are grounds for trusting you beyond the people of the culture we're both alien to. Iago's racist remarks then become simply anything he can grab at to dig Othello to Roderigo, the "white boy." (Henderson, 7)

The conception and casting of Iago were unconventional in another sense as well. It has been the custom to cast actors who seem equally matched as adversaries in the roles of Othello and Iago; in age, they are almost always contemporaries. Scott, however, was struck by the line that gives Iago's age as twenty-eight ("four times seven years," 1.3.310), making him significantly younger than the Moor. Envisioning Othello's relationship to Iago as that of a mentor provided an even more powerful explanation for the intensity of

Iago's desire to destroy Othello's happiness — enormous love has turned to hate. When Scott restaged the production for the 1993 Great Lakes Theater Festival in Cleveland, in an interview with the *Plain Dealer* he proposed a specific scenario in which Othello had rescued Iago when he was a boy, raised him as a son, and saw him married to Emilia before they all came to Venice. We could say that according to this version, events are sent along their tragic course not because Othello fails to believe in Desdemona's love but because Iago loses faith in Othello's love. Scott explains: "Othello's choice of Cassio is purely political. I see Cassio as the epitome of a West Point cadet, unsophisticated about the workings of politics, untried in battle. Othello promotes him but not with any intent of overlooking Iago. He has better plans for Iago later, but being a very private man, he never tells Iago about them." Iago's "devotion and dependency on Othello are such that he can't do without him. When that connection is taken from him, he snaps completely" (Evett, 1993b).[3]

All the modifications to the fabric of the play were to be conveyed without any alteration of the original text. The impact of the nontraditional casting was to be conveyed solely by visual impressions and the effects created when unfamiliar images were juxtaposed with the familiar text. In her review of the production for *Shakespeare Quarterly*, Miranda Johnson-Haddad captures the powerfully transformative effect the altered visual configurations could have on an audience's perceptions of the individual characters and their interpersonal dynamics:

> [B]y far the most significant and provocative visual impressions resulted from the fact that the actors playing Iago and Emilia were both African-Americans. ... Frequently one of the most obvious visual features of a traditionally cast *Othello* is that Othello himself stands out as a solitary figure among the white Venetians; his difference is palpable, and in many productions this difference is further emphasized by Othello's native African or specifically Moorish garb. In this production, however, it was Othello and Iago who stood out together. In scenes involving Othello, Iago, Emilia, and Desdemona, it was Desdemona who stood out. In Cyprus, Desdemona became the outsider, and as the play progressed, we had an increasing sense that she had fallen into a situation where the customs were not her own and she did not know the rules of the game. Emilia's "Is not this man jealous?" was thus more than the commonsense observation of someone with a more objective perspective on Othello's behavior than Desdemona possessed; it was the recognition of someone more familiar with Othello's background and cultural context than Desdemona could perhaps ever hope to be. (Johnson-Haddad, 477)

The casting of black actors in the leading roles of Iago and Emilia, as well as in various nonspeaking parts, was reinforced by the costume design and musical score. Daniel Lawson's costume designs were influenced by North African textiles and clothing. Othello makes his entrance wearing an African robe (specifically a form inspired by the dress of the nomadic North African Tuareg tribe, which includes a headdress that covers the head and all of the face except the eyes), over which he dons a Venetian gown for his meeting with the Senate. The links between Othello and Iago are stated visually by having both wear blouses of brightly colored African cloth that show beneath their black doublets. Both also appear wearing Tuareg turbans and necklaces with crosses, indicating that Iago has also converted to Christianity. Lawson intended the layering of fabrics to reflect cultural layering. He says of Othello, "He has adopted the Venetian conventions, mostly for the sake of appearances, but the fabric closest to his body is always African" (quoted in "Andre Braugher"). Iago, on the other hand, never appears in full African dress, although Emilia wears bright African gowns and jewelry.

The historical and ethnographic details were meant to work with rather than displace the other layers of characterization or substitute for other dimensions of the action. Scott actually found the autumnal nature of the play to be even more significant than the racial issues. Brooks was interested in exploring the ties between racism and sexism and the hierarchy of relationships, noting that "it's too convenient to talk about it simply in terms of color" (Westberg, 7). Braugher was in harmony with the more senior members of the cast, stating, "I don't think it's a play about race, but about pride and love gone bad." His primary concern was to make the character of Iago "a real human being" — "a very proud and loving man" who was reacting to severe emotional pressures (quoted in "Andre Braugher").

For Scott and the actors, it was important that all elements of this "Afro-centric" production be compatible with the dialogue and situations of Shakespeare's text. Scott points out that the rich multicultural nature of the Mediterranean — particularly in cosmopolitan Venice and on Cyprus, an island at the eastern end of the sea — would have made the presence of Moors along the European shores common, especially following their expulsion from Spain in 1492. Consequently, Othello need not have been an isolated figure or unique in becoming partially assimilated into the social and political structures of the state of Venice. The association of Othello, Iago, and Emilia with the Tuareg tribe of Mauritania (Avery Brooks's contribution) not only respected the text but strengthened or enriched its logic. From his study of African cultures, Brooks learned that Tuareg society was matrilineal and women were able to choose their husbands — hence Othello's delight rather than alarm when Desdemona takes the initiative to indicate her interest in him as a spouse. But Tuareg culture also authorized the sacrifice of an unfaithful wife, so that in Othello's mind, Desdemona's death would not have been a passionate murder born of jealousy, but a resolution required by social and religious custom.

Figure 2.1 The 1990–1991 Shakespeare Theatre Company production of *Othello*. Photo: Joan Marcus.

Culture rather than race may have been the primary concern of the artists involved in producing the Folger *Othello*, but once the play had opened, discussions were framed primarily in terms of race — or the absence of race as an issue. The *Washington Post* drama critic, Lloyd Rose, gave the production a very positive review, affirming that the risks taken by the director and cast had resulted in a vital and memorable performance of the play. His enthusiasm, however, was built on a highly questionable foundation, reflected in his bold opening assertion: "With one stroke of nontraditional casting, the director Hal Scott cuts *Othello* loose from racial melodrama and reestablishes it as pure tragedy" (Rose). For Rose, "Iago's racial hostility toward his general and victim, inevitable with a white actor in the role, is removed as a motive, and we get to see his villainy in its sheer malignant egotism." The implicit assumption that racialized attitudes are a relevant factor only when members of different races are placed in direct opposition overlooks the structural and systemic nature of racism and its durable and pervasive effects, which are not suddenly called into being at moments of interracial contact. When asked about Rose's remark, Brooks replied, "On the contrary, a black Iago deepens the issue of race" (Milloy). When he met with black high school students from northeast Washington who had seen the production, Brooks encouraged them to heed the lessons that nontraditional casting had added to Shakespeare's play. He told them: "The lesson of a black Iago is profound for black people. When you betray your brother, you plot your own death, the death of your people, and the death of your culture. We must never forget that we need each other. We must learn to value life again." Apparently this was a point readily understood by his listeners. According to one sixteen-year-old, *Othello* was about "one black man undercutting another. ... A black Iago allowed me to update what was happening in Shakespeare's day with what is happening today on the streets" (quoted in Milloy).

When the production was restaged for the Great Lakes with Delroy Lindo and LeLand Gantt playing Othello and Iago, respectively, the play itself was contextualized by well-publicized events that would foster links with black American history and culture. A day-long symposium entitled "Othello the Moor: Approaching Shakespeare's Majestic Tragedy from African-American Perspectives" was cosponsored by the theatre festival and Cleveland State University's Black Studies Program. In a move contrary to Rose's impulse to cut Shakespeare loose from social concerns such as race relations, the conference sought to examine "the links that unite literature, the performing arts and society's conscience" ("A Cleveland Stage for *Othello*"). Free performances of Lonne Elder's *Splendid Mummer*, a one-man play about the life and career of Ira Aldridge, were offered during the month preceding *Othello*'s run. In the first of several articles reporting on the production, the *Plain Dealer*'s theatre critic, Marianne Evett, characterized the play as "a story of jealousy and betrayed trust that also examines racial divisiveness" and told readers: "Director Scott, who staged the Great Lakes production of *Paul Robeson* in which Brooks starred last season, intends to focus on the racial issues by casting black actors in the roles of Iago, Othello's nemesis, and Emilia, Iago's wife. The casting will add another dimension to Iago's betrayal of Othello's trust" (Evett 1993a). While this may not have been a completely accurate statement of Scott's intentions, judging by the material released for the Folger production, Cleveland audiences were nevertheless being prepared to watch this version of *Othello* in a manner that foregrounded black–white relations. The production concept may have been the same as in Washington, but a different frame had been placed around it.

After noting the innovative casting of Scott's production almost in passing, the reviewers for the New Jersey, Washington, and Cleveland versions inevitably fell back on traditional criteria for discussing the production. Rose, as we have seen, felt the casting eliminated the question of race. In his discussion of the original Rutgers Art Center production, the *New York Times*'s Alvin Klein said only, "Much publicity has attended the casting of a black Iago. Although Shakespeare's setting — Venice and Cyprus — remains unchanged, presumably they are members of a North African tribe" (Klein). In her review for the *Plain Dealer*, Evett wrote: "This *Othello* is different from others because Scott has cast black actors as Iago and his wife Emilia, as well as a few ensemble members. But the idea does not seem revolutionary — it seems perfectly natural here" (Evett 1993c). Miranda Johnson-Haddad, with her scholar's perspective and the more extensive format of *Shakespeare Quarterly* reviews, addressed the problem of how the revised casting functioned visually, psychologically, and semiotically in specific scenes.

With the changes in casting, the most problematic moments are obviously those where the now-black characters utter racially derogatory lines or hear them spoken by others. Where previously Othello was the only target, Iago and Emilia are now implicated, even when the words fall from their own mouths. Act I presents the first challenges, with racial slurs being vindictively and manipulatively cast about by Brabantio, Roderigo, and Iago himself in scene 1. Shortly thereafter, in 1.3, Iago appears to be reacting angrily when Brabantio utters racist slurs and is calmed by Othello's gestures. Before the Venetian Senate, Iago's "solidarity" with Othello is conveyed mimetically through facial expressions and gestures and phenomenally through the material presence of his black body. The contrast between Iago's words and behavior in Act I scene 3 and Act I scene 1 provide evidence of his duplicity and malice no matter how the role is cast, but a black actor is confronted with new choices in deciding how to play the opening scene, which inevitably adds new dimensions to the betrayal. We have already seen Scott's explanation of the exacerbated perfidy, and another common suggestion would be that Iago, tainted by a racial self-hatred fostered by living in a society that considers him inferior, is trying to prove to himself and to others that he has more in common with the white Venetians than with the black Othello. As with all complex plays and roles, Braugher's performance could have accommodated more than one interpretation without disrupting the coherence of the production. Whichever answer makes the most sense to a spectator, the important fact is that suddenly, after decades or even centuries of a circumscribed range of possible characterizations, an entirely new set of interpretive possibilities has been opened up by the casting.

The same is true with a black Emilia. The unfamiliar casting focuses much needed attention on a role that is too often considered of secondary importance. In fact, little or no attention was paid to the effects of switching Emilia's cultural and racial identity in the public discussions of this production. Neither Franchelle Stewart Dorn, who played Emilia at the Folger, nor Jordan Baker (Desdemona) was interviewed for the issue of *Asides* that focused on the winter 1990 season. Dorn's performance drew one sentence in Rose's lengthy review of the production (Desdemona got three), which merely said, "Franchelle Stewart Dorn turns in her usual strong work as Emilia" (Rose). Allying Emilia with Iago and Othello culturally and racially was in fact a key move, serving to define the dynamics between the four major characters as much as did the decision to have a black actor play her husband. If Emilia were still to have been played by a white actress and therefore identified as Venetian, Iago's status in relation to Othello's would change radically, and the entire balance of the play would be drastically altered. Certainly the shock value of Othello's marriage to Desdemona would be significantly reduced if Iago had managed to marry a Venetian woman, even one of appropriately lower social status, before Othello did. The impression of Othello's exceptional stature as an outsider accepted only because of his extraordinary military skills would be dulled if interracial or intercultural marriage were to be perceived as a more common if not welcome practice.

Making Iago and Emilia an interracial couple could have served Scott's overall conception of the relationship between Iago and Othello by strengthening the image of Iago as an ambitious young man who is aggressively trying to advance in Venetian society. We learn at the outset that Iago's abilities, political and otherwise, have not gone unnoticed when he tells Roderigo: "Three great ones of the city, / In personal suit to make me his lieutenant, / Off-capped to him" (1.1.8–10). All he needs is a little extra help from the man he sees as a father figure, who instead seems to thwart his ambitions. But a white Emilia would also undermine the essential premise of Iago's unnatural dependency on Othello by visually and psychologically weakening the sense of bonding in isolation, which is the armature supporting the entire production.

Besides preventing any dilution of the tensions of the Othello–Desdemona relationship, switching Emilia to match Iago also maintained Emilia's subordination to Iago, making *her* increased isolation and dependency on her husband an additional motivation or cause of her betrayal of Desdemona, whether this betrayal is witting or unwitting. Having Emilia and Desdemona come from visibly different backgrounds could convey the message that, under certain circumstances, gender is a stronger source of affiliation than race or cultural origin. Or, if Emilia is conceived of as a character whose sense of identity depends on her associations with others rather than on an independent sense of self, the pained and angry insults she directs at Othello in Act V — "O, the more angel she, and you the blacker devil!" (5.2.140) — could reflect internalized race and class hierarchies. Johnson-Haddad had wondered if Emilia, when she cried that Desdemona "was too fond of her most filthy bargain" (5.2.164), was "adopting the racist language of dominant white Venetian society and thereby participating in both Othello's and her own oppression (much as she colludes with the prevailing male language of domination when she calls Bianca a strumpet)" (Johnson-Haddad, 478–479). Casting Emilia as black could sharpen the portrait of the traditional interpretations of the individual character — eager accomplice, neglected, or abused wife — while contributing to the revised ensemble dynamics of the quadrangle formed with Othello, Iago, and Desdemona.

The Folger production was a great success with general audiences and on the whole well received by professional critics. Most significantly, no one had any quarrel with the fundamental concept of casting Iago and Emilia as black. It is therefore interesting that five years later, when another director, Penny Metropulos, staged a production in which both Othello and Iago were played by black actors, the choice did provoke a highly negative reaction.

The Acting Company

The Acting Company's production of *Othello*, directed by Penny Metropulos, was performed at the Tribeca Performing Arts Center (New York) from May 16 to 25, 1995. Founded in 1972 by John Houseman and Margo Harley with members of the first graduating class of the Drama Division at Juilliard, the Acting Company's mission has been to provide opportunities for younger actors to perform in classic plays and contemporary works, while at the same time building a knowledgeable and diverse national audience for theatre. These twin goals are accomplished through a touring program that focuses on communities where residents have little or no exposure to live performance and theatre arts education. Performances for general and college-campus audiences are supplemented by student matinees, master classes, and performance-based workshops in local middle schools and high schools. As of the start of the 2005–2006 season, the company had performed more than 120 productions before more than 2 million people in forty-eight states and nine countries outside the United States. The company's general practice has been to tour for four or five months and then finish their season with a run in New York City. With its educational and outreach efforts aimed primarily at audiences who have had limited exposure to plays from the classic repertory, the Acting Company's productions tend to be more or less conventional in approach; publicity and program notes accordingly stress commonly received interpretations of the dramas rather than radical rereadings. Plays are most commonly performed in period costume and with minimal sets to facilitate easy transportation.

During the mid-1990s, the company was still made up primarily of younger actors. In Metropulos's production of *Othello*, Ezra Knight had the title role of Othello, Allen Gilmore was cast in the role of Iago, Karen Forbes played Desdemona, and Shona Tucker was Emilia. The production, along with *A Doll's House*, with which it was being performed in repertory, was reviewed by the three major New York City daily newspapers. Clive Barnes's *New York Post* review was the most favorable, largely because he took into account the various constraints and objectives that had shaped the production. It was evident that he and Wilborn Hampton, the *New York Times* critic, had indeed seen the same production, but Barnes consistently put a more positive construction on its different elements. For instance, concerning the overall quality of the performance, Barnes said, "The staging by Penny Metropulos ... is swift and uninflected with any unnecessary scholarship, but is plain and comprehensible" (Barnes). He noted that this approach "admirably serves its purpose, as an introduction to Shakespeare, his piercing insights and his wildfire poetry. You can see Othello plain here — which cannot always be vouchsafed for productions 10 times as fancy." Hampton, on the other hand, wrote: "Under Penny Metropulos's direction, the company's *Othello* concentrates on the big scenes, as through the subtleties of the play were a nuisance. As a result, most of the performances are oddly incomplete, their motivation never fully established, and come to life only in the major confrontations" (Hampton). Both singled out Allen Gilmore's Iago as a weak link. In Hampton's opinion, "As Iago, Allen Gilmore appears undecided about why he hates Othello so much. He speeds through the opening scenes as if he had somewhere else to go and is so pleasant and good-natured that it makes the whole tragedy seem just a misunderstanding" (Hampton). Even here, Barnes softened his criticism by suggesting that the defects in the performance arose from what would be an asset in another context: "One very slight disappointment comes with Allen Gilmore's Iago. I have admired him in the past, but here his subtlety seems sometimes lost in the deep purposeless villainy of Iago's soulless night." There was, however, one point on which the reviews coincided perfectly — neither mentioned that Allen Gilmore is black. With no photographs of Iago accompanying the text of the reviews, readers who had not watched the production would never have known that he was played by an African American actor.

This was not a point that escaped the attention of the *Daily News* drama critic Howard Kissel, who spent most of his column inches complaining about the casting of a black actor in the role of Iago:

This is alas Clever Idea Shakespeare, and the Clever Idea here is to have Iago be black. This distorts the play considerably. If Othello is a black outsider in an otherwise white, racist society (in the very first scene, someone refers to him as 'thick lips'), his plight is immediately understandable. If Othello belongs to an apparently integrated society, he is no outsider, and the play loses its force. Many classical plays are good candidates for nontraditional casting because the characters are larger than life and color doesn't matter. This play, however, is about color. (Kissel)

These reactions stand in marked contrast to the reception accorded Scott's Folger Theatre production. Whereas Scott's casting of a black actor as Iago was always commented on and favorably received (at least in principle), Metropulos's choice was either completely ignored or roundly condemned. Evidently there was fundamental disagreement over which conventions of reception to apply to the Acting Company production. Barnes and Hampton were treating the black Iago as a colorblind choice — a multicultural company's normal practice of casting without regard to race. In the absence of any evidence from the internal codes of the production, it was appropriate to assume that Gilmore's race did not perform any semiotic function and therefore was not a subject for comment. On the other hand, judging by Kissel's use of the term "Clever Idea," he assumed Metropulos was taking a conceptual approach, using Gilmore and Knight's common racial identity to remove race as a factor.

No such confusion had attended Scott's production. On-stage cues were provided by the costumes, which made it clear that Othello, Iago, and Emilia were not just being played by black actors, but that we were to understand that all three were black African characters. Many, perhaps most, members of the audience would have been prepared by the considerable advance publicity. Beyond its normal educational value, offering the public insights into the director's and actors' processes is especially useful when nontraditional casting complicates the semiotic system of a particular production. In such cases, sharing the hypotheses underlying the production does not merely enhance audience appreciation, it signals to the spectators what protocols of reception to apply. In the *Asides* interview, Harold Scott was directly asked to speak about how the Folger production related to his "overall casting philosophy as a founding member of the Nontraditional Casting Board." Scott gave an answer indicating that his strategy for this production was to combine elements of the original "conceptual" and "societal" categories. Scott identified what he had done with *Othello* as "sociological casting ... where certain characters are cast in another ethnicity in order to make a sociological comment" (Henderson, 7). But it was important to Scott that the casting concept be historically justifiable based on the cultural history of the locations where the tragedy was set: "here, by definition, you can put a Black Iago, and a Black Emilia, and Black and Hispanic extras out there besides, because my god, once you see where Cyprus is on the map, to think that it's any pure culture would be folly" (Henderson, 7).

No comparable advance publicity or dramaturgical documentation paved the way for the production of *Othello* directed by Penny Metropulos for the Acting Company's 1994–1995 season. Audiences attending regular Acting Company performances are not provided with the more elaborate explanatory materials available to spectators in theatres like the Shakespeare Theatre in Washington, with their larger budgets and relatively high-income subscription base. Therefore, when faced with a black actor playing Iago in the Acting Company's 1995 production of *Othello*, audience members and critics alike had to rely on various internal and external signals, such as previous experience and knowledge of the company's and the director's practices, to decide whether and how to incorporate this second black presence into the diegetic world of the drama. Although it seemed that in 1995 Metropulos's body of work was not well known to New York critics or audiences, her record reveals a director who is very sensitive to the implications of casting against tradition. Retrospectively, in the absence of any published accounts of the process of creating *Othello*, Metropulos's statement on her nontraditionally cast 2001 production of *The Tempest* for the Oregon Shakespeare Festival may provide the most useful source of illumination for the earlier *Othello*.

In Metropulos's production, Prospero, played by a female member of the company, Demetra Pittman, was now the Duchess of Milan, and the usurper was her sister Antonia. In her program note on the production, however, Metropulos stated: "Gender is not the issue of this production. Casting Prospero as a woman has only helped us explore the themes in a new light" (Metropulos). A woman in the role of Prospero made it easier to make the play more about forgiveness than revenge and to transform Prospero's studies in isolation from a quest for knowledge and power into a search for self-reconciliation. Caliban, incidentally, was played by a white actor, which helped remove the focus from the colonialist aspects of the drama, which have been emphasized in many recent productions. In *The Tempest*, new light was shed on the play's themes as the full implications of gendered difference emerged gradually during the rehearsal process, scene by scene, causing profound shifts in "the play's emphasis and its dynamics" ("*The Tempest*"). Having a black actor in the role of Iago could be expected to affect *Othello* in a parallel manner. Without making race more of an issue than it already is in the text — or a somewhat different issue (as Scott did) — the actors' social sensibilities would enter the production organically rather than conceptually through their interaction with the text and with one another during the rehearsal phase.

Such an approach to casting focuses on using the racial or gendered identities of the actors in the process rather than the product. The spectator is thereby given more freedom and also more responsibility to determine how to read the resulting performances. Not only must viewers decide on a semantic interpretation (the meaning of a particular performance); they must also perform the trickier and less familiar task of selecting a semiotic interpretation (identifying theatrical conventions and codes). These levels or categories of interpretation are identified by Marco de Marinis, who underscores the vital importance of the latter form of interpretation: "While semantic interpretation focuses on the *meaning* of the performance ... which is to say on *what* it is, semiotic interpretation ... mainly focuses on *how* it is, which is to say on the theatrical *signifiers* ... that constitute them" (De Marinis, 14). Semiotic interpretation poses new challenges when nontraditional casting is applied because it is not enough to settle on the traditional *particular* conventions being followed — the conventions associated with given genres, periods, authors, regions, schools, and so on. The different forms of nontraditional casting — colorblind, conceptual, societal, and others — constitute relatively new additions to the codes of particular conventions. Providing spectators with the information needed to determine what particular conventions are being applied as far as the casting is concerned would let them know from the outset whether they should proceed to analyze how the corporeal signifiers fit in among the *unique* conventions of the performance they are watching.[4] By definition, unique conventions are "those that emerge from a given performance, that are present *ex novo*, and that can only be understood through that particular message and performance context. They can often be confusing and ambiguous due to their novelty and originality. This is one of the effects of the constitution or reestablishment of a new code" (De Toro, 56). Once audience members know that the casting of a black actor in the part of a white character has been endowed with semiotic value by the director, they can proceed to evaluate the semantic function of the casting choice.

In the case of Scott's production, the keys to the theatrical or conventional codes were made available to audiences ahead of time. Most important, they were told how to interpret the production semiotically so that they could devote their full attention to interpreting it semantically. Left to their own devices in the case of Metropulos's Acting Company production, three highly competent spectators came to very different conclusions as to how they should perceive the signifiers, and their subsequent evaluations were profoundly affected by these preliminary conclusions. The case histories of the black Iagos confirm that racial positioning and life experiences always work in tandem with specifically theatrical competencies to shape an audience member's readings of productions like the unconventional *Othellos*.

Notes

1. Marowitz's script can be read in dialogue with the tradition of nineteenth-century minstrel show parodies of *Othello* and Jean Genet's *The Blacks: A Clown Show*. Working along similar lines, but without changing the identities of the characters, the American director and educator Shelia Rose Bland proposed a production that would foreground the fact that Othello was written by a white man for white audiences, and Desdemona imagined by a male writer for male actors: "I would direct *Othello* as a comedy, almost as a minstrel

show. The entire show would be played for laughs — even the murders and suicides. I would make Othello the butt of the jokes, and Iago the hero — saving the values of white purity. I would make Desdemona a woman who deserves what she gets. ... I would cast the show entirely with white males, having *Othello* played by a white male in blackface. White males dressed in female clothing would play Desdemona, Emilia, and Bianca" (Bland, 29).

2. Harold Scott's production for the Shakespeare Theatre at the Folger ran from November 27, 1990 to January 27, 1991. An earlier version, with the same actors playing the roles of Othello, Iago, and Desdemona, had played the previous summer at the Philip J. Levin Theater of the Rutgers Art Center. The production was restaged in May 1993 for the Great Lakes Theater Festival in Cleveland.

3. Andre Braugher had just recently completed his training at Stanford and Juilliard when he was chosen by Scott to play Iago. His relationship to Scott and Brooks therefore paralleled the relationship to Othello being envisioned by Scott. Expressing his excitement about the opportunity to work with the two older men whom he respected and admired, Braugher said, "I'm just two years out of school. It's so rare for me to work with *two* mature Black artists ... two incredibly articulate, intelligent, well-informed scholars are *also* very talented artists" ("Andre Braugher as Iago," 5).

4. De Marinis has proposed a tripartite categorization of theatre conventions: the general, the particular, and the unique. A concise definition of the general conventions is given by Fernando De Toro: "General conventions have to do with the *rules* of theatre production in the achievement of fiction. From the moment the spectator enters into the theatre, he/ she knows that a series of conventions distinct from social conventions must be accepted, for a stage production does not provide an exact replica of exterior reality and is not the world exactly as the spectator knows it. ... They are general in that there are no unique forms for theatre production" (De Toro, 55).

References

"Andre Braugher as Iago." *Asides* (Winter 1990): 5.

Barnes, Clive. "No Moor Needed." *New York Post*, May 18, 1995.

Bland, Sheila Rose. "How I Would Direct *Othello*." In *Othello: New Essays by Black Writers*, edited by Mythili Kaul. Washington, DC: Howard University Press, 1996.

Bradley, A. C. *Shakespearean Tragedy: Lectures on* Hamlet, Othello, King Lear, *and* Macbeth (1904). New York: Penguin, 1991.

"A Cleveland Stage for 'Othello.'" *Plain Dealer*, May 20, 1993.

Coleridge, Samuel Taylor. "Comments on *Othello*" (1819). In *Othello: A Norton Critical Edition*, edited by Edward Pechter. New York: W. W. Norton, 2004.

De Marinis, Marco. "Theatrical Comprehension: A Socio-Semiotic Approach." *Theatre* 15 (1985): 12–17.

De Toro, Fernando. *Theatre Semiotics: Text and Staging in Modern Theatre*. Translated by John Lewis. Revised and edited by Carole Hubbard. Toronto: University of Toronto Press, 1995.

Evett, Marianne. "Casting Change Delays Opening of *Othello*." *Plain Dealer*, April 1, 1993a.

Evett, Marianne. "Othello; The Role 'Challenges Everything One Has.'" *Plain Dealer*, May 9, 1993b.

Evett, Marianne. "Mistrusting Happiness until We Destroy It." *Plain Dealer*, May 17, 1993c.

Hampton, Wilborn. "Two Very Different Women in Distress." *New York Times*, May 17, 1995.

Henderson, Liza. "Harold Scott on Color, Cast, Shakespeare, America." *Asides* (Winter 1990): 1, 7.

Jackson, C. Bernard. "*Iago*." In *The National Black Drama Anthology*, edited by Woodie King, Jr. New York and London: Applause, 1995.

Johnson-Haddad, Miranda. "The Shakespeare Theatre at the Folger, 1990–91." *Shakespeare Quarterly* 42 (1991): 472–484.

Kissel, Howard. "Most Unhappy *Othello*." *New York Daily News*, May 17, 1995.

Klein, Alvin. "Striking Performances Light Up *Othello*." *New York Times*, July 1, 1990.

Marowitz, Charles. "An *Othello*." In *Open Space Plays*, edited by Charles Marowitz. Harmondsworth, UK: Penguin, 1974.

Metropulos, Penny. "Director's Note: Creativity, Spirit and True Power in *The Tempest*." Program, *The Tempest*. Oregon Shakespeare Festival, 2001.

Milloy, Courtland. "Black-on-Black Lesson From Hawk." *Washington Post*, December 11, 1990.

Potter, Lois. *Othello*. New York: Palgrave, 2002.

Reed, Henry. *Lectures on English History and Tragic Poetry: As Illustrated by Shakespeare*. Philadelphia: Parry and McMillan, 1859.

Rose, Lloyd. "*Othello*: The Two Faces of Tragedy." *Washington Post*, December 5, 1990.

Rosenberg, Marvin. *The Masks of Othello: The Search for the Identity of Othello, Iago and Desdemona by Three Centuries of Actors and Critics*. Berkeley and Los Angeles: University of California Press, 1961.

"*The Tempest*." *Ashland Daily Tidings*, March 16–22, 2001.

Vaughan, Virginia Mason. *Othello: A Contextual History*. Cambridge: Cambridge University Press, 1994.

Westberg, Chris. "Avery Brooks as Othello." *Asides* (Winter 1990): 1, 7.

Zeisler, Ernest Bloomfield. *Othello: Time Enigma and Color Problem*. Chicago: Alexander J. Isaacs, 1954.

3

Colorblind Casting in Single-Sex Shakespeare

SUJATA IYENGAR

The more precisely the position is determined, the less precisely the momentum is known in this instant, and vice versa. — Heisenberg's "Uncertainty" Principle, 1927

After the so-called Sokal hoax, literary critics should beware of mathematical metaphors. But in this case, the principle I evoke colors my approach and response to colorblind and color-conscious casting: Is it true that the more precisely observers are aware of a character's sex, the less precisely they are aware of the character's race, and vice versa? In a production in which actors may share neither the race nor the sex of the characters they play, what happens? Do audiences notice neither cross-dressing nor what Ian Smith calls (translating the term from Eric Lott's American context) "racial cross-dressing" (see Smith)? Both? Each at different times? Does it make a difference whether the black actor plays a lead or a supporting part? How, if at all, do the race and sex of the observer alter a particular performance and its reception?

Audience members know that upon entering the theatre, we agree to a hermeneutic contract: certain objects, gestures, lights, costumes, bodies, and so on will stand for other objects, other gestures, other lights, other costumes, other bodies, or for something else altogether. This is how Sidney can defend theatre from the charge of lying: "What child is there that, coming to a play, and seeing *Thebes* written in great letters upon an old door, doth believe that it is Thebes?" (Sidney, 124). Sidney's example exposes the semiotics of theatre:

THEBES	=	letters on old door / the scene is set in Thebes
(sign)	=	(form of signifier) / (signified concept)

The word "Thebes" on the old door moves us through time and space; the "great letters" assign importance to the imagined location.[1]

Sidney's child is fluent in a couple of sign systems; she or he is literate and can decode the "great letters" and also knows where to look — on the stage — for information. An early modern audience likewise knew that male actors in dresses (usually) stood for women, or that white actors in blackface make-up stood for Moors. The playful mocking of the conventions of gender impersonation in Shakespeare's cross-dressing comedies and of racial impersonation in *Othello* and *Titus Andronicus* ("Ye white-limed walls!" mocks Aaron [4.2.97], drawing attention to the make-up on the faces of both white and black characters on stage) depends upon the audience's reading the signs of gender and race in the same way.

Present-day casting practices, however, do not offer theatre-goers a clear hermeneutic to decipher *which* signs we should read on stage, and *how* we should read them. Reading race and sex presents a particular challenge to interpretation, and perhaps has done so ever since women began to appear on the English stage. So-called gender-blind and colorblind castings offer further complications. The degree to which a spectator will interpret gender or skin color as interpretable "signs," along with costume, make-up, properties, setting, and other aspects of mise-en-scène, will depend upon the actor or actress playing the role and upon the spectator.

For most critics today — although not necessarily for those in earlier historical periods — Othello is a part for which blackness, or visibly marked racial difference from the majority, is an essential characteristic. There are, however, surprisingly few Shakespearean characters whose skin color seems to be integral to our understanding them. More often, the skin color of an actor functions as a floating signifier, leaving audience and reviewers unsure how or whether to interpret it. For all these reasons, in this essay I focus upon individual responses — of actors and of audience members — in British and American mainstream theatre reviews, and on my own responses to these performances.[2]

Although I have elsewhere suggested that Shakespeare's Cleopatra was played as black and therefore ought to be played by an actress of color on our stages today, I now think that Cleopatra can and should be played as both black and white, and by an actor of "whatever color it please God" (*Much Ado About Nothing*, 2.3.30). But it has taken a performance by a black actress to bring me to this conclusion. A character as theatrical as Cleopatra, in a text so rich, makes hungry where most she satisfies — that is to say, however wonderful the performance, any missing qualities in her make themselves apparent over even an astonishing display. A white Cleopatra makes me notice that the very first description of her in the play is "tawny" and that she describes herself as "black"; a queenly Cleopatra makes me miss her vulgar streak; Mark Rylance's male Cleopatra made me notice Cleopatra's femininity and even her sexuality as a performance, as I will discuss below; and any female Cleopatra must contend with the metadramatic reverberations of "boy[ing] my greatness / I' th' posture of a whore" (5.2.216–217).

Finally, the casting of the black British actress Josette Bushell-Mingo as Cleopatra at Manchester's Royal Exchange Theatre in spring 2005 brought Antony's outraged line to the horsewhipped Thidias, "Henceforth / The *white hand* of a lady fever thee" (3.13.139–140, italics mine) to attention in a new way. Regardless of who plays it, the scene emphasizes the parallels between the overtly histrionic queen Cleopatra, who dies upon a monument, and the seemingly stoic soldier Antony, who "dr[a]nk / The stale of horses" (1.4.61–2); Antony's whipping of Thidias reminds us of Cleopatra's beating the messenger who brings her news of Antony's marriage to Octavia. Both Antony and Cleopatra respond with unreasoning physical violence to the idea of the other's infidelity, punishing a subordinate in place of the errant lover. But Tom Mannion's white Antony employed the "white hand" as a metonymy for Bushell-Mingo's black Cleopatra, a strategy that emphasized his "dislimn[ing]" (4.15.10) and the surprising extent to which his collapse is independent of his lover. Thidias's offense (and, of course, that of Caesar, which underlies it) is against Antony's mistress, not against the queen of Egypt ("she here — what's her name, / Since she was Cleopatra?" [3.13.98–99]). "[S]he here" is a placeholder, standing in the place of a white-handed lady (or of the white-handed wife, Octavia) both physically and psychically. Antony's love "whitens" the hands of Cleopatra, which can then be sullied by an inferior's touch.

Some of these observations are perhaps the cavils of a professional Shakespearean, but they are also the responses of a person of color. Professing "Shakespeare of color," as it were, can be a dissonant experience, and is contextual, contingent, and certainly local, as essays by Ania Loomba, Peter Erickson, Margo Hendricks, and Ayanna Thompson make clear (see Loomba, Erickson, Hendricks, and Thompson).

The 1999 Globe Theatre *Antony and Cleopatra*

Mark Rylance's white Cleopatra, in contrast to Bushell-Mingo's black queen, emphasized not the parallels between Antony and Cleopatra but those between Cleopatra and her women — some might say, between Cleopatra and *all* women, although I myself did not find this production antifeminist. This 1999 Globe Theatre production employed a significant, although unintentional, piece of colorblind or reverse casting by casting the white Mark Rylance as Cleopatra and the black British actor Danny Sapani as her maid, Charmian. Charmian's clever mimicry of her mistress's histrionics and gestures drew attention to the consummate skill of both Cleopatra and Rylance, but for me at least, also seemed to comment inadvertently on August Wilson's arguments that colorblind casting can function as a form of minstrelsy. Arthur Little argues persuasively that Shakespeare's Cleopatra was and should be played as black, and he notes some of the ways in which performances deflect that blackness—onto her attendants, for example (in contrast to Lucan, who talks about maids from various ethnic groups in Cleopatra's retinue) (see Little). I had a strong sense that Sapani's Charmian was in some way personating "blackness" on the Globe stage, as a corollary to Rylance's personation of histrionic femininity. Comments on Sapani's or other players' ethnicity or race were rare in the reviews, but I shall argue that race became apparent at moments in the

Figure 3.1 Mark Rylance and Danny Sapani in the 1999 Globe Theatre production of *Antony and Cleopatra*. Photo: John Tramper.

production when the illusion of single-sex casting came under tension. When a reviewer mentioned skin color or race, it became allied with "sex" as a bodily essential, and opposed to "gender" as social category. At the same time, both race and sex were allied with sensuality, measured as the sexual attractiveness of the performer.

The production was intended to be in some ways a very romantic *Antony and Cleopatra*. Giles Block suggested in rehearsal that Charmian's conversation with the soothsayer voices a "general excitement about the possibilities for marriage," including the possibility of a union between Antony and Cleopatra. Thus, they are not the illicit middle-aged adulterers of Roman propaganda but the inhabitants of "new heaven, new earth," genuinely prepared for a fresh start (Block, quoted in Bessell). Block cut very little of the text, with the notable exception of the character Seleucus and his exchange with Cleopatra. The production notes suggest that this was meant to avoid extra intrigue between Seleucus and Cleopatra — that is, to streamline plot — but it has the added effect of removing any doubt that Cleopatra intends to join Antony. She is absolute for death, her loyalties uncompromised. Her histrionicism is a ploy, but less calculated than in some performances. The production notes thus describe Cleopatra's "lightning mood swings" — that is, they espouse Enobarbus's view that Cleopatra feels her tempests and storms genuinely, that they are not all artifice (Bessell).

The smaller cuts and reallocated lines (listed by Bessell) similarly tend toward romanticizing the lovers. Cutting Antony's lines on the evils his "idleness doth hatch" (1.2.119) removes a sense that he feels guilty, or that he is aware of the self-destructive quality of his love. Condensing Enobarbus's comments about Octavia's "sighs" makes the marriage entirely expedient, with no affection between Octavia and Antony at all, and the "amity" with Caesar entirely illusory. Some reallocations shore up both Antony's military judgment and his steadfastness in love. When Camidius's "we are women's men" (3.7.69) is given to Enobarbus, soon to be "A master-leaver and a fugitive" (4.10.21), the expression of a sense of widespread disgust among Antony's troops becomes an individual's sexist response. Giving Proculeius's "You see how easily she may be surprised" (5.2.35) to Gallus boosts Antony's wisdom, since Proculeius remains as trustworthy as Antony had thought him (left unaltered, the lines comprise another one of Antony's failures, the most notable of which is his attempted suicide).

Gender Trouble at the Monument

Antony's botched suicide was the moment at which reviewers and audiences found it most difficult to suspend disbelief. The actors deliberately made clear to the audience that Eros would not kill Antony, but himself, and Antony's own death stroke, on both the entry and the withdrawal of the sword, was lingering. Audiences laughed on many nights, both during the hoisting of Antony up to Cleopatra "aloft" in the monument and at the sight of Cleopatra without her wig. As Antony was raised up, Iras held the safety rope, while Charmian and Cleopatra pulled. In performance, for various reasons, Rylance developed a flamboyant style of pulling, looking as though he was extending and contracting his entire body. Perhaps this extravagant style prompted the jocular comments of so many of the reviews. Robert Hewison complained of Cleopatra "hauling [Antony up] like a navy on a block and tackle" in a way that he felt "detracted from Antony's death as they crammed into the balcony" (Hewison). An audience member quoted in *The Independent* called the episode "almost a farce" (Hall). Even the otherwise sympathetic John Thaxter commented on the "muscular women-folk" lifting Antony up, but he conceded that the scene "properly [led] to a poignant scene of death" (Thaxter).

Most insistent was *The Times* (London): "Would it help if Cleo and a big, muscular Charmian didn't haul the dying Antony up to the monument quite so beefily? ... Or is there a point beyond which modern audiences find it tough to suspend disbelief in a testosterone-filled heroine?" (Nightingale 1999a). The writer reprised his discomfort in the *New York Times* later that month, singling out "a big, beefy Charmian hauling at the rope" (Nightingale 1999b). Why single out Charmian? Sapani is indeed muscular, but most stage actors are, and Rylance was the one with the exuberant style of hauling. An uncharitable reader might suggest that the reference to Charmian's "beefiness" is a coded racial judgment ("black people are more athletic than white ones, so this actor is too muscular for this role"). I do not think that is the case, at least not intentionally. But Sapani suddenly became visible on stage at this moment; Charmian threatened to upstage both Antony and Cleopatra. Oddly enough, the night I saw the production, I too was mesmerized by Charmian in that scene. This moment of "gender trouble" (muscular "women" hauling up a wounded man) made Charmian's race visible, observable, unmissable, unavoidable.

The only overt reference to Sapani's race that I have found so far in mainstream reviews likewise appears in a complaint about the production's lack of "camp" or prosthetics to evoke femininity. "Rylance is so determined to avoid contemporary associations with drag that he seems not to transform himself at all," writes one reviewer, adding, "Danny Sapani becomes a statuesque Negress, James Gillan a wan wench" (Hewison). The comparison between the "statuesque Negress" and the "wan wench" suggests that both actors, Sapani and Gillan, are simply themselves — their skin colors stand as essential attributes that remain visible through and beneath female costumes. It is a mild shock to see "Negress" in print, however, at least to my Americanized eye. Presumably the reviewer chose it as a deliberate archaism, to go with "wench," and also for conciseness: the word simultaneously marks the actor's "real" race and his performed gender.

Critical discomfort continued with Cleopatra's eulogy on Antony and even her death scene, in an episode that highlights the instability of the theatrical signifier, the difficulty for even sophisticated theatre-goers (such as reviewers) to figure out the meaning behind a particular theatrical sign, in this case Cleopatra's bald, wigless, and damaged head. Following North's Plutarch closely, Rylance decided that Cleopatra should die bareheaded, with evidence of self-mutilation. The production notes outline the discussion, and the make-up artist spent some time trying to create offensive-looking wounds that Cleopatra might have inflicted upon herself in a paroxysm of grief.[3] In performance, however, the gruesome wounds on her scalp evoked the scabs of pox or venereal disease to some audience members, and when she appeared wigless, "[t]here was still the odd giggle" at what one critic took to be a "bald, scrofulous scalp beneath" (Nightingale 1999b). This critic was not the only observer to see Cleopatra's scalp as pock-marked rather than, as was intended, self-mutilated. None of the reviewers seems to have taken Cleopatra's marked scalp as evidence of self-mutilation, seeing instead references to disease, aging, or even imprisonment. One saw "a cropped scalp riddle[d] with alopecia," and another, "a tufty, balding scalp" (Taylor 1999; Billington 1999a and 1999b). Oddly, Hewison compared Cleopatra's wigless Act V appearance to a "shorn-headed ... female collaborator at the end of the Second World War."

The critics' unease with the audience's laughter corresponds in part to my own experience watching the same performance. When I saw the production, Rylance removed his wig (or, perhaps, the wig came off?) immediately after

Figure 3.2 Mark Rylance as Cleopatra in the 1999 Globe Theatre production of *Antony and Cleopatra*. Photo: John Tramper.

"Noblest of men, woo'[d] die?" (On subsequent nights, Rylance seems not to have appeared wigless until his entry in Act V.) My first response was personal and "ethnic": to me Rylance's bald, suicidal Cleopatra suddenly evoked the nineteenth-century *suttee* or Hindu widow, preparing herself to join her husband in death by shaving her head and then destroying herself ("I am fire and air"). After a moment's reflection, I decided that did not fit; how could Cleopatra already have shaved her head, when she did not know for sure that Antony was going to die?[4]

I dwell on this misunderstanding because the confusing relationships among bodily sign, signifier, and signified concept are crucial to understanding how gender- and colorblind casting, or reverse casting, can work or fail to work. The production was hoping that Cleopatra's scalp signified the concept of grief or self-harm through the signifier of wounds, yet reviewers took from it the signified concept of venereal disease through the signifier of pock-marks. In addition, signifiers that had previously floated free of meaning (such as the skin colors of the actors) at times seemed as if they just *might* mean something, since something that had seemed previously to be anchored to meaning now appeared to be floating. Mark Rylance's body signified "Cleopatra" for most of the production, except when the signifier of the wig disappeared, and he signified himself. At the same time, Sapani and Gillan signified Charmian and Iras until the moment of gender trouble at the monument, when they signified a "Negress" and a "wan wench" through a new signifier, "a black man and a white man."

The sexual evaluation implied in Hewison's "Negress" and "wan wench" is deliberate, too, I think. Rylance characterized his skipping Cleopatra by constant movement and energy; I had no problem believing that she could hop forty paces through the public streets. But many critics complained that this childlike physical exuberance substituted for sexual energy (Nightingale called it her "sweetness," a term I find apt). Reviewers understandably often rate the eroticism of a theatrical production on their own responses — think of Charles Spencer's notorious evaluation of a nude Nicole Kidman in *The Blue Room* as "pure theatrical Viagra" (Spencer 1998). Both Frances de la Tour and Helen Mirren played at least one scene with Cleopatra nude or partly unclothed, as if in a last-ditch attempt to prove that the play requires "a woman's part," "an implicit challenge to impudent squeaking boys" (Jays). Hence, perhaps, the repeated complaint from male reviewers that Rylance, despite the lingering kiss he gives Shelley on the lips, lacked "sensuality" or "physical charge" (Nightingale 1999a; Hewison). Hewison suggested that some of this flatness was due to Rylance's own reluctance to play up the necessarily homoerotic overtones of an all-male production, and that Rylance "minimiz[ed] the physical contact between the lovers." There is some truth to this charge; with the exception of that one notable kiss, Rylance and Shelley rarely touched each other on stage, giving his Cleopatra a girlish innocence rather than the knowing coquetry of, say, Bushell-Mingo's or Mirren's. This decision is another point at which the Globe's evocation of "original practices" appears as the red herring that it is.

The Globe claims early modern costume, dance, music, and a single-sex cast as "original practices," and yet to equate all-male casts with all-female ones ignores the social meaning of sexual difference in both our own era and in Shakespeare's (and ignores the still-vexed question of how old in fact the actors playing Shakespeare's female characters were; most theatre scholars argue that the female parts were played by boys, not men). The theatrical experiments currently going on at the new Globe are fascinating enough not to need the spurious credential of "original practices." The restrictions on costume, music, and gender are intriguing and useful; why attempt to justify them in historical terms rather than simply allowing them as experiments in their own right? Furthermore, if single-sex casting is an "original practice," why not perform with a single-race cast (black, white, or Asian), to correspond to the all-white cast of Shakespeare's Globe? Finally, "original practices" need not necessitate removing sexual charge or energy from a production. We know from early modern responses to the theatre that for certain audience members, boy actors put on not only the clothes of women but also "the passions of a woman;" tragedies unmanned men by inducing "womanish weeping and mourning"; and the theatre itself was considered a sink of venery, a market of bawdy (Gosson, E3v, C5r, G5v–G6r). Shouldn't a present-day production claiming "original practices" deal openly with these charges, rather than trying to avoid them? In contrast, as we shall see, the willingness of Cheek by Jowl to embrace both the homo- and heteroerotic implications of single-sex casting in their tenth anniversary production of *As You Like It* gave us a Rosalind and even a Celia shining with desire.

The 1991 and 1994 Cheek by Jowl *As You Like It*

As You Like It, the celebrated tenth anniversary production of Declan Donnellan's Cheek by Jowl Company, was widely and, mostly, enthusiastically reviewed. The "delightful," "enchanting," "ground-breaking" production featured a "captivating" and "extraordinary" Rosalind, played by Adrian Lester (Taylor 1991; Doudai; Coveney; Wardle). The production foregrounded artifice and acting from the very beginning, with a bare stage dotted with actors clothed in black while Jaques delivered his "All the World's a Stage" speech. A smear of mud on Orlando's face evoked the "visceral" degradation to which Oliver had subjected him and foreshadowed the freeing effects of theatre itself and of Arden (Brantley). The set hinted at Arden itself in stylized fashion, with green walls and paper streamers, but only after Orlando's sonnets had already called the world of the imagination into existence (Kingston). The few properties were judicious: spectacles and a book for Rosalind. Imagine Rosalind as a bookish nerd bowled over by a gut-wrenching and transgressive sexuality: the labored jokes about "the good houswife Fortune" (1.2.26) might suggest such a thing, but it was and perhaps still is an unusual way of playing the part.

At the same time, Cheek by Jowl's Arden was no "green world"; some reviewers caviled at the doubling of the Dukes, but it emphasized the ways in which rank and gender could follow the girls into the forest and the courtiers into exile (Ranald). The courtship of Orlando and Ganymede contrasted as a heady liberation. The bond between them played so convincingly that, on seeing Ganymede as Rosalind again, Orlando stepped away in a huff, as if angered at a seeming betrayal (Wardle; Nightingale 1991).

Danny Sapani's race all but disappeared from reviews of the Globe's 1999 *Antony and Cleopatra*, but the blackness of Adrian Lester, Cheek by Jowl's Rosalind, was the subject of scrutiny in many reviews, both in coded terms like those used for Sapani, commenting on the actor's "strapping" body (his height and muscularity), and in overt references to his skin color. One is tempted to speculate that the emphasis paid to Lester's race reflects a surprise or even discomfort with the breaking of the rules of what Celia Daileader calls "Othellophilia" — the tendency, even within supposedly colorblind productions, to restrict black actors to minor roles in Shakespeare that mimic

Othello's language or that emphasize the hypersexual pursuit of a white lover (see Daileader). As in the Globe's 1999 *Antony and Cleopatra*, however, the sexual response of the audience (or of the reviewer) comes into play in both racialized and gendered ways, as does the context of the casting choices of individual productions. The 1991 production featured Adrian Lester as "the only black actor in the company" (Wardle), but the cast of the 1994 revival (and tour to the Brooklyn Academy of Music) was "biracial," altering the meanings of Lester's blackness (Canby). While in the earlier reviews, Lester's blackness and his maleness were simultaneously the greatest obstacles to be overcome in order for him to "become" Rosalind (obstacles linked by his "strapping" size), in reviews of the 1994 revival Lester's race becomes *less* important than his sex and the perceived sexual orientation of the production.

Strapping Lasses

Central to this production was Donnellan's belief that "Rosalind isn't an androgyne. She's a very sexy woman and a very sexy man and both sides have to exist in the play" (quoted in Morris). With this in mind, Donnellan and his cast deliberately eschewed any prosthetics and "avoided any suggestion of camp or of dames" (Donnellan, quoted in Morris), although, as we shall see, reviewers differed in the extent to which they thought that this strategy was achieved at all, on the one hand, or successful, on the other. Donnellan advised Lester, who was complaining that he was "too tall" for the role: "'there are 6 ft. strapping women; what do you do about it?' So the shoulder slips and the knees dunk" (quoted in Morris). Lester thus envisioned from the beginning a transformation from awkward, slouching, "too tall" Rosalind to a Ganymede glorying in his inches.

Two British reviewers likewise called Lester "strapping," marking his height as a factor contributing to the difficulty of playing a convincing Rosalind. One asserted: "Rosalind is a strapping six-footer and her real name is Adrian" (Morris); another added race as another destabilizing factor, describing Lester as "a strapping 6ft. black male actor" (Taylor 1991). The word "strapping" is itself a cross-gendered term, coined in the seventeenth century to describe women whose sexual forwardness makes them masculine, or exotic "sunburnt lasses" or country girls (*OED* 3, obs.), but used now of both sexes (though still with connotations of vulgarity, sometimes ethnically coded; its use is nearly always facetious).[5] U.S. reviewers preferred the term "gangly," in one case describing "a tall gangly man playing a woman in man's clothing" (Brantley), in another, "the kind of tall, gangly young woman who walks in a manner desperately designed to make her look shorter" (Canby).

Reviews took the production's refusal of prosthetics of any kind as a mark of either "a touch of camp" — "pure Widow Twankey" — or of its authenticity, its ability to portray "the giddy ecstasy of love," "love, which both transcends sexuality and includes it" (Rutherford; Church; Billington 1991; Peter

1991). Whatever touches of camp I noticed seemed part of the artificiality of the usurping Duke's court (as opposed to the theatrical *artifice* of the exiled Duke's Arden). Rosalind and Celia moved stiffly, as if constrained by corsets, until released into Arden. Lester's Rosalind hung her head and slouched as if to conceal her height, while Hollander's petulant Celia aped girlishness in the service of a hugely serious crush on her cousin. Once in Arden, however, both Celia and Rosalind discovered an extroverted and exogamic sexuality that brightened the world around them as well as their expressiveness.

To a certain extent, the degree to which reviewers believed that the production worked effectively depended upon whether they thought that the all-male cast "limited" the production's appeal or broadened it. Benedict Nightingale complained that "homo-, bi-, trisexuality is all about," and of the "strongly homoerotic feel"; he found the performance highly camp, Celia's voice "mincing," and argued of Lester's Rosalind, "We never forget the gender behind the gender" (Nightingale 1991). Another reviewer found that Lester failed to "convince as a woman" because he lacked the properties or accoutrements of femininity: that is, what made the production "camp" were not the "big boobs," wigs, and make-up jettisoned by the director as "offensive to women," but their absence (Donnellan, quoted in Hemming). Others found elements of camp to be slight, on the one hand, or inclusive, on the other (if they noticed them at all), because they thought the production brought out that "we are all sexual role-players," that "actors [were] ... communicating a different mode of being," and that the "homosexual undercurrents [were] both male and female" (Billington 1991; Peter 1991; Doudai). And John Peter wrote, *contra* Nightingale: "*As You Like It* is not about sexuality — hetero-, homo-, bi- or trans-."

James Bulman, however, complains that such reviews downplay the production's reliance on "camp" or gay masculinity. Instead, he argues, they constitute an "avoidance behavior" that elides the production's gay agenda, which he contextualizes in light of Britain's then-recent anti-gay legislation (the notorious Section 28 that outlawed the "promotion of homosexuality") and hate crimes against homosexuals. Oddly, he praises Nightingale for acknowledging the production's homoerotic elements but ignores Nightingale's dismissal of those very elements as "limited" (Bulman, 37). Nightingale's is hardly a gay-friendly or queer-identified review. I think Bulman is right that the "gayness" of the production *was* less noticeable to critics in 1991 than in 1994 — but the "avoidance strategy" he finds appears in part because the colorblind and solitary casting of Adrian Lester in 1991 overshadowed the production's relevance to gay theatrical history, as we shall see.

"As black and as tall as Josette Simon"

The comments on Lester's skin color appeared as a corollary to those on his height and sex. Nearly all reviews mentioned race and sex in the same sentence: "the principal boy-girl ... happens to be black" (Church); "a strapping 6 foot black male actor" (Taylor 1991); "the willowy Adrian Lester ... can emerge as the most breathtakingly sensuous Rosalind since Vanessa Redgrave" (Wardle). This final comment re-genders the sexual response evoked by the actor through a comparison to an actress, Vanessa Redgrave. And a couple of "rave" reviews in the British broadsheet press use race to bypass anxieties about gender or sexual orientation raised by Lester's performance: "Lester's as black and as tall as [black British actress] Josette Simon, whom he uncannily resembles in his red and white silks, close-cropped haircut and svelte forest mufti," or "Lester ... bears a spooky resemblance to Josette Simon" (Coveney; Taylor 1991).

The first black British actress to perform major roles for the RSC, Josette Simon was adored by my generation of Britons as Dayna in BBC TV's 1980s space opera *Blake's 7*. Lester and Simon are both indeed tall, black, and beautiful, but it seems bizarre to compare the two actors in this way. Their faces look quite different, perhaps in ways that will sound stereotypical of gender differences as I catalogue them: Lester's jaw is broad, his neck strong, his lips thinner, his skin darker than Simon's, whose chin is dainty and the slenderness of whose neck is usually emphasized by the costumes she wears in character. In this strange comparison, the race of Lester and Simon *undoes* the gender trouble evoked by Lester's male Rosalind; Lester is compelling as Rosalind because he reminds reviewers of another tall, black actor, but one who happens to be female.

Consider the first reviewer's subsequent characterization of Rosalind: "Rosalind is surely ... a portrait of entirely intuitive womanliness. She does not become Ganymede to affect maleness, but to investigate her own femininity. Adrian Lester's extraordinary performance conveys all this" (Coveney). Thus, the "sexually engaged" aspects of the production that the review originally praises become aspects of *heterosexual* love. Lester's performance is "extraordinary" because he becomes not the "androgynous" or "polymorphous" heroine the director imagined (Billington 1991), but a portrait of perfect "femininity," the ideal woman. And the actor's skill at changing sex is measured by his resemblance to an actress whose race he shares. Similarly, although the other reviewer who compares Lester and Simon praises a "comic erotic tension and a sexual ambiguity that's heightened because both players are men" in *As You Like It*, the comparison between Lester and Simon appears as evidence of Lester's skill in "evok[ing] femininity" and even a "frisson" of sexual desire (Taylor 1991). Reviewers, then, noticed Lester's race as a testament to his ability to portray, to become, an ideal Rosalind, *despite* the perceived barriers of race and sex.

It is notable that U.S. reviewers and critics, watching the revived 1994 version with several black actors in the cast, paid less attention to Lester's race than the British reviewers did. One comments only that the cast was "biracial" (Canby), and another lists his blackness only along with a list of Rosalind's

Figure 3.3 Adrian Lester as Rosalind in the 1991 Cheek by Jowl production of *As You Like It*. Photo: John Haynes.

Figure 3.4 Josette Simon as Dayna in *Blake's 7* (1981).

character traits: "a tall, willowy black man in spectacles, blue headband/scarf, and long blue dress, reclining with books on a round black satin pad" (Ranald, 10). This description evokes size, race, and sex, but as attributes of character, rather than of actor, just like the traits of bespectacled bookishness, loneliness, and perhaps melancholy evoked by her props and costume. The headband is both a headband and a scarf, a signifier of both masculinity and femininity. Alisa Solomon suggests that the multiracial cast of the revived *As You Like It* could be seen either as a "liberal integrationist gesture (i.e. race doesn't matter) or as the dominant group wielding its prerogative to dismiss racial identity, which others, as bell hooks has written, are constantly reminded of" (Solomon, 44).

Although Solomon refers to both productions, the 1991 anniversary performances and the 1994 revival, her account conflates them. In fact, race worked alongside and against sexual difference and homoeroticism in different ways in 1991 and in 1994. In 1991, Lester's casting broke the black ceiling encountered by actors of color in classical British theatre, and that taboo substituted in some reviews for the erotic transgression that the production embodied. Whether or not the casting choice was a gesture of "liberal integration," the reviewers certainly did not perceive it that way, regarding "tall, black" Rosalind as an example of color-conscious, rather than colorblind, casting. If we return to semiotics, we see that in 1991, Lester's black skin functioned as a signifier in its own right, one, moreover, that outranked costume and properties in its importance:

Lester's 1991 Rosalind   = black skin / perfect femininity

(sign)   = (form of signifier)/ (signified concept)

Or:

One black actor   = black skin / unique heroine

In 1994, however, black skin could no longer be read as a sign with such assurance, since the cast was multiracial. If Rosalind's blackness was a sign, then so too could be other characters' blackness, whiteness, possible Asian origin, and so on. The semiotic breakdown looks quite different:

Lester's 1994 Rosalind   = skin, specs, book / sexual ambiguity
(sign)   = (many signifiers) / (signified concept)

Or:

Multiracial cast   = many skin colors / bodies do not matter

No longer isolated as the sole black actor on stage, Lester could personify a kind of embodied gender trouble, "an almost giddy awareness of gender's provisionality" (Solomon, 27); "gender [as] simply a choice" (Laris, 301); "an elision of heterosexual and homosexual identities" (Bulman, 36). For some women, the all-male production excluded women and their responses from both the play and the audience, but to others, Lester's Rosalind was both male and female, and the reference to kissing "as many as have beards" in the epilogue was both an affirmation of the boy actor's original masculinity and a mischievous obscene joke evoking female homosexuality (Dusinberre).

Or was the multiracial cast merely another example of the "dominant group ... dismiss[ing]" race as an irrelevance, as Solomon wonders? I did not see the 1994 revival, but I note from a widely disseminated photograph of the final scene (reproduced in Solomon's chapter) that a black actor played Hymen. Perhaps we could read this tableau, too, as the subordination of gay marriage to what Judith Roof has called the heteronarrative — and yet the persistence and proliferation of critical responses from men and women with differing political, academic, and sexual identifications suggests that in some way Lester did succeed in being both male and female, feminist and anti- (or post-) feminist, in being polymorphously perverse sexually and politically.

Bearded Ladies: The 2004 Globe *Much Ado About Nothing*

Just as Rylance's wig became a touchstone of the 1999 Globe *Antony and Cleopatra*, eliciting comments from most major reviewers, and Rosalind's epilogue became a touchstone of Cheek by Jowl's 1991 and 1994 *As You Like It*, so the beards of the all-female cast of the Globe's 2004 *Much Ado About Nothing* became emblems of women's ability — or inability — to portray men on stage: "Female voices issuing from bearded faces sound bizarre" (Peter 1994); "As actresses hung on the false beards and adopt gruff voices and a manly swagger, one is frequently reminded of a mediocre production at a girl's boarding school" (Spencer 2004); "the beards ... seem indecently indebted to borzoi dogs, badgers and bits of Pekinese" (Nightingale 2004). Even the rave from the *Boston Globe* begins with a warning: "One tends to associate bearded ladies with freak shows, not fine theatre" (Gilsdorf). None of the reviewers seems to have noticed that the text explicitly tells us that Benedick (like, presumably, the other men) is bearded. Claudio and Leonato diagnose Benedick's lovesickness by his barbering and painting: "he looks younger than he did, by the loss of a beard" (3.2.40–41).[6] (Contrast *As You Like It*, in which only Phebe's "black silk hair" (3.5.47) receives comment. Rosalind/Ganymede has, appropriately, fewer sex-specific traits.)

What I want to focus on instead are the moments of the 2004 Globe *Ado* at which colorblind casting and gender-blind casting reinforced each other. For me, the sight of Ann Ogbomo playing jealous Claudio to slandered Hero evoked even more strongly the specter of Othellophilia, his strictures in 4.1 even more evocative of Othello's self-hatred: "You seem to me as Dian in her orb, / As chaste as is the bud ere it be blown" (4.1.55–56) resonates with Othello's "[Her] name, that was as fresh / As Dian's visage, is now begrim'd and black / As mine own face" (*Othello* 3.3.391–393). The casting choice also brought out the structural parallels between *Othello* and *Much Ado* — the slandered wife, the gullible lover, the strong-minded female friend — one the comic mirror of the other, but always with the threat of imminent tragedy. The trope of blushing in 4.1 is also racialized within the play, something brought out more strongly by color-conscious casting (see Iyengar, 123–128 *et passim*). This production changed Claudio's racist line, "I'll hold my mind, were she an Ethiope" (*Ado* 5.4.38), to "I'll hold my mind, as I have sworn to do," but keeping it would have emphasized (as did his repudiation of Hero at the altar) the extent of this Claudio's investment in social conformity, regardless of personal cost. The absence of sexual charge in this production, on which many critics commented, was here an advantage, allowing a racial subplot to emerge.

Ann Ogbomo was not, however, the only black actress on the stage. Casting Joy Richardson as Margaret added, for me, a racialized resentment to the latter's acquiescence to dress up in Hero's clothes and to her sullen line, "I have many ill qualities" (2.1.84–85). Isolated upstage from the other ladies in the opening scene, Margaret radiated an anger that suggested an alternative to Claudio's agonized, Othello-like adoption of the dominant culture — almost as if Margaret were the Aaron to Claudio's Othello.

Colorblind Casting as the Racialized Bedtrick

Finally, I want to turn to the device of the bedtrick, or feigned bedtrick. Although *Much Ado* does not include a bedtrick in the sense of *All's Well* or *Measure for Measure*, it does feature the imagined sexual substitution of one woman by another, Margaret in Hero's clothes — in the 2004 Globe production, a black woman standing in for a white one. As Virginia Mason Vaughan has recently noted, the bedtrick in early modern literature often appears as a practical joke involving cross-dressing *and* racial passing.[7] In *Pasquils Jests, or Mother Bunches Merriments* (1604), a "fine boy drest woman like" gulls a "green goose" out of large sums of money. Expecting to sleep with the "woman" in return, the gullible greenhorn goes to bed drunk, but

> in which being laid in his bed, in stead of the faire boy, they had laid a blacke Moore wench by him, with whom I know not how he handled the matter: but in the morning, seeing what a sweet bed-fellow he had gotten, suddenly starting out of the bed, ran to his clothes, and taking them in his hand, ran out into another chamber, crying that hee was vndone, for he had laine with the vgliest thing that euer was, and he feared it was the deuill. (Pasquil, C2r)

This ugly story or "jest" replaces the body of the desirable white woman first with a "faire" youth and then with a "blacke Moore wench"; the "jest" is in the degree of departure from the ideal, the substitution of "one 'monster' with another" (Vaughan, 80). The gull in turn moves the blackamoor wench even

Figure 3.5 Hero and Margaret in the 2004 Globe Theatre production of *Much Ado About Nothing.* Photo: John Tramper.

further from idealized humanity, referring to her first as an object ("the vgliest thing") and then as "the deuill."

The conceit appears again in both a more sophisticated and a more violent form in Fletcher's *Monsieur Thomas* (1639), a play that foregrounds technologies of prosthesis and cosmesis (Frances Dolan's useful term for the ways that early modern women used make-up to assert themselves) on the stage — in particular, the technologies of sexual and racial substitution and the ways in which theatricality confounds both characters' and audiences' distinctions of skin color and gender (see Dolan). Monsieur Thomas goes to increasing lengths to conquer the chastity of his beloved, Mary, while Mary and her friend Dorothy, Thomas's long-suffering sister, respond in kind; references to so-called devils' masks, to paint, and to cross-dressing culminate in the substitution of a black woman for a white woman in bed beside a man disguised as a woman. Thomas's serenade is rebuffed by Mary's maidservant "Madge with a divels vizard roring" (Fletcher, Hv); the red and white "paint" that allows Thomas to impersonate his sister Dorothy casts him instead in the "divels part" (K3r), betrayed by his "Boots on like a Player / Vnder his wenches cloaths" (K3r). The comparison to the player turns the audience into the actors' gulls, stupidly tricked into interest or arousal by the boy actors on stage just as Thomas's old father is the only one convinced by his feminine disguise. The cross-dressed Thomas finally sneaks into Mary's bed to "comfort" her, without realizing that the ladies are aware of his plot and, to confound him, have placed the black maid Kate in bed in Mary's stead. Upon discovering the identity of his bedfellow, Thomas roars "The devill, devill, devill, O the devil" (Lr), beating the maid until her mistress intervenes. Unusually, Kate the blackamoor has some indignant lines in response, retorting: "Pray lye here your self, next Mistris, / And entertaine your sweet-heart" (Lv–L2r). Mary generously offers her "poor Kate" a "petticoat," and swears they will "laugh an houre now" (L2r), but the joke is nonetheless at Kate's expense even more than Thomas's.

Oddly enough, casting a black actress as Margaret, the maid who stands in for Hero, repeats the structure of the early modern racialized bedtrick: theatre makes bodies interchangeable, seemingly able to transcend distinctions of skin color and gender through aesthetics or craft, and yet real-world hierarchies of race and sex persist. I am sure that such associations were far from the minds of those casting and performing in the production. And yet semiotics clarifies that "'All that is on stage is a sign'" (Jiri Veltrusky, quoted in Elam, 7). Elam, following C. S. Peirce, distinguishes among three kinds of theatrical sign — icon, index, and symbol (Elam, 21–31). The Icon means by resemblance or similitude, with varying degrees of realism, so that an actor's body can be an icon for a character's body, but a model ship could also stand iconically for a real ship at sea. The Index means by contiguity or association, an example being the idiosyncratic shuffle that tall Adrian Lester developed to evoke Rosalind's embarrassment at her height. The Symbol means by convention or idea, rather than by physical resemblance: "Peirce's exemplary 'symbol' is ... the linguistic sign" (Elam, 27). To return to Sidney's sign, "Thebes in great letters on an old door," the old door is an icon when someone enters through it (a stage door whose referent is a real door), an index of antiquity, and a symbol (the word THEBES).

Traditionally, the actor's body has been taken for an icon, something that resembles a body in the real world. Gender- and colorblind casting make it obvious that the actor's body is not only icon but index and symbol as well. For reviewer, critic, actor, or director to ignore the social meanings of skin color and embodied gender in either a Renaissance or in a contemporary sense is an act of bad faith. Thus — again, without impugning the motives of those involved, and without denying what I learned from watching these productions on stage or on videotape — I wonder whether the racial bedtrick might itself be a figure for colorblind casting in single-sex productions: we see something that diverts us (in all its senses) because it is an unexpected link in a chain of anticipated substitutions, but that does not question those expectations themselves, or why we have them. For that, we might have to leave Shakespeare behind.

Notes

1. My analysis of theatrical signs is indebted to the germinal work of Keir Elam.
2. I saw the 1991 Cheek by Jowl *As You Like It* on tour at the Swan Theatre, Stratford-on-Avon, in February 1992. I saw the 1999 Globe *Antony and Cleopatra* on a preview night in July 1999, and watched several videotapes of later performances in the Globe's research department. I saw only videotapes of the 2004 Globe *Much Ado*, also in the Globe's research department.
3. Gabriel Egan, electronic mail correspondence with Giles Block, 28 January 2005; quoted with permission.
4. Giles Block had similar misgivings, it seems, thinking that the cue to remove the wig should have been "This mortal house I'll ruin," but Rylance insisted (Egan).
5. Consider this joke story headline from *The Onion*, a satirical newspaper: "Strapping Young Man to Address Congress." Consider also an article from *The Guardian* about female wrestlers that describes a masseuse as "a friendly, strapping lass ... [with] broken English." (Hopps)
6. I thank Fran Teague for reminding me of this.
7. On the early modern bedtrick, see Desens; on the racialized bedtrick, see Vaughan (74–92), who independently analyzes the anecdote in *Pasquils Jests* and the episode in *Monsieur Thomas* alongside other early modern examples to conclude that the racialized bedtrick emphasizes the "ineluctable difference" evoked by black skin in the early modern imagination.

References

Bessell, Jaq. "Findings from the Globe 1999 Season: *Antony and Cleopatra*." *Shakespeare's Globe Research Bulletin*, 2000.

Billington, Michael. "Seeing the wooed among the trees." *The Guardian*, October 14, 1991.

Billington, Michael. "Comedy of Lovers." *The Guardian*, August 2, 1999a.

Billington, Michael. "Comedy becomes Cleopatra." *The Guardian*, August 18, 1999b.

Brantley, Ben. "How to Call a Play into Being by Smearing a Man with Mud." *New York Times*, October 6, 1994.

Bulman, James C. "Bringing Cheek by Jowl's *As You Like It* Out of the Closet: The Politics of Gay Theater." *Shakespeare Bulletin* 22 (2004): 31–46.

Canby, Vincent. "Sunday View: The Evening Is Both Cheever's and Guerney's." *New York Times*, October 16, 1994.

Church, Michael. "*As You Like It*: Lyric Hammersmith." *The Guardian*, December 6, 1991.

Coveney, Michael. "Close encounters of an all-male kind." *The Observer*, December 1, 1991.

Daileader, Celia. "Casting Black Actors: Beyond Othellophilia." In *Shakespeare and Race*, edited by Catherine Alexander and Stanley Wells. Cambridge: Cambridge University Press, 2001.

Desens, Marliss C. *The Bed-trick in English Renaissance Drama: Explorations in Gender, Sexuality, and Power*. Newark: University of Delaware Press, 1994.

Dolan, Frances. "Taking the Pencil out of God's Hand: Art, Nature and the Face-Painting Debate in Early Modern England." *PMLA* 108 (1993): 224–239.

Doudai, Naomi. "An Accent on Comedy." *Jerusalem Post*, December 20, 1994.

Dusinberre, Juliet. "As *Who* Liked It?" *Shakespeare Survey* 46 (1994): 9–21.

Egan, Gabriel. Electronic mail correspondence with Giles Block, January 28, 2005. Quoted with permission.

Elam, Keir. *The Semiotics of Theatre and Drama*. London and New York: Routledge, 1980.

Erickson, Peter. "Taking Shakespeare Personally: A Note on Race." *Shakespeare and the Classroom* 6 (1998): 53–56.

Fletcher, John. *Monsieur Thomas: A Comedy*. London, 1639.

Gilsdorf, Ethan. "Tradition Gets Tweaked at Shakespeare's Globe Theatre." *Boston Globe*, September 8, 2004.

Gosson, Stephen. *Playes Confuted in Fiue Actions*. London, 1582.

Hall, Alastair. "Exit Poll: What Theatre-goers Think of Mark Rylance as Cleopatra." *The Independent*, August 1, 1999.

Hemming, Sarah. "Taking It Like a Man." *The Independent*, November 20, 1991.

Hendricks, Margo. "Visions of Color: Spectacle, Spectators, and the Performance of Race." In *A Blackwell Companion to Shakespeare and Performance*, edited by Barbara Hodgdon and William Worthen. London: Blackwell, 2006.

Hewison, Robert. "Playing Fast and Loose With a Queen." *Sunday Times*, August 8, 1999.

Hopps, David. "Women Grapple with Cultural Shift." *The Guardian*, August 24, 2004.

Iyengar, Sujata. *Shades of Difference: Mythologies of Skin Color in Early Modern England*. Philadelphia: University of Pennsylvania Press, 2005.

Jays, David. "Borrowed Skirts To Call Boys' Own." *Financial Times*, August 29, 1999.

Kingston, Jeremy. "Sorting Out the Men from the Boys." *The Times*, January 27, 1995.

Laris, Katie. Untitled review of *As You Like It*, directed by Declan Donnellan. *Theatre Journal* 47 (1995): 300–302.

Little, Arthur. *Shakespeare Jungle Fever: National-Imperial Re-Visions of Race, Rape, and Sacrifice*. Stanford: Stanford University Press, 2000.

Loomba, Ania. "'Local-manufacture Made-in-India Othello Fellows:' Issues of Race, Hybridity, and Location in Post-Colonial Shakespeares." In *Post-Colonial Shakespeares*, edited by Ania Loomba and Martin Orkin. London and New York: Routledge, 1998.

Lott, Eric. "White like Me: Racial Cross-dressing and the Construction of American Whiteness." In *Cultures of United States Imperialism*, edited by Amy Kaplan and Donald E. Pease. Durham, NC: Duke University Press, 1993.

Morris, Tom. "The Man as a Woman as a Man." *The Independent*, November 24, 1991.

Nightingale, Benedict. "As You Like It." *The Times* (London), December 5, 1991.

Nightingale, Benedict. "Review." *The Times* (London), August 2, 1999a.

Nightingale, Benedict. "A London Season as Unsettling as the Weather." *New York Times*, August 29, 1999b.

Nightingale, Benedict. "Who's Wearing the Trousers?" *The Times*, June 4, 2004.

Pasquil. *Pasquils Jests, or Mother Bunches Merriments*. London, 1609.

Peter, John. "Love Divine, All Roles Excelling." *Sunday Times*, December 8, 1991.

Peter, John. "*Much Ado About Nothing*." *Sunday Times*, June 13, 1994.

Ranald, Margaret Loftus. Untitled review of *As You Like It*, directed by Declan Donnellan. *Shakespeare Bulletin* 12 (1991): 10–11.

Rutherford, Malcolm. "*As You Like It*; Lyric, Hammersmith." *Financial Times*, December 6, 1991.

Sidney, Philip. *An Apology for Poetry*. 1586. Edited by Geoffrey Shepherd. Manchester: Manchester University Press, 1973.

Smith, Ian. "White Skin, Black Masks: Racial Cross-Dressing on the Early Modern Stage." *Renaissance Drama* 32 (2003): 33–67.

Solomon, Alisa. *Redressing the Canon: Essays on Theatre and Gender*. London and New York: Routledge, 1997.

Spencer, Charles. "Room with an Utterly Bewitching View." *Daily Telegraph*, September 24, 1998.

Spencer, Charles. "Women-Only Sex War Fizzles Out." *Daily Telegraph*, June 4, 2004.

"Strapping Young Man to Address Congress." *The Onion: America's Finest News Source*, September 8, 1999 (35.32).

Taylor, Paul. "Meeting the Boys in Lieu." *The Independent*, December 6, 1991.

Taylor, Paul. "Delectable Mark Finds Cleopatra's Sensitive Soul." *The Independent*, July 31, 1999.

Thaxter, John. "*Antony and Cleopatra*: Theatre Review Shakespeare's Globe." *The Stage*, August 5, 1999.

Thompson, Ayanna. "Practicing a Theory/Theorizing a Practice: An Introduction to Shakespearean Colorblind Casting." In *Colorblind Shakespeare: New Perspectives on Race and Performance*, edited by Ayanna Thompson. London and New York: Routledge, 2006.

Vaughan, Virginia Mason. *Performing Blackness on English Stages, 1500–1800*. Cambridge: Cambridge University Press, 2005.

Wardle, Irvine. "All the Stage an Actor's World." *The Independent*, December 8, 1991.

4
Faux Show: Falling into History in Kenneth Branagh's *Love's Labour's Lost*

COURTNEY LEHMANN

Kenneth Branagh has long prided himself on his colorblind approach to casting, for this approach is central to his broader mission of re-creating Shakespeare as a "crossover" phenomenon — indeed, as a screen persona capable of appealing to a mass audience. Appropriately for a British subject, Branagh initially focused his crossover vision on a classless Shakespeare. Well aware of "the barriers that separate Shakespeare ... from a truly popular audience," Branagh made his first adaptation, *Henry V* (1989), with an eye to wooing newcomers in particular (Branagh 1989a, 63). Through a systematic use of cinematic intertextuality, the film continually supplements the untrained ear with the visual idiom of pop culture, encouraging audiences to read the mercurial king as a kind of medieval version of "Batman" (Light, 19). Judging from both the box-office returns and Oscar nominations, *Henry V* successfully fulfilled Branagh's pledge of offering "something for everyone" (Branagh 1989a, 193). Even more ambitious is *Much Ado About Nothing* (1993), which assumes the challenge of adapting Shakespeare through a lens that is not only "classless" but also "colorblind." In an effort to make the Bard more resonant with nonwhite audiences, Branagh pitched *Much Ado About Nothing* as nothing less than a Shakespeare film "for the world" (Branagh 1993, x). The cast, he explained in the published screenplay, would be "as international as possible," presenting the audience with "different accents" and "different looks." As it turned out, however, *Much Ado* was performed exclusively by British and North American actors, whose "different accents" were all but subsumed by the very "different look" of the lone person of color in the production, the African American actor Denzel Washington. Released during the peak of the political-correctness wars, *Much Ado About Nothing* places the utopian burden of a Shakespeare film "for the world" entirely on Washington's shoulders, as his character becomes a synecdoche for all the *other* nonwhite "others" whom Branagh's ostensibly colorblind vision fails to accommodate.

Branagh's casting of Washington as Don Pedro, the film's highest-ranking character, implies that (high) social class can serve as a racial solvent — a strategy that he repeated in *Love's Labour's Lost* (2000). Had Branagh been striving for a historically accurate approach to casting in *Much Ado,* the obvious role for Washington to play would be the film's lowest-ranking character, Don John the bastard, a decision that would neatly explain Don John's dubious parentage as a case of racial miscegenation. But Branagh has always shied away from historical accuracy, preferring a vague approach to period that complements his "anything goes" style. Hence, when confronted with a question about the racial role reversal involving Washington's Don Pedro and Keanu Reeves's Don John, Branagh immediately asserts his colorblind creed, but he does so, significantly, with reference only to Washington: "He's a brilliant actor, very masculine but also very tender. I didn't think beyond that. His being black doesn't work for or against the story. His feud with his half-brother Don John is a filial, brotherly thing, not racial" (quoted in Crawley, 45). As in *Love's Labour's Lost,* however, this colorblind vision can be sustained only by vigilant edits to the Shakespearean text, the most obvious being Claudius's assertion, while standing alongside his best man, Don Pedro, that he would wed Leonato's daughter "were she an Ethiope" (5.4.38). Such omissions reveal not a colorblind but a highly color-conscious approach to Shakespeare, the *un*conscious residue of which, as I have argued elsewhere, emerges in the film's conclusion (see Lehmann). This time adding a scene to Shakespeare's play, Branagh orchestrates a magnificent final song-and-dance reprise of "Sigh No More" in which all the happy white couples, surrounded by fifty or more white extras, celebrate a vision of Paradise Found in the "fairy tale landscape" of timeless Tuscany (Branagh 1993, 83). As the camera cranes progressively higher, we see Don Pedro on the periphery of the scene, watching pensively as he is excluded from the scores of clasped hands that connect all the other characters in the vast morris-style dance. If, in Shakespeare's play, Don Pedro remains unmatched because of his high social class, which makes him "too costly" for these lesser aristocrats (2.1.287), then in Branagh's film, the suggestion — however unconscious — is that Washington's Don Pedro is ineligible for marriage on the grounds of race, for his black skin would interrupt the all-white production values that constitute this vision of utopia, rendering *him,* not his "brother," the film's real bastard.

Perhaps seeking to avoid the charge of tokenism, Branagh employed a less heavy-handed approach to colorblind casting in *Hamlet* (1996), in which actors of West Indian, South Asian, and African descent are sprinkled throughout the ensemble scenes, as well as cast in minor roles as messengers and members of the guard. Yet in his effort to diffuse the stark racial differences that characterize his approach to *Much Ado,* Branagh's *Hamlet* inadvertently produces a vision of racial integration that is more at home in the film's nineteenth-century setting than in its late-1990s era of production. For by casting non-white actors predominantly as "extras" and, at best, as representatives of the Danish "service sector," Branagh's colorful film has greater resonance with the discourse of Orientalism than it does with multiculturalism. Reflecting neither the democratic spirit of the more traditional approaches to colorblind casting advanced by Joseph Papp nor the overtly political bent of contemporary "conceptual" casting practices, Branagh's Shakespeare films ask that we "not see" race *and* that we "not see" racism.[1]

The source of such mixed messages, which exist throughout Branagh's oeuvre, is the utopian mission that informs all of his Shakespeare films — a mission that cannot be fulfilled without first deflecting and, subsequently, exorcising the specter of ethnic antagonisms that Branagh himself embodies as a postcolonial subject. Seeking to escape the escalating violence at the height of the Troubles, Branagh's family moved from Belfast to Reading, England at a time when, Branagh recalls, it was "not a good time to be Irish." "Many of the children at school had older brothers in the [English] Army," he explains, "[e]very death reported on the television news made me try to change even further; I longed just to blend in" (Branagh 1989a, 23–24). In a place where "everyone spoke like BBC newsreaders," Branagh was forced to make a career of acting long before he became a legitimate thespian, by adopting a posture of double consciousness that enabled him to be "English at school" while remaining "Irish at home" (24). Testifying once again to the belief that social class can surmount ethnic caste, Branagh eventually discovered that the residue of his native Ireland — what he referred to as "the accent problem" — could be eliminated by his identification with the middle class, as his voice "gradually took on the twang of suburbia" (23–24). Branagh's eventual admission to the Royal Academy for Dramatic Arts and, later, the Royal Shakespeare Company, both bastions of quintessentially English identity, indicate the success of his ongoing performance. Hence, it is no exaggeration to claim that Branagh has spent the better part of his career as an actor working, quite literally, to "take the Mickey out" of *himself* — an assimilationist strategy that Noel Ignatieff aligns, provocatively, with a symbolic "whitening" process in his book *How the Irish Became White* (see Ignatieff). But racial difference does not simply disappear. Branagh's challenge as a director, then, is to find judicious ways of putting the "Mickey" *back into* his films by "casting" the shadow of his own ethnic difference onto other characters, through whom difference is voiced and, as we have seen in *Much Ado*, summarily rejected.

Hence, the most subtle demonstration of this process occurs in relation to Branagh's construction of British regional identities, which demands not a colorblind reading but a color*deaf* hearing. For example, in *A Midwinter's Tale* (1995), the director-figure, "Joe," becomes a mouthpiece for Branagh's pluralistic approach to dialects when a Glaswegian shows up to audition for *Hamlet*. Seeking to reassure the "fervent young Scotsman" that he will get a fair hearing, Joe informs him that "For me regional accents are ... no problem at all. They are vitally *important in fact. There is no 'set' voice for Shakespeare ... that's ridiculous*" (Branagh 1996, 11). The only Shakespeare film in which Branagh did not cast himself, *A Midwinter's Tale* clearly posits Joe as his stand-in, mimicking Branagh's own assertion that

> we don't try to homogenize the sound of Shakespeare, which again, in its clichéd form, is equated with some kind of overblown theatrical delivery, usually English in accent. ... In casting different groups of people, however, you ... start to create a more level playing field ... from quite different cultural viewpoints. (quoted in Crowdus)

Be that as it may, when *Midwinter*'s Scotsman exclaims in agonizing tones: "Noi iz thah wuntre ov r diskantant," the stage directions in Branagh's screenplay inform us that the auditioner's pronunciation "is unintelligible" and that "Joe tries to smile" but, nevertheless, sends the young man packing (Branagh 1996, 12). Other regional repositories of Branagh's displaced Irish identity include the feisty Welsh Captain Fluellen in *Henry V*, a character whose self-presentation is that of a man "*intemperately* inflamed with ethnic pride" (Lane, 34; emphasis added). Fluellen's behavior, in other words, is judged against the more carefully modulated ethnic identity of his part-Welsh, part-English countryman, King Henry, played — naturally — by Branagh himself.

More disturbing, however, are the ways in which such regional differences are subsequently subjected to a process of constitutive othering — that is, a form of "blackening" against which the desired (white, English) cultural identity is defined. An easily overlooked example of this practice occurs in relation to the depiction of the Irish Captain MacMorris in *Henry V*. The only member of the four-captain squad who emerges from the battle scenes with his face "blackened" (Branagh 1989b, 40), MacMorris invokes "racechange" in the direction opposite of Branagh's lifelong "whitening" process (see Gubar). The appearance of the film's only "Mickey" in blackface not only evokes race as a category of performance in its allusion to minstrelsy — a stage tradition with which the Irish are disproportionately associated — but also suggests the more permanent ontological classification of the Irish themselves as mulattos or "white niggers" (see Ignatieff; Dyer 1997). A category derived from nineteenth-century English and American racism, the denigration of the Irish as "black" was repeated as recently as the 1980s, when the discourse surrounding the British coalfield strikes lumped miners, Irish, and black Britons into the single category of social menace (see Gilroy). In addition to the explicit othering process that *Much Ado* performs vis-à-vis Denzel Washington, then, Branagh's Shakespeare films implicitly generate an ascending scale of whiteness against which British regional identities are evaluated, with the lowest place reserved for the Irish and the highest place, in keeping with the colonial tradition, occupied by the English. Through such strategic displacements of difference, Branagh takes the Mickey out of his extradiegetic performance of assimilation and keeps it out, ensuring his exclusive right to a crossover routine from which there is no turning b(l)ack.

But if ever Branagh were to succeed in creating a truly colorblind Shakespeare film, then the musical is arguably the most powerful generic vehicle for this fantasy, particularly the so-called integrated film musical that began to displace the "revue" style as early as the 1930s. Despite its immediate associations with race, the term "integrated" has always referred to structural properties rather than cultural attributes, denoting a musical in which the song and dance numbers mark a continuation rather than an interruption of the narrative. From a formal standpoint, as many critics have argued, there is no genre better suited to the utopian impulse: any obstacle to the classical Hollywood happy ending is ultimately resolved through the song-and-dance routines. In *Disintegrating the Musical*, Arthur Knight explains how the form of the integrated musical purveys this message about its content: "The cleverness, novelty, and apparent ease with which such difficult conjunctions or dissolves are created fuel the utopian feelings the musical conveys and provide the analogue for how life would feel if all more 'serious' conflicts and contradictions could be similarly resolved" (Knight, 15). That Branagh's intent in *Love's Labour's Lost* is to promote a similar structure of feeling is evident in his response to an interviewer's observation that the songs were particularly "well integrated" into the film: "We worked hard to make them organic, to make them feel part of this story, to reflect back on the scene just happening, and on the scene to come."[2] While touring to promote the film, several of the cast members expressed their surprise at the contrast between these on-screen effects and their off-screen efforts, recalling that only Branagh's "boot camp"-style rehearsals could make everything on screen "seem effortless." The grace with which this illusion of continuity is achieved is precisely what invests the integrated form of the musical with its utopian content — indeed, "the sense that the 'enemy' without," however defined, "can be conquered by the energy from within" (Altman, 191). Branagh's work considerably complicates this formula, for his construction of utopia is continually compromised by the "enemy" *within* his films, against which this "energy" must be matched. Utopia, then, can only be constituted by what gets left over and, more important, by *who* gets *left out*.

Critics agree that within the broad genre of the integrated musical, there are three subgenres: the "fairy tale" musical, the "show" musical, and the "folk" musical, each of which has its own set of conventions and internal variations. Expectedly, the subgenre most identified with the integrated musical's utopian trajectory is the fairy tale musical, the most famous of which are the glamorous Fred Astaire/Ginger Rogers films of the 1930s on which Branagh's *Love's Labour's Lost* is modeled. Tracing its origins to nineteenth-century operettas, the fairy tale musical is defined first and foremost by its setting in some distant, storybook kingdom, which fosters the sense of escapism central to the genre. The tiny walled principality of Navarre featured in *Love's Labour's Lost*, which is located within the larger kingdom of France, is thus perfectly suited to the creation of a Ruritanian setting. In the fairy tale musical, the Ruritanian landscape is a place where politics and love are implicitly conflated; each film undertakes a movement from disorder and fighting in both realms to peace, prosperity, and, of course, pairings, all of which conspire to promote the belief that the loving couples — the chosen few — will prevail over any disturbance to magical harmony. This vision of utopia, as Rick Altman observes, offers a spin on the American dream as a "democratic autocracy" or, even, "benevolent despotism. It is that land, free from material concerns, where charm can indeed replace money as society's standard" (158).

However, establishing a correlation between the affairs of government and affairs of the heart proves more daunting in *Love's Labour's Lost*. Although the play explicitly associates courtship with diplomacy, and more often than not with war, the outside world of *Realpolitik* is not even hinted at until the very end, when Marcade announces the death of the king of France. Branagh negotiates this generic challenge by setting his Shakespearean fairy tale in the interwar period in which Navarre, in the Ruritanian tradition, exists at an idyllic remove from the chaos that is brewing in the rest of France, as Hitler, the world's most malevolent despot, begins his quest for world domination. Quite masterfully, the specificity with which Branagh approaches the film's setting in place and time enables him to retain Shakespeare's downbeat conclusion, which calls for the separation of the lovers — in this case, to go to war — as well as to offer a coda of his own that satisfies the fairy tale ending, by adding a final scene in which the lovers, like the country, are reunited in the wake of V-E day.

In its transition from the more rarified venue of theatre to the mass medium of cinema, the fairy tale musical moved increasingly far from its beginnings in Ruritania, progressively shifting its focus from royal kingdoms to aristocratic households to the gaudy environs of the *nouveau riche* and, finally, to the familiar haunts of the middle class. Altman refers to this phenomenon as a process of "democratization," arguing that the "history of the fairy tale musical thus constitutes a fall by steps from a divine origin" (170). Yet even as the genre was increasingly compelled to represent some aspect of lived experience — typically through the depiction of class antagonisms as so many variations of the rags-to-riches theme — individual films attempted to compensate for this "fall into history" through recourse to nostalgia and, more actively, through song-and-dance numbers that, if only temporarily, sought to reconstitute the rarified social order of a lost golden world (170). As Arthur Knight contends, more than any other film genre, the integrated musical (and the fairy tale musical in particular) embodies the tensions both within and between industrial and social integration in the early twentieth century (15). For if, on the one hand, industrial integration led to the founding of strict labor hierarchies in the interests of mass production, then on the other hand, such distinctions were simultaneously elided by the need to address everyone as potential — and potentially equal — consumers.

Such mixed messages fostered the emergence of societal "mulattos" like the Flapper, whose sexually aggressive combination of masculine and feminine behaviors was a direct consequence of women's integration into the workplace. Moreover, as Attina Grossman explains, the Flapper evinced the fear that gender mobility would threaten other hierarchies, especially those pertaining to sex and race, as suggested by the progressive representational "blackening" of the Flapper as a figure inexorably linked to the Jewish woman, prostitute, and lesbian (167). Such concerns about sexual and, consequently, racial integration peaked during the precarious interwar years following the Great Depression — precisely the period in which *Love's Labour's Lost* is set. Fittingly, then, at a time when Ruritania had never seemed more distant, the films of Fred Astaire and Ginger Rogers launched a vision of utopia in which social and racial fermentation was celebrated and relentlessly controlled. Theirs was a world of reassuring fictions, wherein battles of the sexes ended in happy marriage and a depressed (and repressed) white culture could be liberated by black performance traditions without contamination. When blackness surfaces in the integrated musicals of the 1930s it does so in the form of white impersonation — as blackface routines — or in the form of white fantasy in which black actors appear on screen only in the symbolically segregated space of the specialty number or in the self-policing space of the bass-thumping, thigh-slapping, white-worshipping Sambo. Such whitewashing was crucial to the success of this still burgeoning musical genre, for as Sean Griffin observes: "Without the sense of unity and communal cohesion created by the elision of racial difference, audiences might not have accepted the integrated blend of number and narrative so wholeheartedly" for fear that it might spill over into other, less salutary forms of integration (24).

The Astaire/Rogers films of the 1930s exemplify this vision of cohesion in which "democratization" is associated with class, an infinitely more tractable category than race. Traipsing in on the tattered coattails of the Great Depression, the RKO films featuring this glamorous duo became synonymous with the utopian belief in a universal aristocracy in which charm can indeed replace class. Though both Rogers and Astaire were, significantly, products of middle America and therefore readily identified with the attainability of this dream, it was Astaire in particular who was responsible for its inculcation in the movie-going masses. After all, Fred was just an ordinary guy: far from dashing and a sub-par singer at best, he was as well known for the industry summary of his first screen audition — "can't sing, can't act, can dance a little" — as much as he soon was for a whole lot of extraordinary dancing. But not even talent separated Astaire from the average spectator, for in many of his films he was shown teaching dance in some capacity, and it was not long before life imitated art with the creation of Fred Astaire Dance Studios, "a business," as Altman concludes, "dedicated to the proposition that we can be equal to Fred — or at least good enough to impress our own private Ginger" (171). It was as if all one needed was a top hat and the rest would follow.

Not coincidentally, Branagh screened the most famous Astaire/Rogers musical, *Top Hat* (dir. Mark Sandrich, 1935), for the entire cast of *Love's Labour's Lost* on the very first day of rehearsal, hoping to transport them into a magical vision of the 1930s. In his featurette on the making of the film, Branagh explains that every detail of this fastidiously constructed adaptation — from set to color schemes to make-up — is intended to create "a world that I hope the audience might want to rush into and say: 'Yes — I'd like to be in love in *that* world.'" Accordingly, from its opening moments, *Love's Labour's Lost* exudes the genre's compensatory movement toward nostalgia for a lost golden world, as Navarre emerges as an enclave suspended in space and time, insulated from the rest of France. The lack of specificity with which Navarre is presented is central to Branagh's design, for "utopia" in the integrated musical, as Richard Dyer observes, "is not a specific *place* but a universal *feeling*" (Dyer 1992, 18; emphasis added). By the same token, however, the film's insistent rendering of Navarre as a utopian "no place" clashes directly with Branagh's coexisting desire to set the film in a precise time period — 1939 — on the eve of European entry into World War II. In contrast to films like *Much Ado About Nothing* and *Hamlet*, which demonstrate Branagh's habitual avoidance of period in their vaguely nineteenth-century Ruritanian settings, *Love's Labour's Lost* repeatedly draws attention to its historical moment through the superimposition of newspaper headlines and radio broadcasts on the narrative frame. In discussing this departure, Branagh admits that the specificity of the film's setting makes him somewhat uneasy, chiefly because, in his view, conspicuous appeals to "History" can produce too much distance between the screen and the spectator (*Daily Telegiraffe*). Branagh's solution to this implicit conflict between generic and historical accuracy — that is, between his competing visions of a utopian "no place" and a culturally-specific time — is the creation of a "nostalgia film," a postmodern genre that boasts the best of both worlds: a vision of history subjugated to feeling, or, in Fredric Jameson's words, to "our own pop images and simulacra of that history, which itself remains forever out of reach" (25).

With the enduring traumas of history mitigated by the spontaneity of feeling, *Love's Labour's Lost* sweeps the spectator into a *mise-en-scène* dominated by what I would call "faux history." Creating an impression not of 1939 but of "1939," Branagh's film emerges as a history of the 1930s musical rather than a musical about the history of the 1930s. In fact, it is almost as if the invocation of 1939 is, in fact, a decoy aimed at forestalling the film's inevitable "fall into history." When asked about the set, for example, Branagh explains that Navarre is a "fantasy Oxbridge," modeled on neither Oxford nor Cambridge but on Yale, whose architects attempted to create the look of the university's ancient

British counterparts by distressing the walls with acid; the effect, as Branagh describes it, is "a certain ye olde" feeling (*Daily Telegiraffe*), or the simulacrum of a "history" that, more than out of reach, was *never there in the first place*. Similarly, rather than using actual newsreels as narration devices, Branagh produces parodies of the old Movietone News sequences, which inform the spectator about the farce unfolding in Navarre with the same high seriousness employed to announce the outbreak of war at the end of the film. A clever approximation of the "neutral and reified media speech" that Jameson dubs "blank parody," these "news" sequences employ distressed, grainy film stock, sepia-toned news headlines, and static-filled, radio-transmitted voiceovers as signifiers not of *the* historical past but rather of our contemporary "ideas and stereotypes about that past" (Jameson, 17 and 25). Paradoxically, then, we might conclude that *Love's Labour's Lost* reserves its historical accuracy for the reel rather than the real. Like the tribute to the "show musical" featured in *Footlight Parade* (dir. Lloyd Bacon, 1933), Branagh's film is nothing less than a history of the fairy tale musical genre itself — a history that reflects both the genre's historical democratization and its compensatory, diegetic quest to return to Ruritania.

To this end, *Love's Labour's Lost* deftly weaves references to nearly all of the Astaire/Rogers musicals of the 1930s into the structure of Shakespeare's play, while also cannibalizing stylistic touches from Busby Berkeley, Vincente Minnelli, and Bob Fosse. However, the film provocatively parts ways with Jameson's definition of the nostalgia film in its *purposeful* approach to cannibalization by creating a pastiche vision of the past in which some stereotypes are privileged over others. In its refusal to fall into history, *Love's Labour's Lost* is left with *only* stereotypes and, more specifically, racial stereotypes that expose the film's vision of a universal aristocracy as a sham. Hence, if, as Richard Dyer contends, the musical genre is concerned with presenting the spectator with an impression of "what utopia would feel like rather than how it would be organized", then Branagh's film unwittingly proffers both, for although *Love's Labour's Lost* does indeed present a look — and feeling — evocative of utopia, beneath the glitzy surface of this "faux show" lurks a deeper organizational principle, which reveals the extent to which reel Ruritania may be found only when real democratization is lost (Dyer 1992, 18).

Dirty Dancing

Branagh's utopian mission in *Love's Labour's Lost* is to create a world in which there are no barriers to love. His pairing decisions within the film reinforce this vision not in the typical fairy tale musical style of pairing members of different social classes, but rather, quite explicitly in terms of race. Two of the four couples are racially mixed: Longueville is played by the lanky, fresh-faced, all-American kid Mathew Lillard and Maria by the black British actress Carmen Ejogo, the London-born daughter of a Nigerian father and Scottish mother; Dumaine is played by Adrian Lester, a black Birmingham native, and is matched with Emily Mortimer, the classic English beauty who plays Katherine. Predictably, Branagh reserves the only "English" pairing for himself, matching his Berowne with Natascha McElhone's Rosaline, while the couple's American counterpart is formed by Alessandro Nivola's King of Navarre and Alicia Silverstone's Princess of France. Clearly, then, Branagh intends his musical to be not only formally but also racially "integrated." What is especially interesting about these *particular* pairings is the fact that, when the women adopt disguises to humiliate their wooers, the pattern of integration is skewed, for the two black actors wind up together and three white couples spring from the "confusion." If, as Lacan argues, the truth has the structure of a fiction, then what is revealed by such masking episodes is critical to determining the success of Branagh's integration strategy in *Love's Labour's Lost*.

In the musical, song-and-dance routines become masks in their own right, functioning not just to conceal but also to reveal what narrative alone cannot convey. Indeed, one of the central reasons why musical films became so popular in the 1930s was that the representation of sexuality, which was banned by the Production Code by 1934, could be disguised in intimately choreographed dance routines (Altman, 159). At the same time, however, the forbidden desires that dance functioned to hide could be safely revealed in suggestive — but appropriately ambiguous — lyrics, as in Ginger Rogers's performance of the song "Music Makes Me Do the Things I Never Should Do." Branagh's film revolves around a similar shell game occurring within the musical numbers; the difference is that whereas the songs he chooses conceal racial difference, the dance routines increasingly undermine this whitewashing effect, revealing blackness to be the central production value for representing sublimated sexuality.

Significantly, all of the composers and lyricists represented by the soundtrack of *Love's Labour's Lost* — George and Ira Gershwin, Irving Berlin, Jerome Kern, Cole Porter, and Oscar Hammerstein, as well as lesser-known writers like Jimmy McHugh and Dorothy Fields — are identified with musicals that reflect an act of racechange. Branagh's song selection, however, explicitly avoids those musicals that are associated with this cultural fantasy. For example, the Gershwin brothers' most famous musical is the all-black operetta *Porgy and Bess*, but Branagh chooses songs from noncontroversial musicals like *Lady Be Good*, *Shall We Dance*, and *American in Paris*. Similarly, Irving Berlin, a practicing Jew, engaged in a form of racechange when he penned *Easter Parade* and *White Christmas*, musicals that validate the white Anglo-Christian identity which, in the real Berlin across the Atlantic, Hitler was championing to genocidal extremes. Despite its setting on the eve of World War II, Branagh seeks to avoid this association by hand-picking Irving Berlin musicals that revolve around class as opposed to religious creeds: *Top Hat*, *Follow the Fleet*, and *Annie Get Your Gun*. This pattern is repeated for Jerome Kern, whose most famous musical, *Showboat*, is forever associated with the Negro spiritual sung by Paul Robeson, "Ol' Man River." *Love's Labour's Lost*, by contrast, features songs from the less popular musicals *Roberta* and *Swing Time*. Particularly in the case of *Swing Time*, the title of which invokes the musical genre's debt to black music, Branagh's song choice is explicitly attuned to the most staid and controlled, indeed, the "whitest" of song types, the ballad — specifically, the old standard "The Way You Look Tonight" — rather than to the overt racial content of numbers like "Bojangles of Harlem." Significantly, the lyricists who partnered with Kern on songs from *Roberta* and *Swing Time*, Dorothy Fields and Jimmy McHugh, were known in the industry for their ability to employ a black idiom. Fields, for example, authored the "black" jive song "Diga Diga Doo," while McHugh wrote the black-cast musical *Blackbirds of 28*; predictably, Branagh never credits these songwriters in discussing the musical origins of *Love's Labour's Lost*. Even Cole Porter, whose lyrics continually encode the literally unspeakable desire of a gay composer writing for the most heterosexist of genres, is neutered by Branagh's song selection. For although Branagh showcases Porter's best-known musical, *Anything Goes*, the song he chooses is the sweet, naïve ballad "I Get a Kick Out of You" rather than the overtly naughty importunings of "Let's Misbehave."

In *Love's Labour's Lost*, misbehaving becomes the province of dance rather than song. At first, however, the whitewashing effect of the film's song choice extends to the dance numbers themselves, reflecting what Richard Dyer identifies as the "aspirational" quality of whiteness.[3] An ontological desire that does not correspond to the rest of the racial spectrum, the aspiration to whiteness in *Love's Labour's Lost* is evinced by the shared desire to be like Fred and Ginger. For example, the first number, "I'd Rather Charleston," shows the four male characters in an ensemble performance that intermittently produces a mock chorus line effect — a dance strategy which, like its female can-can counterpart, is meant to elide distinctions between individuals in order to create the illusion of a single body, or a vision of "whiteness as a coalition" (Dyer 1997, 51). This effect is enhanced by the removal of the neckties that distinguish the men from one another, as all of them appear uniformly outfitted in white shirts uninterrupted by a color-coded accessory — a costuming decision that could be interpreted as a form of "whiteface."[4] The four women are treated similarly in their first ensemble number, "No Strings," which begins as a pajama party in their tent and ends in a giant swimming pool, where they too have the opportunity to shed their color-coded pajamas (made to match their respective wooers) in order to sport gold lamé bathing suits. As the women engage in Busby Berkeley-style synchronized swimming maneuvers, flashing their white teeth and gliding, gilded bodies, we see the faint outline of the fairy tale musical's vision of a universal aristocracy in which money — indeed the gold standard — is surpassed by grace and charm as the basis of a new, more democratic social standard.

Importantly, however, as early as the first "mixed" number, in which the men are paired with the women and hence sexual tensions are introduced into the choreography, we see this (white) coalition begin to unravel. That the dance numbers become increasingly identified as a racially marked space is announced by the men's ongoing removal of clothing — sports jackets, ties, academic gowns, and finally the shirts on their backs — an act that connotes not only the increasing freedom of expression permitted by dance but also the mounting association of this liberal sexuality with (nonwhite) skin color. In the first of the film's partner dances, "I Won't Dance," the men prance about their women with a certain giddy awkwardness, in the same order of appearance employed throughout the film: Berowne is shown first, followed by the King, Longueville, and last Dumaine. With the exception of Dumaine, the men look foolish and unskilled in courtship as the women continually elude their grasp. However, when Dumaine is shown momentarily catching up with Katherine, he aggressively pins her up against a barred wall, his hands gripping iron bars on either side of her face, as she stares back at him with a mixture of fear and intrigue. In less than five seconds of screen time, we see the allegedly predatory sexuality of the black male vis-à-vis white women, as well as an allusion to the prisons that house disproportionate percentages of black men in the Anglo-American penal system.

Appropriately, given the binary logic of the fairy tale musical's battle of the sexes, *Love's Labour's Lost* provides us with a female complement to this scene, in which Maria (pronounced "Mariah" to give the name a "black" inflection) acquires the active sexuality that the musical genre generally forbids (white) women to embody. In the prelude to the next number, "I've Got a Crush on You," each of the men enters the library while gazing lovingly at a picture of his longed-for lover, pausing to cast off his academic robe and sing a line of the song. Whereas Berowne and the King are shown gushing over the photographs in their hands, the photos that Dumaine and Longueville hold are framed in racially specific ways: Dumaine's white girlfriend is pasted into the white pages of a book, while Longueville's black girlfriend is attached to the black underside of his academic cap. Both details imbue these tokens of cross-racial couplings with an aura of necessary secrecy that Berowne and the King are not compelled to perform. More disturbing, however, is Longueville's behavior when it is his turn to serenade Maria's image, as his demeanor undergoes a violent shift from sexually naïve to sexually explicit. Indeed, although the other men passively adore their photos in an upright position, Longueville lies prone on a desk, whispering lines that, considering the unorthodox beauty of his "dark Lady," cannot help but come across as a racial insult: "It's not that you're attractive, / But oh my heart grew active." Worse, Longueville's voice begins to rise with the word "active" and, when he sings the next line — "When you *came* into viewwwwww!"—he thrusts his pelvis up and down, wriggling with orgasmic anticipation. There is nothing even remotely subtle about this moment in a film wherein the men are otherwise painfully reserved, prone to shuffling their feet, shrugging their shoulders, and simply acting "swell." The only explanation for Longueville's behavior, then, is a racial one, as if the hypersexuality historically ascribed to the black female has rubbed off on him in his first dance with Maria.

As the privileged white impersonator of black sexuality, Longueville, as Dyer might observe of this episode, can experience what forbidden modes of "being, physicality, [and] presence might be like, while also dissociating [himself] from the non-whiteness of such things" (Dyer 1997, 80). But "ain't *I a Lady?*" we might hear Maria whispering through the walls, as a variation on Sojourner Truth's famous theme, for *only* skin color distinguishes Maria from the other identically dressed women, whose chastity the men treat with the utmost respect. This scene offers the first example of the phenomenon of "black surrogacy" in Branagh's film, reflecting the historical shortcut, as Toni Morrison defines it, through which white culture has often sought to resolve its own internal conflicts, by projecting them onto a "blank darkness" (Morrison, 38). In keeping with Morrison's contention, perhaps the most troubling aspect of Longueville's behavior is that Maria is not even permitted to own this assertion of her sexuality, for Longueville occupies both sexual positions as he projects his fantasy of Maria's response — "on the bottom" — to him "on top." In this oblique way, Branagh invokes the black-cast musicals, otherwise absent from his tribute, that rose to prominence alongside the Astaire/Rogers films of the 1930s. As Arthur Knight observes of many of these white-financed, so-called race-musicals, despite the casting novelty they introduced into the genre, the films themselves offered a limited number of variations on the same old derogatory song and dance, serving not to contest racist representation but to reify whiteness as the cultural standard. In Knight's view, such films, which situate blackness within the impossible aspirational logic of white imitation, fall under the category of "mastery of form" rather than the more subversive practice of "deformation of mastery." Paraphrasing Houston A. Baker, Knight explains that "the master of form 'lies,' while the deformer of mastery 'scandalizes'" (174–175).

In keeping with Branagh's colorblind vision for *Love's Labour's Lost*, Adrian Lester's performance as Dumaine falls largely within the confines of the white-identified practice of mastery of form, as he, too, is represented as longing to "be like Fred Astaire" — that is, to "just blend in" with the rest of his cohort. But the complexity of this assignment is revealed in Branagh's instructions to the actor upon awarding him a solo. "You've got a whole number, do whatever you like," he told Lester; but this freedom was granted on the condition that Lester "do the thing with the chairs" — the signature Astaire move — which, Branagh implies, none of the other actors can pull off. In one respect, Branagh's desire to liberate Lester's talent from the constraints of the less-talented ensemble reinforces the stereotype that black people are naturally better dancers than their white counterparts; but in another respect, Branagh clearly seeks to whitewash — that is, to circumscribe — Lester's performance by insisting that he perform "the thing with the chairs," which becomes a synecdoche for the aspirational quality of whiteness. Importantly, both readings belie Branagh's colorblind vision in *Love's Labour's Lost*.

Moreover, by awarding the *only* solo in the entire film to Adrian Lester's character, Branagh pays him a compliment that, albeit unintentionally, is associated with the implied racism of the "specialty number" tradition. Although the specialty number served to showcase black talent, it also segregated the black performer from the rest of the cast, enabling such sequences to be readily cut from films seeking distribution in the Jim Crow South. True to the film's replication of the history of the musical rather than the historical 1930s (although in this particular case the two are quite similar), Lester's rendition of "I've Got a Crush on You" begins by mollifying the potentially apprehensive white viewer, presenting the audience with a performance of uncritical "whiteface" as the ballad he sings and the balletic moves that accompany it clearly identify him as a master of (white) form — especially once he does the Astaire "thing with the chairs." But following this classical routine, the music shifts to a swing interlude in which Lester's Dumaine performs an extraordinary series of acrobatic dance moves to match the upbeat tempo of the song. Although this impressive specialty number caters to stereotypes about black male physicality, its also suggests that Lester's subsequent "return to (white) form" is a kind of "deformation of mastery," for the contrast between the swing routine and his abrupt shift back, at the end of the song, into the studied reserve of the ballad seems to parody his companions' lesser and simultaneously more labored abilities. In fact, having witnessed *just how much better* Lester's Dumaine is than the others, it is hard not to acknowledge, in the subsequent ensemble numbers, the visible effort that he puts into "dancing down" to the level of the others. In so doing, Lester's performance invokes the tactical response of black dancers to the prospect of appearing alongside famous white leads, the precedent-setting example of which is the Nicholas Brothers' performance with Gene Kelly in *The Pirate* (dir. Vincente Minnelli, 1948). Instructed not to outshine Kelly, the Nicholas Brothers turned such stage directions into a kind of inside joke, by subtly *playing through* — as Lester does throughout the film — the mask of masking their talent (Hill and Hines, 95–96). In such a context, as Sean Griffin observes, the specialty number could be interpreted as a variation on the challenge dance, upstaging "not only the white male" lead but also establishing "the white viewer [as] the outsider" to this invitation-only performance (11).

Branagh has repeatedly acknowledged the centrality of masks to his performing ethos. In fact, his first encounter with masking — specifically, with blackface — changed the course of his life and art. Recalling his brother's performance in a school play, Branagh claims to have been so "transfixed" by his brother's impersonation of "a blacked-up American minstrel" that his decision to become an actor was "ignited" by this mask of burnt cork, which embodies the performance of racechange to which he has dedicated himself ever since (Branagh 1989a, 16). In this context, Branagh's elimination of two of the three masking sequences contained in Shakespeare's play is particularly conspicuous, especially given that he opts to include them as "extras" on the DVD menu. The pageant of the Worthies, in which the lower classes are abused by their aristocratic audience and Don Armado is humiliated for his foreign accent, is an easy candidate for removal from the film, given the centrality of "different accents" and "different looks" to Branagh's production ethos. More importantly, the decision to eliminate a scene that represents the Lords and Ladies as indecorous and unsympathetic characters is vital to the thematic trajectory of the fairy tale musical, which promotes the idea of a universal aristocracy only to the extent that this new social order trickles down from the real, existing aristocrats.

The disappearance of the mask of the Muscovites is somewhat harder to explain, as is the manner in which Branagh films this scene in the first place. In the play, the entrance of the Russian maskers is preceded by "Blackmoors." Although Branagh has, for obvious reasons, chosen not to include this Orientalizing vision of blackness in his adaptation, he appears to have transferred its racist content to the representation of the suitors themselves. A striking departure from the typically Slavophilic representation of Muscovites as blonde and graceful, the King and his men portray bumbling brutes, uniformly outfitted with thick black beards and unkempt black wigs that clearly resemble Afros — a literalization, perhaps, of the swarthy "black Russian." Historically, whereas the Russian term "Africantsy" or "Negry" is used to denote people of African descent, the word "chernij," meaning "black," has been used as a derogatory description of the darker, non-European inhabitants on Russia's southern and eastern margins, whom "authentic" Russians have long considered to be unruly and uncivilized. In the deleted mask scene, this association between blackness and primitivism is evoked by Longueville, who demands requital of his affections by falling on his knees and thumping his chest while grunting "Ugh! Ugh! Ugh!" Longueville's impersonation of a distinctly primal sexuality — ostensibly sanctioned by the mask of blackness he wears — reflects a conflation of "chernij" and "Africantsy," black Russian and native African, and functions to reserve whiteness for the more dignified forms. More than any of Branagh's earlier Shakespeare films, *Love's Labour's Lost* gravitates toward a division of labor that belies the fantasy of colorblind casting with the recognition that some masks *cannot be removed*. This is, after all, what ultimately distinguishes a Kenneth Branagh from a Denzel Washington, or, in *Love's Labour's Lost*, from an Adrian Lester and a Carmen Ejogo, whose blackness becomes increasingly visible as the film's fall into history draws near.

I've Got You under My Skin

The fall into history featured in *Love's Labour's Lost* is really more of a fall into sexuality, for the one aspect of this fastidiously constructed film that consistently eludes Branagh's control is the rising sexual tension endemic to the musical genre. Apropos of the combative spirit that characterizes the fairy tale genre, sex is sublimated in confrontational dance routines; sexual tensions are typically introduced in a "challenge dance" and resolved in a "romantic dance" — the latter signaling that "the search for pleasure has won out over the more conventional respect for morals" (Altman, 173). In fact, the romantic dance corresponds directly to the rhythms of sexual pleasure, as the melody rises and falls until it at last swells toward a crescendo and then falls again in conjunction with the exhausted energies of the dancers. The song that Branagh selects to serve this function in *Love's Labour's Lost* is "Let's Face the Music and Dance," the romantic dance from the Astaire/Rogers film *Follow the Fleet* (dir. Mark Sandrich, 1936). But unlike all the other routines in Branagh's adaptation, which are deliberately choreographed to recall the elegant, understated intimacy of Fred and Ginger's screen chemistry, this number is modeled on the sexually explicit work of Bob Fosse. In contrast to the soft postures, fluid lines, and wide-angle camerawork that characterize the other numbers, here the bodies are taut, alternately erect and prone, as rapid cutting reveals groping hands, licking tongues, thrusting hips, and heaving bosoms in a montage of body parts intended to evoke the violent, fetishistic camerawork of hard-core pornography. In short, there is no mistaking the "sex" in this scene as *just* a dance.

That this dance number is unequivocally positioned as *the* climactic sex scene in *Love's Labour's Lost* is made all the more obvious by the immediate cut to the women smoking cigarettes at the bar, all of them glowing with post-coital satisfaction. More interesting than the sheer explicitness of this song-and-dance routine, however, is the way in which it exploits black surrogacy to represent illicit sexuality. Indeed, a better title for this number would be "Let's Blackface the Music and Dance," for the men wear black masks throughout the number, a sartorial flourish that invests their tense, stalking movements with a distinctly menacing if not overtly criminal aura, consistent with the representation of Dumaine's predatory sexuality earlier in the film. Significantly, Branagh notes that "Let's Face the Music and Dance" was the song that inspired his musical adaptation of Shakespeare in the first place, citing the "very dirty drum beat" as his point of affective entry into the number and, eventually, into his conception of the film itself. Especially in conjunction with the reference to drums — a signifier of the primal and impulsive — the term "dirty" is particularly striking, because it drapes Branagh's image of this dance routine in a veneer of otherness, indeed, a constitutive blackness, that makes its performance of sexuality possible. For just as drums have long served as musical shorthand for the "savage" African rhythms that are the antithesis of "civilized" European melodies, references to dirt, as Richard Dyer contends, have historically functioned as ontological slang for "black" (see also Saakana). Dyer traces the origin of this association to the (white) Anglo-Saxon Protestant creed that the body is dirty and the dirty body is black, both inexorably tied to "the fate of the sensuousness" that constitutively falls away from the world of whiteness (Dyer 1997, 75).

Branagh's disproportionate investment in the relationship of "Let's Face the Music and Dance" to his film is underscored by the promotional materials for *Love's Labour's Lost*, all of which show the couples dressed in the costumes worn for this number. A distinct exception to the formal dress code that dominates the rest of the film, the attire featured in this "dirty" number is, significantly, largely comprised of undergarments: the men sport white, "wife-beater" undershirts with black pants, while the women wear teddies and fishnet stockings. Revealing much more than flesh, these costuming choices serve as a signal that, if only "for two minutes traffic of the stage," all of the performers get to wear their inner "other" or, in Branagh's case, "brother," on the outside: all of them, that is, except for Dumaine and Maria — for this is, importantly, a *faux* show. Indeed, what separates the costumes shown in the promotional materials from those worn in the actual dance is a single accessory: the black eye-masks that are added to the routine, which mark the performance as conspicuously artificial, as a self-conscious display of blackness. Hence, neither Adrian Lester's Dumaine nor Carmen Ejogo's Maria is permitted ownership of this representation. In contrast to the representation of the other women, whose arched backs and open mouths denote their ravishment and ecstasy, Maria is repeatedly shown with her partner's hands about her neck, in a tableau far more suggestive of sexual violence than pleasure. Equally disturbing is the series of intercuts to Dumaine, who occupies the same feminized position as the women themselves in this scene: he repeatedly snaps his head backward as though he were bracing himself for penetration. And what better way to diminish the threat Dumaine poses to the other suitors' masculinity than to objectify, feminize, and subdue him as though he were one of the girls, punishing him in this "anything goes" dreamlike sequence for aspiring to upward mobility through interracial marriage? What else explains why black men were castrated *after* they were lynched, if not the threat of an uncanny, transubstantial sexuality that somehow survived the death of the physical body? More historically accurate than he ever intended to be, Branagh's rendering of this scene suggests the cultural leaps that could convert Dumaine, decades later, into an Emmet Till.

Perhaps the most crucial point to make about the role of this scene in *Love's Labour's Lost* is the fact that, as the film's "romantic" dance, this erotic number should also serve as a *resolution* dance, indeed as the prelude to marriage in both the fairy tale musical and Shakespearean comedy. But the interjection of masks causes everyone to wind up with the "wrong" partners: Berowne pairs off with the Princess, the King joins Rosaline, and Longueville is matched with Katherine, while Dumaine and Maria, the film's two black characters, are coupled. I would argue, however, that this "confusion" *is* Branagh's resolution to the mounting sexual tensions that he refuses to deal with honestly, for these mismatches exorcise the specter of miscegenation haunting the film by representing all of the couples having sex with their "own kind," enabling them to return to their original pairings with a clean conscience, having purged the dirt that lurks just "under their skin." In other words, the ultimate function of this scene is to present sex as something that, as Ginger Rogers's song goes, one shouldn't do unless the right partner comes along. It is no wonder, then, that Branagh's selection of romantic dances does not extend to the final Astaire/Rogers musical of the 1930s, *Carefree* (1938), for the song that fulfills this role is, ironically, "I Used To Be Colorblind" — a confession that Branagh is clearly unwilling to make. Pairing all the couples according to race, Branagh, faithful to the tradition of the 1930s musical, makes sex in his utopia separate but certainly not equal.

The Faux Show

By way of conclusion, I want to suggest that the film ultimately moves away from sexualized, racial othering toward, simply, sexual othering. Boyet, the effeminate companion to the Princess and her ladies, is the figure who comes to occupy this position at the very end of *Love's Labour's Lost*. In a film genre fueled by a relentless heterosexuality that settles for nothing less than the mandatory matching of all possible mates, Boyet literally has no place — indeed, no partner — in the musical's quest for utopia. Rather, he represents the structural impossibility around which this social fantasy revolves; his elimination, then, as Slavoj Žižek might observe, is "acceptable insofar as it prevents the disintegration of the social fabric" (73). Indeed, Branagh dis-integrates Boyet from the rest of the cast by visibly pairing off characters who are not the subject of such unions in Shakespeare's play, going so far as to change the character of Holofernes to Holofernia so that "she" can be partnered with Sir Nathaniel. Additionally, the film frequently employs homophobic in-jokes to deflect the latent homoeroticism of the all-male ensemble numbers, which feature gags that represent men getting caught in an accidental clinch, a pregnant pause, or even a kiss with other men. Beyond the diegesis, Branagh takes care to ward off inquiries into his own sexuality by repeatedly making jokes about "wearing tights," as if he were anticipating the charge of "guilt by association" with a performance genre dominated by gay men. But Branagh goes one step further in his constitutive othering of Boyet, fashioning him as the film's representative of what Douglas Greene refers to as the "queer traitor."[5]

A character who appears in virtually all of Branagh's films — from Scroop in *Henry V* and Don John in *Much Ado* to Osric in *Hamlet* and even Branagh's

Iago in Oliver Parker's *Othello* (1995) — the queer traitor is a figure who elides the distinction between homosexuality and treason. In fairness to Branagh, however, the reading of Boyet through this lens is not completely unearned in *Love's Labour's Lost*, for Boyet is in fact the "double agent" who sets the men up to woo the wrong women. Moreover, after the betrayal is revealed in Shakespeare's play, Berowne rebukes Boyet in a way that proclaims his deviant, "queer" status by associating him with women's underwear — if not necrophilia — in the condemnation "a smock shall be your shroud" (5.2.479). But in the film, Branagh bests Berowne's insult in an interpolated scene that splices real war footage into a fabricated shot of Boyet fleeing the Gestapo. Seconds later, the "smocks" he chases — the ladies he serves as they flee for their lives — do indeed prove to be his shroud, when a bullet fired by the Gestapo fatally pierces his back. Worse than the fate of the queer traitor in Branagh's other films, Boyet is made to die the death historically reserved for cowards. Hence, the fall into history that Branagh so judiciously seeks to forestall in *Love's Labour's Lost* is exceedingly short-lived. In this one single flash of violence, the historical enemy of the Axis powers and the fictional "enemy within" the film's representation of the Allied camp of straight men are brutally condensed into Boyet, the dirty queer whose elimination shores up the symbolic community around which fascism and the integrated musical are structured. Left to rot in the ghetto somewhere beyond the gates of Branagh's Ruritania, Boyet is nothing less than the film's honorary Jew.[6]

Despite the climactic reunions and utopian feelings with which *Love's Labour's Lost* ends, then, Branagh has ultimately provided us with one too many glimpses of how his utopia would be organized. But as we sing along to the infectious melody of the film's final celebratory song, "There's No Business Like Show Business," we might listen for the beat of a different, distinctly "dirty" drummer, who calls Branagh's colorblind bluff with a variation on this theme: "There's no utopia like myopia." And that's faux show.

Notes

1. For an informative reading of contemporary approaches to the categories of nontraditional casting defined by Harold Scott's Non-Traditional Casting Project (colorblind, cross-cultural, conceptual, societal), see Pao.
2. All of Branagh's comments on *Love's Labour's Lost* may be found in the Daily Telegiraffe site dedicated to the making of the film: http//:members.tripod.com/~Daily Telegiraffe/branaghloveslabourslostmakingof.html. Due to the length of the URL, I will hereafter indicate this site in the text as *Daily Telegiraffe.*
3. This assumption is discussed throughout Dyer's *White.*
4. For a thorough discussion of the accessories associated with contemporary performances of whiteface, see Gilbert.
5. Working with Alan Bray's observations on homosexuality in the English Renaissance, Greene offers a brilliant reading of this preoccupation in Branagh's oeuvre.
6. For a comprehensive exploration of the deviant sexuality, feminization, dirt, and disease associated with the figure of the Jew in Nazi ideology, see Harrowitz and Hyams.

References

Altman, Rick. *The American Film Musical*. Bloomington and Indianapolis: Indiana University Press, 1989.

Branagh, Kenneth. *Beginning*. New York: St. Martin's, 1989a.

Branagh, Kenneth. *Henry V, by William Shakespeare: A Screen Adaptation by Kenneth Branagh*. London: Chatto and Windus, 1989b.

Branagh, Kenneth. *Much Ado About Nothing by William Shakespeare: Screenplay, Introduction, and Notes on the Making of the Movie by Kenneth Branagh*. New York: W. W. Norton, 1993.

Branagh, Kenneth. *A Midwinter's Tale: The Shooting Script*. New York: Newmarket, 1996.

Crawley, Tony. "Much Ado about Ken 'n' Em." *Film Review* (August 1993): 45.

Crowdus, Gary. "Branagh Breathes New Life into Classics." *Insight on the News*, January 15, 1996.

Dyer, Richard. *Only Entertainment*. London and New York: Routledge, 1992.

Dyer, Richard. *White*. London and New York: Routledge, 1997.

Gilbert, Helen. "Black and White and Re(a)d All Over Again: Indigenous Minstrelsy in Contemporary Canadian and Australian Theater." *Theatre Journal* 55 (2003): 679–698.

Gilroy, Paul. "British Cultural Studies and the Pitfalls of Identity." In *Black British Cultural Studies: A Reader,* edited by Houston A. Baker, Manthia Diawara, and Ruth Lindeborg. Chicago: University of Chicago Press, 1996.

Greene, Douglas. "Shakespeare, Branagh, and the 'Queer Traitor': Close Encounters in the Shakespearean Classroom." In *The Reel Shakespeare: Alternative Cinema and Theory*, edited by Lisa S. Starks and Courtney Lehmann. Madison, NJ: Fairleigh Dickinson University Press, 2002.

Griffin, Sean. "The Gang's All Here: Generic versus Racial Integration in the 1940s Musical." *Cinema Journal* 42 (2002): 21–45.

Grossman, Attina. "The New Woman and the Rationalization of Sexuality in Weimar Germany." In *Powers of Desire: The Politics of Sexuality*, edited by Ann Snitow, Christine Stansell, and Sharon Thompson. New York: Monthly Review Press, 1983.

Gubar, Susan. *Racechanges: White Skin, Black Face*. Oxford: Oxford University Press, 2000.

Harrowitz, Nancy, and Barbara Hyams, eds. *Jews and Gender: Responses to Otto Weininger*. Philadelphia: Temple University Press, 1995.

Hill, Constance Valis, and Gregory Hines. *Brotherhood in Rhythm: The Jazz Dancing of the Nicholas Brothers*. Oxford: Oxford University Press, 2005.

Ignatieff, Noel. *How the Irish Became White*. London and New York: Routledge, 1995.

Jameson, Fredric. *Postmodernism, or, The Cultural Logic of Late Capitalism*. Durham: Duke University Press, 1991.

Knight, Arthur. *Disintegrating the Musical: Black Performance and American Musical Film*. Durham: Duke University Press, 2002.

Lane, Robert. "'When blood is their argument': Class, Character, and History-making in Shakespeare's and Branagh's *Henry V*." *ELH* 61 (1994): 27–52.

Lehmann, Courtney. "Much Ado about Nothing? Shakespeare, Branagh, and the 'National-Popular' in the Age of Multinational Capital," *Textual Practice* 12 (1998): 1–22.

Light, Alison. "The Importance of Being Ordinary." *Sight and Sound* 3 (1993): 16–19.

Morrison, Toni. *Playing in the Dark: Whiteness and the Literary Imagination*. New York: Vintage, 1993.

Pao, Angela C. "Changing Faces: Recasting National Identity in All-Asian(-)American Dramas." *Theatre Journal* 53 (2001): 389–409.

Saakana, Amon Saba. "Culture, Concept, Aesthetics: The Phenomenon of the African Musical Universe in Western Musical Culture." *African American Review* 29 (1995): 329–340.

Žižek, Slavoj. *Enjoy Your Symptom! Jacques Lacan in Hollywood and Out*. London and New York: Routledge, 1992.

5

When Race Matters: Reading Race in *Richard III* and *Macbeth*

LISA M. ANDERSON

As a young undergraduate theatre major in the mid-1980s, I auditioned for my college's summer theatre program. Like many of my classmates, I was in love with the theatre and imagined myself in a career (or at least an avocation) as an actor. I searched for a monologue that might be appropriate, but I wanted to choose one that was not a "black" monologue, not one written for a black female actor. In retrospect, I did not choose the best monologue; it was from James Baldwin's *Blues for Mister Charlie* and was probably unfamiliar to the directors. It also did not really give me much with which to work. It was not my poor choice of monologue, however, that kept me from earning a role in that year's summer theatre. I was told that there were no parts for black actresses that summer, so they could not cast me. Enraged, I dropped my theatre major in favor of political science and vowed to become a playwright and write good roles for black women.

In my experience in my high school drama club, race mattered, but not so much. The faculty advisors/directors of the drama club had no problem casting me in a role that did not specify someone of a particular race. However, that was not my experience in the musical theatre club, which "insulted" me by casting me as Bloody Mary in our production of *South Pacific*. Raised in primarily white suburbs, attending predominantly white schools, I was accustomed to being one of the few blacks, even the only one. I also thought, rather emphatically, that race did not matter unless race *mattered* — if the play was about race, then race should be part of casting; otherwise, the best actor should be cast for the job.

I am part of the first generation to feel the full impact of the legal changes brought by the civil rights movement of the 1950s and 1960s. I benefited from changes in laws that allowed me to live in my neighborhood, to attend my schools (both public and private), and to be accepted at a highly ranked college. I believed in integration — I certainly lived it. I believed that race should not determine opportunity (and I still do). But I also think I believed that race did not always matter, and that it should not matter when it came to issues like casting. After all, I had felt the effects of race-based casting, and it kept me from the opportunity to play roles I wanted to play.

I might still believe that race is irrelevant in casting were it not for a number of experiences that have shown me that race is never irrelevant when it comes to mimesis and the act of watching a dramatic performance. As part of American culture, we may believe in the abstract idea of a colorblind society, but we are actually anything but colorblind. I will first discuss the idea of "colorblindness" as it is in fact lived in American culture. I will then discuss two productions of Shakespeare plays that used colorblind casting; specifically, I will examine the ways in which the casting affected the audience's perception of the characters and the experience of watching the plays.

The Myth of Colorblindness

Culturally, we have translated Martin Luther King, Jr.'s famous phrase about being judged "not by the color of [our] skin but by the content of [our] character" to mean that color — a sign for race — should not, and does not, matter. Such a statement begs the question: What exactly does it mean for race not to matter? Invariably, a world in which race does not matter is a world in which race, and its signifier skin color, do not *mean* anything. Such a world would have no meanings attached to differences in skin color, and it would not have a history in which race was a central category.

Obviously, in the U.S. cultural context, differences in skin color, signifying differences in "race," have been profoundly significant in our history. From the earliest encounters with "Indians," to the transformation of indentured servitude to chattel slavery based upon race, to the Exclusion Acts and Japanese internment of the 1940s, *race* has been a central category. Race was a deciding factor in citizenship. Laws against interracial marriage were designed to keep the "white" race "pure." Race always already has meaning in a U.S. cultural context; this is undeniable.

As much as we might want to deny its salience, the United States was founded with race as a meaningful category. One's race determined whether one could be a citizen, whether one could vote or own property. Slavery, in its U.S. form, was based on the idea that enslavement was the "natural" status of the biologically inferior peoples of Africa. Conflicts about race, discrimination, and racism characterized much of the history of the twentieth century and continue to be significant issues into the twenty-first century.

August Wilson's argument against colorblind casting deals squarely with the fact that race is, and has been, a salient category in U.S. culture. Race is not only about skin color; race is a cultural construct. As such, while racial dividing lines have been used to discriminate, they have also served to create an identity for those who are racialized. The common history of African ancestry and varieties of racial discrimination (Jim Crow, redlining, etc.) have created the identities "African American" and/or "black." Wilson says, "I believe that race matters — that is the largest, most identifiable and most important part of our personality. It is the largest category of identification because it is the one that most influences your perception of yourself, and it is the one to which others in the world of men most respond" (14).

Race has also created and sustained cultures. The fact of its social construction does not negate the positive effect of such an identification for those who live with discrimination. Part of Wilson's argument is that race carries culture with it. In other words, there is cultural specificity to a broad "African American culture." Wilson states, "We decorate our houses. That is something we do in common. We do it differently because we value different things. We have different manners and different values of social intercourse. We have different ideas of what a party is" (27). That cultural specificity is elided when colorblind casting is employed.

Colorblindness ultimately signifies assimilation. When white students claim that they "don't see color," or that a racialized person is "just a person," they are reading the racialized-other as being like them: "white." While they deny that they see color, they do in fact see it; it is a part of their cultural ontology to see race and to assess people according to race. We are not blind to race (color); it is one of the ways in which we categorize our lives. Indeed, as Tamie Kanata notes, "by saying that 'I don't see color,' one is affirming of and sometimes *granting others the freedom* which they deserve to make their skin color invisible" (157). The reality of the visibility of skin color remains, however, even if the racialized person is "whited." To assume that we can watch a theatrical production and ignore the racial identities of the actors on stage is to assume the impossible. As Janice Peck notes, "ideologies of race already present in society ... are part of the material social conditions into which we are born, and within which we acquire racialized identities and identifications, develop understanding of others based on racial positioning, and interpret social relationships through racial categories" (92).

Race in the representational arts — theatre, film, and television specifically — continues to be contested. We assess the number of people of our specific racial/ethnic identity in primetime television programs each year: How many Latinos? How many Asians? How many blacks? Have we gained ground or lost it? We question the choice to cast a white person in a role that calls for an Asian. We wonder how quickly the black/Latino/Asian/Native American character will die. We wonder why the characters in *Friends* did not know any people of color in New York City.

Although it began as an effort to eliminate white privilege, colorblindness has become another mask behind which racism and what Patricia Hill Collins refers to as "controlling images" are maintained (see Collins). The practically ubiquitous claim to have rendered race invisible has not made race irrelevant. Colorblindness requires that we ignore three hundred years of history, or if not ignore them, render them meaningless. We must pretend that racism as an institution in the United States has not created significant differences in the real lives of real people. In many situations of colorblind casting, it asks that we mentally erase three centuries of images that have shaped and continue to shape the racial sign system in which we live. In the two cases I examine here, I demonstrate that while our intentions may be good, the insidious nature of our racial sign system continues to reinscribe itself. The effects of this reinscription can range from merely distracting to quite discomfiting.

Theatre Semiotics and Race

The theatrical stage is always a semiotic system, for everything that we put on stage has meaning and is coded to direct an audience toward a particular understanding. At the root of the system of any particular production are the cultural and social codes of the society in which the production is created. Therefore, at the root of these two productions is the sign system understood in general in both British and American cultures. In both contexts, race is a significant element of the sign system; it has social, political, and economic meaning. Blackness signifies race; blackness also carries with it three centuries of sedimented meaning. This is true for both men and women (because those sedimented meanings are differentiated by gender), and race on the stage has had and continues to have significance beyond skin color.

The semiotics of race in the U.S./British context looks for ways to both understand and account for the ways that skin color signifies. One of the things that skin color signifies is "the space of difference [that] is a historically and culturally constituted borderland between the perceptual/conscious and the unconscious" (DeLauretis, 56). This difference is experienced as corporeal; to be black is to be different. Stuart Hall, using Franz Fanon's *Black Skin, White Masks,* posits that race is inscribed on the body, in the skin; "*epidermalization*: literally, the inscription of race on the skin. This armature of 'race' provides the black subject with that which elsewhere Fanon calls an alternative 'corporeal schema.' But, as he always insists, this schema is cultural and discursive, not genetic or physiological" (1996, 16). Blackness is not only discursive; it is also cultural, and thus its meanings emerge from and function to maintain that culture.

Western representation of blackness on the stage has its own history. The nineteenth-century minstrel shows, which represented black men as lazy, ignorant, and often deceitful and black women as mammies and light-skinned prostitutes, laid the foundation for the theatrical representation of blackness as pathological. Even the classic Shakespearean texts that include black characters (Othello, Aaron) rely on stereotypes of black men, especially those stereotypes that represent black men as aggressive, transgressive, and violent. Representations of the black "buck," "coon," and "Tom" became standard characterizations on stage that moved quite readily to the screen upon the development of film. These images become part of our racialized discourse;

as Stuart Hall notes, "the astonishing persistence of the basic racial 'grammar of representation' is documented [in critical studies of race in American film] — of course, with many variations and modifications allowing for differences in time, medium, and context" (1997, 251).

Even as the black body is racialized, it is also sexualized; in this specific context, we must take up the meanings of the black *male* body. The sexualization of the black male body marks its deviance not only as one of color but also one of sexuality; the black male body is one that is sexually deviant. The iconic signifiers of race — brown skin, curly hair, flat nose, thick lips — "are signifying elements in the discourse of racism" (Hall 1996, 21). Thus, as Hall notes,

> It is not the status of racist discourse as "scientific" but the fact that its elements function *discursively* which enables it to have "real effects." They can carry meaning because they signify, through a process of displacement, further along the chain of equivalencies — *metonymically* (black skin — big penis — small brain — poor and backward — it's all in the genes — end the poverty programme — send them home!). That is, because their arrangement within a discursive chain enables physiological signs to function as signifiers, to stand for and be "read" further up the chain; socially, psychically, cognitively, politically, culturally, civilisationally. (Hall 1996, 21 and 24)

These signifiers signify not only race but also the stereotypes of the black man — the Tom, the Coon, and the Buck. Particularly of interest to me, in the context of this essay, is the invocation of these icons within these particular productions.

As much as we may abhor the negative stereotypes of blacks that became standard fare in theatre, they remain part of the consciousness of the audience that enters the theatre to watch a play. The presence of a black actor on stage recalls other representations, other plays; this fact remains when we watch a production that attempts to *unsignify* race by casting without apparent regard to it. The nature of these "controlling images" inherited through our culture, particularly those that are racist, is to persist, to reemerge, and to defy attempts to render them powerless. Because of their persistence, rather than ignoring race (or pretending to ignore race), it is incumbent upon artists (particularly directors) to consider the ways race *in performance* signifies for an audience. The audience always brings with it an understanding of the signifying systems of identity when entering the performance space. There is always a period of adjustment to the sign system of the director; the audience must observe the signs, noting whether or not, or in what ways, to retain the common social significance in this particular production.

When audience members encounter a situation in which they must decode the production's signifying system, they do not leave their cultural codes behind. If, for example, the director chooses to use a blue-tinted light to signify that the time period of the play has shifted to the past, the audience still understands that this is a blue light; whatever other signification there may be to this particular color of light (cold, for instance, or nighttime) is not transformed. It remains even as the audience adds the concept "blue = ten years earlier" to its understanding for this particular production. Similarly, the meanings of blackness do not disappear simply because a director chooses to pretend that skin color and race do not signify anything in our culture.

There is another aspect to the idea of shifting codes and significations; it is sometimes used deliberately by a director in order to make a point. A director might choose to cast both male and female roles in a play with female actors in order to highlight gender, sexism, and power. One might, as was famously done in Caryl Churchill's play *Cloud 9*, cast males in female roles (Betty, the Victorian wife played by a man in drag) or a white man in the role of an African, in order to make a point about power, race, and gender in the twentieth century. An audience accustomed to looking for meaning in this way will search, sometimes in vain, for the meaning behind the "altered" casting (not what one would normally expect). When the choice to cast a play is not done deliberately with this kind of audience challenge in mind, the audience may still look for this kind of meaning in the play's casting. It is in this audience practice (decoding the political or social significance of "altered" casting) that the good intentions of colorblind casting slip from the director's control, and where the use of colorblind casting can reinscribe racist images even while attempting to present a nonracist perspective.

Disruptions: *Macbeth* at the Globe

In May 2001, I was able to see *Macbeth* at the Globe Theatre in London. It was a nontraditional production, set in the 1920s with a "gangster" theme accompanied by jazz. The set was a curious affair; aside from the theatre structure itself, there was a long black tabletop suspended by cables from the ceiling, and a complement of black café chairs. The costumes recalled a formal party during the 1920s, with the women in long gowns and the men and witches in tuxedos. Cummerbunds were of various colors, depending on the character; Duncan's was gold, and Macbeth's was, for a time, red.

The set pieces and the costumes (and the music) were clearly nontraditional, set in a time and place neither Shakespeare's nor Macbeth's. As audience members, we understand that when a director sets a play in a particular period, she or he is trying to illuminate something about either the script or the period in which the play is set. The set was highly symbolic. While this is true of most sets for Shakespeare plays, which typically take place in multiple locations, for this play the simplicity of the set pieces created among the audience members a consciousness about the symbolic nature of everything put on the stage.

When nontraditional or colorblind casting is used in a context like this one, the audience is expected to perform two different types of interpretation.

On the one hand, we are asked to look for meaning in the things that are put on stage. We look for ways to differentiate between the "good" and "bad" guys — which actors are playing Malcolm, Donalbain, Duncan, Banquo, Macduff, and so on. Because the choice of costume, black tuxedos, made differentiation by costume difficult, we searched for any subtle difference between them that would help us understand the play. This was particularly true for me, since I had not read *Macbeth* in several years and needed help filling in the details. On the other hand, we are asked to rely on our cultural understandings of meaning to further understand the production. We must combine the general cultural significations that we carry with us into the theatre with the very specific theatrical significations designed for this particular production. With a simple set, we look for the meanings in the director's choices. How does Macbeth relate to, say, Chicago in the 1920s and the lives of gangsters? For me, as someone from the United States, the inter- and intra-family conflicts and murders among members of the Mafia correlate well with Shakespeare's play. For me, the director's concept was not too distracting. His casting, on the other hand, was.

The majority of the cast was white, as one might expect in a Shakespeare company. There were two black actors in the company, and they were cast in the roles of Duncan's sons, Malcolm and Donalbain. As far as gender is concerned, two of the witches were male and one female. Since male witches are not outside the realm of possibility, this choice was not distracting. In contrast, the choice to cast both Duncan's sons with black men puzzled me. First, the incongruity of biology stands out. It seems rather silly in 2006 to argue about the casting of family members with people of different races, but there remains the reality that biological inheritance shows on the body. Duncan's having two dark-skinned black sons is biologically impossible. However, I knew that the director was trying, and so I accepted the fact that he cast two black men in the roles of Duncan's sons. The second aspect is that the two black actors in the company were cast as brothers. That seems to imply that there *is* some significance to this particular casting; they could not be their father's children (racially), so it was odd to me that they should be cast as brothers, and not in two very disparate roles. Even when we pretend that race is irrelevant, it finds ways of sneaking in through our unconscious and preconscious sense-making. It would have been possible for the director to cast either Chu Omambala or Mark Springer in other roles so that they would not have played kin. Something was at work, though, when the only two black men in the company were cast as brothers. On the one hand, the audience was asked to believe first that they could be Duncan's sons, and on the other, the audience was given these two actors as brothers.

Obviously, I found this incongruity annoying, but it seems that I was the only one. While the reviewers agreed about the poor quality of the production, they ignored the cross-racial casting. One reviewer praised Omambala's acting:

"Only Chu Omambala, in the ungrateful role of Malcolm, tries to force some interest into his lines" (Macaulay). Neither Omambala nor Springer is mentioned in any other review. The reviewers from *The Times*, *Independent*, *Daily Telegraph*, and *Financial Times* were distracted by the jazz music and the costuming. Charles Spencer, in his review for the *Financial Times*, highlighted the degree to which the director, Tim Carroll, used symbolism. He complained:

> No one does anything as ugly as fight, or stab, or maim. Each member of the cast carries a stone. When someone is killed, his assassin takes his stone and drops it into a cast iron bucket. When you hear the metallic boink, he's snuffed it. In the same ungory manner, Duncan's blood is represented by gold tinsel, and at the fateful supper where Macbeth is confronted by Banquo's ghost, everyone wears novelty party hats. (Spencer)

Clearly, Carroll's production asked the audience to understand the significations of gold tinsel and dropped stones. It stands to reason, then, that an audience member might ask, "What is the significance of Malcolm and Donalbain both being black actors?" If everything else on stage means something, then this must mean something as well. If the actors' race means nothing, then how do we as an audience differentiate between signifiers that mean something and signifiers that do not?

Four years after seeing the production, I still puzzle over this seemingly meaningless choice in a production where so many other objects were deeply infused with meaning. Although it is not offensive, the understanding of this particular production requires that the audience understand this particular sign system, in which some codes are consistent with our everyday cultural sign system and some are not. In the sign system that Carroll created, the audience learned, for example, that gold tinsel is a sign for royal blood (gold, hence royal, and liquid-like movement, blood). This is a signification outside our everyday signification, in which we might expect either fake blood or, at least, red tinsel. On the other hand, the signs of gender remained consistent with those of contemporary Western European culture; the women wore dresses, the men wore dinner jackets, and the witches — neither one nor the other — wore dinner jackets and weird glasses. Unlike gender, race was evidently no longer a sign; the skin color of the actors playing Malcolm and Donalbain did not signify anything in the concept of the play.

Malcolm, Donalbain, and Racial Signifiers

In investigating the semiotics of this production, we can also consider whether or not the *meaning* of the black Malcolm and Donalbain might still emerge as somehow coded to their race. Clearly, the meaning of their race is not related to the "race" of Duncan. So we consider what the choice of these actors for these parts might lend to their characters; in other words, do the roles of Malcolm and Donalbain signify something about the actors' race? We also consider the iconic images of black maleness and examine whether or not the production plays into, or draws upon, the stereotypes of the Tom, Coon, or Buck.

Reviewing the text discloses little that might spur a director to attempt to make the actors' race a sign for something about Duncan's sons. There are some elements that might have meaning, but they do not seem particularly inventive, nor do they retain meaning in the context of the production's sign system. When Duncan is murdered, Malcolm and Donalbain are in shock. While Macbeth feigns outrage that makes him kill the guards, and Lady Macbeth swoons, Duncan's sons do not have an emotional response at hand. In order to avoid being considered suspects, they quickly leave Macbeth's castle for Ireland and England, but their flight immediately makes them suspect; Macduff explains to Ross that "Malcolm and Donalbain, the King's two sons / Are stol'n away and fled, which puts upon them / Suspicion of the deed" (2.4.25–27).

One might stretch to consider that race influences the relative guilt or innocence of a suspect; when Malcolm and Donalbain, the two black men, flee the scene of the crime, they are considered suspects. However, this is not solely racial; in most circumstances, anyone's fleeing the scene of a crime implies guilt. It is also necessary that Duncan's sons, who are his logical successors, leave in order for Macbeth to accede to the throne of Scotland. It requires a bit of a stretch to think that this is the underlying significance of the casting of Omambala and Springer.

Although Malcolm and Donalbain have their revenge on Macbeth, they are not alone in their plotting against the usurper. Macduff and Ross also suspect foul play in the murder of Duncan, which is confirmed by the murder of Banquo. Macduff fears that he may be next on Macbeth's murder list, and he goes to join Malcolm in England. In a conversation with Macduff, Malcolm claims that he would be no better king than Macbeth; his lust for women, land, and money makes him unfit to be king. We learn quite quickly that Malcolm's confession is merely a test to gauge Macduff's loyalty, and that he is quite the opposite of what he has just confessed. While the first self-description that Malcolm gives to Macduff might echo stereotypes of blacks, there is nothing in this scene, or in Malcolm's actions or words here, that makes the actor's race significant.

It is Malcolm who attempts to console Macduff when word arrives that Macduff's wife and children have been murdered; it is Malcolm who directs the army to cut branches from Birnam Wood to disguise their march to Dunsinane. In short, there is no significant textual signification that might incline a director deliberately to cast Duncan's sons as black. Neither Malcolm nor Donalbain is the self-sacrificing Tom, the comic Coon, or the threatening, violent Buck; in short, their roles do not enable the use of stereotypes. The sign system employed by the director requires its audience to understand race to signify nothing, while all other elements of a contemporary American or

English culture maintain much of their meaning. One might refer to the colorblind casting of this particular production as "full of sound and fury, / Signifying nothing" (5.5.26–27). Yet, as audience members, we are left hopelessly to sort through the possible meanings; we have to work hard to ignore race as a sign on stage.

Black Buck as Villain: *Richard III*

While the production of *Macbeth* had its difficulties around the issue of colorblind casting, a production of *Richard III* in Chicago in 1996 was actually disturbing in its use of the practice. It is this kind of colorblind casting that reveals the extent to which Americans are anything but colorblind. As in the more recent production of *Macbeth*, reviewers of the Chicago production never mentioned the race of the actor playing Richard, or the implications of the ways in which race actually signified in the production.

As in many colorblind productions, the number of black actors was small. Typically, they are not given lead roles, but they may take major roles. This production of *Richard III* broke with that practice by casting a black actor in the lead role. In this case, it also meant that this particular black actor was cast in the role of a villain. In and of itself, the choice of a black actor to play a villain is not necessarily problematic. In fact, the use of a black villain might have been offset by the casting of other black actors in various roles in the play. The director went halfway there; there were two other black actors cast in the production. Unfortunately, they were both cast as Richard's henchmen, the two murderers.

What the actor playing Richard on the stage signified was far greater than what the character of Richard signifies in the play, or what a white actor as Richard might signify. Indeed, to consider the character of Richard as a black man invites a bevy of stereotypes of black men in the United States. Shakespeare's Richard is a malformed, conniving, evil murderer who will do anything to gain power. A black Richard adds another level of signification that cannot help but recall representations of black men throughout the history of American theatre and film. The most salient of these stereotypes is that of Black Buck. As Donald Bogle states, "The black brute was a barbaric black out to raise havoc. Audiences could assume that his physical violence served as an outlet for a man who was sexually repressed" (13).

Richard's pursuit of Anne in 1.2 recalls the aspect of the Black Buck, the black man who is "oversexed and savage, violent and frenzied as [he] lust[s] for white flesh," sexually pursuing white women (Bogle, 13). Richard's unrelenting attempts to convince Anne to marry him take place while she is accompanying her dead husband's body to burial. Richard's presence is unwanted; Anne knows well that it was Richard who orchestrated her husband's death. His badgering recalled to me the figure of Silas Lynch in D. W. Griffith's *Birth of a Nation*, who pursues Elsie Strongman with similar fervor. For both men, the acquisition of this particular woman is access to power. As Kobena Mercer writes, "The primal fantasy of the big black penis projects the fear of a threat not only to white womanhood, but to civilization itself, as the anxiety of miscegenation, eugenic pollution and racial degeneration is acted out through white male rituals of racial aggression" (185). Inadvertently, this particular production captured the signifiers of the icon of the Black Buck within the performance.

The characterization of Richard as deformed, and therefore as a type of defective human, reflects a history of the representation of the black male body as something not quite human. Richard's self-hatred, in any circumstance, appears normal. Textually, Richard experiences his body as the source of his hatred; his deformity engenders the scorn, pity, and fear of those around him. His external appearance, as "deformed," reflects the internal nature of Richard. Even though he can be (and has been) named the Protector, his disfigurement makes it impossible for him to be king. This is particularly true in Britain, where the ability to be king required physical health and wholeness, for the body of the nation was reflected in the body of its ruler (see Figes). In this production, Richard's attempt to take power creates a situation in which the nation begins to reflect him; it becomes deformed and dark as Richard murders his relatives in order to gain power. In the production, the idea of a dark and broken England was evoked by a set filled with pieces that "[took] the form, literally, of a vast ship of state, with a raw wood deck and trap doors and a great expanse of overhead beams," lighting that was dim, and an atmosphere filled with fog (Weiss). The red lights that symbolized Richard's murderous reign succeeded in highlighting the visual differences between Richard and the two murderers, on one hand, and the rest of the (white) characters, on the other.

Race emerged as a visual dividing line between the "good" and "bad" characters. Blackness as a signifier for evil was unconsciously invoked by the director; the audience and reviewers, by their avoidance of the subject of Richard's race and the signified meanings of blackness, implied that this casting choice was not a deliberate effort on the part of the director to signify evil through the race of the actors she chose. The figure of a black Richard III in the context of an otherwise all-white cast displaces our revulsion at Richard's physical deformity — his hump — onto his racial difference.

As with the Globe production of *Macbeth*, mention of the *race* of Richard and his henchmen was absent in published reviews of the play. Like the London critics, the Chicago reviewers were full of critique — some of it harsh — of the production. Their reviews made me wonder if their negative responses to the play were not partially a reflection of the discomfort of the reviewers, who understood that they were supposed to "ignore" the actors' race. One reviewer critiqued Brendan Corbalis's performance thus: "But with his slight figure and bearing — and the petulant moodiness of a naughty boy with little more than a very nasty streak of maliciousness — he fails to believably galvanize the relentless slaughter carried out in his name" (Weiss). The reviewer for the *Chicago Tribune* also saw Corbalis as "fairly bland and ineffectual" and attributed part of the problem to the director's casting and concept:

> As the great crookback, Brendan Corbalis has been given a formidable hump (which at one point he bares in ugly detail). But he hasn't been given a real focus on the part. He tries playing it sexy, as a seducer of women. He tries playing it for sly comedy. He tries, in his closing moments, for pathos. None of it works well. Neither Corbalis nor Gaines [the director] appears to have a solid grip on this character. Perhaps she was too busy focusing on the theory she expresses in a program note: "The very masculine world of politics and war in *Richard III* must be understood, it seems to me, through the women of this play and the feminine side of nature they represent" (Christiansen).

None of the reviewers mentioned that Corbalis is black; it is certainly not because they did not see his race. It does make me wonder to what extent their responses to his performance were the effect, however unconscious, of the reviewers' struggle to avoid noticing the images that Corbalis's performance recalled for them.

The production also did not call upon, or recall, the history of black performances of Shakespeare, in particular of *Richard III*. One of the earliest was that of the African Grove's controversial production in 1821, with Richard played by James Hewlett. It is understood to have been a well-done production, which made it possible for the white audience members to associate blacks with the accomplishment of performing Shakespeare well. For those whose goals were to maintain racist notions of blacks (particularly of their lack of intellect), the African Grove's production was actually dangerous; they worked hard to shut the production down. This production was immortalized in Carlyle Brown's fictionalized play *The African Company Presents Richard the Third* (see Brown). Richard has also been played by such noted black Shakespeareans as Ira Aldridge, Paul Molyneaux, J. A. Arneaux, and Paul Winfield. Like many others in Shakespeare's tragedies and histories, Richard is a particularly coveted role that enables an actor to demonstrate his talent. Unfortunately, none of this was apparent in the Chicago production, and for the most part, audiences are unaware of the African Grove production or of the celebrated black actors who have played Richard.

Race and Meaning

The pursuit of an antiracist society is without question important. It remains important, particularly as our society has yet to overcome its assumption of white supremacy and attendant racist attitudes. The erosion of the legal rights gained during the civil rights movement has made it almost acceptable to continue to hold racist views of blacks. The effort toward colorblindness has not reduced or eliminated racism; rather, it has reinforced whiteness as neutral, "raceless," and "colorless." We remain acutely aware of race, and of the privileges that a "lack" of race (i.e., whiteness) bestows. We are unable to pretend that a black person, on stage or in a film, is not a black person. The actor's blackness precedes him or her, evokes the history of race in our culture; without any effort, the meanings of blackness filter through our consciousness. We work to ascertain the meaning of *this particular* blackness, while other meanings remain present.

In these two instances, we can see the ways in which the meanings of blackness interject themselves into our activity as audience. We can also see how colorblind casting can either invoke the stereotyped images of race or avoid doing so. In some ways, the practice of colorblind casting attempts to change what Stuart Hall calls the "representational regime of racial difference" (1997, 256). These two productions also reveal the necessity of understanding that we live in a culture that has not been able to achieve racial equality. We are always subject to the binary structure of racial stereotyping; the black/white binary is reaffirmed in the case of the production of *Richard III*. The "*range* of racial representations and the complexity of what it means to be black" is not expanded in this production of *Richard III* in the ways that it is in *Macbeth* (Hall 1997, 272–273).

Can the dominant regime of representation be challenged, contested, or changed? Can we unfix the meanings of blackness? Colorblind casting is an admirable effort to create opportunities for actors of color to play roles not specifically written for their particular race — that are, in fact, written as white characters. When the actor's race is used deliberately as part of the director's concept for the play, it can be an effective tool in revealing racism and the meanings of race. For example, the director of *Richard III* might have chosen to highlight the casting of Corbalis as Richard in order to expose the ways in which cultural representations of black men are still stuck in the old negative stereotypes. She might also have carefully considered her casting, and rather than cast the only other actors of color as Richard's henchmen, cast one or both of them in opposition to Richard. A deliberate defamiliarizing reveals the *use* of the stereotype; but such a technique is used transparently, informing the audience (perhaps through a program note from the director) of the use of the cultural meanings of race as a device. Careless casting, however, has the potential merely to reinscribe the racist controlling images that we, as artists and scholars, have worked so diligently to eradicate.

References

Bogle, Donald. *Toms, Coons, Mulattoes, Mammies and Bucks: An Interpretive History of Blacks in American Films.* 3rd ed. New York: Continuum, 1996.

Brown, Carlyle. *The African Company Presents Richard the Third.* New York: Dramatist Play Service, 1998.

Christiansen, Richard. "Major Hump Keeps Richard III from Succeeding." *Chicago Tribune,* April 23, 1996.

Collins, Patricia Hill. *Black Sexual Politics: African Americans, Gender, and the New Racism.* London and New York: Routledge, 2004.

DeLauretis, Teresa. "Difference Embodied: Reflections on *Black Skin, White Masks.*" *Parallax* 8 (2002): 54–68.

Figes, Eva. *Tragedy and Social Evolution.* New York: Persea, 1976.

Hall, Stuart. "The After-Life of Frantz Fanon: Why Fanon? Why Now? Why *Black Skin, White Masks?*" In *The Fact of Blackness: Frantz Fanon and Visual Representation,* edited by Alan Read. Seattle: Seal, 1996.

Hall, Stuart. "The Spectacle of the 'Other.'" In *Representation: Cultural Representations and Signifying Practices,* edited by Stuart Hall. London: Sage, 1997.

Kanata, Tamie. "'I Don't See Color — We're All Just Human Beings': Phenomenology of Students' Online Discourses on Race, Ethnicity, and Prejudice." Ph.D. dissertation, Arizona State University, 2003.

Macaulay, Alastair. "Globe Lives Down to Usual Expectations." *Financial Times,* June 7, 2001.

Mercer, Kobena. "Reading Racial Fetishism." In *Welcome to the Jungle: New Positions in Black Cultural Studies,* edited by Kobena Mercer. London and New York: Routledge, 1994.

Peck, Janice. "Talk About Racism: Framing a Popular Discourse of Race on Oprah Winfrey." *Cultural Critique* 27 (1994): 89–126.

Spencer, Charles. "A Macbeth that Fascinates for 15 Minutes." *Daily Telegraph,* June 7, 2001.

Weiss, Heidi. "Richard III Lacks Firepower." *Chicago Sun-Times,* April 22, 1996.

Wilson, August. *The Ground on Which I Stand.* New York: Theatre Communications Group, 1996.

6

Ira Aldridge, Shakespeare, and Color-Conscious Performances in Nineteenth-Century Europe

KRYSTYNA KUJAWINSKA COURTNEY

When discussing the use of colorblind casting in Shakespearean productions, one has to examine the complex semiotics of race. In the context of the United States and the United Kingdom, the presence of a black actor onstage may be interpreted through various disparate lenses that recall the histories of these countries, including the history of slavery, the ongoing battles for racial equality, and the history of the exploitation of black bodies (public lynchings, minstrel shows, etc.). These interpretive lenses, however, are not universal. An examination of the Continental reception of the nineteenth-century black Shakespearean Ira Aldridge will complicate our understanding of both the performance of blackness and the semiotics of blackness. Although Ira Aldridge is one of only thirty-three distinguished actors — and the only actor of African American descent — who is memorialized by a bronze plaque at the Shakespeare Memorial Theatre at Stratford-upon-Avon, and who has a theatre named after him (at Howard University), he is not given his due in scholarship. British and American historians tend to view Aldridge as a perfect example of the Strange, the Unknown, the Other.[1] But the archival materials about Aldridge's reception on the Continent may challenge us to think about how our theories of theatre semiotics need to be developed in both historical and global contexts.

Indeed, in Aldridge's case the theatrical records and criticism that praised and venerated him during his life came mostly from the non-English-speaking countries he visited on his tours. Named by *Gazeta Wielkiego Xsiestwa Poznanskiego* as "a star of the first magnitude" in 1853, he was, according to the *Kurier Warszawski*, "greeted by crowded houses everywhere, and princes and people were eager to see him, while honours, orders and medals were showered upon him."[2] The composer Richard Wagner noted the clamor to watch Aldridge's play in the theatre; the writer Théophile Gautier wrote about his enchantment with Aldridge's performances in his famous *Voyage en Russie* (1895); and Taras Shevchenko drew his portrait as a token of their friendship.[3]

The Continental reception of Aldridge's performances was inseparable from the political and cultural milieu of each country he visited. Though many countries were not involved in the problems of slavery, they had their own political and social concerns, which they frequently treated as a reflection of the enslavement of Africans in the Americas and other colonies. The discrimination against blacks and their fight for emancipation seemed to many Europeans synonymous with their own struggle for national government and ethnic equality.[4]

Aldridge's visits in Poland and Russia are good examples to study the ways social and political debates affected the reception of Aldridge as a black actor. An analysis of Aldridge's reception on the Continent reveals how color-conscious his performances were. Not only were these performances interpreted as being about Aldridge's race in particular and the black race in general, but they also were read as being related to the social, cultural, and political struggles over nationality and ethnicity on the Continent. Though the questions of race and Shakespeare as an international writer constituted a permanent point of reference in Aldridge's career in Central and Eastern Europe, his Otherness became a frequent excuse for discussing national and ethnic concerns.

Becoming an "African Prince"

Born in New York City on July 24, 1807 and educated for a few years at the Second African Free School, Aldridge was employed in his youth in various menial jobs in the city, including a brief period as a costume carrier for a visiting British actor. Aldridge was also involved in several small dramatic productions staged by the black acting company known as the African Grove Theatre of Manhattan, where he fell in love with the theatre and decided to become a professional actor. Since he could not fulfill his ambition in the United States, he emigrated to Britain, where he was fortunate to secure an engagement at London's Royal Coburg Theatre (now the Old Vic) in October 1825. During his almost twenty-five-year career in Britain, he did not have a long London run in the patent theatres (Covent Garden and Drury Lane), which to many British actors at that time would have been the surest sign of professional recognition. Aldridge's attempt to achieve that recognition at Covent Garden (1833) brought him a devastating rejection (see Waters). For the rest of his career in Britain, the tragedian's professional life depended mainly on tours. In 1852–1867 Aldridge toured many European countries, where he was accorded the recognition due to an outstanding Shakespearean tragedian. He died in the middle of rehearsing *Othello* in Lodz (Poland) in 1867.

Aldridge's career falls into three distinct parts. In the United States, he became fascinated with theatre and Shakespeare and experienced his first encounters with racial prejudice and hatred.[5] In Britain Aldridge was treated as a star that glowed from afar, since he was not recognized by the establishment of the capital. His Continental triumphs were, however, remarkable, and his acting tours evoked an unprecedented interest in Shakespeare.[6] In contrast to his reception in Britain, where the color of his skin made Aldridge "unworthy" to perform Shakespeare's roles in the legitimate London theatres, in Continental Europe his presentations were received with enthusiasm and admiration.[7] He played in the most prestigious theatres, and he was received with adoration by both the social-cultural elites and the common people. Aldridge's performances on the Continent coincided with Europe's "discovery" of Shakespeare's works: the first half of the nineteenth century was the time when his plays became accepted as a source of universal values, psychological, philosophical, spiritual, and moral. Europe was beginning to appropriate Shakespeare's dramas, and in many cases the dramatist himself, as a national figure for quite disparate cultural, social, and political reasons. Translations and adaptations of Shakespeare's plays appeared; luminaries published their scholarly and critical studies of Shakespeare; and visual artists and creative writers were inspired by Shakespeare and his works.

It was, however, the popular culture of performance that enabled the propagation of Shakespeare's dramas to the general public. Given the high rate of illiteracy in nineteenth-century Europe, the theatres constituted the most accessible means of reaching a lower-class audience. In addition, while other traveling Shakespeare performers (e.g., Adelaide Ristori, Ernesto Rossi, Tommasi Salvini) usually toured only in major cities and performed various dramatists' works, Aldridge visited the provinces and played only Shakespeare's tragedies, sometimes in tandem with Isaak Bickerstaff's comedy *The Padlock*.[8] One critic from Odessa wrote in 1866:

> It is already some years that Aldridge, in the role of a strolling missionary of art, has enlightened the Russian public with the light of the immortal creations of Shakespeare: at the moment there is not one provincial city, it seems to me, not one well-known fair in Russia, where the light of Shakespeare's genius has not penetrated, thanks to this traveling tragedian. (*Odesskiy Novosti*)

Though many people attended his performances because they wanted to see a black actor, Aldridge also exposed them to Shakespeare's texts. It is not surprising that for many critics the black tragedian became the first Shakespearean actor, and many of the people who saw his performances addressed him as "Ira Aldridge, the Great Interpreter of the Ever-Living Shakespeare" (Mortimer, 7).

While during Aldridge's Continental tours the actor's talent and professionalism were casting a spell on theatre-lovers in one country after another, the physical presence of his black body triggered not only fascination but also debates about race and Otherness. Very early in his career Aldridge was labeled the "African Roscius." The name "Roscius," a reference to the glory of

Quintus Roscius Gallus, a Roman slave who became an actor, was customarily bestowed on paramount theatre performers.[9] Though it is impossible to say whether that *nom de théâtre* was the idea of Aldridge's first managers or his own choice, the name must have appealed to him. Aldridge used it throughout his career: the assumption of the phrase "*African* Roscius" signals the actor's explicit awareness of and participation in the ongoing debates about the enslavement of Africans.

In 1849, Aldridge's first biography was published as *The Memoir and Theatrical Career of Ira Aldridge*.[10] According to the memoir, the tragedian was apparently a son of the chief or prince of one of the Senegambian tribes, whose family endured hardship and degradation because of their skin color.[11] It is impossible to say who was responsible for this romantic provenience. It might have been "invented" by the *Memoir*'s author, or as Marshall and Stock believe, it might have been written at the tragedian's suggestion. The biographers base their assumption on the fact that the actor was aware of the value of publicity and treated the "story of Aldridge's life" as a significant part of his European tours. The *Memoir* became known worldwide when it was translated into German (1853), Russian (1858), and French (1866).

Though critics usually discount the biographical value of the *Memoir*, both its ideological and "fairy-tale" dimensions provided a certain cultural capital. The invented story of his origin may be interpreted as the actor's attempt to fight racial discrimination. Kevin Gaines explains and justifies dissembling (silence, evasion, and distortion) in the presentations of African American family histories:

> African American men and women dissemble to survive in a racialized world not of their own making. ... For educated blacks, the family, divisive memories of the violence, and humiliation of slavery and segregation were and remain at the heart of the uplift ideology's romance of the patriarchal family, expressed by black men and women's too-often-frustrated aspirations to protect and be protected. (Gaines, 5)

In a British society strictly regulated by class and race identity, Aldridge found a way to affirm his fitness for approval and assimilation. After all, much of the appeal was based "on the victim's right, like Oroonoko, to riches through his noble birth" (Disher, 108).

The life of Oroonoko, the first character Aldridge played in Britain (1825), might in fact have become a model for his family story: the actor "abandoned" his American origin and became an African, a descendent of a Senegalese king. His newly assumed identity was not just a simple promotional act, though it did help to attract an audience; it was also a complex performative act. John Coleman described Aldridge's arrival in Derby in 1848, where he was to play Othello and was billed as the son of an African prince:

> As I reached the market place I saw the prince [Aldridge] driving the High Street in his carriage, and a very princely affair it was. The coachman on the box, the flunkeys behind, and the distinguished looking coloured gentleman inside attracted crowds as it leisurely rolled along.... He, or the carriage, or both drew a crowded house. (Coleman, 91)

Only later, when Coleman came to know Aldridge better, did the actor tell him that "the gorgeous equipage had been in pawn at the railway station," and it was only through the kindness of the officials that Aldridge was permitted to borrow it "to parade through the town, for the purpose of attracting the audience" (Coleman, 91). By accepting or maybe "inventing" his family story in the *Memoir*, Aldridge "uplifted his race" by implicitly challenging many British cultural and moral tenets.

In his Continental tours fashioned as an "African Prince," Aldridge became perceived as the representative, and later as a living metaphor, of the Dark Continent. Though many people still associated him with the situation of blacks in overseas colonies, the American abolitionist movement, the Civil War, and black emancipation, all these issues were perceived through the prism of European nationalism, which frequently involved a radical drive for liberation from political and social oppression.

Reading Blackness/Reading Aldridge

Russia and Poland, like other European countries, had been exposed to a vigorous debate on the concept of race in the nineteenth century. Fueled by the Enlightenment classificatory systems of Carl von Linne, better known as Linnaeus (1707–1778) and George Louis Leclerc, comte de Buffon (1707–1788), the Romantics attempted to define and categorize the exquisite colors, forms, and architecture of nature in its disparate living forms.[12] Their concerns with nationality and ethnicity, the local and the particular, led Romantic thinkers to believe the landscape and climate of Europe were better than those of the other continents. This enabled them to construct Europeans as the superior race (see Bernal, 198–223). The concept of "race" became inseparable from classifying and categorizing individuals in relation to their physical appearance, skin color, hair texture, anatomical form, and other physical features.

Aldridge was never ashamed of his racial origin, as if he were aware of the cultural confusion his race and professionalism created in the minds of his audiences. After acknowledging and assuming his African identity early in his career, the actor signed most of his letters as "An Actor of Color known as the African Roscius" or "African Tragedian."[13] All his playbills and theatrical announcements in Europe stressed his racial provenance. Aldridge fashioned himself as "An African," and this self-fashioning found its culmination in "the write-ups of adventures of the 'black artist,' the portraits, brochures, life sketches" based on the *Memoir*, which the actor included in his promotional materials during his Continental tours (*Czas*, 2 November 1854). By purposefully drawing attention to his race, Aldridge turned it into cultural capital which, at least initially, caught people's interest: his race constituted a substantial part of his carefully orchestrated theatrical event. In Poland, audiences wholeheartedly accepted his promotional strategy. For example, the reviewer of his appearance in Warsaw treated the commercialization of the actor's racial origin as an additional asset to his performance (*Tygodnik Illustrowany*).

Encountering a black actor for the first time aroused curiosity, but it also left prospective theatrical clients in a state of suspense: they went to the theatre eager to find out whether their initial wonder would turn into hatred or love. Yet after his first encounters with the public, audiences and critics recognized Aldridge as a theatrical star. They began to evaluate his art, not the fact that he was "the Negro" (*Czas*, 2 November 1854). The actor was aware of his cultural role. On 30 October 1852, Philippe Edouard Devrient noted in his personal diary that Aldridge came back on stage after the performance and pronounced an epilogue "in which he implored respect for his race ... with dignity, modesty, with moving insistence, without any pretension" (quoted in Mortimer, 193).[14]

In Poland, where Africans appeared for the first time in the seventeenth century as court pages, people did not have substantial daily exposure to people of African ancestry.[15] The situation was, however, radically different in Russia, which in the seventeenth century was involved in the trade in African children from Turkey.[16] From the eighteenth century to the first half of the nineteenth, the number of blacks in Russia increased significantly, though the relatively few African slaves brought to Russia were primarily for ornamental display in wealthy households. The households of Russian tsars sometimes included between ten and twenty-five black pages (see Gnammankou).

In addition, at least part of the Russian public became knowledgeable about Africa and its inhabitants because of the country's religious, diplomatic, and economic interactions with sub-Saharan Africa, especially Abyssinia (Ethiopia). Information about Ethiopia was disseminated through the writings of Russian scholars, clergy, and politicians. References to blacks and the African continent were also present in literature and in paintings. Several groups of Russian scientists and officials who visited the "Dark Continent" published their reports (see Zabrodskaia, 52–73). People talked about two blacks, Nelson and Claude Gabriel, who were in the service of the first American ambassador to Russia in 1809, John Quincy Adams — president of the United States from 1825 to 1829 — and who fled during a stay in Saint Petersburg (see Gnammankou, 71). Thus, at the time of Aldridge's visits to Russia, the African presence in the country could be felt from the banks of the Neva to Saint Petersburg and the Caucasian mountains.

At the time of Aldridge's visits to Poland, the country's knowledge of Africans was growing, mainly through various scientific or pseudo-scientific publications and travelers' reports. Short articles, travel accounts, poems, and stories on Africa appeared in respectable popular dailies and periodicals, and authoritative sources, such as encyclopedias, also helped to construct a racial discourse. Orgelbrand's *Encyklopedia powszechna* (1859) offers an example of the nineteenth-century Polish construction of blackness:

> Negroes inhabit the whole of Africa from Nubia and Assyria to the lands of Hottentots and Bushmen. ... The blackness of their skin is their most distinctive feature; it differentiates them from other races. Their skin color does not result exclusively from the intensity of their exposure to the sun: ebony-like skin color can be found in the tribes, which live far from the equator. ... Because the Negroes have an inclination to sexual pleasures and a lazy style of living, they have not played any important role in the world civilization. ... Their occupations, though they barely deserve such names, include animal herding, fishery, and agriculture. Their religion is primitive: they worship animals, and fetishes, and they have witch doctors and shamans. Their language is elementary: its vocabulary consists only of the words that designate sensory objects. (Orgelbrand, 518)

Struggling to define "them" (the Africans) in the context of "us" (Europeans), the encyclopedia compilers nevertheless conceded that

> the Negroes should not be seen in a completely negative light. ... [Negroes] can attain a higher level of civilization, as there are numerous examples of consummate artisans, talented farmers, and traders. ... It seems that the local conditions of hot climate, unfriendly soil, sand, and water, which separate them from other nations, deprive the Negroes of any external stimulation and that is the reason why they have not yet emerged from the primary state of civilization. (518)

Some of Aldridge's reviewers took advantage of the preexisting notion that education and exposure to the achievements of white culture could bring Africans to a higher level of civilization. Baffled by his theatrical genius, the critics explained it as the result of the Western acculturation. One Polish writer assured his readers that though Aldridge's origin was African, "he was brought up and educated in England" (*Tygodnik Illustrowany*). Similarly, A. Urusov, a Russian lawyer, informed his readers that "Aldridge is not a savage Negro, captured only yesterday, but a Negro who has received in Europe an aesthetic education" (*Russkii Vestnik*).

Informed by nineteenth-century racial discourses, the Polish desire to divide and rank, and in effect exclude, was not exceptional. It demonstrated the widely circulated conceptual core of the construction and theorization of race and difference. The first reactions to Aldridge in Saint Petersburg (1858) reflected this popular practice. Mikhail Pogodin (1800–1875), an eminent right-wing intellectual and a famous historian, wrote:

> General opinion puts the Negro at the lowest level among the members of the human family. He is forced to accept the mental and moral superiority of his white brothers, as if they were of nobler blood. Look at Aldridge ... he is an African, with a swarthy face, dark skin, kinky hair, dilated nostrils, guttural speech. He does not attract us with an exquisite form, such as we are accustomed to; external beauty does not help him to create a favourable impression in the beginning to gain him friendship. Moreover, he speaks a foreign language. (quoted in Durilin, 37–38)

Throughout his review, Pogodin attempts to force the Other, the Unknown that is defined in shifting cultural margins, to occupy a fixed place in a system of shared belief. His anxiety to present Aldridge, the subhuman, revealed tensions and contradictions in the Russian belief system. Yet the power of Aldridge's acting made the reviewer come to terms with his equivocal feelings, since he presented "with astonishing clarity the minutest and finest nuances of the human emotions which the greatest master and clairvoyant Shakespeare portrays" (quoted in Durilin, 38). In his review, Pogodin made what was in effect a fiction of difference, but he accepted this fiction even as he praised the power of Aldridge's acting.

At the time of Aldridge's tours in Continental Europe race "was no longer," as David Lloyd says in a different context, "an arbitrary mark or a cultural distinction but it rather consisted in, and of, natural signs written on the body itself" (Lloyd, 69). What came to distinguish one people from another was not their religion, their degree of "civilization," their customs, or their beliefs but rather their anatomy and external appearance. Aldridge's anatomy was of a particular interest to his audience. Reminiscing about his artistic achievements, Kazimierz Kaszewski located his body in the context of its anatomical structure: "His [Aldridge's] appearance, not so much represented by a Negro as shown by an Ethiopian type from old descriptions: he was tall and of strong stature, his breast eminently developed and a well-shaped head rested on his powerful shoulders" (Kaszewski, 580). In 1853, *Dziennik Warszawski* recommended his performance to its readers, but it also described the actor as an "athlete of a surprisingly strong stature."[17]

The interest in Aldridge's anatomy was so compelling that it became the object of a chronometric study. The followers of this pseudo-scientific and biased methodology claimed that a clear relationship existed between the size of human skulls and the shape of human brains and, as a consequence, racial difference and social status. The black's cranial capacity, facial angle, and brain volume or brain weight were regarded as an indicator of innate capacity, which was presumed to be analogous to that of apes. In 1858, while on tour in Odessa in Russia, Aldridge consented to having his head measured by the American consul. The consul concluded his elaborate study with a statement that "the head of this eminent colored man is very much larger than the average size for a white man, which, as is generally known, is above the Negro type of head." Since Aldridge's head did not reflect the parameters of "a typical Negro," the consul came to the conclusion that "his head, like that of Fred Douglass, is an isolated case and proves only rare possibilities or outcroppings from common stock," and he dismissed it as a biological aberration (quoted in Marshall and Stock, 154).

In Poland and Russia, as in Britain, Aldridge's sexuality, too, became the object of white men's concern. Rumors were spread about his uncontrollable violence toward his Desdemonas in the bedroom scene: people gossiped that he was notorious for fatally injuring his leading ladies. The talk about particular relationships between Aldridge and white women resulted from the popular stereotype of African male virility and prowess. "Folded within the scientific accounts of race," Robert Young points out, the nineteenth-century European "assumption and paranoid fantasy was endlessly repeated: the uncontrollable sexual drive of the non-white races and their limitless fertility" (Young, 180–181). The anecdotes about Aldridge actually "suffocating" his Desdemonas and his seemingly uncontrolled, fierce acting inspired satirical drawings, which appeared in the Russian and Polish press.[18] The actor's portraits were inspired by the racial attitude to the Other. Since Africans aroused popular interest for their savagery rather than their docility, Aldridge was presented as a "barbarian superman" who could throw Iago in the air with one hand and leap several feet high. His assertive figure was sharply contrasted with those of his Desdemonas, who were little, frightened creatures. Though in the drawings the overpowering presence of the black actor is grotesque, it also evokes amazement.[19] These grotesque presentations of Aldridge disclose a significant element of nineteenth-century racial dynamics in Europe. This collision of diametrically opposed reactions to Aldridge became the organizing principle of the Russian and Polish satirical pictures: the viewers were simultaneously to deny and to embrace his humanity.

Many Polish and Russian theatrical reviews reveal that as a nonwhite, Aldridge was both feared and desired. Following the early evolutionists, who often explained race in terms of a chain of being, moving from vegetable matter through the ranks of animals to the white European male standing atop the pile, closest to God, they dehumanized Aldridge, the African, by constructing him as somehow closer to nature or even subhuman. In their descriptions of his performances, attention was paid to Aldridge's "peculiarly fiery racial temperament" and his "style of acting bearing the imprint of a distinct individuality verging upon primitive nature" (Alexandrowicz, 579). Praising the actor's artistic achievement, the *Kraukauer Zeitung* compared him favorably with white actors. Yet this acclaim was also based on prejudice. "Thanks to his complexion," the journalist said, Aldridge was "able to reach a naturalness unattainable by other actors, even if they had used all the soot of the earth." These opinions show the mechanism of the export of nineteenth-century European ideas of difference onto the Other in racialized hierarchies of self/other, white/black, civilized/savage, rational/primitive. By translating their fantasies of the unknown into seemingly rational structures, some of the critics attempted to define and contain an ambiguously threatening or alluring Aldridge/Other by inventing his allegedly inborn characteristics ("savagery"). They used these characteristics to explain his professional success, because they simply could not understand his acting style.

"A True Othello"

From the onset of Aldridge's career, spectators were convinced that in the actor "the animal nature dominates human nature," and that "the disagreeable natural intonations which border on animal sounds and are continually repeated" provided sufficient proof that Aldridge was the real Othello, who also was a "ferocious beast, child of the desert" (*Kraukauer Zeitung*). The color of Aldridge's skin made many people believe that he was the embodiment of Othello as Shakespeare had created him: he was "a natural African" (*Kurier Lubelski*). A reviewer for a German newspaper stated: "After this Othello it would be an anti-climax to have to see an ordinary Othello again" (quoted in Marshall and Stock, 181). In addition, the qualities attributed to the fictional character Aldridge most often played seemed to be reflections of the actor as a human being. Aldridge was, like Othello, an exile from his native land, and he married a white woman. Consequently, some critics found it difficult to apply their accepted canons to Aldridge. Treating him as the very incarnation of Othello, they frequently blurred the boundary between the flesh-and-blood actor and the dramatic character.

Pauline Wilkonska, a novelist and an eyewitness to his performances in Poznan (1853), wrote in her memoir that only in the performances where the "Negro was playing a Negro" could one experience "the totality of acting [Othello]" (101). An 1854 review in *Czas* (9 November 1854) stated that "it is the first time we have seen a true Othello," while the reviewer in *Pamietnik muzyczny i teatralny* assured his readers that "Othello is a perfect fit for Mr. Aldridge" because "he himself is a Negro." The "Negro essence" that became so significant in Aldridge's performances frequently ignited discussion on Shakespeare's attitude to race. Some critics still believed that the subject of interracial sexuality made *Othello* unfit for stage presentation. Consequently, they tried to prove that Othello was not really black. "Shakespeare's Othello is not a black Nubian or a native of hot Senegal," wrote the critic for *Czas*, "he is simply a Mauritanian in the service of the Venetian Republic, and only in disdain and comparison did the author use the expression 'black' several times to stress his blackness" (9 November 1854).

Charles Lamb's opinion that the "courtship and wedding caresses of Desdemona and Othello," even in blackface, was "revolting," was not exceptional (207). Although some in the Polish audience shared Lamb's opinion, they changed their attitude after watching Aldridge's performance. "We must admit," as the reporter for *Czas* (9 November 1854) pointed out, that "by the third scene we paid tribute in our souls to the true talent of an artist and we ceased to be amazed at the audacity of Shakespeare, who made the proud daughter of a Venetian senator fall in love with 'a black devil,' as Emilia calls him elsewhere, when the newly awakened jealousy stirred his African blood and roused even that noble lion to anger." The same critic attempted to explain the passion present in Aldridge's acting as an expression of his race, finding beauty in the actor's allegedly "ugly features" and the "sonorous organ of his voice," which "became gentle to a murmur, and his strong eyes melted with tenderness." Deeply impressed that "at the moments of utmost elevation," Aldridge presented "the fury of a wild beast, but not a scuffle: a howl, and not a shriek in his voice," the critic concluded, "so must have been Othello when the poet's genius created him."

The other blacks engaged in the European performing arts were limited to the circus or boxing ring, where they were treated as exotic aberrations. But Aldridge demanded respect: he was a serious actor, a Shakespearean tragedian, who played in the best of the Continental theatres. He became "the first Negro" to earn unparalleled success in a very difficult profession. In his *Memoir*, Aldridge describes that profession as one that requires "the acquirements of a scholar, the conception of a poet, and the accomplishments of a gentleman ... united in one individual before he can become eminent as an actor" (19).

At the same time that the very character of his profession put him in the limelight, the audience went to the theatre to "stare" at him, to magnify Aldridge's blackness. In this sense, his black visibility was revolutionary: by elevating his race to the domain of art, he broke strictly prescribed cultural conventions. A reporter for the journal *Iskuysstvo* still could not come to terms with the idea that Aldridge was a full-fledged Shakespearean tragedian. He confessed that the announcement of his performances in Moscow made simple people "somewhat incredulous and skeptical, deeming that the singularity, unprecedented as [they] believed it was in dramatic history, of a Negro assuming the stock and buskin, together with the tendency of the multitude to praise any novelty, however extravagant, that it chose to set up for worship." Because Othello had been played in blackface in England before Aldridge's appearance, the actor disrupted the tradition of presenting Shakespeare's character with European features (see Cowhig). His performances stressed the contrast between the black anatomy of Othello and the European whiteness of Desdemona. In Poland and in Russia, the shock effect must have been enhanced by the fact that the spectators were less experienced with blackface in the theatre: in a way, Aldridge introduced black characters into the history of these nations' drama.[20]

Reading Whiteness/Reading Aldridge

Although Othello was Aldridge's trademark, in Poland and even more often in Russia, the actor continued his experimentation with whiteface roles. He started this practice in Britain, where he played white characters in melodramas, such as William Tell in *William Tell* by James Sheridan Knowles, Dirk Hatteraick in *Guy Mannering*, a theatrical adaptation of Sir Walter Scott's novel, an outcast pirate hero in *Bertram, or the Castle of Aldobrandt* by C. Maturin, Rolla in *Pizarro* by Richard Brinsley Sheridan, Alessandro Massaroni in *The Brigand* by J. R. Planche, and the Monster in *Frankenstein* in H. M. Milner's adaptation of Mary Shelley's novel. Later the actor turned to Shakespearean plays such as *Macbeth*, *The Merchant of Venice*, *King Lear*, and *Richard III*.

According to Marshall and Stock, Aldridge's whiteface productions constituted one of the "most revolutionary steps" the black actor took in his advance into white culture. "In playing white parts," the biographers maintain, "he used white make-up and a wig, possibly a beard ... which completely transformed the black into white" (Marshall and Stock, 87–89). Though they state that "in the matter of make-up Aldridge based himself primarily on the demands of the play and not his own desire to appear as a Negro in these roles" (95), his whiteface performances evoked scurrilous criticism in England. When it was advertised that he would play a white part in the Surrey Theatre, one reviewer responded:

> The unhappy Nigger has been facetiously advertised for a *white part*. ... Chalk and plaster of paris have, however, failed as much as his native soot, for not all the whiteness in the kingdom will transmogrify the unseemly nigger into the shadow of a genius. This man seems to rely solely on color for his inspiration, and imagines that though nature has made him an Othello, he has only to resort to the paint-pot to become a Romeo. Talent is, however, not to be thrown in, in distemper colours, and not twenty coats of paints would make an actor of the black whom we have so wholesomely flagellated. Instead of hearing that a play is in rehearsal, we shall be told that the *die is cast*, and that instead of such an actor being about to study a certain part, the African Roscius will shortly be painted for a new character. (*Figaro in London*)

In other words, in Britain, Aldridge's whiteface performances enraged some members of the audience because his performance was regarded as subverting the tenets of racial essentialism. For this critic, no amount of paint could make Aldridge into a Romeo.

The situation assumed another dimension when the tragedian played his whiteface productions on the Continent. The critics stressed that these presentations confirmed the actor's genius — he showed that he could subdue his passion and display a more sophisticated acting technique. According to Ludwig Sittenfeld, Aldridge "achieved a true artistic success" and "surprised everybody with his calmness and the simplicity of the representation" (56). The audience appreciated his elaborate make-up. Gautier was particularly impressed with Aldridge's "whiting up" as King Lear:

> A flesh-coloured headpiece of papier maché, from which hung some silvery locks of hair, covered his woolly thatch and came down almost to his eyebrows like a helmet; an addition of wax filled in the curves of his flat nose. A thick coat of grease paint covered his black cheeks, and a great white beard enveloped the rest of his face and came down over his chest. (Gautier, 254–255)

The fact that Aldridge did not whiten his hands, "which showed below the sleeves of his tunic," was read as a sign of "caprice" (Gautier, 255). Although it is possible to interpret Aldridge's black hands as a plea to remember the real color of his skin, it is also possible to read this gesture as a comment on black minstrelsy practices: white actors never made up their hands.

Though neither the reviewers nor the commentators interpreted Aldridge's performances of *Macbeth*, *King Lear*, and *Richard III* as political, social, or cultural commentaries, these plays were banned by the tsarist censors.[21] When many people in Russia were punished for political reasons by the totalitarian regime, any play that threatened to shatter the seemingly endless hegemony of the current regime was regarded as subversive. The nineteenth-century censors were particularly concerned with material that could be viewed as threatening the existing socio-political order. The theatre, which gathered together large crowds, introduced an immediate potential danger to public order when seditious plays were presented on stage. In addition, it was generally accepted by the censors that the impact of the spoken word was far more inflammatory than the impact of the same text in print (Goldstein, 116–118). Despite the fact that Aldridge was prohibited from continuing his productions in the main Russian theatres, he went on to stage them in the provinces.

The Merchant of Venice was Aldridge's only whiteface performance that evoked political, social, and cultural debates. Critics generally agreed that his interpretation was highly original, since "in Shylock he [Aldridge] did not see just a Jew, but a man persecuted by age-old hatred, and he expresses his feelings with wonderful force and truthfulness" (quoted in Golden-Hanga, 13). In his performance, Shylock was a tragic figure and a majestic outcast from society. Polish reviewers also understood Aldridge's interpretation of Shylock as a comment on a pariah who had been socially and culturally marginalized by prejudice. "Being himself a representative of a despised race," Ludwig

Sittenfeld stated, "he [Aldridge] could strongly and truly portray the feelings of wronged Jews" (56). His Shylock was a tragic figure who reacted with horror at the thought of becoming a Christian, and when he played that part in one Russian town a delegation of local Jews officially thanked him for his sympathetic portrayal (Marshall and Stock, 288).

The Politics of Performance

During his tours, Aldridge often faced complicated political situations that required him to display unusual sensitivity to the human suffering caused by ongoing despotism and persecution. The actor was frequently caught in an impossible quandary: he played under the auspices of the most ruthless political regimes, trying to win the approval of the people. Hated in Poland, the rulers of Russia, Prussia, and Austro-Hungary, the three partitioning powers, extolled Aldridge as an actor and a man, and they attempted to appropriate his successes for their own political and cultural agendas by awarding him with honorary titles and medals. It is no wonder that during his first visits to Polish towns, the local revolutionary factions treated him with suspicion. During his 1854 stay in Krakow, there was a general trend to boycott Aldridge's performances because the public wished to show their dissatisfaction with Austro-Hungarian social and cultural policies (Estreicher, 512). His 1862 appearance in Warsaw was seen as a visit by a Russian agent (*Gazeta Wielkiego Xiestwa Poznananskiego*, 28 May 1862). Aldridge had to draw the attention of Polish theatre-goers despite their initial prejudice, and he was successful. The power of his theatrical skills made the spectators fill all the seats in the auditoriums, and the newspapers enthusiastically reviewed his performances.

There appears to have been a direct correlation between the nature of Aldridge's reception in Poland and Russia and the prevailing social and political climates. Indeed, Aldridge's reception in these countries had political reverberations for his audiences that the British and American press perhaps could not understand. Yet these reverberations have to be seen within the context of severe censorship, which varied greatly in intensity. In Poland, the Austro-Hungarian, Prussian, and Russian empires were concerned mostly with the Polish revolutionary movements, so any attempt to criticize the occupying regimes was severely punished (Szyndler, 102–108). Consequently, the Polish press was not allowed to draw any analogies between the situation of Aldridge's fellow blacks in the United States and the situation of the Polish people in their country. The Russians faced similar problems. Any references to American slavery as an analogue of Russian serfdom meant imprisonment, a sentence to labor camps, or exile in some faraway part of the empire. Yet in both countries the censor allowed, and even encouraged, reporters and commentators to voice open condemnation of slavery and of America as the land of oppression.

The publication of Harriet Beecher Stowe's *Uncle Tom's Cabin* caught European readers' attention, and it contributed to discussions of Aldridge's acting within the context of American slavery. Since his Polish tours coincided with the appearance of the Polish translation of Stowe's book, Aldridge's Mungo, the black character in *The Padlock,* which the tragedian frequently played in Europe, was compared with her rendition of slaves' lives.[22] The *Czas* reporter maintained that in that play his "picture of Negro slaves in the West Indies" was more realistic and "certainly more true than the one in [her] sentimental work" (11 November 1854). Aldridge must have been aware of the sympathy for American slaves expressed by some reviewers and critics. When he returned home from his first sojourn in Russia, he apparently sent a letter to the critics: "In my person you have shown your sympathy and love for my oppressed people" (quoted in Marshall and Stock, 244).

Aldridge's audiences in Russia also knew *Uncle Tom's Cabin.* In 1858, the year of Aldridge's first visit, Zvantsev, the actor's biographer, who watched his performances in Saint Petersburg, interpreted Aldridge's performance of Othello as the actor's comment on slavery:

> From Othello is torn the deep cry, "Oh, misery, misery, misery!" and in that misery of the African artist is heard the far-off groans of his own people, oppressed by unbelievable slavery and more than that — the groans of the whole of suffering mankind. (Zvantsev, 3)

In addition, the critic came to the conclusion that in the play Iago represented "the present-day Europeans," who by slavery tried to "tame ... the leonine and at the same time childlike nature" of Africans:

> Seeing before us the tamed Othello in the net of the tamer, seeing the wild lion in the power of the educated European (the Iago of contemporary history), one involuntarily thinks of the many generations of black people suffering under the whip of American slave-traders. (Zvantsev, 34)

The fact that Aldridge, as a black man, achieved great successes at the time when his compatriots had slave status in the United States helped to attract people to theatres to see Shakespeare's plays. That attraction contributed to ongoing discussions of American slavery and emancipation.

Considering the strong elements of protest in his art, Aldridge's ability to continue performing in Poland and Russia for nearly a decade is in itself remarkable. Part of the explanation for his survival is that the protest was present mainly in his art. Though the revolutionary elements of Polish and Russian society turned Aldridge/the Other into a commentator on their current political, social, and cultural events, the actor was never engaged in any revolutionary activity. He did not maintain any contacts with the radicals who voiced special interest in his work. The only exception was his friendship with Taras Shevchenko, a Ukrainian poet who had been released from a sentence of lifetime military service, which had been imposed for his writing satiri-cal verses offensive to the censors.[23] The political interpretation of Aldridge's performances resulted from the audience's eagerness to take advantage of the black actor's presence and his willingness silently to inspire and acknowledge these interpretations. In Aldridge's behavior and appearance, spectators found hidden allusions to and metaphors for political and social oppression, such as slavery, serfdom, and national partition. The Russian and Polish responses to his acting demonstrate that in the nineteenth century Aldridge, as a mere "Negro," was not only one of the best and most effective emissaries of Shake-speare, but also a compelling representative of the antislavery movement and an effective ambassador for the politically, socially, and culturally abused.

Notes

1. Early in my research I discovered that most works on Aldridge's life are selective, biased, and/or fragmented. Of the many biographical works, two are of special significance. Herbert Marshall and Mildred Stock's *Ira Aldridge: The Negro Tragedian* is generally regarded as the most comprehensive biography written in English. It appeared in 1958, so almost a century had to pass after Aldridge's death before his story became researched. In 1995 *"Speak of Me As I Am": The Story of Ira Aldridge*, by Owen Mortimer, Mildred Stock's volunteer research assistant, appeared. Although the research of Marshall and Stock was thorough and painstaking, they were well aware that they had not been able to tell the whole story. In their "Prologue" they admitted that "there still remained some missing links": the tale was "not complete in all its aspects" (8). The same concerns are present in Mortimer's work.

2. *Gazeta Wielkiego Xsiestwa Poznanskiego*, 23 January 1853; *Kurier Warszawski*. If not indicated otherwise, all translations are mine.

3. The long list of those who knew Aldridge includes not only his professional colleagues, such as Ellen Tree, Edmund Kean, Charles Kean, J. Philip Kemble, and Madge Kendal (Robertson), but also eminent personalities from other walks of life: Sir Walter Scott, Tyrone Power, Sir Edward Bulwer-Lytton, Hans Christian Andersen, Franz Liszt, Charles Dickens, Jenny Lind, and Leo Tolstoy. After Aldridge's tours in Continental Europe, his albums were filled with photos of eminent Russian, Ukrainian, and Mongolian women and men, who usually expressed in their signatures their appreciation of his acting. See Charles Deering McCormick Library of Special Collections, Northwestern University, Box 2, Folder 1.

4. Yet, the prejudice, freedom, and solidarity the American antislavery representatives spoke about were completely different from the emancipatory aspirations and drives of Continental Europeans. Blacks in America wanted to be full-fledged citizens within the nation's social and political fabric, while the subjugated Europeans, especially in the cen-tral and eastern parts of the Continent, wanted their own national culture, their own schools to preserve their respective histories and traditions, their own autonomous gov-ernment conducted in their national language, and eventually complete independence. Both groups shared a desire for liberation from their oppressive regimes, but the aims of their fights diverged. American slaves fought for cultural integration, while many Euro-pean nations and ethnic groups fought for separation to enjoy a self-governed identity.

5. Thompson presents many documents that point out not only various forms of racial dis-crimination directed toward the African Theatre, also known as the African Grove, but also its subversive nature. See also McAllister.

6. It was Aldridge who first brought Shakespeare to Serbia (1858), where he played Richard III, Othello, and Macbeth at Novi Sad, then a part of the Austro-Hungarian Empire. His visit also hastened the foundation of the National Theatre in Belgrade. During his visit to Krakow in 1858, Aldridge staged *Richard II* for the first time in Poland, and his visits inspired the first translation of *Othello*, in which he performed in Warsaw (1862). His per-formances of *Richard III* and *Macbeth* were the first productions of these plays in Russia. Aldridge was also the first actor to perform Shakespeare in Constantinople (1866).

7. It was only during his Continental tours that Aldridge played whole texts of Shakespeare's plays. While he was in his twenties and thirties in the United States and Britain, he mainly did scenes or selected speeches from Shakespeare as part of a long bill. Aldridge was nearly forty when he first attempted the whole of *Macbeth*, and he was at least forty-one when he finally ventured a complete *Richard III*. Thus, he took on most of his full-scale Shakespearean roles in middle age. In his youth he played only *Othello* in its entirety, and Shylock in a popular four-act version of *The Merchant of Venice*. (I am grateful to Dr. Mortimer for this information.)

8. Produced in 1768, this play, whose plot is loosely based on Miguel de Cervantes's novel *The Jealous Husband*, was apparently as popular as Thomas Gray's *The Beggar's Opera*. *The Padlock* brought fame to Charles Dibdin (1745–1814), a comic actor who was the first Mungo, a black servant. His performances of Mungo and his songs, especially "Mungo, here, Mungo there, Mungo everywhere," became catch phrases. His Mungo was a disrespectful and presumptuous though music-loving slave. Aldridge's way of staging this character was diametrically different. His Mungo was funny, but he also provided an extensive commentary on the spreading fashion of American blackface minstrelsy and its British variant, while criticizing slavery. See Lindfors 1993 and MacDonald.

9. Shakespeare makes reference to this figure in *Henry VI* Part 3: "What scene of death has Roscius now to act" (5.6.10). Richard Burbage (c. 1567–1619) was apparently the first English actor labeled "Roscius." Later that name was applied to Thomas Betterton (1635–1710) and David Garrick (1717–1779). For further discussion see Lindfors 1996.

10. The twenty-eight-page *Memoir* was published in London by Onwhyn, Catharine Street, Strand and was printed by Frederic Ledger at the same address. Its flyleaf has a quotation from *The Merchant of Venice*, when the Prince of Morocco introduces himself: "Mislike me not for my complexion / The shadowed livery of the burnished sun" (2.1.1–2). The front page gives the price of the publication as "sixpence."

11. The *Memoir* narrates that Aldridge's father was taken by a Protestant missionary to New York and brought up there in Christianity. When he returned to his motherland, his father attempted to regain his land but was forced to flee because of political problems. Eventually he reached the plateau of southern Africa, where his wife gave birth to Ira. Two years later he found himself on the coast and was luckily taken on board a ship sailing to America, where he became pastor in a Negro parish.

12. An increase in ethnological data that resulted from the voyages of exploration in the latter half of the eighteenth century, especially the three great circumnavigations by Captain James Cook (1769–1775), also contributed to the growing interest in the study of human differences (see Pratt, 15–37).

13. See, for example, his correspondence with theatre managers in Britain, now in the Charles Deering McCormick Library of Special Collections, Northwestern University, Box 1.

14. In fact, Aldridge followed this practice in many of his performances in Continental Europe. For example, the Polish press noted that he gave an "epilogue" after his appearance in the Poznan theatre in 1853 (*Gazeta Codzienna*).

15. The discourse of slavery, however, was not a novelty in Poland. It surfaced in 1801–1803, when some five thousand Polish soldiers were sent by Napoleon to quell the Haitian revolution. Following the official French line, the soldiers initially viewed the black revolutionaries as rebels; yet they soon realized that the former slaves were fighting for the same ideals to which they, the Poles, aspired. The black insurgents, for their part, quickly learned to distinguish the Poles by their language and uniforms; when captured by them, the insurgents often received better treatment than they would otherwise. Napoleon's military debacle in the Caribbean was widely discussed at home, and the Haitian fighters became perceived as equals in the struggle for freedom and independence (see Askenazy, 316–317). In 1825, Poland experienced another wave of interest in issues of slavery when Tadeusz Kosciuszko, the country's national hero, who had actively participated in the American War of Independence, spent his fortune on the liberation and education of black American slaves (see Kuczynski, 37–38).

16. One victim of this traffic was the maternal great-grandfather of the great Russian writer Alexander Pushkin, Ibrahim or Abraham Hannibal, who became a source of the Russian public's interest in Africa.

17. The descriptions of the actor's body reflected nineteenth-century artists' and connoisseurs' admiration for the heroic proportions of black bodies, which they scrutinized as if they were ancient Greek or Roman statues. Hugh Honor demonstrates that many nineteenth-century artists employed blacks as their sitters, despite the common association of their skin color and physiognomy with ugliness (23–60).

18. *Syn Otchestva*, 27 October 1858; *Kurier Niedzielny*, 12 June 1862.

19. Discussing early European encounters with the Other, Stephen Greenblatt calls this kind of amazement "a primary or radical passion ... that precedes, even escapes, moral categories." When we are amazed, he continues, "we do not yet know if we should love or hate the object at which we are marveling; we do not yet know if we should embrace it or flee from it" (20).

20. Before Aldridge's appearance, there had been no plays written with any black roles in Poland. In Russia there had been one instance: in the eighteenth century Iakov Knizhin had introduced one black character in his tragedy *Didona* (1769), yet that part had always been performed in blackface (Karlinsky, 132–135).

21. Nicholas I personally controlled and censored the theatre, even the supervision of the repertory and the assignment of roles to actors (Goldstein, 128–131). Narzymski, a Polish dissident of that period, outlined the basis of the censors' reasoning and explained why Shakespeare's *Macbeth*, and by analogy his other tragedies, were classified as politically dangerous: "The stage is neither a religious pulpit, nor a university dais or a political tribute: yet it performs all these functions, since it possesses means to control social and moral powers. ... In *Macbeth* the poet does not present any dogmas, but he envisions this great idea of Divine Justice according to which the punishment is inherent in the crime itself. ... Though Shakespeare does not make any political comments, his *Macbeth* makes clear this significant and as old as the hills truth: crime gives birth to despotism, and despotism feeds itself on crime" (Narzymski, 185).

22. A year after its original publication in 1852, the Ossolinski Publishing House, one of the most prestigious publishing houses in Poland, produced the first Polish translation of *Uncle Tom's Cabin*. In 1853 a journal in Vilnius, at that time a Polish town, issued an abridged version for children. The same year another two-volume edition of Stowe's book was issued, with realistic drawings, by the Warsaw Blumental Publishing House.

23. Describing their friendship, Maria Trommer states, "It is undoubtedly the power of destiny that brought and drew together two flaming, kindred souls, the two persecuted slaves from countries far apart, who succeeded in escaping from the brutality of their environment into a human world." In her highly emotional short monograph, Trommer describes the circumstances of their first meeting. By singing, dancing, and embracing, they apparently could understand each other without an interpreter. Shevchenko taught Aldridge some Ukrainian serf songs, which the actor incorporated in his productions of *The Padlock*, singing them in Ukrainian and playing his guitar. After Shevchenko's premature death, Aldridge visited Ukraine to put flowers on his friend's grave. See also Miller and Makaryk.

References

Monographs and Essays

Alexandrowicz, J., ed. *Wielka encyklopedia powszechna ilustrowana* [Great Complete Encyclopedia Illustrated]. Warsaw: Sikorski, S, 1890.

Askenazy, S. *Napoleon a Polska* [Napoleon and Poland]. Warsaw: Towarzystwo Wydawnicze w Warszawie, 1919.

Bernal, Martin. *Black Athena: The Afroasiatic Roots of Classical Civilization*. London: Free Association, 1987.

Coleman, John. *Fifty Years of An Actor's Life*. 2 vols. New York: James Pott, 1904.

Cowhig, Ruth. "The Importance of Othello's Race." *Journal of Commonwealth Literature* 12 (1977): 153–161.

Disher, Maurice. *Blood and Thunder: Mid-Victorian Melodrama and Its Origins*. London: Frederick Muller, 1949.

Durilin. "Ira Aldridge." Translated by E. Blum. *Shakespeare Association Bulletin* 17 (1942): 37–38.

Estreicher, K. *Teatra w Polsce* [Theatres in Poland]. [1873] Vol. 2. Warsaw: PIW, 1953.

Gaines, Kevin. *Uplifting the Race: Black Leadership, Politics and Culture in the Twentieth Century.* Chapel Hill: University of North California Press, 1996.

Gautier, Théophile. *Voyage en Russie.* Paris: Charpentier et Fasquelle, 1895.

Gnammankou, Dieudonne. "The Slave Trade to Russia." In *From Chains to Bonds: The Slave Trade Revisited,* edited by Doudou Diene. New York: Berghahn, 2001.

Golden-Hanga, L. *Africans in Russia.* Moscow: Novosti, 1966.

Goldstein, J. *Political Censorship of the Arts and the Press in the Nineteenth Century Europe.* Basington and London: Houndsmills, 1989.

Greenblatt, Stephen. *Marvelous Possessions: The Wonder of the New World.* Oxford: Oxford University Press, 1991.

Honor, Hugh. *The Image of the Black in Western Art: From the American Revolution to World War II. Black Models and White Myths.* Vol. 4. Cambridge, MA: Harvard University Press, 1989.

Karlinsky, Simon. *Russian Drama from Its Beginnings to the Age of Pushkin.* Berkeley: University of California Press, 1985.

Kaszewski, Kazimierz. "Ira Aldridge." In Alexandrowicz 1890.

Kuczynski, A., *Wsrod buszu I czarownikow: Antologia polskich relacji o ludach Afryki* [In Bush and Among Shamans: An Anthology of Polish Narratives on the African Peoples]. Wroclaw: Zaklad Narodowy im Ossolinskich, 1990.

Lamb, Charles. "On the Tragedies of Shakespeare, Considered with Reference to Their Fitness to Stage Representation" [1811]. In *Life, Letters and Writings of Charles Lamb,* edited by Percy Hetherington Fitzgerald and Thomas Noon Talfourd. Vol. 4. London: W. W. Gibbings, 1892.

Lindfors, Bernth. "Ira Aldridge, 'The African Roscius.'" *South African Theatre Journal* 10 (1996): 71–84.

Lindfors, Bernth. "The Signifying Flunkey: Ira Aldridge as Mungo." *Literary Griot* 2 (1993): 1–11.

Lloyd, David. "Race under Representation." *Oxford Literary Review* 13 (1991): 62–94.

MacDonald, Joyce Green. "Acting Black: *Othello,* Othello Burlesques, and the Performance of Blackness." *Theatre Journal* 46 (1994): 231–249.

Makaryk, Irena. "Calibans All: Shakespeare at the Intersection of Colonialism." In *Multicultural Shakespeare: Translation, Appropriation, Performance,* edited by Yoshiko Kawachi and Krystyna Kujawinska Courtney. Lodz: Wydawnictwo Uniwersytetu Lodzkiego, 2003.

Marshall, Herbert, and Mildred Stock. *Ira Aldridge: The Negro Tragedian.* New York: Macmillan, 1958.

McAllister, Marvin. *White People Do Not Know How To Behave at Entertainments Designed for Ladies And Gentlemen of Color: William Brown's African and American Theatre.* Chapel Hill and London: University of North Carolina Press, 2003.

The Memoir and Theatrical Career of Ira Aldridge. London: J. Onwhyn, 1849.

Miller, D. L. "A Momentous Meeting — Ira Aldridge and Taras Shevchenko." *Ukrainian Quarterly* 10 (1964): 127–132.

Mortimer, Owen. *"Speak of Me as I Am": The Story of Ira Aldridge.* Wangaratta, Australia: privately published, 1995.

Narzymski, J. "Slowko o teatrze, znaczeniu tegoz i moralnosci scenicznej" ["A Word on Theatre, Its Meaning and Stage Moralism"]. *Tygodnik Wielkopolski* 15 (1871): 185.

Orgelbrand, S., ed. *Encyklopedia powszechna* [Complete Encyclopedia] [1859]. Vol. 12. Warsaw: Wydawnictwo S. Orgelbrand, 1991.

Pratt, Mary Louise. *Imperial Eye: Travel Writing and Transculturalism.* London and New York: Routledge, 1992.

Sittenfeld, Ludwig. *Geschichte des Breslauer Theatres.* Wroclaw, 1909.

Szyndler, Bartłomiej. *Dzieje cenzury w Polsce do 1918 roku* [The History of Censorship in Poland up to 1918]. Kraków: Krajowa Agencja Wydawnicza, 1993.

Thompson, George. *A Documentary History of the African Theatre.* Evanston: Northwestern University Press, 1998.

Trommer, Maria. *Ira Aldridge, American Negro Tragedian and Taras Shevchenko, Poet of the Ukraine: A Story of a Friendship.* New York: 62 Brooklyn, 1939.

Waters, Hazel. "Aldridge and the Battlefield of Race." *Race and Class* 45 (2003): 1–30.

Wilkonska, Paulina. *Moje wspomnienia o zyciu towarzyskim na prowincji w Kongresowce przez Pauline Wilkowska spisane* [My Recollections on the Social Provincial Life in the Congress Polan Recorded by Paulina Wilkonska]. Poznan: Nakladem L. Merzbacha, 1875.

Young, Robert. *Colonial Desire: Hybridity in Theory, Culture and Race.* London and New York: Routledge, 1995.

Zabrodskaia, M. P. *Russkie puteshestvenniki po Afrikie* [Russian Travelers in Africa]. Moscow: Geografia, 1955.

Zvantsev, K. *Ira Aldridge, bibliographicherski ocherk* [Ira Aldridge. Biographical Narrative]. Saint Petersburg, 1858.

Newspaper Articles

Czas (Kracow), 2 November 1854; 9 November 1854; 11 November 1854.

Dziennik Warszawski (Warsaw), 7 February 1853.

Figaro in London (London), 10 May 1833.

Gazeta Codzienna (Warsaw), 4 February 1853.

Gazeta Wielkiego Xsiestwa Poznanskiego (Poznan), 23 January 1853; 28 May 1862.

Iskuysstvo (Moscow), 14 November 1862.

Kraukauer Zeitung (Kracow), 15 January 1858.

Kurier Lubelski (Lublin), 25 August 1866.

Kurier Niedzielny (Warsaw), 12 June 1862.

Kurier Warszawski (Warsaw), 10 August 1866.

Odessky Novosti (Odessa), 3 February 1866.

Pamietnik muzyczny i teatralny (Warsaw), 14 May 1862.

Russkii Vestnik (Moscow), 15 October 1862.

Syn Otchestva (Moscow), 27 October 1858.

Tygodnik Ilustrowany (Warsaw), 24 May 1862.

II
Practicing Colorblindness:
The Players Speak

7

My Own Private Shakespeare;
or, Am I Deluding Myself?

ANTONIO OCAMPO-GUZMAN

As more theatre is being produced by the ever-growing Latino population in the United States, and as more Latino actors are trained to perform Shakespeare, I think it is crucial to add our perspective to the discourse on colorblind casting. I am an actor, director, and teacher originally from Bogotá, Colombia. I have been playing with Shakespeare in the training studio, the rehearsal studio, and on the stage since my teens. From the beginning, I have played with Shakespeare in both English and Spanish. Until recently, I believed I had mastered Shakespeare — the language, the stories, the characters — and made him my own. But after engaging in some fascinating conversations about the cultural politics of Shakespeare, I have been wondering: Have I been deluding myself? After much pondering and intellectual toil, I would like to offer my complex and occasionally contradictory observations, thoughts, and revelations to the vital conversation contained in this collection.

As an artist and not as a scholar, I want to include the following elements in the dialogue about colorblind casting. First, by sharing several tales about my own training and experiences as a Shakespeare player, I hope to articulate why I believe that Shakespeare has been fundamental in both my artistic and personal growth. Second, I will examine the use of Shakespeare in contemporary, "multicultural" theatre projects. My main goal is to ask if I have been deluding myself about Shakespeare's universality. Part and parcel of this examination is a new conceptualization and articulation of my Shakespearean experiences that is more defined politically and culturally. Perhaps making Shakespeare one's own is more than just mastering the language, stories, and characters. In order for socially defined minorities to make Shakespeare our own, we must address how playing with Shakespeare affects our complex contemporary lives.

The Player

The first time I played with Shakespeare was in my high school English class. I went to the Anglo-Colombian School in Bogotá, a private school sponsored in part by the British Council. Most of my teachers were adventurous young

English women and men who loved teaching and traveling. My ninth-grade teacher, Mr. Brown, loved three other things: Shakespeare, Monty Python, and beer. I was irrevocably infected. In Mr. Brown's class, I played Friar Lawrence in the "Romeo, Romeo, come forth, come forth thou fearful man" scene. Amazingly, my first experience with Shakespeare was also my first experience as a bilingual performer. I seem to remember being more interested in my costume — my father's bathrobe was passing as the Franciscan monk's habit — than in the words I was speaking. I remember it being lots of fun. I also remember that I was very good at it, even if English was not my first language.

During my senior year, I was cast as Henry Irving in Christopher Durang's *An Actor's Nightmare*, and I had to deliver Horatio's "Two nights together have these two gentlemen" speech. That was my first experience in being coached to speak Shakespeare. I cannot remember my teacher's name, although I do remember her excitement as we unraveled the meaning of the lines beyond the mere affectation with which I was speaking them. I also remember thinking that this language worked in bizarre yet fascinating ways: it apparently went around in circles, but at the same time it was amazingly precise and thrilling.

During the years of my acting training at the Teatro Libre School in Bogotá, I played several Shakespearean roles, including Puck, Petruchio, Iago, and Lady Macbeth. Those explorations were more about character and emotion than language, because it is nearly impossible for Shakespeare's words to operate on a similar level in any other language than English. Still, it was fertile ground for a young actor. To be able to tap into the darkness of greed, ambition, hatred, and fear to bring to life characters that were so huge in the history of theatre: it gave me a certain pride to think that I, a Colombian actor, could play Shakespeare.

One afternoon, for some fundraising event, I was asked to read two Shakespeare sonnets in both English and Spanish. Although I cannot remember the exact sonnets now, I do remember how attentive the audience was when I read them in English. They looked at me differently, as if the foreignness of the English words made them even more attentive to me. In Spanish they were listening to what I was saying, but in English they were attentive in a different manner. I also remember a different physical sensation when I read in English: I was actively seeking more understanding from my audience. In a sense, I cared more about them than about the sonnets. These memories have just come to me as I write this, and I wonder if that was the first time the idea of playing Shakespeare in both languages was planted in my brain.

Fast-forward a number of years; it is 1995, and I am about to go onstage at the Strand Theatre in Boston as Julius Caesar in Shakespeare & Company's New England Tour production. About 1,500 high school students fill the venerable house with buzzing energy. It is our biggest house so far on the tour, and my fellow players and I know that they will be a tough crowd. Most of them are inner-city kids, and many are Latino. At the beginning of each performance we give some historical information and then state our names and the characters we play. After each name, the crowd applauds politely. Jeff Plitt, a handsome actor from somewhere in New England who plays Mark Antony, gets a thunderous reception. When it is my turn, I go out, look out at the huge auditorium, and decide to show off not only my big, Linklater-trained voice but also my rich Colombian accent. I look for audience members who look particularly Latino, and I dart my introduction at them: "My name is Antonio Ocampo, I'm from Bogotá, Colombia, and I AM Julius Caesar." I am not nearly as good-looking as Jeff, but I brought the house down. There was something more than just plain actor's vanity in this: I realized that as a Latino actor, I had a great opportunity to show these high school students that playing Shakespeare was not reserved for white actors. I think they understood this point, and that is what caused them to erupt in thunderous applause.

I came to this country in 1993 to participate in the month-long Intensive Training Workshop at Shakespeare & Company in Lenox, Massachusetts. The experience changed my life, not only as an actor but also as a person. What is most amazing about the aesthetic and the training of Tina Packer's indomitable company is the first basic step: find yourself through what you are speaking. I was being trained to reveal who I was through the speaking of Shakespeare. The first days of these training workshops are spent in intense sessions called, appropriately, "Basics." Each participant selects a piece of text to which he or she has some kind of connection. I chose Shylock's "Hath not a Jew eyes" because I had witnessed Antony Sher's Shylock in London the year before and had been profoundly moved by the humor and the sorrow of his performance. I thought that since I shared some of Shylock's experience as an outsider and a foreigner, the speech could work well for me in the training studio. I was the first one up to work on it. I displayed what I had been taught before — character and emotion. I used everything at my disposal — my voice, my body, my imagination — to indicate that I was a Jewish father who carried a huge grudge and now sought vengeance. I used everything except the words and my experiences. After some intensive coaching, I acknowledged how I had been picked on, insulted, and generally discriminated against for being a Colombian. The rage, sorrow, and loneliness I carried within became available to me. When I was almost spent and completely vulnerable in my own experience, I was asked to speak the lines again. It was a mind-blowing experience. I was using words written four hundred years earlier, words in my second language, and yet they were so accurate in revealing my predicament to others. I have not been the same actor, or the same director, or the same teacher since that experience. Shakespeare became my own because my own personal and emotional growth came through his words.

After "Basics" I was cast as Macduff in the "my pretty chickens and their dam" scene to continue the training. All the conflicting feelings about the civil war in Colombia — my family members and acquaintances being hurt, my uncle being kidnapped, and my impotence to alter these events — became superb fuel for me. After the last presentation of the scene, I could not stop weeping out of sheer joy and pride. I would now call myself an actor because I now knew how to tap into these personal experiences. More important, Shakespeare played an integral part in this personal and intellectual growth. Shakespeare helped me uncover these emotions and gave me a vehicle to create compelling theatre from them.

I spent three years training, acting, working, and growing in Lenox. It was a spectacular experience for me. Certainly performing in *Julius Caesar* at the Strand was a highlight. Another highlight was performing as Antigonus in Cecil Mackinnon's workshop production of *The Winter's Tale*. Cecil had us all seated onstage during the Sicily act. I remember the experience of the opening night. There I was onstage, Colombian and accented, along with superb actors who had inspired me beyond measure: Tod Randolph as Hermione, Michael Hammond as Leontes, and, especially, Lizzie Ingram as Paulina. Not only did I feel lucky and grateful, but also I felt a sense of belonging. Although I was not a native English speaker, or one of the company's top actors, I could share the stage with them, and I could play with them. Once again, I found that playing Shakespeare did wonders for my self-esteem.

I moved to Boston in 1996 and, as fate would have it, I found that teaching at the university level was my ticket to stay in this country. Kristin Linklater, one of the founders of Shakespeare & Company, was Head of Acting at Emerson College, and since I was finishing my training as a teacher of her approach to voice, she hired me. Ten years later I am still an artist in academia, still teaching Shakespeare, directing it, and occasionally playing it on the stage. At Emerson I had another revelation about the power of Shakespeare. I met Yuka Nakayama, a delightful young woman from Japan who came to train at Emerson in the late 1990s. Because of her pronounced Japanese accent, she very seldom got cast and her huge talent was overlooked. In my senior Shakespeare class, Yuka played with Margaret of Anjou's texts — perhaps because Margaret was herself a foreigner living in England — and the results were astonishing. Her initial fear of Shakespeare was simply the assumption that her English would not be good enough for it, but after weeks of exploration, she found the power and beauty of the language and was able to show us what an accomplished actress she really was. I contacted Yuka recently; she is working as an actress in Japan. She writes to me that "the experience is still most memorable. I remember the feeling of being strong and admired for my acting, not for how I spoke English. And it wasn't about making better sounds at all. I remember the joy I felt at being one with Margaret ... at last, I was an actress. Although I very seldom act in English here in Japan, those feelings and memories remain." Conquering Shakespeare, Yuka felt an unparalleled pride in her success. Shakespeare was helping young actors, like Yuka, find material to have powerful expressive experiences regardless of whether or not English was their first language.

Bilingual Shakespeare

My most important and most complex Shakespearean experience to date came in April 2005, when I directed a bilingual production of *Romeo and Juliet* as part of Florida State University's School of Theatre 2004–2005 season. For years I had been wondering what would happen if I encountered Shakespeare in my two languages at the same time. Would my creativity operate in different ways? Would my understanding of the play deepen? Would my fragile sense of belonging deepen? I was fortunate to have the support of the administration, faculty, staff, and students at FSU in this enterprise, as well as several talented young bilingual actors. Above all, I had Frankie Alvarez, a Cuban-American senior in the Bachelor of Fine Arts track. Building on the assumption that the story of the lovers is universally known, I sought to investigate whether anything new would be illuminated in the story by playing it simultaneously in English and Spanish.

The translation, however, posed a huge challenge. Years earlier in Colombia, I had discovered the famous Pablo Neruda version, *Romeo & Julieta*, but coming back to Shakespeare in Spanish was very strange after all my years of playing with Shakespeare in English. At Shakespeare & Company, I experienced the immediacy and precision of Shakespeare's words. But now, I discovered that the figures of speech that make the rhetorical devices so visceral and effective in English were flowery and uncommunicative in Neruda's adaptation. It just did not carry the dark side of the play, especially in the domestic violence of Lord Capulet and the explicit sexuality of Mercutio's lines. It was clear that for the experiment to work, I would need to translate it myself.

The easy part was selecting which sections to do in Spanish. Since I had a bilingual Romeo, and since the Montagues have much less stage presence than the Capulets, it made sense to have them be the Spanish speakers (I called them the Montescos). I assumed that our audience, predominantly English speakers, would be able to follow the few scenes between them, which would be the only scenes entirely in Spanish. For the true "Spanglish" experience, the exchanges between Romeo, his cousin Benvolio, and his page Baltasar were in a combination of both languages. They used English for their bawdy jokes and returned to Spanish when arguments got serious. Also, when characters would address the audience directly, it would be in English, whereas more intimate thoughts would remain in Spanish. In other words, Romeo would speak in Spanish to Juliet when he wanted to be especially attentive.

Frankie grew up in Miami, where the two languages coexist openly in everyday life. Although he had easy access to Spanish sounds, he fell into the common trap of thinking in English (his primary language) and translating the thoughts into Spanish (his original language). Because of this, during rehearsals he was reciting his lines and not really generating thoughts and feelings in both languages, which of course was vital for the success of the production. The solution was pretty simple, really. I had to direct him in Spanish for the Spanish scenes and in English for the rest. Frankie and I began to communicate very precisely as we simultaneously thought in English and Spanish. He recently wrote to me that his largest challenge was thinking in "Spanish during the Spanish parts. It was hard to let myself do that, because for years I had only thought in English. The point that I finally stopped translating words into English in my head and started to really think in Spanish, was a major factor in the development of Romeo. That is when my body and energies became more open and much more playful." The process was exhilarating, and a great learning experience for both of us. We discovered a precision of thought in our communication because we were using two languages. The challenge of meeting Shakespeare in both our languages was making us better theatre artists.

Playing with Shakespeare has indeed been meaningful and enriching to me on several levels. As an actor and director, it gives me great pride that I can master him whom so many call the greatest playwright in history — he who is called "universal." Playing with Shakespeare, anchored in the Shakespeare & Company aesthetic, I learned how to be a more compelling actor, a better listener, and a better thinker. Shakespeare not only has demanded that I be more personally invested in my work but also has contributed to my emotional development. For a Latino actor, mastering Shakespeare is an additional source of self-esteem, because I am able to master a language that so many native English speakers find challenging. It has been extremely beneficial for me to succeed at the constructed standard of my adoptive culture. As a teacher, I have been able to create similar experiences for young actors, including others whose first language is not English, prompting a sense of self-esteem and artistic worthiness similar to that I have felt since my early years at Shakespeare & Company. Without a doubt, Shakespeare has been a significant part of my artistic and personal life.

The (Possible) Delusion

That is all very well, but am I being deluded? I am fully aware of how much Shakespeare has meant to me, but I am also aware how unexamined my experience has been to date. I must analyze why Shakespeare has been so unquestionably special to me personally. Why is he a landmark of my adopted culture? And how do I reconcile that fact with the current multicultural theatre practices that I support as a Latino artist?

On a very basic level, I recognize that yes, indeed, there are pieces of Shakespeare that are as phenomenal as Beethoven, Picasso, Martha Graham, and García Márquez. There are elements of Shakespeare that rightly place him among the wonders of human creativity, and as such, I have as much right to enjoy and work with him as any other artist in the world. But I must also recognize that there is a lot of his work that is questionable. There are aspects of Shakespeare that are offensive to a twenty-first-century liberal sensibility: sexism, racism, xenophobia, and homophobia. Some of it is very weak theatre, and many scenes simply do not work on stage today, which is why most of us who direct it end up cutting, adapting, updating, and manipulating it in order to have a compelling evening of theatre. In my respect and admiration, have I forgotten to illuminate those aspects of the Bard for myself as well as for my students? Have I been unknowingly manipulated by a social construct that I have not yet examined? Why, as a Colombian theatre artist, have I not challenged myself to work with any of the greatest playwrights in the Spanish-speaking canon? Why, as a Latino teacher, do I not challenge non-Anglo students to master the playwrights in their own languages?

My experiences at Shakespeare & Company were immensely eye-opening on many levels, certainly as an artist, discovering my deep intricacies and the tools to create compelling theatre with those raw materials. It also taught me about the cultural make-up of this country and the role that art plays in it. It brought to my attention two intriguing concepts I had never before encountered: arts in education and multiculturalism.

Shakespeare & Company's renowned Education Program is committed to bringing the plays alive for students and schoolteachers and to demystify the notion of Shakespeare as "boring" and "foreign." They not only situate Shakespeare in the Renaissance but also use his plays to teach students about inquiry, humanity, and the importance of the arts. They use Shakespeare to investigate the stories that we must hear, and to teach students about what we all must do as members of a community. Fully invested in this aesthetic, I put it into practice during my years in Massachusetts and witnessed its power in action. It has certainly permeated all my encounters with Shakespeare. I am convinced that devoting a similar effort to Sophocles, Lope de Vega, Anton Chekhov, Henrik Ibsen, García Lorca, or even Tennessee Williams, Tony Kushner, or August Wilson would not have had the same impact. There is something unparalleled in the way Shakespeare inquired about the world that makes it possible for us to do the same through his lens. I believe it stems from Shakespeare's language; his words are powerfully precise and intensely revealing. The rhetorical devices used to persuade, argue, and comprehend the world of Hamlet, Lear, Romeo, Cleopatra, and Brutus are immensely beneficial to the education of young students. Shakespeare makes us more articulate, more able to name our experiences, and better equipped to shape the experiences of our lives. When so much of our culture turns superficially visual and disposable, it is imperative that we inculcate our youth with the love of knowledge and passion for learning, the clarity and precision of thought, and the need for inquiry in which Shakespeare, at his best, excels. Even writing these words now, I do not think I would have been able to comprehend and articulate all these complex thoughts if I had not struggled with Shylock, Macduff, Richard III, and others. They have helped me become a better thinker, listener, and speaker. In that respect, I am a champion for Shakespeare to be seminal in the education of our youth. For exactly the same reasons, I am a champion for Shakespeare to be seminal in the training of young actors, regardless of their heritage and ethnicity.

I have come to realize, however, that my championing of Shakespeare does have a limit. I have been very fortunate that in my training at Shakespeare & Company I was always allowed to sound Latino. No one ever suggested that my English was not good enough for Shakespeare. We did a great amount of voice training, based on Kristin Linklater's "Freeing the Natural Voice" approach, in which an actor's voice is freed from the limitations of habit and psycho-physiological disconnect. But we never engaged in the kind of speech and accent reduction that permeates much of actor training in this country. Even at the dawn of the twenty-first century, I have witnessed countless auditions and performances in which American actors of diverse ethnicities struggled through Shakespeare in a horrific semblance of "received pronunciation," as if they had been instructed that in order to do Shakespeare they must sound British. I have taught at professional conservatories where students of diverse ethnicities and linguistic backgrounds are trained to speak Shakespeare in a uniformly heightened style, with strict adherence to a certain standard of pronunciation and strict observance to iambic pentameter even when the text does not follow it. Their sounds, even when their native language is English, are corrected to meet this standard, which of course has not been examined in generations. This is an oppressive and deluded aesthetic.

Regardless of linguistic history and background, it is imperative for an actor to achieve three main vocal objectives. An actor needs to be heard by the audience; an actor needs to be understood by the audience; and an audience must be able to follow an actor's train of thought. Voice training must be designed to help the actor achieve these goals with maximum efficiency. I contend that if the free and natural sounds of an actor are replaced to fit a constructed standard, the actor's psycho-physiological instrument is negatively affected. To tell someone that the way he or she sounds is not good enough, and specifically not good enough for Shakespeare, is oppressive. If Shakespeare is a paragon of human creativity, we all have a right to access him from our own identities. If Shakespeare holds the mirror up to nature, it ought to reflect our current cultural spectrum and the sounds and colors of our contemporary culture. These thoughts lead me to multicultural theatre and the notion of colorblind and "colordeaf" casting of Shakespeare.

I assume that multicultural theatre is one where many cultures are represented by the theatrical experience, and not only onstage. I assume that multicultural theatre means theatre that tells stories from different cultural perspectives, from playwright to designer, director to performer, and audience to critic. If so, then the question that I must wrestle with next is: What is the purpose of having people of different cultural and linguistic backgrounds perform Shakespeare as a multicultural experience? What do I aim to illuminate by that practice?

I believe that theatre artists across the nation have good intentions when we aim to expand the impact of the work through nontraditional casting and a multicultural perspective. On one level, we aim to celebrate those of us who are not white, those of us whose linguistic inheritance is not English. But I also know that there is something else at play. The more multicultural a company is, the better it can present itself to its funding agencies. This is something I suspected while at Shakespeare & Company and which I later confirmed when I worked as a development associate for the Boston Center for the Arts. If arts organizations can prove that they are "serving" minority constituencies, then they can present themselves as more worthy of funding. Furthermore, it appears that if cultural organizations serve minorities by exposing them to the established "sacred cows" of the dominant culture, they are further rewarded with funding. In other words, theatre companies that present Shakespeare to inner-city youths (especially those of color) often get the most grant money. But, I wonder, do cultural organizations serving minority constituencies exploring their own cultural heritage get similar funding support? I am afraid that overall, as painful as it seems, the answer is no. That revelation makes me wonder further: If I get cast only because I am not white, is that an act of racism? Am I being exploited for my race, regardless of my talent? Looking back at my experience at the Strand Theatre, however, I wonder if there is any cultural value in the fact that Latino students saw themselves represented on the stage in a performance by a Latino actor. Am I in some way contributing to their education and opening their eyes to the possibility of participation? Is it so wrong to be proud that I succeed at doing something once reserved only for Anglo actors? I am not sure what to make of these contradictory reactions, but I think it is important to have a frank discussion about them.

I must return to my original questions: What is the purpose of colorblind and colordeaf casting? How much does having a cast of many hues actually illuminate a Shakespearean story onstage? Does it contribute at all to new understandings of the plot and the relationships presented on the stage? In my second summer at Shakespeare & Company, I was cast on the Mainstage playing the kitchen wench Luce, in drag, in *Comedy of Errors*. It was a very fun role to play, and it was great to be on the Mainstage. The twin Dromios were played by Kenny Ransom, a tall, lanky, agile, handsome black actor, and Jonathan Croy, a tall, stout, agile, handsome white actor. I assume that this was a nontraditional casting choice, as opposed to a colorblind practice. I imagine the point was to illuminate that brotherhood and the recognition of one's doppelganger can cross skin color. But if so, why just the servants? The masters were white, and one of them even dyed his hair to better match his twin. Also, the lines about being beaten constantly and unfairly by his master were spoken by the black Dromio. Our Adriana was also black, and she was wonderfully funny. As the evening progressed, and she got more and more frustrated with the day's confusions, she lost her poise and began to sound more "ghetto." A possible reading of this nontraditional casting choice was that she had constructed a particular way of speaking that allowed her to fit into her white husband's world; but when tested, her true sounds came out. Not only that, the couple had a Latino maid who dressed in drag. I think I was funny as Luce, but I know it was just for laughs. It is hard to say what the audience saw, since I was onstage. But from my perspective, the whole experiment was interesting on the surface, and indeed very funny, but not very moving on a visceral level. It was a good idea on paper, a good intention in the director's mind, but it did not manifest itself well onstage. It did not truly address the cultural or racial suppositions it seemed to breach. The colorblind casting did not illuminate anything new in the story. If anything, the performance posed questions it was unwilling to answer.

My production of *Romeo and Juliet* also did not really illuminate the play in new ways. We were very fortunate that our first preview audience was a group of high school students, bused in for the performance. Teenagers at a play do not lie: they do not suspend their disbelief easily, and they will not be polite if bored. For that reason, they are extremely dangerous and rewarding audiences. As they filled the theatre, I was very nervous, wondering how the bilingual experiment would work out. I could gauge that very few of the students were of Hispanic background, but I knew that several were studying Spanish, and I hoped that our experiment might be an added treat for them. The reception of the play by these high school students was overwhelming. They enjoyed the play immensely, and to my perception, were able to relate to the characters and the story in a surprising way. We got several comments such as "I never thought this could be so much fun." Yet, to my great disappointment, playing in two languages simultaneously was not the big deal I hoped it would be. It had an effect on how the students listened, but it really did not illuminate anything new in the story of the play. One young student told me that she was able to understand the "old" English better because from time to time she had to listen more intently to compensate for her lack of Spanish.

This reminds me of the afternoon when I recited the sonnets back in Bogotá. Maybe being bilingual allows us to be more efficient in our use of language, not only in the speaking of it but indeed, in the listening to it. And that is why I think these students were able to enjoy the play so much: they were really being "audiences," hearing the play, as Elizabethans would. "Let's go hear a play" was the phrase used by the Elizabethans, not our "Let's go see a play." Shakespeare wrote for an audience who participated fully in the performance, an audience eager to hear and enjoy language — words, reason, and rhetoric — through which the human predicament is illuminated. These high school students certainly were that: they played along with us as an important element, and the actors had a fantastic time because the audience was alive with them, responding to and returning energy. The bilingual experiment had a positive effect on the educational experience of these students, but I am not convinced that it helped illuminate the actual story or the relationships in new ways.

To my even greater disappointment, our predominantly adult and predominantly white audiences did not respond nearly as generously. Generally speaking, the adult audiences were very resistant to the untraditional delivery of the text and to the bilingual experiment. I had endeavored to make the language as visceral and powerful as possible, not a mere intellectual feast of beautiful sounds. There is a lot of sexuality in the play, and I had brought that to the foreground as well: our audiences did not seem to enjoy that. Possibly, they had a preconceived notion of what is "good and proper" Shakespeare, and my production did not match it in sounds, sights, or actions. We did not even have a balcony! And overall, they did not respond to the bilingual nature of the play; some even felt alienated by the Spanish. The worst possible comment I received was from one of the board members, who said to me that she thought the use of Spanish was "cute." With a broad smile, she said how much it served our "minority" students. Her words cut through me. "Cute" spoke of my experiment being superficial, and possibly even arrogant. It made me cringe that this board member infantilized my experiment, as if the exploration of the "sacred cow" by the ever-present Latino theatre artist was a necessary evil, but a silly one at best. Her words suggested that my attempt to make Shakespeare my own was not even worthy of attention; instead, she viewed it as a futile exercise and a misguided interpretation of the Bard of Avon. I learned that even in the theatre, even at an academic institution, there is linguistic as well as racial discrimination. I must accept that some in the audience were not open-minded enough to enjoy different languages. We had dared to toy around with one of the paragons of white, Anglo theatre, and they were not amused.

Maybe this sort of experiment would have worked better in a more urban setting than Tallahassee. And yet, on a certain level, I am to blame for the experiment failing. I committed a huge mistake: I decided not to give any specific context to the bilingual nature of this world because I did not want to make a political statement, just an artistic one. Given the fact that the prevailing language of the play was English, there needed to be a significant political context to explain why one of the most powerful houses in this world used a different language. Without this clearly examined and defined context, playing *Romeo and Juliet* in both languages made no sense to the story of the play. Maybe it would have served the story better to have the linguistic and cultural differences between the two families be at the center of their brawl. Maybe it would have been a more compelling challenge for Prince Escalus to keep two disparate cultures from erupting into constant civil strife. Maybe it would have been more meaningful to have two young people from clearly defined different backgrounds fall in love to illuminate the transcendent nature of love, and to use the two languages to deepen their connection further. Overall, I believe this bilingual *Romeo and Juliet* was a positive educational experience, but not a very compelling artistic one because, just like the *Comedy of Errors* production, it remained unexamined.

I do not think I have been deluding myself. Instead, I think I have been wearing horse blinders which I must now remove. I do know I have mastered Shakespeare's theatre, but I need to examine its cultural politics much more deeply if I am going to find its true significance for me, my students, and my audiences. The cultural politics have to begin with the possibility of participation. Shakespeare's stories are very deeply anchored in worlds that are racist, homophobic, and xenophobic. Nontraditional casting is absurd unless the structure of the worlds represented in the plays is thoroughly examined and reinvented to contextualize colorblind and colordeaf casting choices. I must tackle Shakespeare in a new way, with more awareness of the cultural politics of performance and a deeper examination of my own participation in that performance — as a Latino artist living and creating within a culturally diverse society. Only then will I truly make Shakespeare my own.

8

In The Blood: William Shakespeare, August Wilson, and a Black Director

AYANNA THOMPSON INTERVIEWS TIMOTHY DOUGLAS

Timothy Douglas and I corresponded about this collection via e-mail for a few months in 2005. It was apparent that Douglas's voice needed to be included in the collection because of his unusual resume: Douglas began his career as an actor in Shakespeare & Company, but he has most recently been noted for his direction of plays by August Wilson, Suzan-Lori Parks, and Lynn Nottage. As Douglas himself jokes, his resume consists of "50 percent dead white playwrights and 50 percent living black playwrights." Coming from a black actor and director who has managed to perform in and direct both colorblind productions of Shakespeare and black-specific theatre projects, Douglas's personal reflections on the state of casting in the twenty-first century are not just pertinent but invaluable. This interview was conducted over the phone on December 6, 2005. The transcript of the interview has been edited solely for length.

AYANNA THOMPSON: What projects are you currently working on?

TIMOTHY DOUGLAS: I am right in the middle of several new projects. I just finished a production of *Crowns* at City Theatre in Pittsburgh. And I am in pre-production for four projects: the first is *Intimate Apparel* by Lynn Nottage. I am going to be doing a co-production with Indiana Rep and Syracuse Stage. And I am actually working right now with Lynn and two other playwrights, Catherine Filloux and Joe Sutton, on a Katrina project. We don't know what it is going to be yet, but we are all heading down to New Orleans in two weeks to start talking to people. And then I have a *Twelfth Night* for the Latino Shakespeare Company, a *Pericles* for the Julliard School, and a new translation of Ibsen's *Rosmersholm* for a company here in New York called Oslo Elsewhere.

AT: Does colorblind casting play a role in these productions that you have coming up in the future?

TD: It does. It is interesting. With the Latino Shakespeare Company, this is their inaugural production and so we have been talking about it. They feel strongly that as long as I make every effort to cast Latino actors they are open to mixing the company up. So with a play like *Twelfth Night*, I am not so concerned what implications there may be depending on a particular actor's perceived race because of the issues of that play — the politics don't get near race, as far as I can see. I am still working on getting the play ready. But I am not concerned about that, as opposed to an *Othello* or an *Antony and Cleopatra*. But I always remain sensitive to, once it is cast or as I'm casting, what a contemporary audience, bringing their biases, will read into this actor being a particular race, or perceived race. I don't do this to the point of pandering, but, at the same time, I am careful not to fly in the face of people who collectively are going to have a problem with it, at the expense of the story I am trying to tell.

AT: It is interesting how much audience perception comes to bear on this because the original idea behind colorblind casting was that the productions themselves would help change those biases and perceptions. Now it seems as if you have to think about it in the reverse.

TD: Well, I feel that way. I have been talking to more and more people about it, and what is not coming up in conversation often enough is just how the theatre and all creative arts are affected by the culture and the times we live in. The more conservative ideas that have come across this country since the idea and promotion of nontraditional casting are so different. At the time when these casting issues first came up, it was such a great idea to cast blindly and nontraditionally because it was at a time when people were much more open to accept new ideas. Now we're just stuck. It was such an exciting time when nontraditional casting started coming into demonstration. It actually illuminated older plays, especially Shakespeare. But the lack of respect for arts in this country — our government pretty much telling us they don't value the arts with the continued cuts to the NEA and all of the forms of support — is not encouraging. This is having a direct impact on our perceptions. So if there is going to be any hope for the performing arts theatre to have an impact against this huge wave of cuts it has to be so precise and specific in the casting, including being diligent about where nontraditional casting is going to have an impact. But for me the bottom line has to be that the casting is not at the expense of the story being told.

AT: How have you seen it used at the expense of the story being told?

TD: By someone whose heart is absolutely in the right place, usually a director, who wants to support nontraditional casting and employ artists of color, who doesn't think through the casting, and who just hires the best actor for the role. This is an ideal, and I am all about that. But there are certain examples in casting where it goes against the story. For instance, I was troubled by the Folger Shakespeare Theatre's production of *Othello* with Patrick Stewart, where they did the photo-negative casting. Conceptually it was a great idea. Patrick Stewart is a fantastic actor. I absolutely loved hearing him do Othello. The bigger message sent to me — even though they hired more black actors — was that I was being encouraged to lay aside my continued awareness that this nation has yet to come to some kind of agreement — or address the rift that still exists — about the legacy of African slavery. At least this has not been dealt with on a level on par with how we have dealt with the Holocaust or how we've dealt with the internment of Japanese Americans in World War II. There is not even a national monument of note that deals with African American slavery: it does not exist. So until we come to some fundamental understanding, I go to see something like this and it says to me "Oh, we've dealt with that. So we are all past that. So just look at this play, and what we've done, and just look at the relationship." But I can't as an American: I sit there and I see race. And I see the white man getting the best lines!

AT: There is the sense now that we are in a post-racist era: that is the conservative line. Racism doesn't exist anymore so therefore we don't even have to be attentive to race issues. I think productions like that seem to fuel that conservative agenda.

TD: That is what I feel as well. What is interesting about that — I was having this discussion the other day — I was doing a workshop about a new play that deals with the legacy of the perception of the black American family, the institutionalized idea of the absent black father and the super black mother, and how do we deal with that broken thing. And there were some very, very intelligent and passionate young artists there. And one woman said, "For my generation, for how we were raised, we don't have a visceral connection to that civil rights movement and to what that struggle was about. As artists we were coming up at a time when the hip-hop culture intermingled all races around a central cultural phenomenon." So it is a dilemma because I don't want to be someone who keeps harping on something that may have found a way to heal. She didn't feel she has the same issues I do, and I think that's great. But then I wonder, "Do you really know your history?" I want to support her open mind and her willingness to be in a place for healing and colorblindness, but I have this need to feel that it is all coming from a very authentic and considered space. I am really torn.

AT: But how do you approach the topic of colorblind casting with your casts? As an academic and not a performance artist, I always wonder if there are frank and open discussions once you are in production with your cast — when it has already been cast, either colorblindly or not. Does the topic come up in your discussions about how you are staging certain scenes, or what you are afraid of, or things you want to avoid, or things you want to emphasize because of the race of your cast? Do you have those discussions with your cast?

TD: My MO is that it tends to show up pretty deeply into the process. The most recent example for me was my *Marriage of Figaro* that I did last year at the Juilliard School. The play was cast for me because it was a fourth-year student project. The Countess happened to be played by a white actress, and Suzanne, who is a wonderful role and basically the female lead, but a servant to the Countess, was played by a black actress. I sort of allowed myself to relax my issues because I was handed this cast, and that is what I had to work with. But as we started to unearth the truth of the play first and then the truth of the characters and the relationships, the more personal it got, especially in a scene where the Countess, after she is confronted by Suzanne, says, "Enough. Get my hat!" And one day, when the actresses were being wonderful actresses, digging deeply into the relationship, when she said, "Get my hat," we were all like, "Oh!" And although they were acting, it was real. Suzanne stood there for a long time; she literally could not walk across the room to get the hat until she could swallow it. Then we could talk about it. It really is such a murky thing when we get into race and authentic relationships because it really was about what was going on between these two women: the added fire was the color of their skins. These two actresses were very close with one another, and really adored each other, and I think it scared them — that these feelings came up. The feelings were authentic and they were about power; it wasn't about race. But they are so intertwined; you can't see one for the other in this country at the moment.

AT: So when it came up, how was it discussed?

TD: I had to lead the discussion, and I don't dictate. So I said, "Let's talk about that. I couldn't help but notice the color of your skins at that moment. How do you feel about that?" And they were like, "Oh my God, yeah." And they were very concerned for one another at that moment. "You know I was just acting," that sort of thing. I said, "The audience is looking at you. I think this is a part of the world we have created. I don't think we can avoid it. I am not interested in going any deeper into it than it wants to be to make this successful storytelling. But I think what I just witnessed, if it is okay with you, I'd love to stay open to that place and allow yourselves to go there in that moment, and stay open to other moments where that might be the case as well." And they were like, "Is that okay?" And I said, "Well, I understand the question" — because I think they thought that might be insulting to some people in the audience, to see that played out — and I said, "Well, it's real. As an artist, that is what I am doing in the business. We have to reflect the honesty of what is being portrayed here, and it is influenced by the culture we live in. That is our job." And they got that. This moment also served to break through to a deeper level that influenced the entire performance, all the way through, not just that moment. Even though we did not make this play about race — it was definitely a play about class — and because they were being so honest and not ignoring real specific cultural feelings about who they are as people, the authenticity and the impact of this thing was very powerful. The beauty of being an actor on the stage is that even though they were having very real experiences, the words of Beaumarchais kept them safe and kept the audience from imploding. They may have gotten angry, but we could always go back and point to the play, the story of the play, and the text and ground our discussion there. But the casting also allowed us to have the harder discussion.

AT: The art can facilitate the harder discussions that are often left unsaid.

TD: Which, again, is the purpose of our job, I think. That is about as prescriptive as I get with the discussion about nontraditional casting and race with my casts.

AT: Have your ideas come out of your own acting experiences? I see that your career began in Shakespeare & Company. How did you come to be a member of that company?

TD: Shakespeare & Company is a member-driven company: you have to be invited to be in the company. There were very intensive workshops offered. Tina Packer looked at texts and decided that the American actor is much more suited to speaking Shakespeare's texts than any other English-speaking people since the Elizabethans. Tina Packer and Kristin Linklater, who was developing voice and text work, formed a true partnership in developing this company of actors and performance aesthetic. In 1986, as the company continued to grow, Tina decided it was time to do her take on *Antony and Cleopatra*. She thought it would be great to cast all the Egyptians with African American actors, of which I was one, and all the Romans white. Her intent, as I understood it, was to trigger deeper, unspoken, perhaps unconscious cultural tensions about the history of this country, specifically the legacy of African slavery. She knew something was going to happen, and her intention was to be responsible with whatever came up, and through the text, and through discussion, and through authentic communication, illuminate or address these issues. She thought that she could give these issues a voice so that people wouldn't implode, which so often happens when discussions of race happen directly.

So in 1986 she did not have many black company members, that was one issue, and also the company was not that large, and *Antony and Cleopatra* requires a huge cast. Up to that point, you had to do a month-long intensive, and it was intense: fourteen-hour days, six days a week, for a month locked up with sixty other people. The team of facilitators was very trained and filled with integrity so there was always somebody to deal with the issues that came up. No one was ever left to their own worst devices when it really got difficult. And it was very emotional and exhausting and all that wonderful, churning stuff. It was from these workshops that you could be invited to do the productions in the summer. There were really no exceptions; you had to go through the training before you could perform on the main stage.

But then came *Antony and Cleopatra*, and they needed some black people fast. I was just graduating from Yale Drama School — I was there as an actor — and I had begun to audition in the spring. Now at Yale, two of my voice teachers were Shakespeare & Company members. So I had a visceral working knowledge of the aesthetic, at least from the voice-work point of view. So it wasn't completely unfamiliar to me. I went in to audition for Tina Packer, and she had me do four pieces, and I remember her comment to me was "Wow, you can do Shakespeare really fast." So she hired me, and I was one of about ten people in that company who had never spent time with the company before, who had never done the workshop training. But I was also the only newbie who actually had experience with the work. So even though it was really hard, and foreign, and crazy, at least I understood what was going on. And that is how I got into Shakespeare & Company.

AT: We have talked previously about the extraordinary circumstances of that 1986 production of *Antony and Cleopatra*. I was wondering if you could elaborate on those circumstances now.

TD: In *Antony and Cleopatra*, I was the soothsayer. I also played the clown who brings the snake to Cleopatra, and Michelle Shay played Cleopatra. Whatever play happens to be worked on, the company will play out the relationships of that play. It is either going to happen on the stage or off, but it is going to happen. When I go to see a show, and if the show is not quite working, I am really interested in hanging out with the company and there it is: there's the show. So in *Antony and Cleopatra* most of it happened off the stage because we rarely got to complete the show. The rain was the biggest issue because over the course of the summer most of the performances were canceled because of the rain: out of thirty-six planned performances only five were finished without any delay and only thirteen more were finished at all. We would attempt to rehearse in small spaces; we couldn't get the entrances; people were on top of each other; and we were getting frustrated. As an actor, not being able to finish rehearsal and feel like you know what you are doing, this stuff builds up and you just start snapping. The normal measures that Tina and the team usually used to address these emotions and conflicts were not available to them because of the hugeness of this production and the problems we were having getting it up. So we would all leave rehearsal frustrated, and we lived forty minutes away. We all had to carpool, and we were all on top of each other. And we were in this giant house; and it was always raining; and there is no town and nowhere to go; and we were all on top of each other; and shit started to come out. It did not take long for the frustration to come out. We were all artists — we were all in the same boat and we are all reasonable people — but that does not do anything to what we feel emotionally.

So as our responses started to happen, it didn't take long for people to feel — whether they could articulate it or not — that it started to become race-related. It had to do with, "Oh, white man, you are so privileged. You don't understand that you are sharing a house. I know you are used to having your own apartment when you do an out-of-town gig, but you signed a contract and we are living communally." And people have habits; it is not easy to live with people you don't know. I couldn't help noticing how all the black folks would hang out together and be loud, and we had culturally specific ways of being that were different from our white counterparts in that house. And we felt ourselves being studied. We felt the resistance of joining in our conversations. I must say we did not go out of our way to create a whole house community because we needed to have some sense of sameness because we were in the Berkshires, and because we were in the Shakespeare experience, and because we were so miserable. We sought each other out. We felt that it began to be perceived that we did not want to hang out with the white people. And we saw that judgment, and we made no effort to address it as a group because we were like we can address it and take care of them and make them feel more comfortable around us, or, we can make each other feel more comfortable because we are miserable. And then we would make these attempts at these nightly poker games and that really helped because we love game playing. But again, even though we played nickel, dime, quarter, there was money involved and people's personalities come out when they start losing. And nothing untoward happened, but in that closed environment, in that pressure cooker, a lot more was read into everything. And then we would go back to the theatre, and we would start to work some of this out. And just as Tina was about to try to shape it and facilitate it in a way that was healthy for everybody, it would downpour — in the middle of a sentence. Tina couldn't even get through a scene to work it out. It was so tense. It was so tense the whole time.

AT: Did the season end without the tensions being released or addressed? Did you just go your separate ways thinking it was a horrible experience?

TD: There was great effort to address it. One of the MOs of Shakespeare & Company is to sit the entire company down on a consistent basis — staff, cast, everybody involved in any given moment — and just talk. We are asked to stay in that room until everyone feels that whatever is up has been worked through. And so you have more than half of this company who is not used to this, who find it masturbatory, who find it manipulative because they are not used to communicating that way. That is the way Shakespeare & Company works — and I fell right into it because I love working things out that way — but that is not for everybody because they do not want to reveal. They are actors and they do their work, but they don't have to tell you about themselves. And the other side of that is that people don't want to be perceived as being a problem or a complainer because that could affect their castability later. So people were not willing to talk about things that were pissing them off. So at one point Tina realized that there were diminishing returns so she just sort of gave up the compulsory feedback sessions, and anybody who needed to talk about whatever — whether it was in a group session or privately — were welcome to do so but many people chose not to. There was really something wrong there, and all of us recognized it. We were able to demonstrate it in proportion to the degree of our pissed-off-ness. If we were really pissed off, it was hard to do the show and people did not have a good time doing it. But if we were only mildly pissed off, we could find the moments in the show to let go. And we would be like, "This feels good," and then it would downpour and we would have to stop.

AT: We have talked previously about your growing frustration with the company because you were expected to represent so much. As you said to me before, you were 50 percent of what made Shakespeare & Company a multi-racial company!

TD: Yes, I was 50 percent of what made Shakespeare & Company a multi-racial company. There were two of us that were consistently asked back. Well, that's not true. Tina was asking other people of color back, but people didn't want to come. The next summer (1987) because of the joy and the growth that I got in a special clown workshop, I was not concerned that I was only playing Starveling, the Tailor in *A Midsummer Night's Dream*: I had a great time. The following season (1988) we did *As You Like It*. Karen Allen played Rosalind in that production; she became a company member. And I played Le Beau, Amiens, and Hymen. The value both for me and for the company was that I can sing, and so I played all the roles that required singing. And Tina hired this amazing composer; there was amazing music. I had great songs to sing in this show, but I was in service — it was mostly about the singing and I didn't have much of a role. But, again, I had a great time and I got to premiere that music, and I got a lot of attention for that. But I wasn't taking a role and investigating it from beginning to end — the in-depth, down in the dirt way that Shakespeare & Company works. I never got a role that allowed me to do that. The following season I stepped out because I had begun my formal voice training with Kristin Linklater to become a voice teacher. So I was at the company, but I was following Kristin, serving as a voice coach, and teaching for the company. So I didn't perform that summer, but that was really because I wasn't asked to do anything. Then in 1990 it was a remount of *As You Like It* because the company was in trouble and it was such a big hit: they brought it back and knew they could make some money. And I revised the same roles.

AT: So you've done the Soothsayer, Starveling, and what you call "service roles," and you had been at the company for five years?

TD: Yes, there were diminishing returns for me. And that was the summer of the Showdown at the O.K. Corral. Tina had gone away to do some lectures or residency, and she came back after not seeing the show for a couple of weeks and she clearly thought the show was unraveling and she wanted to give some notes. But she was pissed. She was under a lot of pressure. I understand what she was going through. But she came in before the show, and she said, "Look, I have some notes. You guys are letting it fall apart. Just take the notes. I don't have time to talk about it. Just take the notes." And we were actually having a good time and we were into it until she came in with that. And we were Shakespeare & Company and we were supposed to be wide open; so her words felt like a knife in the heart. So she was rattling off these notes, and literally she gives me a note and I didn't understand it. So I raised my hand to ask a question (which you don't do at Shakespeare & Company because you just speak when you feel like speaking), and she said, "Just take the fucking note. Why do you have to be so difficult? Just take the fucking note." And I was like, "Oh, no, no, no." And suddenly for the first time, I had a very different response: I was having an *Antony and Cleopatra* response. And I hadn't felt that in five years. I didn't say anything because we had to go on. She was taking a long time with notes, and we had a show to do. I let nothing affect my performance. I am that kind of actor, and I have never had anything affect the focus of my performance. An hour later I am onstage, and I am standing in the scene (I don't have any lines at the moment), and all I am doing is thinking, "I can't believe she got in my head. This has never happened before. I am still in that room. I'm not even here on the stage, in the scene that I am in." And that had never happened to me before, and that just did me in because I did not know what I was going to do. But I got through it.

Later, when it was intermission and places were called, I was walking and I could feel that someone was lurking on the staircase but I couldn't see who it was. And I was startled a little bit and jumped because it was dark. And I turned a little bit, and it was Tina. So I looked at her, but I was just startled. I didn't think there was anything behind my look — other than being startled and not knowing there was someone there. So I looked at her and I clocked her, but I didn't say anything because I was still mad: I knew if I said anything, I would SAY something. So I just turned away and started to walk to places, and from behind me I hear, "Why do you hate my ideas? Why do you look at me like that? Why do you hate me? What have I done? You hate me so much!" I just stopped. Now I am wearing — I am dressed for Le Beau — and I have on these platform shoes, these bumblebee stockings, and I have this huge big, French-style Napoleon hat. I was not dressed for this confrontation. And I said, "Lady, you don't mean that much to me. What makes you think I am that concerned about you? You're not that important in my life."

We went at it. She goes, "Why are you are so upset with me?" And I said, "It was no big deal. Why did you come in like that? It wasn't a big deal. I just didn't understand the notes."

And then we got to it, and it just came out of me. I didn't know I felt like this way. I was frustrated. I definitely felt I wanted more substantial roles, but I was also aware of how amazing the actors who were consistently cast in the meatier roles were. I felt they were amazing, but I did feel that I was ready. But I didn't realize how frustrated I was about that until this conversation. It just came out, "I am really getting tired of being 50 percent of what makes this a multicultural and multiracial company."

And she said, "Well, I am just as frustrated as you are. But I can't keep them. I can't get the people of color to come back. I ask people to come back, but they won't come. I need you to help me with that. I need you to help me understand why. I need you to help me recruit more people of color."

And I said, "First of all, I wouldn't ask any person — white, black, or any other race — to come here in the condition the company is in right now: it is too challenged. I wouldn't encourage anyone to come here, and I think you know what I am talking about. This makes me feel really under-appreciated because clearly in your mind I am doing more work than is being asked of the other company members, and yet it is not being reflected in my casting." That is how it came out.

To be fair to her, I don't remember what she said directly to that, but we went on to talk about why people of color wouldn't stay at the company. And I was able to articulate, "Even though your intention, Tina, is total inclusion and to work through the conflicts that are a result of race consciousness and misunderstandings and the current climate we live in, it is not enough to invite people of color here and think that it is all going to happen magically. In me, you have found someone who has worked on himself and worked through a lot of this stuff on his own, and so I understand your language and I can speak your language. And I can work through, on my own, things that you don't have time or the company doesn't have resources to address, but that doesn't mean that it is not there." This was news to her. It was a revelation to her, and actually I had never articulated this before. It was coming out in this conversation, and she understood that. And she asked, "What can I do?" And when I said, "I don't know," she said, "But I need you to help me." And I said, "That is not my job, and again, you are asking me to do more — markedly more — than anyone else in this company. And on a very basic level, I am not being compensated for that fairly." And she heard that.

So that was when the revelation happened. That is when I had this little out-of-body experience in which I kind of stepped aside and someone spoke through my body and said, "Black people have nothing to teach you about this rift between the races. We have no information for you that you can use. It needs to be you going back and looking at your own culture and ancestry to get underneath that vibe that said that it was okay to enslave another people and then to continue to ignore it all these hundreds of years. When you can understand that, you will understand everything you need to understand about black people in this country."

AT: It is not our job to teach it to you.

TD: We are participants, inextricably, but white people think we are holding out on them. But they need to realize the thing they need to connect the dots does not come from us. That investigation is feared because they think we will beat them over the head, stab them in the back, and take retribution. But actually we are not that interested. It would be such a relief not to be under this fucking microscope.

God bless Tina, she just took all this in. And I had to take it in too because I had never thought that before. So we just stood there in silence for a long time, and then the stage manager came and grabbed me because it had been ten minutes and we had to start the show. What a relief. That is when I stopped performing with the company. I did go back the following summer and continued to teach for the workshops. I still stay in touch, and I talk to Tina all the time, but we have never picked up that conversation again.

AT: But it does seem that these are precisely the conversations that have gone unsaid. So how true can productions be if there are these unspoken tensions that we can't get past?

TD: There is a fair process. I feel that I have absorbed the practice of addressing that question as I am working. My experience has taught me that these issues can only be addressed from a platform that is completely steeped in authenticity and the willingness to speak what Tina often referred to as "the unspeakable." The person has to feel completely valued and honored. They have to feel that whatever they say is going to be taken as part of the whole person's expression and not be used against them to single out one aspect of their philosophy. We must listen to the whole person with our whole being and acknowledge that we are all very complicated beings that don't exist fully on one principle. So that is why in the example from *The Marriage of Figaro*, I said that it is not until I feel that each person is absolutely present and willing to be authentic that I specifically and literally address all the different issues, including the one about race perception. For me, that is the only way that it can happen in any meaningful way.

AT: When you decided that you were no longer going to be an active member of the company, were you paying attention to the colorblind casting debates between August Wilson and Robert Brustein?

TD: Yes.

AT: It must have felt surreal to read about these debates as you were going through your own issues in supposedly colorblind productions of Shakespeare. You have become a very important director of August Wilson's plays, and Wilson ends up playing a large role in many of the essays in this collection — the contributors keep coming back to Wilson's words. So the connections between Wilson, Shakespeare, casting, and race are enmeshed, and you end up representing how enmeshed they can be for someone in the arts. When you started directing Wilson's plays and approaching the topic outside of Shakespeare & Company, how did you make this transition?

TD: Like every meaningful thing in my life, it was made for me by God. I never uttered the words to anyone, "I want to direct." I never said those words to anyone. So when the opportunity came into my life, it was clear to me that this was designated for me and this was my life's work until it leads to whatever it is leading: I am not convinced I am a career director.

August communicated to me that he was not initially a man of the theatre: he was an artist, a poet, a writer. When he transitioned from poetry to plays, he was very excited by the dynamic of the dialogue and so started his own theatre collective in Pittsburgh with some friends of his who all were great, great artists, but not of established American theatre. So August had only been black-specific; he had only been black theatre-specific, and yet he has had this profound impact on American theatre. And he was never tempted to move away from any of the first principles he believed in. He hadn't done it, and he didn't have to. So I just always understood that about him, and I agree with a lot of what he says. And where I disagree, I am aware that he and I had very different journeys, and I have seen things and experienced things that either he hadn't or he simply wasn't interested in: things that I have found great value in, including this idea of people of color moving through a Eurocentric playwright and finding valuable lessons in it and being able to illuminate it. I think August's primary issue was, and forgive me for stating the obvious, that we are just not honoring black theatre; we are not honoring our black artists; and we don't have the representations in mainstream American artistic institutions of black artists that reflect the amount of talent that is there. What is the resistance to that? To me it is no mystery: it is not just theatre; it is every aspect of this nation. We just have not dealt with that. So it just reflects back in the theatre. He was just outraged by that, and God bless him for being so vocal about it.

But I never felt that I was in opposition to August Wilson, and he knew my work. Unbeknownst to me, he had been traveling around seeing productions of my shows. That is how he came to pick me to do *Radio Golf*. It was his decision; I did not even know he was paying attention to me. August knew what my career had been — and I think it has been fifty-fifty, I'm doing 50 percent dead white playwrights and 50 percent living black playwrights — but we never talked about it. We never talked about it. He never brought it up, and my feeling was that if he knew my history then he didn't feel that my beliefs were going to get in the way of being able to interpret his work. And because of the circumstances around *Radio Golf*, in terms of the timing of it and the enormous task of it, I was afraid of opening up a can of worms — a potential can of worms. Although Wilson was terminally ill at that point, he did not know it then. The extraordinary circumstances had to do with the fact that Wilson was finishing the play as I was directing it, while simultaneously spending time at the bedside of his dear friend, Ben Mordacai, who passed away shortly after the play opened. I didn't want to open that because that was what our relationship would be about, and we had to get that play up. So I decided we are going to do *Radio Golf*, and when the dust cleared I planned to take August to lunch one day and talk about all of these things that I had always wanted to talk to him about. There was a blessing and a wisdom in that, and I just accept it because it was all just so bizarre. That voice came from the same place that said that thing to Tina — you know about investigating their own culture. That inner voice is so strong in me, and sometimes it just smacks me upside my head and pushes me away and says, "No, I am taking over because you are not listening to me." And it was at that level that said, "Don't get into this. You've got to get this play up. Later." So I guess I've got to wait until I make my final transition, or maybe August is going to start talking to me [from beyond the grave]. Who knows?

AT: That sounds like a play in and of itself! Can you talk about your most recent productions of Shakespeare?

TD: I've done *Richard III* at the Folger Shakespeare Library. And then I've done two productions of *Pericles* in schools, one at the University of Southern California and one at DePaul University. I just did *Love's Labour's Lost* this past summer at the Utah Shakespearean Festival, and that was cast for me. They're trying, but I was their first black director in their forty-four-year history. So I didn't expect too many black actors, and I had one in my show and I think there were two in the company. They've got work to do. I totally took them to task on that one, and they did not offer anything in their defense. I decided that I am going to take them on. I am not leaving them alone. I am going to keep calling. Not that they necessarily need to hire me again, but I am like, "Are you attending to it? Are you attending to it?" I am going to make sure that people of color are auditioning because — that is the other thing that's happened — the disillusionment is so great, especially among actors of color, they stop seeking out opportunities. History has taught them there is not much for them.

AT: Exactly, instead they are looking at Suzan-Lori Parks's wonderful plays, which I see you have also directed, and August Wilson's, where they feel that at least they are going to have a shot.

TD: It is obvious that black actors are going to have a shot at Wilson and Parks, but what is happening is that I am calling for certain people from the agencies — "bring so and so in" — and they say, "No, I am not going in because there is nothing for me there." That's happening. People are taking themselves out in addition to being ignored.

AT: Really. Why is this happening?

TD: It is a two-part thing because part of that is that actors don't want to leave New York and Los Angeles anymore. Because of the lack of funding and the lack of opportunities, people don't want to leave town for two months at a time for fear of missing an opportunity. That is part of the reason why certain people are refusing to audition for certain things. The other part is that the several clear and forward-thinking artistic directors and directors who are specifically asking for actors of color — "I want people of color. I want to mix this cast up. I want something different" — are having a hell of a time getting people in to read because people don't BELIEVE it.

AT: That is fascinating. Actors of color no longer believe that Shakespearean productions are truly colorblind. Can you talk more specifically about your experience at the Folger doing *Richard III*?

TD: That was great. That was 1995, and it was my first professional production. And it was truly the first and last time for me personally that this idea of nontraditional casting was just the greatest thing ever. It was just such a joyous experience. It was the first season after the Shakespeare Theatre Company, Michael Kahn's company, had moved out of the Folger Library and went into their own space. And the Folger wanted to continue producing Shakespeare. So they partnered with a lot of different companies, and this was the Traveling Shakespeare Company. Michael Tolaydo, who was our artistic director — a British actor — wanted to play Richard.

AT: Was this a colorblind production?

TD: It was. I got to cast it, and it was one of those situations where I just cast the best actors for the roles, and it was all D.C.-based actors. I had a black woman who played Lady Anne (Aakhu Freeman), who was fantastic. We learned so much about that relationship because of the actress *and* because she was black. The actor who played Edward was an African actor who lived in D.C. (James Brown-Orleans), and he was amazing. It was never a thing with the company, the reviews, or the Folger Library: it was just like they wanted a good production of *Richard III*. In D.C. in 1994 the theatre community was about honoring their local talent, especially the actors of color. It was also about honoring an American aesthetic that included everybody. I got this feeling that that was a drive in D.C. at the time, and I still feel that when I go down there.

AT: You said earlier that the cultural and political climate was right for allowing a truly nontraditional cast to succeed at that point. Can you expand on that?

TD: I definitely think that was true, and up to that point it was true for the majority of the American theatre-going public. But in D.C. it was especially potent because it is such an international city. It was essential that *Richard III* be a good production of *Richard III* because a D.C. audience is not as aware of "Oh, that's a black person so what is he saying about the role." That is not the first question in D.C.

AT: So what is your suggestion for a colorblind production of Shakespeare? What advice do you have for actors and directors, and how do you make it so that the frank conversations about race are not just a burden for the actors of color?

TD: It is such a hard question. The reason it is hard is because I can feel myself maturing, and as I feel myself maturing, I can feel myself becoming less flexible. And so I am not sure if I am answering this question from an idealistic point of view or from a crusty point of view. I want to remain open; I want to keep my heart open; I want to believe in the potential for the human race to improve and heal and in the ability for us to honor each other. And that really comes from my spiritual background, which I am deeply immersed in and from which all of my best work comes. I don't hide that in rehearsal. I demand that people speak from their higher selves. I will honor anything that comes up, including transgression, but we are not going to leave it there. Because that is the environment that I try to create — and I have been very blessed to be successful in that — shortly after the first few days of rehearsal people are talking from their authentic selves. By speaking that truth, everyone must also include their feelings, perceptions, and frustrations about who they are as people, how they are perceived by gender, race, politics, and all those things. By the time that I engage them in that level of discussion, race is just part of the whole person. So in that sense the burden remains on the people of color to provide information that white people in the room may not know, but it does not become a defense of the race or defense of principles. Everybody in the room is allowed to form his/her own philosophy and shift his/her philosophies based on new information and new experiences. So that is how I do it, and that is what I believe the über-answer is.

AT: Do you think that there are some productions where the play itself will facilitate this more or less than others? At the beginning of our conversation you said, "Well, it is *Twelfth Night* so those issues are not as prevalent as they would be in *Othello*."

TD: Particularly in Shakespeare, the politics of the play will shift and be in counterpoint to whatever the particular politics of the land are in that location at that moment. Shakespeare constantly shifts. For me, this idea of colorblind casting depends on where the play is performed. When the play is performed in America — and it really depends on where it is being performed in America — it elicits and deals with issues having to do with race, or cultural differences perceived as racial differences. Then the casting has to be very careful: I don't think it can be colorblind, but it can be nontraditional. And for me those are two different things.

AT: If you were invited to direct *Othello* somewhere and you had no say in the casting, would you do it?

TD: Well, it depends. Now what was interesting about *Love's Labour's Lost* — this is not quite the same point, but it makes my point — is that they cast a black actor in the role of Mercade, who represents death. And I was like, "Okay?" So I thought about that. He is the only black actor. This is the bonus — when I have no say in the casting and something like this happens — this is where the people of color in my productions really benefit the most because the play becomes about that character for me. I have to solve that character first to make the play work. So I will never forget the look on those poor people's faces, hiring this black man for the first time, when I came out there. They asked, "Tim, so we are all gathered, and we were wondering what is your concept for the play? What is *Love's Labour's Lost* about?" And I said, "It's about death." And this was the play cast in the season to be the comedy. This was the comedy, sandwiched between *Romeo and Juliet* and *Dr. Faustus*, and I said, "It's about death." Very few people can solve the last ten minutes of that play. It just completely becomes a different play and it seems to have nothing to do with anything that went before it. So I had to start there. It wasn't just about the black actor, but it made me realize, focusing on him, that I had to start there. And the whole point of the thing was that there was an awareness of mortality. The young folks were driven to make something of their lives

because of their constant existential awareness of death. Actually, in performance it became very funny because it was very real and compelling. I say all
this because it was all inspired because I looked at that black actor, and I knew
I had to solve his role first. It opened a doorway for me to look into the play in a
way that was surprising to a lot of people. I never shared this with anyone else,
but it was because the actor was black: and that is how I got to it.

So in terms of *Othello*, if I can solve it, meaning solve it for me, absolutely I
will do it. If I can get through it and not feel that I am performing some kind of
mental gymnastics to make it work because of the complications of the casting, I will jump at it. I can't shut down. I have to keep finding ways. But I am so
frustrated, especially at conservatories where I work once a year to keep that
muscle oiled, but often I don't have any say in the casting. But I like to walk in
thinking, "Can I solve it? Can I solve it?"

AT: So you must see part of your job as making them realize the implications of their casting decisions, right?

TD: Absolutely. As the conversations come up, as the difficult feelings and
interactions come up, my job is to not ignore it and to be there to discuss it.
"Oh, that black guy at the front of the room. Well, if he can do it, then — ."
Looking at my resume, there are so many people who have not met me who
think, "Either he is a really respected black director who people really trust
with the classics. Or, he is a white guy who has the nerve to do all these black
plays." Either way they want to know me!

AT: Your resume is amazingly diverse. It is so impressive.

TD: I have never had to ask. I actually now have to attend to make sure I
am keeping in the loop with the new black plays that are coming through.
I have to attend to that now because I haven't been pigeonholed. The question that keeps coming up, especially in training centers, is when will we start
mixing up August Wilson's plays. When will we see white people in that? My
answer is: "When we have dealt fundamentally with the conundrum between
the races in this country, then we can see that." But do we have to wait? Maybe
we should start with the theatre, as we are meant to do, shedding light and
holding up the mirror. But it is very prickly for me. I am not ready to address
that yet. With that said, when I am teaching acting classes I absolutely give my
white actors August Wilson.

AT: Really?

TD: I would be negligent as an educator if I did not bring that into the
classroom.

AT: But it is fascinating to think that something that is appropriate in the
classroom would not be appropriate on the stage.

TD: For me it has to do with the fact that the American cultural perception
is that audiences would never go for it. But I should never say never, because I
have been surprised by things like this many times. Perhaps I am perpetuating
this stereotype by even saying it. I am open to it if the actors are really good

and the director gets those relationships in line. Now that I am talking about it, I don't know, maybe I need to give it a shot. I need to try it.

AT: I will be the first in line to see it! Thank you, Timothy, for your time and generosity. Good luck with all of your future projects.

III
Future Possibilities/
Future Directions

9

Civic ShakesPR: Middlebrow Multiculturalism, White Television, and the Color Bind

RICHARD BURT

"Skin tone soon becomes irrelevant in performance."
— Errol Hill, *Shakespeare in Sable*

Citizen Shakespeare

In an interview on the *Tonight Show* that aired on August 26, 2004, First Lady Laura Bush told host Jay Leno that she wanted to bring Shakespeare to gangs in the United States in order to increase literacy and, presumably, reduce violence.

> Mrs. Bush: Well, one thing that I'm going to go to later today is a Shakespeare program, "Will Power to Youth," it's called, it's here in Los Angeles. And it's a way to use acting and Shakespeare to get kids into—
>
> Leno: Will boys really want — Shakespeare, come on. (Laughter.)
>
> Mrs. Bush: They actually love it. Think about Shakespeare. It's bloody.
>
> Leno: It's bloody, yes.
>
> Mrs. Bush: All those things that boys might like.
>
> Leno: See, I couldn't see myself — "Hey, you gang-bangers, come on over here for some Shakespeare." (Laughter.) Seems like it would be tricky to do.
>
> Mrs. Bush: Well, these maybe aren't gang kids.[1]

Leno's skepticism flew in the face not only of a longstanding Americanization of Shakespeare but also of a more recent broad effort by the Bush administration to harness Shakespeare. Laura Bush made her remarks about Shakespeare to Jay Leno while she was on a tour across the United States and Mexico in support of her husband George W. Bush's "Helping America's Youth" initiative, focusing particularly on boys and supported by Bush's reallocation of federal tax dollars to faith-based charities. One could easily read the Bush administration's use of Shakespeare as part of a concerted, far-reaching Republican right-wing multicultural agenda in which racism is disciplined in order to create a better-functioning workforce. That is, Shakespeare is not presented as part of white high culture but as open to all races and cultures. That is why colorblind casting has played such an important role in the groups Bush has supported.

Laura Bush's public relations Shakespeare efforts, or "ShakesPR," have reinforced those of a new National Endowments for the Arts (NEA) program entitled "Shakespeare in American Communities," begun in 2003 under NEA chairman Dan Goia to "bring professional Shakespeare productions and related educational activities to more than 150 small and mid-sized communities in all 50 states."[2] For the first time in its history, the NEA funded a program the NEA itself created.[3] In addition, the NEA promotes their conspicuously multiracial *Shakespeare in American Communities* educational booklet and has produced two documentaries about this program. Moreover, a Shakespeare program run by teacher Rafe Esquith at Hobart Elementary School in Los Angeles is the darling of conservatives such as Abigail and Stephen Thernstrom (see Thernstrom). A Public Broadcasting System *P.O.V.* documentary entitled *The Hobart Shakespeareans* (dir. Mel Stuart, 2005) shows how Esquith teaches his fifth-grade Latino and Asian students to perform full-length productions of *Henry V* and *Hamlet*. Esquith's book *There Are No Shortcuts* (2003) is explicitly directed to parents and "concerned citizens" as well as teachers.

The right-wing slant of Laura Bush's Shakespeare initiative may be further adduced by taking note of the formation of a civic American Shakespeare by the Bush administration that has transnational, imperialistic dimensions. In January 2003, the Department of Defense distributed copies of *Henry V* to GIs as they were being mobilized to invade Iraq. Soon after Bush ordered the Iraq invasion that began in March 2003, neoconservative pundits and Bush administration hawks such as Kenneth Adelman began linking Shakespeare and Iraq, often comparing Bush to Shakespeare's Henry V, tendentiously regarded by these pundits as a failed prince who made good as a warrior king.[4] In 2004, after the Pentagon allocated one million dollars (under special congressional authorization), NEA Shakespeare productions began touring military bases in the United States, beginning with *Macbeth* and *Othello*. All of the NEA theatre companies producing plays had multiracial casts and used colorblind casting.[5] The documentary *A Dream in Hanoi* (dir. Tom Weidlinger, 2003), about a bilingual and binational production of *A Midsummer Night's Dream* in Vietnam, tied the Shakespeare production to French and American economic reforms, especially to disciplining the Vietnamese labor force to get them to work longer hours and take fewer breaks.

In addition, Shakespeare plays have been performed in elementary school programs and by U.S. prison inmates since the 1990s; several such productions have been the subject of film documentaries, including *Colors Straight Up* (dir. Michèle Ohayon, 1997), which gives an account of a now defunct Shakespeare musical and dance adaptation of *Romeo and Juliet* with Watts teenagers, entitled "Watts Side Story," and *Shakespeare behind Bars* (dir. Hank Rogerson, 2005).[6] The latter film follows a group of prisoners, about half of them white and half of them black, at the Luther Luckett Correctional Complex in LaGrange, a minimum security prison, as they rehearse a race- and gender-blind production of *The Tempest* over a year and finally perform it as part of a rehabilitation program. The Prospero-centered production is ostensibly apolitical. Yet the documentary, perhaps inadvertently, shows that the prison's method acting approach to Shakespeare works in a quite Foucauldian manner as a means of getting the prisoners to police themselves: they do therapy with one another, confess their crimes to the camera, and try to forgive themselves for their crimes. No political explanation of crime or critique of the penal system is ever voiced in the documentary. The premise of the Shakespeare program is that gender and race are superficial (hence the prison uses race-blind and gender-blind casting).

If for Laura Bush, prison wardens, and the like, Shakespeare is supposed to function as a prophylactic against kids joining gangs and going to jail, Shakespeare also works as a backup to redeem kids who turn to crime and have consequently been imprisoned, giving new meaning to the words "institutional Shakespeare." In a Foucauldian nightmare inversion of Orson Welles's New Deal Federal Theatre Project Shakespeare productions, such as the 1935 all-black cast of *Voodoo Macbeth*, civic Shakespeare is no longer a means of expanding civil rights but an enticement to subjugation. Government-sponsored programs in disciplinary institutions including urban schools, the military, and prisons, and government-sponsored television programs and films about them are designed to integrate minorities and poor whites by warehousing them into service sector, low-income Mcjobs. Humanism and the performing arts are used to legitimize dehumanization.[7]

Raising the Color Bar/d

The preceding account needs to be seriously qualified, however, in a number of ways. Shakespeare has been so thoroughly penetrated by capitalism that the consequent variations, spinoffs, and citations mean that no government program can monopolize his value. The Bushes' attempt to construct a right-wing civic Shakespeare has hardly been a success. By late 2004, when it became clear that the mission in Iraq was not accomplished, the analogy between Shakespeare's Henry V and Bush was reversed by a number of commentators who pointed to Henry V's Machiavellianism and the epilogue noting the loss of France after Henry V died. Perhaps coincidentally, the 2004 season of the NBC series about the Vietnam War, *American Dreams*, did several episodes about a production of *Henry V*, which is assumed by the characters to be an antiwar play. In addition, the celebration of the Hobart Shakespeareans comes off as their own dumbed-down Shakespeare, as if the only way to save the idea of "great" books and avoid considering questions about gender, race, and class in Shakespeare's plays and their performance history is to reduce the plays to single themes, such as the colorblind nature of love.

More interesting for the purposes of this essay is that a far from monolithic, traditional Shakespeare is being harnessed by prison wardens, the Bush administration, and its neoconservative apparatchiks; rather, what I call Hy-Bard-ity, a mix of traditional and modernized Shakespeares, is in play. Shakespeare takes on elastic form. Captions below the Laura Bush photos describe the "Will Power to Youth" *Romeo and Juliet* production as a "performance" and a "rendition," suggesting that it is both the original play and an adaptation of it. One photo caption explains that "students in the program write their own versions of Shakespeare's plays, create the music, costumes and construct the sets for each production."[8] Bush (and her webpages) clearly has no interest in identifying and valuing one kind of Shakespeare as institutional and another as a degraded simulacrum of it. Post-Victorian "bloody" Shakespeare is fine with Mrs. Bush, just as NEA Chairman Dan Goia says he does "earthy," original Shakespeare productions. When it comes to Bush government Shakespeare, neither authentic Shakespeare nor racial authenticity matters much.

Figure 9.1 Laura Bush's colorblind Shakespeare. Photo: Krisanne Johnson.

While a critique of the Bush ShakesPR is important, my interest in this essay lies in the ways Shakespeare's Hy-Bard-ization calls attention to commonalities between Shakespeare on the Left and Right. Consider the way both Bush and others have modernized images of Shakespeare while introducing multiracial casts. In a photo on the "First Lady" webpage of Laura Bush visiting "Will Power to Youth" in Los Angeles, she stands next to an NEA poster with Shakespeare wearing blue dark glasses. This move to make Shakespeare hip bears a striking similarity to the image of "Bill" Shakespeare with dark glasses on the official film website for Baz Luhrmann's *William Shakespeare's Romeo + Juliet* (1996), which makes the Capulets Hispanic, except for Juliet, and the graffiti Shakespeare spray-painted at the beginning of *The Street King* (dir. James Gavin Bedford, 2002), a Hispanic modernized spinoff of *Richard III*.

Moreover, colorblind casting practices have become the established, unquestioned, and unexamined rule. For example, *Within a Play* (dir. Mark P. Ring, 2004), a documentary about a U.S. production of *Hamlet* touring in Taiwan, stars a black actor as Hamlet. At a press conference in Taipei, a Taiwanese reporter wants to know why a black actor was cast as Hamlet. The director responds not with an explanation but with a shrug of his shoulders, as if the question were totally bizarre. To see Laura Bush's Shakespeare as somehow a faux multiculturalism, a cooptation or containment of Shakespeare's truly subversive energies, both ignores the way her rainbow Shakespeare is "politically correct" and begs the question of just what an authentic, progressive, anti-imperialistic American multicultural Shakespeare would be, and

Figure 9.2 Baz Luhrmann's shaded Shakespeare (1996).

Figure 9.3 James Gavin Bedford's shaded Shakespeare (2002).

how it would differ from Bush's.[9] Indeed, one could argue that Bush's multiculturalism only exposes the racism that underwrote multicultural accounts of racial difference all along. As Walter Benn Michaels argues, "The modern concept of culture is not ... a critique of racism; it is a form of racism. ... Our sense of culture is characteristically meant to displace race, but ... culture has turned out to be a way of continuing rather than repudiating racial thought" (Michaels, 683). It is worth asking if race now makes a difference when it comes to casting Shakespeare — and, if so, how?

Color Band of Brothers

To address these questions, I suggest that the discussion of the politics of civic ShakesPR as a vehicle of multiculturalism be framed in terms of ShakesPR's promotion through middlebrow mass media, especially television, largely because television is typically viewed as the most powerful of mass media. I use the term "civic ShakesPR" rather than "public Shakespeare" because "civic" raises issues about citizenship, immigration, and commerce related to the mediatization of literature in general and its promotion via middlebrow culture in particular.[10] Civic ShakesPR demands a significant rethinking on several fronts of what has come to be known in academic circles as political Shakespeare in particular and political criticism in general.

- In attending to civic ShakesPR, one must examine — dare I say it — a marginal area of Shakespeare performance that has received almost no critical attention: televisual Shakespeare.

- In attending to civic ShakesPR, one must refuse to oppose academia, high culture, and politics, on the one hand, and the professional class, middlebrow culture, and apolitical self-improvement, on the other. According to John Guillory, middlebrow culture (which he identifies with televisual and other mass media adaptations of canonical literary works seen on PBS's *Masterpiece Theatre* and the like) is resolutely antipathetic to politics in the United States: "Middlebrow culture ... sees culture as a means to individual self-improvement and has long since divorced such improvement from the area of political citizenship" (Guillory, 90). Yet the Bush Shakespeare agenda reworks both ends of Guillory's opposition between politics and culture, fully exploiting the mediatization of literature and theatre. For Laura Bush and the Bush administration, civic ShakesPR is both apolitical in appealing to Shakespeare's "greatness," producing apolitical interpretations and performances of Shakespeare's plays and poetry, and political in linking education to citizenship and immigrant assimilation.

- In attending to civic ShakesPR, one must acknowledge that there is a left-wing middlebrow culture as well, as both Left and Right tend to share the same ambivalence about television as either "a great democratic leveler in providing information to the public" or a "dumbing-down that ... comes with 'passive' viewing rather than 'active' reading" (McAlister, 244). Left-wing films about television that cite Shakespeare, such as *Quiz Show* (dir. Robert Redford, 1994) and *Good Night, and Good Luck* (dir. George Clooney, 2005), link whiteness, high culture citation, and civic highmindedness, regarding the entertaining, commercial aspects of television as a threat to the public interest and the intellectual journalist or academic. Academic accounts of the public sphere often mime this account of television: as public funds are linked with corporate and private sponsorship, so the argument goes, television is said to produce a phantom, undemocratic public sphere (or its supposed inversion in active fan subcultures) (see Burt 2006b).

- In attending to the politics of civic ShakesPR and multiculturalism, one must historicize the medium of television as well, taking into account the centripetal pull of vertical integration of new media and the centrifugal pull of the proliferation of new media screens.[11] Owing to the broadcasting deregulations that began in the 1980s and new media technologies, older TV series are widely available on cable rebroadcasts and on DVDs as well as via Internet television. The fantasies about civic ShakesPR and multiculturalism that have played out in commercial TV, notably middlebrow situation comedies involving a class production and/or discussion of a Shakespeare play, are now more readily accessible than ever before.

- In attending to civic ShakesPR, one must understand that civic television is white. I say "white" not only because the kinds of PBS *Masterpiece Theatre* programs Guillory mentions are adaptations of canonical works written by white, usually English authors, but also because avowedly civic programming is almost entirely composed of white people who, when talking about multiculturalism and Shakespeare, address a presumptively white viewer.

- In attending to civic ShakesPR on white television, one must acknowledge the fantasies of multiculturalism and register Shakespeare's Hy-Bard-ity, his crossing over races, nations, and cultures. Civic ShakesPR is both a transnational unconscious of the United States and a U.S. cultural imaginary of race and multiculturalism.

- Finally, in attending to civic ShakesPR in television and other mass media, one must analyze allusion rather than adaptation or citation. In addition to framing scenes of recitals, readings, theatrical rehearsals, and theatrical performances of Shakespeare plays, many television programs (and films) also often cite promotional, paratextual, and para-Shakespearean materials such as posters, movie theater marquees, busts, letters of the alphabet, character names, scripts, book covers, photographs, illustrations, or websites. These citations are "blind" not only in being barely visible references to Shakespeare and race but also in being encrypted, effectively buried, and hence meaningful, like symptoms.[12] The Shakespeare margins are not located in one place. As in Freud's unconscious, there is no performance topography that may be mapped; rather, Hy-Bard-ization is a dynamic process, and how one kind of Shakespeare circulates across different racially defined or inflected materials is what, in my view, demands analysis. Similarly, the paratextual Shakespeare does not have one location, but is "a transitional zone between text and beyond text" (Genette, 407). The framing of theatrical Shakespeare in another medium, be it film or television, doubles questions about casting (how a film is cast and how characters in the film are cast in a Shakespeare play) and helps make visible the ways in which Shakespeare, as a site of a capitalized American transnationalization, and race operate in national fantasies about "America" both within the United States and beyond its borders, like a traumatic kernel that can never be fully symbolized.[13] Though Shakespeare episodes vary in their aesthetic complexity, they nevertheless reward close reading, sometimes of a hyper, excessive kind. The episodes are sometimes in dialogue with a much older theatrical Shakespearean performance history and help make aspects of that history visible that have not been noticed and that, once noticed, challenge prevailing historicist and postcolonial accounts of Shakespeare and race.

Lowering the Color Bar/d

In the remainder of this essay, I want first to address some of the theoretical implications of framing the politics of civic ShakesPR in terms of middlebrow mass media by articulating a series of critical impasses that constitute what I call the color bind of Shakespeare's Hy-Bard-ization, or colorization. I will then explore some consequences of the ways in which the history of Shakespeare, race, and performance might be rewritten by examining three Shakespeare-related white television episodes that engage civic ShakesPR: *Othello*-related episodes of *The Lone Ranger* and *Have Gun — Will Travel*, with nearly all-white casts (Tonto, played by Jay Silverheels, being the one exception), and the final episode of the third season of *The West Wing*, with a multiracial cast.

In my view, the 1990s debate over race-based casting and race-blind casting has clearly been decided in favor of the latter, and, in consequence, has morphed in the later 1990s into a debate over the end of race, with left-wing academics challenging the conservative argument that race is over by saying that it is not.[14] This shift in the debate from casting to the end of race has left Shakespeare critics in what I call a color bind: in an effort to preserve or maximize the antiracism potential of Shakespeare and early modern race studies by historicizing Shakespeare, these critics have succeeded in universalizing race along Manichean lines. The anti-essentialist move to make race into a prosthetic performance that can be resignified, for example, makes race a historical constant; while black resignifications always challenge a supposedly all-white original Shakespeare and are always supposedly subversive because they perform a "real" blackness; conversely, white performances involving blackness are always under the gaze of a "white, imperial eye."[15] Unlike earlier critics of Shakespeare and race, who thought one kind of casting practice was bad and another good and celebrated the transition from one practice to another, critics now condemn virtually every particular casting of black roles, whether the actor is white or black, and applaud every all-black performance of Shakespeare.[16] Whether a white actor plays Othello as a light-skinned Moor (Orson Welles) or as a dark-skinned West African (Laurence Olivier), his performance will be called racist. If a good-looking black actor like Laurence Fishburne plays Othello, his body will be said to be exploited.[17] Whitening Othello is regarded as racist, but so too is blackening Othello.[18] Whether a black Shakespeare performance is colonial or postcolonial, antebellum or postbellum, it is typically recuperated as sly mimicry and a performative subversion of white Shakespeare.[19] Along similar lines, white anxiety about black masculinity is said to explain why white actors play Othello, whether in blackface or not.[20] As is generally the case in cultural studies, any criticism of multiculturalism, any narrative of changes in race and racism, is understood only as a backlash. Whereas these earlier critics thought they could prescribe the correct practice, critics now police productions they take to be politically incorrect.

I call the current state of affairs in criticism a color bind in part because universalizing race means that Shakespeare critics end up paradoxically supporting a case for racism. For starters, the arguments about Shakespeare and race noted above are frequently nonsensical. For example, if white male anxiety holds for all white males at all times, the very idea of a backlash is meaningless since such anxiety would always be present. Similarly, arguments that the black bodies of actors playing Othello are being exploited because they are commodified have no purchase. What body in the commercial media of theatre, television, and film is not commodified? Left-wing multiculturalists and antiracists share the same account of race as conservatives: both define the end of race in the same way, as the end of inequality and discrimination, and they differ only in thinking that race has or has not yet come to an end. Moreover, current work on Shakespeare and race is arguably more conformist than the Bush administration's Shakespeare.

The color bind of universalizing race to combat racism has produced color blind spots, by which I mean a lack of attention both to a wide range of Shakespeare materials related to race, to casting practices other than blackface, race-based, and race-blind, and to the way these practices may be understood. Recent accounts of the historical specificity of Shakespeare and the universality of race have produced a narrow account of race in Shakespeare, and a canonical set of Shakespeare citations. Accounts of Shakespeare and race remain focused on African American casting largely as a consequence of being Shakespeare-centric, focused on the black characters Aaron and Othello, with some attention to Shylock, Caliban, the changeling boy, the Muscovite disguises in *Love's Labor's Lost* and the Dark Lady of the Sonnets.[21] Similarly, performance criticism of *Othello* has attended almost exclusively to U.S. and U.K. performances and canonical film adaptations.[22] Consequently, no performance histories of *Othello* include discussions of Shakespeare in television such as the "Lamont as Othello" episode of *Sanford and Son*, blaxploitation films like *Othello: Black Commander* (dir. Max H. Boulois, 1982), and interracial pornographic film adaptations such as *Othello: Dangerous Desire* (dir. Joe D'Amato, 1998) and *Hotel O* (dir. Roy Karch, 2001).[23] Similarly neglected are Shakespeare's appearances in black television programs such as *What's Happening!*, *The Cosby Show*, *Cosby*, *Martin*, *My Wife and Kids*, *The Steve Harvey Show*, *That's So Raven*, *The Proud Family*, *Parent Hood*, *The Famous Jett Jackson*, and *Romeo!*, among others.[24] Casting theatrical Shakespeare productions does not raise the same kinds of issues raised about casting in television and film more generally because calls to integrate film and television have involved greater representation of actors of color, never race-blind casting, which has been limited to theatrical performance; hence race-blind productions of Shakespeare always appear in films, for example, that do not use race-blind casting.

Moreover, critics have two related color blind spots when it comes to Shakespeare, race, and performance: whiteface cosmetics and nation-blind casting. Critics in Shakespeare studies and in theatre and film studies more generally have productively attended to whiteness and performance in order not to confine race to people of color. Yet discussions of white performance ignore the practice of using whiteface cosmetics and are invariably locked into a white/black binary, with blacks "acting white" assimilated to existing notions of racial passing.[25] Though the practice of blacks wearing whiteface has continued in films like *White Chicks* (dir. Keenan Ivory Wayans, 2004), blacks doing whiteface Shakespeare is such a deep-seated taboo that it has become unthinkable and an all but forgotten practice.[26] Black actors using whiteface to perform Shakespeare dates back to the war of 1812, however, when an African-American sailor in Dartmoor prison played Juliet in whiteface with a black Romeo.[27] Ira Aldridge played Shylock and King Lear in whiteface. Similarly, the less famous actor Morgan Smith followed Ira Aldridge to England, where he played Othello, Richard III, Macbeth, Hamlet, and Shylock. He called himself "the coloured American tragedian," but "more than half his roles were nonblack, for which he appeared in whiteface" (Hill and Hatch, 64). Whiteface makeup was clearly not about passing, since the actors' racial identities were advertised and known to their audiences. Nor was the use of whiteface consistent. Ira Aldridge stopped whitening his hands at one point when playing the white roles of Shylock and King Lear. Metaphorical instances of whiteface are even more clearly not about passing, as when Buckwheat wears a blonde wig when playing Juliet in the Little Rascals' production of *Romeo and Juliet* in *Pay As You Exit* (dir. Gordon M. Douglas, 1936). Whites wear whiteface as well. In *Stage Beauty* (dir. Richard Eyre, 2004), for example, the male and female actors playing women's roles in Shakespeare's plays all wear white makeup.[28] Moreover, whiteface is still often used in Asian Shakespeare productions (and in non-Shakespeare productions and films) (see Sun).

A second, related blind spot is the practice of nation-blind casting. Laura Bush's use of a cultural import, Shakespeare, as a way of constructing a national imaginary to be used both for national consumption and for transnational export echoes the ways in which Shakespeare performance and Shakespeare cinema have both become transnationalized as well as colorblind in their casting. Sometimes foreign actors do not disguise their accents. For example, in Kenneth Branagh's *Much Ado About Nothing* (1993), *Hamlet* (1996), *Love's Labour's Lost* (2001), and *As You Like It* (2006), American actors speak with American accents. In *Shakespeare in Love* (dir. John Madden, 1998) and *Stage Beauty*, however, the American actors adopt English accents. There has been no debate over this casting practice like that over colorblind casting, of course, and indeed, nation-blind casting seems invisible. Yet it is worth noting that the nation-blind casting occurs in the recognizably Shakespeare film adaptations, while the attempts at passing occur in the fictional, romantic biopics about Shakespeare.

My sense is that what counts as race is now in flux. If race and racism are not over, a certain way of thinking about race and performance is, except perhaps in English departments. A film spinoff of *Othello*, *Black and White* (dir. James Toback, 1999), registers this shift, exploring precisely the way in which white kids have taken up black styles of speaking and mannerisms even as racial inequalities between whites and blacks persist.[29] Identity politics still persist in performance, but in ways that now often seem incoherent. What amounts to a taboo on representing racial antagonism, I would argue, comes out of a white liberal utopian fantasy. This fantasy may have unintentionally racist effects. For example, in the television version of *The Tempest* (dir. Jack Bender, 1998), set in the Mississippi Bayou during the Civil War, the African American actor Harold Perrineau Jr. plays a slave named Ariel while a white actor plays Gator-man, the equivalent of Caliban. The casting thereby avoids the potential for a racist interpretation of Miranda's attempted rape (along the lines of D. W. Griffith's *Birth of a Nation*) at the expense of using Caliban to explore a colonial reading of the play. As the issue of theatre, television, and film casting has been more or less settled, racial signifiers have become empty. There is now no consistent way of differentiating a racially marked Shakespeare of color from a racially unmarked white Shakespeare, if there ever was. As a modernized film adaptation of *The Taming of the Shrew*, the blacktopian[30] *Deliver Us from Eva* (dir. Gary Hardwick, 2003) does not significantly differ — apart from the skin color of its cast members — from the white spinoff *10 Things I Hate About You* (dir. Gil Junger, 1998). The two film spinoffs even share the same black actress, Gabrielle Union. Similarly, *Deliver Us from Eva* does not differ significantly with respect to how it modernizes *The Taming of the Shrew* from the earliest all-black spinoff of the play, *The Framing of the Shrew* (dir. Arvid E. Gillstrom, 1929).

Though the history of Shakespeare's performance is a history of the play's revision and fragmentation, a fantasy of an authentic Shakespeare has persisted across races in the United States until recently. Nineteenth-century African American Shakespeare actors were invested in a legitimate Shakespeare, just as white actors were. Henrietta Vinton Davis was advertised in 1883 in Boston as "the first lady to publicly essay a debut in Shakespeare and other legitimate characters" (Hill and Hatch, 65). Ira Aldridge even went so far as to bowdlerize the Shakespeare plays in which he performed in order to make them respectable. Similarly, a black church-sponsored production of *Othello* in the race film *Paradise in Harlem* (dir. Joseph Seiden, 1939) is said to be for the betterment of the community, and Lem, the character playing Othello, says he wants to give up his blackface cabaret act and do Shakespeare (for which he does not blacken up). In 1981, a *Fame* television episode (season one, episode seven) involved a black drama student anxious about playing

Othello and wanting help to do the language right. As late as 1991, the film *True Identity* (dir. Charles Lane) contrasts the desire of an African American character, Miles Pope (Lenny Henry), to act in *Othello* to his refusal to do the demeaning work demanded of him by a white director in television. While betraying stereotypes about African Americans in electronic media, *True Identity* remains quite faithful to a theatrical performance tradition of *Othello* in which Othello is played by a black actor. Along similar lines, James Avery and NPR are invested in distinguishing Avery's work (to pay the rent) in *Fresh Prince of Bel Air* and his portrayal of Othello in 2005.[31]

Yet this high-minded notion of colorizing not just Shakespeare but television programming and films more generally as a vehicle of racial integration and assimilation has involved not only an idealized notion of an authentic Shakespeare as the pinnacle of high culture (ignoring "low" Shakespeares) but has also made race relatively insignificant in Shakespeare performance. Marginal, Hy-Bard-ized Shakespeare materials require a rewriting of the performance history of Shakespeare and race that does not involve mythic transitions, either a Fall or a Redemption from one kind of more or less liberated or more or less repressive practice to another. Closer attention needs to be paid to the ways the end of different kinds of casting taboos also involves the introduction of new taboos, and these taboos do not work uniformly in a progressive direction. The shift to multiracial casting as the default position in itself might seem to be unwittingly racist because it is the dominant, white practice; only minority theatre companies remain invested in segregated casts (and sometimes colorblind casting). "White" companies are all multiracial. But to support segregated companies would of course now only seem racist. The option open to Orson Welles in 1935 — directing either all-black Shakespeare productions like *Voodoo Macbeth* or all-white productions, no matter how subversive they might be — is no longer open to whites.

Black Masked Man Othello

I would like to focus on a particular blind spot relating to white television and racially marked Shakespeare. Narratives of minority actors in Shakespeare plays that focus on firsts (the first black actor to play Othello; the first black actor to play Othello in the United States; the first black actor to play Othello at the National; the first black actor to play York in *Henry VI* at the RSC, and so on) to show how the color barrier has been broken cannot explain the diversity of white Othellos on TV, even when casting was still almost all white. Consider, for example, two television western episodes involving contradictory versions of Othello and married Shakespearean couples that aired on U.S. television within a year of each other. In "Outlaws in Greasepaint," the final episode of *The Lone Ranger* television series (1957), the Lone Ranger takes off his black mask to disguise himself as Othello wearing black greasepaint, to catch two former traveling Shakespearean actors turned robbers. In "The

Moor's Revenge," an episode of *Have Gun — Will Travel* (1958), Vincent Price plays a traveling Shakespearean actor who performs Othello as white while the actor's white wife (Patricia Morison) plays Desdemona.

In "Outlaws in Greasepaint" (episode 221, June 6, 1957), black make-up proves to be superior to white. The Lone Ranger (Clayton Moore) disguises himself as Othello in order to catch a married couple, De Witt and Lavinia Feversham, both members of a defunct Shakespearean repertory company who have turned to robbing Wells Fargo offices for a living. The episode begins in Pine Valley with the Reverend Prospero and his daughter Miranda asking directions of a bank teller as the bank closes for the day; once inside, they proceed to rob the bank. The camera cuts to a poster in close up that says:

> Coming Soon
> The Famous Manhattan Repertory Company
> Distinguished Traveling Players
> In the works of Shakespeare
> Featuring De Witt Feversham as Hamlet
> With his wife Lavinia Feversham as Ophelia

When Tonto (Jay Silverheels) explains that the most recent robbery was done by Reverend Prospero and Miranda, the Lone Ranger notes, "The characters from Shakespeare's play *The Tempest.* ... Always in disguise and using Shakespearean names." The doubling of robber and Shakespearean role is a dead giveaway. When Feversham tells the Lone Ranger his name is "Horatio Mon-

Figure 9.4 Scamming Shakespeare: *The Lone Ranger* (1957).

tague," the Lone Ranger smiles and says, "Thanks for giving yourself away so quickly. Montague is Romeo's last name. Horatio is a character in *Hamlet*."

The Lone Ranger searches his room, but does not turn up any stolen goods. When Lavinia returns to her room, the Lone Ranger pretends to be De Witt by coming out as Othello in blackface with a black wig, beard, turban, and earrings. Lavinia is deceived and lets it out that they have been hiding the goods in a trunk with a false bottom. Apparently, blackface is just as good a disguise as the Lone Ranger's black mask. Though earlier De Witt told Lavinia, as he was trying on beards, she "shall be the one to choose which disguise I shall wear tonight. Mercutio, Othello, Shylock," she now says it is ridiculous to rob dressed as Othello and Desdemona, since previously they have worn disguises such as a Civil War soldier and his daughter. In other words, an interracial couple will not be convincing. The interracial taboo, though not made explicit, is cued by her earlier pose as a Southern belle.

By limiting their disguises to white roles, either Shakespearean or extra-Shakespearean characters, the Fevershams are unable to elude the Lone Ranger. He sees through her pose as a Southern belle at the Wells Fargo office, and again, near the end of the episode after they have escaped by disguising themselves as grandfather, daughter, and baby granddaughter (a doll) riding in a covered wagon. Although the Lone Ranger lets them go as if he has fallen for their act, he soon stops and tells Tonto who they really are, saying "I've worn a disguise long enough to recognize make-up when I see it." White make-up is detectable; black is not. Only after the point is made explicitly does the Lone Ranger go after them again and arrest them. Though the Fevershams' acting involves accents and vocal mimicry, it is their inability to use make-up that proves them to be both bad outlaws and bad actors. By contrast, playing Othello, the equivalent of the black mask, enables the Lone Ranger to legitimate himself as an agent of the law rather than the robber Lavinia perceives him to be when she asks him why he is "wearing that mask" after he stops them in their wagon. The mask effectively becomes a transracial prosthesis in establishing the Lone Ranger as an agent of the law and moral good. "Who was that black masked man?" the tag line at the end of the episode almost seems to ask.

Othello, White Negro

In "The Moor's Revenge" episode of *Have Gun — Will Travel* (season 2, episode 54, December 27, 1958), the hero Paladin's black clothing and his links to Othello are similarly central, but they are more complicated by the series's emergent antiwestern elements (the antiracist, urbane, and hard-boiled hero dressed in black rather than white, for example). Guest star Vincent Price plays a traveling Shakespearean actor, Charles Matthews, who performs Othello without make-up while Matthews's white wife, Victoria Vestris (Patricia Morison), plays Desdemona. Though all the actors are white, the episode's racial unconscious, I will maintain, is registered in a series of opposites that are also doubles.

"The Moor's Revenge" episode begins by opposing San Francisco and San Diego as venues with audiences capable of appreciating Shakespeare. The episode opens with a poster of "The Tragedy of Othello / The Moor of Venice" in a theatre hallway, followed by a shot of Matthews and Vestris taking a bow after *Othello* has ended and then a shot of Paladin dressed in a suit, applauding. San Diego is posed as the anti-Shakespearean Other of San Francisco in a dinner conversation the three have afterward. The Shakespeareans tell Paladin that though the rest of their troupe has returned East, they will go to San Diego to perform Shakespeare by themselves. Paladin tells them not to go, advising that "a cattle town during a roundup can be an extremely dangerous place. ... Believe me. They're not looking for the kind of entertainment you're prepared to offer in San Diego." Vestris is skeptical, thinking that Paladin is fabricating a story about the Wild West, and avers that Shakespeare is universal: "For your information Mr. Paladin, *Othello* has moved audiences for two hundred years. I don't think our audience in San Diego will be any different." Matthews adds, "We have yet to find an audience, Mr. Paladin, that is not receptive to Shakespeare." Rather than being a civilizing force, however, the vain and increasingly defiant actors have to be tamed as much as their San Diego audience.

Once in San Diego, Vestris and Matthews discover that Paladin was right. The San Diego Opera House is in fact a saloon, and a sign over the door advertises Matthews as a comic, and Vestris as "beauty unadorned" whom the patrons can "see ALL of." Victoria comments in disgust, "Charles, we'll be playing in a saloon. This isn't a theatre. It's a saloon!" Doubling the action of *Othello*'s plot, the two actors become increasingly violent. Vestris rips up a somewhat revealing poster of her as Cleopatra, and Matthews is stopped from ripping up another poster of Vestris by a gunshot from Paladin's rival, the gunslinger Ben Jackson. *Othello* threatens to become the occasion for violence. Though Paladin is generally nonviolent and Jackson is a violent killer, the two are also doubled first and foremost by their appreciation of *Othello*, or at least of Vestris. During the performance of the death scene of *Othello*, the camera tracks left to show the performance over the shoulder of Paladin, sitting at one end of a row, then right back across the same row before stopping in a more tightly held shot over the shoulder of Jackson.

The death scene begins with Othello's lines from 3.3/4:

O curse of marriage,
That we can call these delicate creatures ours,
And not their appetites!
Her name is now begrimed and black.
O, now, forever

Farewell the tranquil mind! Farewell content!
Pride, pomp and circumstance ... Farewell!
Furnish me with some swift means of death.

During this speech, the camera cuts to Ben Jackson as the word "black" is heard in voice-over, then to Paladin, watching Jackson. So blackness connects Desdemona, now dressed in white, and Jackson, who is also like Othello in becoming jealous of the attention another man pays to the woman he loves (he is mistaken in thinking that Vestris and Matthews are not married). When Jackson pulls out a gun and says to Matthews, "I'll furnish you with some swift means of death," Paladin throws a chair at him and a brawl ensues. It stops after Paladin enters into a visual triangular relation to Matthews and Vestris, standing in front of the couple and ready to fight anyone else in the saloon. Paladin hands Jackson's gun over to Matthews, who says he does not know how to use it. In a version of the comical "Moor's Revenge" promised in the newspaper ad, Matthews accidentally fires the gun.

This suspension of violence and the comical harmlessness of it, which is and is not *Othello*, allows the death scene to proceed, with Paladin and Jackson agreeing to draw guns after it is over. But instead of sorting out and settling the difference between Paladin, as the white cowboy who uses fists but not guns, from the irrationally violent "black" Jackson, the *Othello* death scene continues to link the two hired guns; moreover, the performance is interrupted once again, such that Paladin is and is not Othello, both white and a "white negro."[32] The camera tracks back to Jackson as Othello gets angrier

Figure 9.5 Black jealousy/White Moor: *Have Gun – Will Travel* (1958).

with Desdemona, and the camera focuses in a tighter shot on the right side of Jackson's face as the death scene continues. Instead of whitening a black Othello, however, Paladin blackens a white Othello (Matthews) while distancing him from another white Othello, Jackson.

The performance of the death scene from *Othello* is also doubled. The saloon death scene falls into two parts, separated by the brawl. The seriocomic interruption of the brawl between the death scene doubles the performance itself, signaling the retitling the play *The Moor's Revenge* and calling it a "comedy." The episode flags nineteenth-century minstrel versions of *Othello* and bizarre British "travesties." *Dars de Money* (c. 1880), for example, reduces the final scene of *Othello* to a comic brawl. Pushing the point further, we could say it signals the problem of comedy in *Othello* itself (see Bristol). Just as the performance location shifts from San Francisco to San Diego and from opera house to saloon, so it shifts from stage to floor, with chairs replacing the bed, and the audience encircling the performers. And just as the insertion of the line about Desdemona's blackness being read when she has changed from a black dress into a white one echoes the opening transition from the poster to the curtain call, so Desdemona's death seems to be the end of the performance, as the audience applauds. Only when Matthews motions the audience to stop does he recite Othello's final speech to end the performance. Similarly, Paladin is the first to applaud after she dies. Paladin applauds a second time after Othello dies, but then stops suddenly.

By the end of the episode, everything is sorted out as it usually is in the series. Shakespeare is as well received in San Diego as he is in San Francisco, and a gunfight is averted. Not wanting to take advantage of Paladin's sore hand, Jackson postpones the fight indefinitely. Still, a number of questions remain: Why these doublings and repetitions? Why use *Othello* rather than another play like *Hamlet* or *Romeo and Juliet* in the first place? And why do it white rather than in blackface? Answers to these questions do not lie only in TV casting codes or practices excluding nonwhites, since TV *Othellos* were not uniform, as the *Lone Ranger* episode makes clear. And Shakespeare could also work in cross-racial plots. In "Lady in the Stagecoach," a *Have Gun — Will Travel* episode (season 2, episode 57, January 17, 1959) that aired two weeks after "The Moor's Revenge," the Boston-educated Paladin and an Apache princess's shared knowledge of Shakespeare, particularly *Romeo and Juliet*, saves them and three racist white stagecoach passengers from being killed by a robber.

At risk of seeming to over-read "The Moor's Revenge" episode wildly, I want to suggest that the doublings and repetitions are about a foreclosure of race and Shakespeare, especially *Othello*, that marks Shakespeare's Americanization. The opening shot that skips over the *Othello* performance from poster to applause and the premature applause for the death scene at the saloon are instances not just of dramatic economy but of televisual foreclosure. Even more telling, if far more subtle, however, is a small detail involving the spelling of Matthews's name and a plot hole involving Paladin's decision to go to San Diego and not show Matthews and Vestris an even racier newspaper advertisement for the San Diego performance. The actors' names are also crucial to Jackson's misinterpretation and jealousy. Jackson mistakes a husband for a lover because the two actors have different stage surnames. In all these cases, Matthews is spelled with two *t*s. In the advertisement Paladin keeps from the actors, however, Matthews is spelled with one *t*. The ad reads:

BEAUTY — FUN — BEAUTY The Luscious Victoria Vestris For Whom A Lust-Maddened Monarch Gave Up His Throne. And Charles Mathews, King Of The Comics, In That Rollicking Comedy, "The Moor's Revenge." SHOCKING — SAUCY — NAUGHTY Playing All Through The Cattle Run. San Diego Opera House. L. Bellingham, Manager.

In addition to asking why the spelling is different here, we may also ask why Paladin does not show the actors the advertisement. And why does he fold it up again and then cover it over with his calling card, echoed by the series's theme music?[33] And why is this version racier — "shocking — saucy — naughty" — than the actual advertisement in the saloon, which bowdlerizes the "cunning whore of Venice" as the "cunning woman of Venice?"

The moment showing the single-*t* spelling is also a moment of open repression and literal cover-up that alerts the viewer to the actual Charles Mathews, who spelled his name with a single *t*. Mathews was a nineteenth-century English vaudevillian who did one-man shows, including Shakespearean speeches. Mathews's first wife was an English actress called Madame Vestris, and both traveled together to America (Mathews, 82–87).[34] The ad also renames Lucia Vestris as Luscious Victoria Vestris. And oddly enough, Madame Vestris was persuaded to go to America with Mathews by one Mr. Price, "the proprietor of the New York and other principal theatres" (Mathews, 286). Price shut down a *Romeo and Juliet* planned by Ira Aldridge because, Aldridge maintained, Price was "jealous of the success of the 'real Ethiopians'" (McAllister, 170). Mathews did play the role of Othello, though not in San Francisco. Adding to this admittedly bizarre series of what may only be coincidences is the fact that Mathews taught Shakespeare to the first professional African American Shakespearean, James Hewlett, on board a ship. When Hewlett imitated Mathews or wrote about him, Hewlett spelled his named with two *t*s (reprinted in Thompson, 119, 121, 145, 146; cf. 147–148).

I follow out this chain not in order to suggest, in what would no doubt seem a paranoid fashion, that the episode encodes some secret history about Mathews and Hewlett. I want to use it to show that both doublings in the episode and in theatre history prior to it show the uncanniness of Shakespeare's racial history in the United States, a history that entails a series of imitations and doubles from across races (white to black) and nations (America to

England), and within races (black to black) rather than oppositions between a foreclosed, whitened revision or repression of history and real black history, or between white colonizer and black colonized. The full uncanniness of this fascinating and sad history is beyond the scope of this essay. Suffice it to say that in addition to imitating Mathews, Hewlett emulated Edmund Kean's Richard III after Kean met a bad reception from whites and a positive one from blacks in Boston in 1825, and Hewlett thereafter cited Kean in titling himself "Shakespeare's proud representative" (White, 81, 140–141). Ira Aldridge, Hewlett's junior and sometime colleague, followed suit, titling himself "Mr. Keene" (sic) for the first six or seven years of his career (White, 163; Potter, 109). More pointedly, Hewlett and Aldridge both called themselves "the African Roscius," even though they were both of mixed race and married white wives. And the African American tourist William Wells Brown saw a man in London, "neither white, nor black," perform Othello; this actor claimed to be an African prince and also called himself the "African Roscius" (Brown, 203).

The racial unconscious of "The Moor's Revenge" does not take us to an original theft of African American Shakespeare but reveals that Shakespeare's performance history always has an unconscious, uncanny dimension involving a complex, even vertiginous circulation of black Americans taught by white English actors, who in turn imitated African American actors for English audiences, and who were then imitated by African American actors, who were imitated by other African American actors, and so on. Indeed, the double status of the saloon *Moor's Revenge*, both comic parody and serious performance, and the multiple allusions to *The Moor's Revenge*, from two antiracist Restoration plays (Aphra Behn's *Abdelazer, or The Moor's Revenge* and Edward Young's *The Revenge*) to nineteenth-century racist parodies and travesties, calls into question the standard history of American Othellos as a whitening of blackness, which starts with minstrel adaptations such as *Dars-de-Money, Alexander DoMar, Othello: An Interesting Drama, Rather!* (1850), and Maurice Dowling's 1834 *Othello Travestie*, and reads all subsequent performance history in light of its "shadow."[35] This standard academic account, which focuses on racist exclusion of African Americans from legitimate Shakespeare, occludes the transatlantic and transracial prehistory of African American Shakespearean performance (Hewlett came from the West Indies, for example, and ended his career in Trinidad). Paladin's white Negro Othello offers an avenue to a fuller understanding of performance than one based on Judith Butler's deconstruction of original and copy (Butler, 298–319).

Hung Be the Heavens with Black Shakespeare

If "The Moor's Revenge" destabilizes any notion of an original Shakespeare and a parody of a white Othello and a black Othello, "Posse Comitatus," the last episode of the third season of *The West Wing* (episode 322, May 22, 2002), goes even further in linking race to what I call faux Shakespeare; that is, the Shakespeare referred to in the show does not actually exist, but, in this case, viewers are apparently not supposed to notice. This season of the show also introduced a black actor playing a White House staffer in response to charges that the cast of the show was not racially diverse.[36] Both Shakespeare and race come into play as the final episode involves a turn toward the right in terms of foreign policy in the wake of 9/11. In the final episode, "Posse Comitatus," President Jed Bartlet, a liberal-minded, Clinton-like Democrat, gives an illegal order to assassinate a terrorist Arab defense minister of the fictitious country of Qumar, a former protectorate of Britain. This plotline merges in the season finale with another plotline that involves the murder of a male Secret Service agent (Mark Harmon) assigned to protect the female press secretary while she and Bartlet attend a British production of an amalgamation of some of Shakespeare's history plays entitled *The Wars of the Roses* at the Booth The-atre on Broadway, New York City, which combines period dress with modern military costumes.

The play and the assassination are obviously meant to parallel each other, but the Shakespeare history plays, especially a scene shown with Margaret triumphing over York, suggest a related parallel between the developing romance of the Secret Service agent and the press secretary and *The Taming of the Shrew*. Shots of red and white roses are seen several times, most con-spicuously in the President's office before he talks to his psychoanalyst about what is reported to be a five-and-a-half-hour play (Bartlet displaces talk of the assassination with talk of the play), and after a Secret Service agent is shot and killed in the final sequence.

"Posse Comitatus" relates faux Shakespeare to racial coloring as a way of emphasizing Bartlet's turn to the right. The blackening of Shakespeare coin-cides with the blackening of the presidency. Although not clearly marked as such in the way that Qumar is a clearly fictionalized Arab country (regularly vilified on the series), the British Shakespeare Company is a fabrication, and *The Wars of the Roses* is unlike *The Wars of the Roses* staged at the RSC by Peter Hall (1963–1964) and Michael Bogdonov (1986–1989). Viewers familiar with Shakespeare's history plays may notice something odd when Bartlet men-tions that the production is made up of the unlikely combination of "*Henry V, Three Henry VI,* and *Henry VIII.*" In addition to showing scenes from the first tetralogy, the "Posse Comitatus" episode shows *The Wars of the Roses* ending with an interpolated song entitled "Patriotic Chorus" that was not written by Shakespeare. A young black actor credited as "Young Boy" (Adrian Diamond) sings the non-Shakespearean song alone on center stage: "England arise! Join in the chorus! / It is a new made song you should be singing. / See in the skies, flutt'ring before us / What the bright bird of peace is bringing!" The rest of the cast then join him in singing the rest of the song. The interpolated song has a bizarre, perhaps vertiginous connection to Shakespeare via the 1983 RSC production of Charles Dickens's *The Life and Adventures of Nicholas Nickleby*, an actual hit in London's West End and on Broadway and filmed as a television miniseries, in which a theatre troupe does an adaptation of *Romeo and Juliet*.[37] "Patriotic Chorus" is sung by the theatre troupe after the performance of *Romeo and Juliet* ends. Further marking the *West Wing*'s *Wars of the Roses* performance as fake in ways unnoticeable to the average viewer, writer and producer Aaron Sorkin even included fake blurbs below the marquee poster and a fake playbill for the production, shown being held by the press secretary.

The authenticity of the Shakespeare performance is similarly complicated by the indeterminacy of its nationality. Though the production company is said to be British, the cast is American and they speak in American accents. A flag in the performance, on the left of the stage, has an eagle that looks very much like the one on the U.S. presidential seal. The performance of what is actually supposed to be a Victorian song further complicates the nationality of the production since it is performed as red, white, and blue streamers are waved by the chorus, evoking the American flag. The episode makes quite clear that the production is not a musical, a genre in which Shakespeare has frequently been adapted in the United States (see Teague). One white staffer describes it as "five hours of King Henrys with musical interludes and a dinner break." Bartlet is even more pointed when responding to his psychoanalyst, who concludes that "it's a musical": "No, but there's going to be singing from time to time. And one of the songs is a song I love. I can't think of the name now, but it's an Edwardian. They should be singing it in the dining hall at Christ College at Cambridge. The chorus is 'and victorious in war shall be made glorious in peace.' I was just singing it this morning."

In order to understand the significance of both the performance of fake Shakespeare and the casting of a light-skinned black actor to begin the post-performance chorus after the Shakespeare performance is over, we need first to examine how the episode connects race and Shakespeare from the start. Charlie Young (Dulé Hill), a black staffer, is the first person to talk to Bartlet about the play, explaining to the President that "this is nontraditional Shakespeare." Bartlet responds: "What does that mean? It sounds modern." Young explains, "The director uses music and song and theatrical devices along the way." Bartlet: "Well, it doesn't sound bad." Bartlet is identified both with a blackened Shakespeare and with a fake Shakespeare, undercutting the opposition between dark-skinned Arab terrorist and white U.S. President. Initially, Shakespeare seems to be white. At the beginning of the final episode, a television monitor next to a white newscaster shows a photo of Bartlet with the caption "I Heart New York: Bartlet and the Bard." Bartlet is specifically aligned as a Democrat with Shakespeare, in contrast to his opponent, Republican Governor Ritchie (James Brolin), who goes to see a Yankees game instead of *The Wars of the Roses*. Yet, as we have seen, Bartlet is also identified with the interpolated song performed at the end, which he refers to as "my song." In the second of the final three episodes, a black admiral named Fitzwallace (John Amos), the most hawkish of the cabinet members and the one who makes and leads the case for assassination, invokes the battle of Agincourt along the way.[38] The cast of the play seen in the Shakespeare scenes is all white, even though York has been played in an RSC production by a black actor. Yet the poster for the production has a black background and is seen at night, and the first line heard is "Hung be the heavens with black." The racial meaning of the word "black" in this line was articulated as early as 1840, when a newspaper published a poem by an African American poet about the English actor Edward Shales performing the role of Richard III, which used the "Hung be the heavens with black" as its title (Cockrell, 90).

The more fake the Shakespeare becomes, the more black he becomes as well, though blackness takes different shades. The light-skinned young black actor echoes the dark-skinned black staffer who told the President that the play is modern, as well as a young dark-skinned black man whose "Big Brother" is the Secret Service agent who is shot and killed. The last shots of the episode show Bartlet's face progressively in darker shadows until he steps out of his theatre box and stands motionless behind a curtain, becoming a distorted, deformed black silhouette. Exeter's line about Henry V, "We mourn in black," which was muffled in voice-over as the camera cut to the theatre hallway earlier in the episode, returns, as it were, in this final shot.

President Bartlet is both aligned with a binational (U.S. and U.K.), modern, and traditional, English and American, white and black, or Hy-Bard-ized Shakespeare, and he literally and metaphorically becomes blackened as he preserves the republic by violating international law and his own executive order prohibiting the assassination of a foreign leader. Earlier in the final episode,

Figure 9.6 Black Bartlet: *The West Wing* (2002).

Bartlet invokes Machiavelli's *The Prince*. Given that *Henry VI, Part Three* ends with the murder of Henry VI by Richard, duke of Gloucester, the *West Wing* episode implies that the answer to Bartlet's question "Which Plantagenet do I resemble most?" is Dick Plantagenet, a.k.a. Richard III. In the *West Wing* episode's analogy between our post-9/11 and post-Camelot world of realpolitik and permanent wartime, on the one hand, and Shakespeare's post-Henry V world of the English Civil War, on the other hand, Bartlet, like Richard III, sets "the murderous Machiavel to school" (3.2.193). Like Richard III and the fake Shakespeare production, Bartlet compromises and rules by deception in the shadows; and like Richard III, Bartlet "might crush all obstacles, and throw them down, / That stood betwixt [his] shadow and a crown." Bartlet's Kennedy-like liberal idealism and belief in moral absolutes give way to violations of international law and the merger of professional theatre and political theatre.

We can also understand how far right the *West Wing* is willing to go in making Bartlet into a dark and deformed Tricky Dick III by understanding how the *Wars of the Roses* parallel fits into the Secret Service agent's murder and why it follows the scene with Margaret stripping York of the paper crown she has placed upon his head. The white Secret Service agent, who is called "slow-witted" by his African American "young brother," is also feminized. He is not only a brother rather than a father but also is shown to be a failed Petruchio, wooed by rather than wooing the press secretary, a single mother with a teenaged daughter. The agent dies not so much a brother who sheds his blood on St. Crispin's Day but as a failed white brother and failed romantic partner/stepfather. In contrast, Bartlet stands at a marked remove from domesticity. His wife does not appear in this episode and is only seen once, in a photograph on Bartlet's desk. A harder President emerges at the end of the season finale as a leader baptized in the fire of illegal machine gun bursts, whose moral darkness is figured by blackness. Yet black characters also provide a positive, idealizing counterpoint to Bartlet's dark Richard III. The young black actor, who sings a very positive song about peace and prosperity, appears to be cast nontraditionally, as if fast-forwarding past the English Civil War to a seemingly still enduring British Empire. The hawkish African American Admiral Fitzwallace also helps shape a mythological contrast between Henry V and Richard III. In celebrating the battle of Agincourt as an example of the good old days of chivalrous combat, the admiral with a Scottish name (shades of *Braveheart*'s William Wallace?) neglects to mention that Henry V ordered that the French prisoners be killed. Even as blackness is embraced by a white President in ways that mark him off from weaker men, African American characters are enlisted in articulating an idealized, softened version of what Bartlet is doing as he takes a sharp turn to the political right.

The Remains of Race/The Remains of the Play

In this essay, I have turned to reframing the enlistment of a civic ShakesPR by Left and Right and the color bind of Shakespeare, race, and performance by focusing primarily on television episodes that frame Shakespeare as a remainder: characters rehearse or perform in scenes from the plays; paratextual and promotional materials also encrypt and allude to Shakespearean performance history. Focusing on para-Shakespeare materials as blind spots, one gets a fuller understanding both of the way promoting Shakespeare is both civic and commercial, on the one hand, and on the other, of the ways in which race and racialized performances are used to sell Shakespeare to students, especially students of color. Attending to marginal, obscure Shakespeare materials which have an eccentric relation to Shakespeare's plays, one sees a parallel between Shakespeare's circulation and race: like Shakespeare, race remains, as a leftover which both does and does not signify. Yet it is precisely because of their eccentric pull that these marginal materials deepen our understanding of Shakespeare's performance history in the United States and enable a critique of some of the blind spots in academic middlebrow fantasies and narratives about Shakespeare, race, mass media, and performance.

Notes

1. A photo of Bush and Leno and a transcript of the interview are posted on the White House website: http://www.whitehouse.gov/news/releases/2005/04/images/20050426-5_leno9jpg-515h.html.
2. See http://www.shakespeareinamericancommunities.org/home.html. On citations of Shakespeare by U.S. politicians, see Garber.
3. The controversy of this move was discussed by Richard Burt, Tom Cartelli, and Douglas Lanier in a National Public Radio interview (Chicago syndicated show "Odyssey" with host Gretchen Helfrich) on "Shakespeare in America," April 28, 2003.
4. On the *Henry V* and Bush analogy, see Scott Newstrom's excellent article.
5. For descriptions of the theatre companies and links to their websites, see the NEA Shakespeare in American Communities webpage: http://www.nea.gov/national/shakespeare/Companies.html.
6. For a lengthy and informative article on the program, with interviews and photos (by Andy Nelson), see Wiltenburg. See also Raidonis; Kelly 2001a and 2001b; and Hayes.
7. On multicultural imperialism, see Kaplan and Pease; Kaplan; McAlister; and Winkler.
8. See the *Step into Shakespeare* website affiliated with Will Power to Youth: http://www.stepintoshakespeare.com.
9. Avowedly left-wing citizens may well like Laura Bush's politically correct Shakespeare. See, for example, an episode of the liberal PBS program *NOW* that aired on September 2, 2005. In the second segment of the program, host David Brancaccio introduced parts of *The Hobart Shakespeareans* documentary: "Next time somebody moans about the messed-up state of our schools in America, I want you to think about this amazing guy: Rafe Esquith, educator. He teaches at Hobart Elementary in a tough part of Los Angeles. He gets fifth graders, many new to English, doing Shakespeare that'll make you cry."
10. See especially chapter 22, "Manufactured Publicity and Nonpublic Opinion: the Voting Behavior of the Population," in Habermas. For a useful critique of this view, see Robbins.
11. For developments related to television and digital media, see Karnitsching; Albergotti and McWilliams; *New York Times* Editorial Board; and S. Collins.
12. On cinematic encryption, see Conley; Cohen; and Petro.
13. On the traumatic kernel, see Žižek.

14. Conservatives have adopted the metaphor of colorblindness to advance their argument that race has ended. Race is over, so the conservative argument goes, because equal skills and equal knowledge are supposedly available to all, and, moreover, supposedly translate into equal opportunity for employment and earnings. See, for example, Cose and D'Souza.

15. See, for example, Hodgdon. Hodgdon wonders, "how a Spike Lee or a Cassie Lemons might tackle Shakespeare's *Othello*. Might they, one wonders, frame up a visual — and aural — field that would enable seeing its racial ethics and textual erotics with a difference?" (104). Yet why should these directors be imagined as having the capacity to do *Othello* differently, except for the fact that they are black? A racist essentialism paradoxically underwrites Hodgdon's fantasy of an antiracist *Othello* film.

16. See, for example, Starks; Royster 1998; Daileader; and Chatterjee and Singh.

17. Consider Ania Loomba's rhetorical use of comments by black actors who have played Othello. Loomba gives authority to their comments about the racism of Shakespeare's *Othello* by virtue of their blackness. The issue of the play's racism or antiracism is reduced to a question of whether it is challenging or reinforcing white stereotypes about black males (110–111).

18. On whitening Othello as racist see, for example, Henderson. On blackening Othello as racist see, for example, Cartmell.

19. For a typical example, see Over. Over cites Judith Butler to argue that performance is always a copy, an imitation, and finds that a "similar dynamic was present in the African Theatre, where subversive possibilities were presented by Brown and Hewlett through their 'imitations' of well-known white performers" (78). For a more nuanced account of the African Theatre and James Hewlett, see White.

20. See, for example, Rippey. Note how Rippy shifts from indefinite to definite articles so that "a white masculine psyche in crisis" (27) quickly becomes universalized as totalizing "the white male psyche" (31).

21. See, for example, the essays in *Shakespeare and Race* (Alexander and Wells).

22. See, for example, Vaughan and Potter. I discuss a number of examples of African American Shakespeare in Burt (2002).

23. Even Douglas Lanier (2005a) does not mention these materials in his fine essay in the Sourcebooks Shakespeare edition of *Othello*. Francesca T. Royster (2003) has explored this area, however, in relation to blaxploitation films and *Antony and Cleopatra*.

24. I have catalogued Shakespeare episodes from all of these programs in *Shakespeares after Shakespeare: An Encyclopedia of the Bard in Mass Media and Popular Culture* (Burt 2006).

25. The following devote attention to both the reality and metaphor of whiteface performances but never discuss the material cosmetics used to create them: McAllister; Foster; Knight; Pelligrini; and Cockrell.

26. The practice of blacks doing whiteface in the theatre came to an end when Roscoe Lee Browne filed a discrimination lawsuit after being told he would have to perform for the Seattle Repertory Theatre in white roles wearing whiteface (Hill and Hatch, 464).

27. A white American sailor named Benjamin Palmer held in Dartmoor prison during the War of 1812 claimed to have "witnessed a tall strapping negro, over six feet high, painted white, murdering the part of Juliet to the Romeo of another tall dark skin" (Bolster, 102–130).

28. For a discussion of this film, see Burt 2006a.

29. The film's link to *Othello* is spelled out in a classroom scene where white kids and black kids talk about not being what their race expects them to be. The teacher (Jared Leto) ends the class by mentioning Shakespeare's *Othello*: "Iago, who has no identity, says 'I am not what I am.'"

30. By "blacktopian" I mean film and television programs that invert the norms of white programming and film: in Blacktopia, the world is populated almost entirely by black people who have access to wealth.

31. The copy for the July 12, 2005 NPR interview with Avery reads: "James Avery is best known as Philip Banks, the wealthy uncle of Will Smith's character in the 1990s TV series *The Fresh Prince of Bel-Air*. But his work encompasses a broader range, from movies to voicing animation to his latest role onstage in a California production of William Shakespeare's *Othello*": http://www.npr.org/templates/story/story.php?storyId=4748045.

32. Norman Mailer's "The White Negro: Superficial Reflections on the Hipster" in *Advertisements for Myself* (1956, 337–358) had appeared only a few years earlier.
33. Each *Have Gun — Will Travel* episode is broken up into three parts, each followed by commercials. In some episodes, the card appears at the end of the first part, as it does in "The Moor's Revenge."
34. Mathews was also the basis for Vincent Crumels in Dickens's novel *The Adventures of Nicholas Nickleby*.
35. See MacDonald and K. Collins. Douglas Lanier (2005b) expands this account into an overarching account of all race-related Shakespeare performance in the United States.
36. According to Andy Dehnart, "Back in 1999, Kweisi Mfume, president of the NAACP, blasted prime-time television's 'virtual whitewash in programming' of black characters and actors. He was reacting to the 1999 prime-time lineup, which had not one black or minority performer in a leading role in any of 26 new programs. The networks reacted — and fast. Shows without black actors added them. *The West Wing*, for example, on NBC, quickly cast Dulé Hill as the president's personal aide."
37. In the televised version of *Nicholas Nickleby*, see the end of episode 4. The connection to *Nicholas Nickleby* also suggests that U.S. and U.K. Shakespeares cannot be properly contrasted as fake versus authentic. U.K. Shakespeare is already more or less fake, involving rewritings and reinventions.
38. Fitzwallace says, "The battle of Agincourt. This was the French fighting against the English archers. This was like a polo match. The battles were observed by heralds and they picked the winners. And if a soldier lay down his arms he was treated humanely. And the international laws that you're talking about, this was where a lot of them were written. At a time and a place where you could tell the difference between wartime and peacetime."

References

Albergotti, Reed, and Gary McWilliams. "The Elephant in your Living Room." *Wall Street Journal*, November 12, 2005.

Alexander, Catherine, and Stanley Wells, eds. *Shakespeare and Race*. Cambridge: Cambridge University Press, 2000.

Bolster, Jeffrey. *Black Jacks: African American Seamen in the Age of Sail*. Cambridge, MA: Harvard University Press, 1997.

Bristol, Michael. *Big-Time Shakespeare*. London and New York: Routledge, 1996.

Brown, William Wells. *The Travels of William Wells Brown, Including Narrative of William Wells Brown, a Fugitive Slave* (1848), edited by Paul Jefferson. New York: Markus Wiener, 1991.

Burt, Richard. "Backstage Pass(ing): *Stage Beauty*, *Othello*, and the Makeup of Race." In *Shakespeare on Screen*, edited by Mark Thornton Burnett and Ramona Wray. Edinburgh: Edinburgh University Press, 2006a.

Burt, Richard. "Selling Out Shakespeare." In *Shakespeares after Shakespeare: An Encyclopedia of the Bard in Mass Media and Popular Culture*, edited by Richard Burt. Westport, CT: Greenwood, 2006b.

Burt, Richard. "Shakespeare, More or Less?" In *Shakespeares after Shakespeare,* edited by Richard Burt. Westport, CT: Greenwood, 2006c.

Burt, Richard. "Slammin' Shakespeare in Acc(id)ents Yet Unknown: Liveness, Cinem(edi)a, and Racial Dis-integration." *Shakespeare Quarterly* 53 (2002): 201–226.

Butler, Judith. "Imitation and Gender Insubordination." In *The Lesbian and Gay Studies Reader*, edited by Henry Abelove and David Halperin. London and New York: Routledge, 1993.

Cartmell, Deborah. "Shakespeare and Race: *Othello* I.iii." In *Talking Shakespeare: Shakespeare into the Millennium*, edited by Deborah Cartmell and Michael Scott. Basingstoke and New York: Palgrave, 2001.

Chatterjee, Sudipto, and Jyotsna Singh. "Moor or Less? The Surveillance of *Othello*, Calcutta 1848." In *Shakespeare and Appropriation*, edited by Christy Desmet and Robert Sawyer. London and New York: Routledge, 1999.

Cockrell, Dale. *Demons of Disorder: Early Minstrels and their World*. Cambridge: Cambridge University Press, 1997.

Cohen, Tom. *Hitchcock's Cryptonymies*. 2 vols. Minneapolis: University of Minnesota Press, 2005.

Collins, Kris. "White-Washing the Black-a-Moor: *Othello*, Negro Minstrelsy and Parodies of Blackness." *Journal of American Culture* 19 (1996): 87–101.

Collins, Scott. "Some Television Reruns Hit Their Prime on DVD." *Los Angeles Times*, November 13, 2005.

Conley, Tom. *Film Hieroglyphs: Ruptures in Classical Cinema*. Minneapolis: University of Minnesota Press, 1991.

Cose, Ellis. *Color-Blind: Seeing Beyond Race in a Race-Obsessed World*. New York: Harper Collins, 1997.

Daileader, Celia. "Casting Black Actors: Beyond Othellophilia." In *Shakespeare and Race*, edited by Catherine Alexander and Stanley Wells. Cambridge: Cambridge University Press, 2000.

Dehnart, Andy. "Don't call it a comeback." Salon.com, May 23, 2001: http://www.salon.com/ent/tv/feature/2001/05/23/black_tv/index.html

D'Souza, Dinesh. *The End of Racism: Principles for a Multicultural Society*. New York: Free Press, 1995.

Esquith, Rafe. *There are No Shortcuts: How an Inner-City Teacher — Winner of the American Teacher Award — Inspires His Students and Challenges Us To Rethink the Way We Educate Our Children*. New York: Pantheon, 2003.

Foster, Gwendolyn Audrey. *Performing Whiteness: Postmodern Re/Constructions in the Cinema*. Albany: State University of New York Press, 2003.

Garber, Marjorie. "Character Assassination: Shakespeare, Anita Hill, and JFK." In *Media Spectacles*, edited by Marjorie Garber, Jann Matlock, and Rebecca Walkowitz. London and New York: Routledge, 1993.

Genette, Gerard. *Paratexts: Thresholds of Interpretation*. Translated by Jane E. Lewin. Cambridge: Cambridge University Press, 1997.

Guillory, John. "The Ordeal of Middlebrow Culture." *Transition* 67 (1995): 82–92.

Habermas, Jürgen. *The Structural Transformation of the Public Sphere: An Inquiry into a Category of Bourgeois Society*. Translated by Thomas Burger. Cambridge, MA: MIT Press, 1989.

Hayes, Steve. "Shakespeare Goes to Prison: Slouching toward Agincourt in an L.A. County Lockup." *American Theatre* 13 (1996): 82–84.

Henderson, Diana. "Othello Redux?: Scott's *Kenilworth* and the Trickiness of 'Race' on the Nineteenth-Century Stage." In *Victorian Shakespeare*, vol. 2, edited by Gail Marshall and Adrian Poole. Basingstoke and New York: Palgrave Macmillan, 2003.

Hill, Errol, and James Hatch. *A History of African-American Theatre*. Cambridge: Cambridge University Press, 2003.

Hodgdon, Barbara. "Race-ing *Othello*, Re-engendering White-Out, II." In *Shakespeare, the Movie, II*, edited by Richard Burt and Lynda Boose. London and New York: Routledge, 2003.

Kaplan, Amy. *The Anarchy of Empire in the Making of U.S. Culture*. Cambridge, MA: Harvard University Press, 2002.

Kaplan, Amy, and Donald Pease, eds. *Cultures of United States Imperialisms*. Durham, NC: Duke University Press, 1993.

Karnitsching, Matthew. "AOL to Offer 'Vintage' TV Free — With Ads." *Wall Street Journal*, November 14, 2005.

Kelly, Philippa. "'Make not your thoughts your prisons': Shakespeare in a Different Place." *Shakespeare* 5 (2001a): 10–13.

Kelly, Philippa. "The Shakespeare Redemption." *American Theatre* 18 (2001b): 32–35, 134–135.

Knight, Arthur. *Disintegrating the Musical: Black Performance and the American Musical Film*. Durham, NC: Duke University Press, 2002.

Lanier, Douglas. "'It is the green-eyed monster': *Othello* and Pop Culture." In *Othello*, edited by Marie Macaisa et al. Naperville, IL: Sourcebooks, 2005a.

Lanier, Douglas. "Minstrelsy, Jazz, Rap: Shakespeare, African American Music, and Cultural Legitimation." *Borrowers and Lenders: The Journal of Shakespeare and Appropriation* 1 (2005b): 1–29.

The Life of Charles James Mathews; Chiefly Autobiographical with Selections from his Correspondence and Speeches. Vol. 2. Edited by Charles Dickens. London: Macmillan, 1879.

Loomba, Ania. *Shakespeare, Race, and Colonialism*. Oxford: Oxford University Press, 2002.

MacDonald, Joyce Green. "Acting Black: *Othello*, Othello Burlesque, and the Performance of Blackness." *Theatre Journal* 46 (1994): 231–249.

Mailer, Norman. *Advertisements for Myself*. New York: Putnam, 1959.

Mathews, Charles. *Memoirs of Charles Mathews*. Vol. 3. Edited by Mrs. Mathews. London: Richard Bentle, 1849.

McAlister, Melanie. *Epic Encounters: Culture, Media, and U.S. Interests in the Middle East, 1945–2000.* Berkeley: University of California Press, 2001.

McAllister, Marvin Edward. *White People Do Not Know How To Behave at Entertainments Designed for Ladies and Gentlemen of Colour: William Brown's African & American Theatre.* Chapel Hill: University of North Carolina Press, 2003.

Michaels, Walter Benn. "Race into Culture: A Critical Genealogy of Cultural Identity." *Critical Inquiry* 18 (1992): 655–685.

Newstrom, Scott. "Step Aside, I'll Show thee a President: George W and Henry V?" PopPolitics. Com, May 1, 2003.

New York Times Editorial Board. "The Eternal Now of Television." *New York Times*, November 11, 2005.

Over, William. "New York's African Theatre: Shakespeare Reprinted." In *Shakespeare Without Class: Misappropriations of Cultural Capital*, edited by Don Hedrick and Bryan Reynolds. New York: Palgrave, 2000.

Pelligrini, Anne. *Performance Anxieties: Staging Psychoanalysis, Staging Race.* London and New York: Routledge, 1997.

Petro, Patrice, ed. *Fugitive Images: From Photography to Video.* Bloomington: Indiana University Press, 1995.

Potter, Lois. *Othello.* Manchester: Manchester University Press, 2002.

Raidonis, Laura. "'Here is not a creature but myself': Shakespearean Reception in Solitary Confinement." *Shakespeare Yearbook* 12 (2001): 122–130.

Rippey, Marguerite. "All Our *Othellos*: Black Monsters and White Masks on the American Screen." In *Spectacular Shakespeare: Critical Theory and Popular Cinema*, edited by Courtney Lehmann and Lisa Starks. Madison: Fairleigh Dickinson Press, 2002.

Robbins, Bruce. *The Public Sphere.* Minneapolis: University of Minnesota Press, 1993.

Royster, Francesca T. *Becoming Cleopatra: The Shifting Image of an Icon.* New York: Palgrave, 2003.

Royster, Francesca T. "The 'End of Race' and the Future of Early Modern Cultural Studies." *Shakespeare Studies* 26 (1998): 59–69.

Starks, Lisa. "The Veiled (Hot) Bed of Race and Desire: Parker's *Othello* and the Stereotype as Screen Fetish." *Post Script: Essays in Film and the Humanities* 17 (1997): 64–78.

Sun, William. "The Power and Problems of Performance across Ethnic Lines: An Alternative Approach to Non-Traditional Casting." *Drama Review* 44 (2000): 86–95.

Teague, Fran. "Swingin' Shakespeare from Harlem to Broadway." *Borrowers and Lenders: The Journal of Shakespeare and Appropriation* 1 (2005): 1–9.

Thernstrom, Abigail. *No Excuses: Closing the Racial Gap in Learning.* New York: Simon and Schuster, 2003.

Thompson, George, Jr. *A Documentary History of the African Theatre.* Evanston: Northwestern University Press, 1998.

Vaughan, Virginia Mason. *Othello: A Contextual History.* Cambridge: Cambridge University Press, 1994.

White, Shane. *Stories of Freedom in Black New York.* Cambridge, MA: Harvard University Press, 2002.

Wiltenburg, Mary. "Acting with Conviction." *Christian Science Monitor*, July 24, 2002.

Winkler, Martin, ed. *Classical Myth and Culture in the Cinema.* Oxford: Oxford University Press, 1991.

Žižek, Slavoj. *The Sublime Object of Ideology.* London and New York: Verso, 1989.

10

Gestures of Performance: Rethinking Race in Contemporary Shakespeare

MARGO HENDRICKS

In October 2002 I was invited to join a group of Shakespearean scholars and actors in a workshop organized by Lynette Hunter and Peter Lichtenfels held at the Globe Theatre, London. The workshop, "Fifth Wall," was conceived to foster conversations between theatre practitioners and literary scholars on a variety of issues often viewed as dividing the two groups, especially in the area of Shakespearean playtexts. The session I was involved in, "Gesture and Language," was lively, filled with contradictions, and, in the end, it fostered greater understanding of the complexities of Shakespeare's dramatic language and its performance. As someone intrigued by the performance of racial identities in general and in productions (theatrical and film) based upon Shakespeare's playtexts, I found great appeal in the idea of adding gesture to my theoretical exploration of race and Shakespeare. As is the case with nearly all intellectual conversations, there is a turning point when an elusive connection between ideas suddenly materializes, becoming solid, focused, and intelligible. This point occurred in the session when Alan Cox[1] spoke about improvisation as part of the rehearsal process, "what [he] called 'making rituals' that went on 'all the time'" (Arden, Hendricks, and Hunter, 63). It was not so much the notion of rituals but the making of them and the importance of gesture to that making that animated the conversation; it was the realization that, in the process of creating theatrical or performance cultures, writers, actors, directors, designers, and stage crews all participate in the making of rituals that become not only associated with Shakespearean playtexts but also become a necessary component of their performance.[2] The relationship between ritual and gesture, as Cox's observations throughout the workshop indicated, is a synergistic one, and this synergy is very much a manifestation of the actor's body.

"Gesture," Adam Kendon writes, "is a name for visible action when it is used as an utterance or as a part of an utterance" (Kendon, 7). By "utterance," Kendon means "any ensemble of action that counts for others as an attempt by the actor to 'give' information of some sort" (7). Furthermore, utterance "is any unit of activity that is treated by those co-present as a communicative 'move,' 'turn' or 'contribution.' Such units of activity may be constructed from speech or from visible bodily action or from combinations of these two modalities" (7). Gesture, then, "is the visible bodily action that has a role in such units of action" (7). More precisely, Kendon writes that gesture refers to "a movement of the body, or any part of it, that is expressive of thought or feeling" (7–8). In other words, gestures are deliberate uses of bodily movements that add significance or meaning to spoken language. And, he concludes, "it is through the orientation of the body and, especially through the orientation of the eyes, that information is provided about the direction and nature of a person's attention," as well as "about the nature of their intentions and attitudes" (1).

Very few of the theatrical practitioners and scholars involved in the "Fifth Wall" workshop would disagree with Kendon's definition of gesture, or "that gesture is a vital aspect of communication," yet there was an acknowledgment of an "inbuilt difficulty of communication ... [on] the topic of gesture itself" (Arden et al., 61). As Annabel Arden reminded participants in the "Fifth Wall" workshop, a simple gesture can profoundly affect the way a performative moment is understood. Describing a moment in a production of Caryl Churchill's *A Number*, "a play about family relations, breakdown and divorce," Annabel Arden remarks that "at one point Gambon simply glanced at the wedding ring on his hand and the audience thrilled to the suddenly charged air of that small detailed action." It was, Arden continued, "the 'perfect gesture' for that play. For the practitioner, the body itself is a gesture" (64). Arden went on to observe that "the body animates the text," to which I replied "if the body animates the text, 'the text animates gesture'" (61).

The "Fifth Wall" workshop was the catalyst for this essay. In the process of reflecting on the ideas, comments, and challenges posed by Shakespearean actors and directors during the workshop, I began to consider the possibility that "racial identity" is more often than not a gestural act of performance, especially in Shakespearean playtexts; not only does gesture make visible a character's "intentions and attitudes," it also may make visible a race for the performing body (whether it is the actual actor playing a character or the character itself). Furthermore, I came to understand that both the theory and practice of colorblind (or nontraditional) casting, whether in theatrical or cinematic productions of Shakespeare's playtexts, cannot escape this gestural act. In the discussion that follows, I want to address two questions. First, how does one (actor, director, or costume designer for example) go about gesturing race into existence in a performance? And second, if I am correct in arguing that race is merely gestural, why do we continue to debate directorial decisions about casting Shakespeare's playtexts, whether on the stage or in film?

Sensing Race

In a course I taught on race, a student posed a simple query that kept the members of the class in animated discussion for some time: How does a blind person know race? The question is profoundly complex and perhaps incapable of truly being answered. Yet undaunted, we worried the problem until we reached something of a resolution that, in retrospect, seems apropos to the topic of this essay: in truth, a blind person could not know race as a sighted individual would, given that the current definition of race is predicated upon physical cues accessible through sight. Thus a blind person would have to be taught to use her auditory and tactile senses to recognize race (voice, facial features, and hair would have to be the basis for knowledge). Of course, there are problems with a tactile mode of racializing, as most people would not willingly allow themselves to be subject to an exploratory examination by a stranger so that the stranger could identify them "racially." In addition, one class member pointed out, there are people of African ancestry whose hair, skin color, and facial features are such that the blind person could mistakenly classify them as another racial category. So my class decided that the auditory sense would have to be the principal means by which a society guides a blind individual's initiation into racial consciousness and ideology. Listening to speech and discerning differences between individual speakers might be a better method for the sight-impaired person to categorize racially those around him. Hence, dialect, tonal timbre, pronunciation, and vocabulary would be the predicates for articulating racial difference. Noting and classifying the differences (in effect, recognizing accents and/or dialects) becomes part of the racial and ethnic taxonomy that allows a sight-impaired individual to know races without actually seeing race.

This method has its flaws, however, most notably in performance venues such as stage and film. In her insightful essay "False Accents: Embodied Dialects and the Characterization of Ethnicity and Nationality," Angela Pao illustrates that the "racial" or "ethnic" voice is a highly problematic proposition within performance spaces. Beginning with a discussion of an anecdotal account of the "dubbing" of "Oriental intonation" (i.e., that of American speakers of Asian languages) for "authentic" Chinese accents, Pao illuminates the ways in which contemporary performance media (television, film, and stage) help to sustain racist racializing practices (see Pao). The dialects or accents are nearly always of nonnative speakers of English, and the English is either unintelligible or comically "broken" (i.e., nonstandard). To many African Americans this terrain is quite familiar. In addition to the complication of skin color, linguistic patterns among a large segment of the African American population in the United States have also made racial identification appear relatively easy. In his article "Slammin' Shakespeare in Acc(id)ents Yet Unknown: Liveness, Cinem(edi)a, and Racial dis-integration," Richard Burt unwittingly falls into the ideological trap about language and race that Pao so cogently exposes in her article.

Burt's aim in the essay is "not only to fill a missing gap in Shakespeare and black film criticism but also to show that such materials invite theorizing

Shakespeare, race, and film in terms of 'cinem(edi)a,'" especially the notion of "authenticity" in relation to Shakespeare's playtexts and their continued circulation within contemporary American culture (201). While Burt rightly criticizes those who assume an "authentic" Shakespearean performance (that is, a visually "correct" rendering of Elizabethan stage performance, albeit a performance that now includes women), he does undermine his own interrogation by arguing that sound is racially marked: "In my examples of Shakespeare cinemedia, the simulation of liveness requires the synchronization of visual and *aural* racial signifiers (in order to achieve cinematic or televisual realism)" (Burt, 208; emphasis added). As a reading of his essay reveals, what Burt means by "aural" racial signifiers in this context is the difference between English as spoken or pronounced by whites and English as spoken by blacks.

As I note in another essay dealing with Shakespearean performance, "The idea that one can always 'tell' a black person by voice and speech assumes that there is a singularity in voice for all blacks. Variables in speech pattern, timbre, tone, and vocabulary are as distinct between black people as they are between non-black people" (Hendricks, 521). Furthermore, as a result of the deep influence of hip-hop culture across the globe, the so-called black American speech pattern is increasingly heard internationally. Within the United States, many white, Asian, and Latino young people (suburban and urban) are "speaking" with what Burt would define as an "aural racial signifier." What is more striking is the fact that the so-called black voice has served as a political bridge across ethnicities and nationalities. In essence, the language of hip-hop culture is emblematic of what Pao describes as "what once would have been perceived as an unrealistic or 'unnatural' matching of body and accent has become or is in the process of becoming a common phenomenon" (Pao, 369). Pao continues:

> This is what has happened with British South Asians who speak English not with Indian or Pakistani accents, nor with the standard British accents, but with the regional accents of the industrial cities of the Midlands or with the ethnic Japanese from South America who speak English with a Spanish accent. It is what is beginning to happen with the children of Chinese immigrants who learn Irish before they have mastered English, or with Arab Americans who speak with regional rather than General American accents. (Pao, 369–370)

Pao's discussion of accents has serious implications for stage and film casting, especially the former. As she rightly argues, "As things stand in American theatre, unless experimental casting is being used as part of the production concept, racially authentic casting (sometimes rather broadly defined) has become the rule, with the character's ethnic identity being commonly constituted through empathy and an appropriate accent" (Pao, 369). The idea of colorblind or nontraditional casting, not surprisingly, has its more vocal critics among the groups that are most often marginalized in United States theatre.[3] One voice, that of the late African American playwright August Wilson, stands out in opposition to the concept of colorblind casting. In a talk given at Princeton in 1996, Wilson raised the stakes on the idea of colorblind casting. His talk *The Ground on Which I Stand*, first printed by the Theatre Communications Group and reprinted in 1998 in the journal *Callaloo*, was, as two writers observed, "potent and provocative enough to transform a long-smoldering brushfire into a flaming feud" (Saltzman and Plett 1997). About colorblind or nontraditional casting August Wilson argued:

> To mount an all black production of *Death of a Salesman* or any other play conceived for white actors as an investigation of the human condition through the specifics of white culture is to deny us our own humanity, our own history, and the need to make our own investigations from the cultural ground on which we stand as black Americans. ... The idea of colorblind casting is the same idea of assimilation that black Americans have been rejecting for the past 380 years. For the record we reject it again. We reject any attempt to blot us out, to reinvent history and ignore our presence or to maim our spiritual product. (Wilson, 30–31)

Though Wilson acknowledged that playwrights such as Shakespeare influenced "the ground on which [he] stands," it is race that matters (11). For Wilson, colorblind casting does not disrupt but rather reiterates ideologies about black cultural inferiority.

Despite Wilson's concerns, the issue will not disappear, and such casting decisions remain fraught and much debated. For example, when the actor Bob Devin Jones was cast as Don John in Saint Petersburg, Florida's American Stage's Shakespeare in the Park production of *Much Ado About Nothing*, he was questioned about accepting a role as a villain: "A friend asked me ... 'so what I want to know is what does it feel like being the only African-American and also playing the villain?'" (quoted in Fleming). The unspoken concern behind the query, as Jones noted, was the potential for "negative racial stereotyping." Director Justin Emeka, a student in the University of Washington's School of Drama, took a different approach to the issue of nontraditional or colorblind casting. Emeka directed a multicultural cast in his production of *Macbeth* and deployed his cast "to incorporate race and culture into the telling of the story" (Wick). Emeka conceptualized his production in terms of the U.S. Civil War and its aftermath. He depicted the witches as "newly freed slaves" and Macbeth as a "fierce northern general"; Duncan was a "Lincolnesque figure hated by Macbeth's southern belle wife"; and "Banquo is an African-American soldier equal to Macbeth in merit who has been held back because of his race" (Wick).

Like many other directors, Emeka treated Shakespeare's playtext as a working palette, making "bold choices, bold edits" to tell a story about betrayal and a "nation divided" because of race. In making his decisions, the director sought to "go beyond so-called 'colorblind casting,' a system that encourages the casting of non-white actors in roles traditionally played by whites without any alteration in those roles" (Wick). Emeka argued:

> "When colorblind casting began it was progressive, because it was letting people of color into the theater. … But really what you're saying with that is, 'We'll let you be white and act like you are just like everybody else.' There's something that's kind of dehumanizing about that. This production for me was an experiment in saying, 'Let's not just let black actors in; let's incorporate their culture into the world, the telling of the story.'" (quoted in Wick)

In essence, according to the writer of the article, Emeka viewed his casting decision as an opportunity for "black actors to play what he calls black roles" (Wick). One of the unknowns in Emeka's production is whether he retained Shakespeare's language intact — that is, whether the actors spoke Shakespeare's actual words, or whether the director modernized the play's language to reflect the modernity in which the play was set ("bold edits"). In other words, did the actors deploy Southern and black accents or dialects and American colloquial language, or did they adhere to the tradition of speaking the Jacobean verse that Shakespeare wrote?

What is striking about Justin Emeka's comments on his production decisions is that they are achingly familiar responses within the debates surrounding nontraditional and colorblind casting. On the one hand, the director seeks to validate the idea of Shakespeare's universality with a multicultural cast; yet, on the other hand, he also wants to repudiate that notion by localizing his production in "black" American culture. In many ways, productions of this type are weighed down by the still problematic discourse of race in theatrical performances of Shakespeare's playtexts. Race in this context is always a priori located in skin color, and with rare exceptions that color is "black." When a director seeks to disrupt what she or he sees as the racism that shadows both Shakespearean playtexts and their performances, more often than not the director disturbs the surface rather than disrupting it. The director's efforts (no matter how brilliant or diverse the cast) may not effectively redefine the language, gestures, and ideologies of the plays and their characterizations to achieve directorial aims. This is not to argue that Shakespearean language somehow transcends political agendas; rather, political agendas are often blind to their own limitations. The end result is a curious culturally schizophrenic position on casting that can satisfy neither side of the debate.

Even when a production is not explicitly framed in the familiar binary terms of black and white, race often becomes part of the conceptualization of the production. The Stratford Festival of Canada's 2003 staging of *Pericles* exemplifies this situation. In her review of the play, Margaret Jane Kidnie writes that "all modern productions of *Pericles* are challenged to find suitable, and suitably resonant, cultural and performance traditions within which to locate the figure of Gower" (Kidnie, 307). The director of the production Kidnie is reviewing "transposed and extended Pericles's journeys, originally along the eastern and northern Mediterranean coast to Arabia and India, to the far East" (311). How the playtext's "constantly changing locale" (and, I would argue, ethnicity or race) was conveyed was through costume design:

> Pentapolis, where the members of Simonides's court dressed in kimonos and geta sandals, was Japanese, while the bare-chested men wearing white turbans and off-white lengths of cloth wrapped around their waists visually located Ephesus in Indonesia. Female actors draped head to foot in black chadors or burqas with full-faced views, and male actors dressed in kaffiyehs and loose robes with dark cloaks, belted and trimmed with heavy embroidery, created Antioch as a blend of Arab influences. (Kidnie, 311)

Props such as hookahs and "hand-held fans for the geishas" served to reiterate the ethnic or racializing process that marked the production.

Just as with the Saint Petersburg and University of Washington productions, the cast of Stratford's *Pericles* was "multicultural." In a footnote, Kidnie quotes from an e-mail sent by the director, Leon Rubin: "I decided early on to locate the play mainly in the Far East and I insisted appropriate actors would be cast. ... I wanted to use a richly multiculturally-influenced cast with diverse looks and cultural roots. I feel Stratford should be doing this" (317). Thus Kidnie writes, "*The Adventures of Pericles* told its audience a story about self and the foreign other. The neutral body was defined by the white male courtiers of this Greek Tyre, the place Pericles called home, and this body functioned as the normative perspective — the constructed I/eye — through which we read the exotic, often dangerous markings of race, gender, and ethnicity" (313). For Kidnie, Rubin's concept, while fascinating to watch, was troubling for its "miscues" and "heavily overdetermined in terms of [the] race and ethnicity" of bodies ("the kechak chorus in Ephesus or the kimonoed court in Pentapolis, for instance, seemed not Indonesian or Japanese but European or, equally distracting, African" [317]). In the end, Kidnie argues, "the conception shaping the exotic, marked body in this Ontario production ... presented a stereotyped and imprecisely executed treatment of race and culture that did little to challenge assumptions that the 'real' Shakespearean body is white and of European (preferably British) descent."[4]

Kidnie's essay, like Richard Burt's "Slammin' Shakespeare," represents a useful starting place for my consideration of race as a gestural act. In both essays, the performed body is a body to be read and, ideologically, made meaning of in relation to cultural intersections with Shakespeare's playtexts. How we read that body is very much determined by its movements, gestures, and its appearance — make-up, costume, and, of course, the actor's body. To illustrate this point, I want to turn to three films that draw upon or make reference to Shakespeare's playtexts: Julie Taymor's *Titus*, Baz Luhrmann's *William Shakespeare's Romeo + Juliet,* and Andrzej Bartkowiak's *Romeo Must Die.* Specifically, I will look at three instances of what would be viewed as highly charged moments in the films: the cinematic image of Aaron at the party celebrating the marriage of Tamora and Saturnius in Taymor's *Titus*; the opening scene of Luhrmann's *Romeo + Juliet*; and Han's entrance into Silk's Club in *Romeo Must Die.* My aim is to expand our understanding of these films as mediations of race in Anglo-American culture.[5] More importantly, my reading of specific scenes in these films is my attempt to register the significance of the gestural performance of racial identity in contemporary productions of Shakespeare's playtexts.

"It's in the way that you use it"

One of the more striking figures in Shakespeare's *Titus Andronicus* is Aaron the Moor. In the playtext, Aaron sits as the ominous figure of doom, the Satanic instigator of Titus's fall, and the emblem of unbridled lust. Recent essays have dealt adroitly with the depiction of Aaron as a highly marked racial/racist figuration. What I want to explore in Taymor's film of Shakespeare's playtext is the importance of gestures to the construction of Aaron's racial identity. The African American body of the actor portraying Aaron (Harry Lennix) immediately localizes the relationship between Moor and skin color for the film's audience. Yet like Shakespeare's playtext, there is ambiguity about Aaron's racial identity that skin color cannot overwrite. Thinking about Aaron's status before his capture by the Romans, we must realize that we do not know much about Aaron and his relationship to the Goths, except that he is the lover of Tamora the Queen. This lack of knowledge provides Taymor and Lennix an opportunity to interject a "nobility" into Lennix's portrayal of Aaron. The result is a complex and paradoxical villain. Taymor's film, in ways not possible just with a reading of the playtext, highlights the complex range of racial signifiers the actor's — and through him the character's — body can project. During a panoramic shot of a wild party scene (clearly celebrating the union of Tamora and the Emperor Saturnius), the cinematic spectator catches her first glimpse of Aaron: he is standing alone, a glass of wine and a cigarette in hand, gazing out at the tableau before him — clearly an outsider yet very much part of the court. How the actor is positioned (above the crowd, on a step or a ledge) makes the specific object of his gaze somewhat mysterious: Is he merely a spectator of the excess of the Roman court, or is he studying his mistress with her new husband?

The shot of Aaron is extraordinary in that it is framed by erotic Greek vase paintings recapitulated on the walls of the chamber and in the excesses of the party, yet he is clothed in dark blue trousers (Turkish in design, loose-fitting but tapered at the ankles) and a robe or caftan of the same hue, belted with a sash and held together by a circle of gold. Aaron's garments and his tonsured look give him a priestly, ascetic image (one need only recall the costuming of *The Mission*'s Jeremy Irons and Robert De Niro to know whence Aaron's clothing derives its Jesuit appearance). The clothing totally encompasses his body except for his face and hands, giving him a priestly air, disrupted only by the glass of wine held in his hand. What is notable about Aaron is the positioning and movement of his body. Aaron's right forearm is bent at the elbow and hidden behind him, almost as if he is hiding something. His body leans slightly to the right, as if he is a member of the party yet not entirely of it. What is most interesting about the moment is the gestural way in which Aaron holds his glass. Aaron's pinky finger, second finger, and thumb hold the glass, while his middle and first fingers hold the cigarette. The camera lingers briefly on the shot, Aaron's hand and the glass prominent in the spectator's gaze. What we notice almost immediately is the elegant length of the actor's fingers and the way they hold the glass.

The hand animates our sense of who Aaron is — two fingers pointing upwards toward, but not directly at, his face, drawing attention to the contrasting blackness of his tie and the whiteness of his shirt, which in turn brings attention to his brown face. Were we to mask his face so that the only visible part of his body is his hand, we would find that the shade of Aaron's hand is quite similar to those of the server just below him and the woman seated near the server, and Aaron's racial identity would be relatively unintelligible. We do,

Figure 10.1 Aaron's gesture: *Titus* (2000).

however, see Aaron's face and with it the racializing effect of the hand's gesture, as, in the shot, the hand occupies almost the same visual space as his face.

The hand, in Taymor's film, is a profoundly racializing motif.[6] Aaron's hand directs the gaze to the predicates within the film that mark Aaron's blackness, his foreignness, his refusal to become assimilated into Roman society: on the one side is the room filled with white people (Romans and Goths), on the other side are his scarred face, his alien clothing, his brown-skinned hand elegant against the clear glass, the militaristic stance, the look of disdain on his face. When Aaron moves, it is to stand in front of a white pillar, a movement that heightens our awareness of the fact that he is the only dark-skinned person in the room. As Aaron repositions himself in front of the pillar and he crosses his arms, we realize that the glass is no longer in his hand — a cinematic gaffe, as we do not see him give the glass to another or put it down. What we do notice is that a flicker of uncertainty crosses his face as he watches his mistress being kissed by her new husband.

The effect of Aaron's gestures is both paradoxical and achingly familiar in the representation of people of African ancestry in the performance of racial identity. The bodily cues affirm his identity as an outsider, marginalized in both his color and position, as well as his powerlessness as he watches his mistress and her new husband. The paradox is that Taymor's and Lennix's vision of Aaron is one of nobility — in effect, the noble Moor that is Othello — and not the barbaric savagery that Shakespeare's playtext constructs and with which Taymor opens and concludes the film.[7] Aaron's villainy, then, becomes a study in contrasts for Taymor as, apparently, she seeks to ameliorate — or at least mediate — the problematic ideology that associates Aaron's blackness with evil. Unfortunately, her intervention is constrained by Shakespeare's playtext and the performative gestures Lennix uses that draw attention to and connections between his color and his identity as a racialized villain. Aaron's Moorishness (his racial identity) becomes located, interestingly enough, not in Lennix's skin color but in the actor's body and the way he uses it.

A similar tactic occurs in Baz Luhrmann's *William Shakespeare's Romeo + Juliet*. In the opening scene of the film, the rival Montague and Capulet "gangs" arrive at a gas station simultaneously. Because a van (filled with school girls and a nun) blocks each gang's view of the other, neither group is aware of the other's existence. Again gestures and costuming contribute to the defining of "ethnic" or racial differences: the Montagues are dressed in bright shirts with Christian iconography. In contrast, the Capulets appear as dark, menacing figures. The first figure we see, Abra, is dressed in dark clothing (black leather jacket and black trousers), his dark hair and beard giving him a very sinister appearance. Across the gas station, the rivals posture, flourishing guns and exchanging words. The exchange ends with Abra flinging his jacket off his shoulders and flashing a malevolent grin, his upper teeth encased in silver with the word "Sin" inscribed in the metal. One of the Montague boys, a frightened expression on his face, falls back into their car as Abra yells "Boo!" The confrontation escalates until Benvolio walks out of the restroom; he draws his gun and the two Capulets freeze. This scene is all about gestures: the constant waving of guns, the darting glances, and the woman's purse striking the head of a Montague. As the tension mounts between the Montague boys and the Capulets, all the audience hears are the clicks of the guns' safety catches being released, until the squeaking of a hanging metal sign overrides all other noises. In between the squeaks, a scratchy sound occurs and Benvolio turns toward it.

What Benvolio, and the audience, hears and then sees is Tybalt Capulet (played by John Leguizamo) striking a match and lighting a cigarillo. Just as with Aaron, what stands out are the hand gestures that draw attention to Tybalt's face. The match is held delicately in a vertical position between Tybalt's first and middle fingers; his thumb provides support beneath the two fingers to keep the match upright while the second finger is bent parallel to the middle finger and the little finger is vertical. The cigarillo is brown and creates a chiastic contrast between Tybalt's hand and his face in profile. Its brownness emphasizes the delicate, almost effeminate gesture Tybalt makes and, importantly, the dark tuft of hair just below his full lower lip. The next shot (and sound) is the match falling to the ground and hitting Tybalt's metallic heel as he turns toward Benvolio and the others. The actor's face occupies the left side of the screen, and a caption, "Tybalt CAPULET Prince of Cats Juliet's cousin," the right side. If in the initial shot Tybalt's racial identity was ambiguous, we are under no illusions with this second one. The dark eyes, the sideburns with a single curl, the shadow of a mustache, and the small goatee often seen on Latino men, as well as his suddenly slightly darker skin, all serve to mark him racially.

In a gesture that adds emphasis to his characterization, the actor smiles and slowly draws open his jacket. Like the lighting of the cigarillo, this gesture is crafted with exquisite elegance and deliberation. Tybalt's fingers become signifiers of meaning: they point simultaneously to an image of Christ (with stigmata) on a reddish brown shirt, and to Tybalt himself. The fingers of the right hand direct our gaze to Tybalt's belt even as they make clear he is drawing the jacket open. The fingers of the left hand, closed in a gesture of self-referential pointing, shift our gaze to the face of Christ, which bears a slight resemblance to the actor performing Tybalt in the color of his skin and his garment. Like the right hand, the fingers of the left hand are also performing the task of revealing what is inside the jacket. The next two frames explode on the screen as Tybalt exposes the gun hidden inside his jacket pocket and its twin concealed at his waist. Again, his hands are the performative measure by which Tybalt's racial identity is marked. As the actor draws a gun and aims it, his hands dominate every movement he makes for the remainder of the scene.

Figure 10.2 Tybalt's gesture: *Romeo + Juliet* (1996).

The shoot-out is vividly choreographed, leaving the audience breathless and knowing that what they are watching is a race war.

My third example is taken from the film *Romeo Must Die* (2000) staring Jet Li and the singer Aaliyah. Similar to Luhrmann's film, Bartkowiak localizes the *Romeo and Juliet* plot in contemporary America. The film depicts the violent conflict between rival ethnic families in twentieth-century Oakland, California. One family is Asian (the father emigrated from China), and the other is African American. The conflict clearly is orchestrated by Mac (Machiavelli), the aide to the African American kingpin O'Day, and Kai, the aide to Ch'u, a Chinese American gang lord. Our hero Han Sing, a former police officer imprisoned in Hong Kong for crimes committed by his father, receives word that his brother Po has been murdered. Han escapes and travels to Oakland to find Po's killer. The film is primarily a showcase for Jet Li's martial arts skills. Thus, the storyline is neither original nor complicated. The screenplay by Eric Bernt and John Jarrell locates the narrative in a contemporary California city noted for its changing demographics (at the time of writing this essay, Oakland is approximately 36 percent African American, 24 percent white, 22 percent Latino/Hispanic, and 15 percent Asian). The white presence in the film, interestingly, is minimal, although it is clear that the economic power does for the most part reside with Roth (a white developer, though his name signals his potential Jewishness). Han successfully exposes the double dealings of Mac and Kai, and, after confronting his father with the fact that he (Han) knows that Ch'u is responsible for the murder of Po, Han wins the girl (Trish O'Day) and walks away.

What makes the film interesting to Shakespearean studies, as well as critical race studies, is its rewriting of the *Romeo and Juliet* narrative. Set in a violent world of guns, drugs, and class conflict, *Romeo Must Die* uses Shakespeare's storyline as an attempt to redefine our perceptions about race.[8] Asian Han and African American Trish find themselves attracted to each other despite the emerging racial or ethnic conflict between the two families. Because Jet Li's martial skills are the reason for the film, the film's development of the romantic relationship between Han and Trish is at best superficial (much like that of *Romeo and Juliet*). Throughout the film "racial" identity is marked whenever there is interaction between Asian and African American. The actor's skin color and linguistic accent or dialect define each character's racial subjectivity in familiar and predictable ways. Yet there are two moments where the template for racialization is disrupted, and it is gesture that effects this disruption.

After her brother is murdered, Trish seeks Han's aid in finding the killer. Han shares with Trish information (a list of addresses) he has discovered in his investigation of his brother's death. One of the addresses is the club Po visited just before his death. Han persuades Trish to take him there. As the couple starts to enter the club, Trish stops Han and checks out his appearance. She removes her cap and places it on his head. With a slight grimace, she turns the cap around so that the brim is worn backward. "Now you're giving me some b-boy flavor," she says. Han looks puzzled and says "What?" As the two walk towards the club, Trish smiles, "Hip-hop." A serious expression on his face, Han repeats the phrase "hip-hop." Trish smiles again: "Yeah, hip-hop." Han stops and takes gum from his pocket. The camera shot captures both Trish and Han, facing each other, as he clearly is about to offer her some. Their hands are close yet not touching, his slightly raised above hers, her fingers close ready to receive his gift. He gives her the gum and says, "I know hip-hop." In what is clearly to be read as parody, Han grabs his pants at the waist and readjusts them as he swivels his hips before engaging in a "black" swagger as the couple walk into the club. Han's gestures situate him simultaneously in two racial typologies, one ethnic (Asian) and one performative (African American). Han's performance as a "black man" can take place only through bodily gestures: wearing the cap backward, gum chewing, the walk, and facial expression. Gestures do not make Han Sing black; rather, what they do is allow him to perform black — where black is not skin color but gestural movement.

The second moment when race and gesture become indistinguishable occurs at the film's conclusion. Han's father has committed suicide after being confronted by his son. As Han walks slowly from the house, police rush past him. Standing next to a police car is Trish, only her face visible. She hurries up the steps toward Han; when she reaches him, her hands are extended toward him as if to embrace him, yet she gently touches his hands; then her fingers move caressingly up his arms until they come to rest on his cheeks — her eyes dreamily gazing into his as she inquires about his well-being. The camera

Figure 10.3 "I know hip-hop": *Romeo Must Die* (2000).

Figure 10.4 Blending differences: *Romeo Must Die* (2000).

lingers on Trish's face, yet it is her fingers on Han's face (fuzzy in the image) that speaks volumes for the way race is simultaneously a factor and not. We cannot help but notice that the color of Trish's fingers virtually blends into Han's face. The film ends with Trish and Han embracing, then walking — hand in hand — away from Ch'u's. Our ability to use skin color to define and differentiate between the two lovers is rendered useless, and thus the race war is ended: Romeo and Juliet live, to beget a new racial model.

Unlike *Titus*, colorblind or nontraditional casting in *William Shakespeare's Romeo + Juliet* and *Romeo Must Die* serves to illuminate the performative nature of race. In each film gestures seem to override words, animating the body in directions that question the validity of our assumptions about the fixity of race in Shakespeare's playtext — and, I would argue, in our world. Gestures such as Jet Li's "b-boy" moves make it clear that racial identity can be easily assumed and performed, rendering color a negligible element of that identity. Just as important, the hand gestures of Lennix and Leguizamo remind us that even when color and phenotype are deployed as predicates of race, they too must be performed. In other words, the physicality of race must be made visible if race is to have cultural and ideological weight. Simply stating that race is skin color without localizing and valorizing that statement renders the notion meaningless. To speak of a "black voice" or an "Asian dialect" or "traditional Shakespearean performances" is to ask an actor to physically gesture into existence or awareness that voice, dialect, or performance.

I have focused on three filmic engagements with Shakespeare's playtexts as a way of suggesting that perhaps it is moot whether colorblind or nontraditional casting should be undertaken. The cinematic (as well as other media) engagement with Shakespeare's playtexts has redefined the notion of "traditional" (i.e., as done according to Elizabethan and Jacobean theatre practices) performances of Shakespearean characters. What changes the dynamics of power in each film is a gesture that is at once metaphorical and racializing. By bringing Shakespeare's playtexts down from the stage into the audience by means of the cinematic eye, directors such as Luhrmann, Taymor, and Bartkowiak have shifted the level of meaning and knowledge that an audience must bring to bear on its apprehension of Shakespeare's dramas. What the cinematic eye reveals is that race in Shakespearean performance has no meaning until it is gestured. And this, rather than the merits of nontraditional or colorblind casting, is what makes Jet Li's performance so Shakespearean even if the screenplay is not Shakespeare's playtext.

To return to the workshop on gesture that gave rise to this essay, Lynette Hunter cogently argued, "Gestures cannot be 'aware' unless there is reciprocity, an answering gesture, so that actor and audience (or another actor …) engage in this process of bringing into intelligibility at their particular location in space and time, their situatedness" (quoted in Arden et al., 81). To animate the text, we must animate the body, and in animating the body we cannot help but gesture. Just as important, we need to understand the ways rituals associated with both the stage and cinema complicate how racial identity is and can be performed in productions of Shakespeare's playtexts (including their adaptation and evocation). What seems even more apparent now, when we consider the ways Taymor's, Luhrmann's, and Bartkowiak's films make use of Shakespeare's playtexts, is that gesture is to race what language is to Shakespeare: a necessary means to an end. And what that end is, not surprisingly, is what makes performing Shakespeare's playtexts exciting possibilities.

Notes

1. Alan Cox is an actor and director who has worked in the Royal Shakespeare Company (RSC), National Theatre, and the Globe Theatre in London, England.
2. I have enlarged the list of usual suspects to include those who work behind the scenes because it is also their skill that enables the visual magic of the theatre.
3. I use both terms because, while nontraditional casting can include colorblind casting, it also refers to casting across gender, ethnic, and other categories of social identity. Color- blind casting refers solely to physical appearance.
4. Kidnie compares Rubin's efforts to those of the RSC and the National Theatre in London. She states that "so-called 'colorblind casting' is at the heart of a contested theoretical debate, some critics objecting that race on the modern stage is never invisible, others arguing that it tends to require actors, regardless of their racial and cultural backgrounds, to conform to a particular, supposedly 'neutral' accent and style of delivery. That said, it also allows talented black actors such as Ray Fearon ... and Adrian Lester ... to play lead roles once reserved exclusively for white actors" (318). She goes on to cite "racially and culturally diverse" productions at Stratford's Studio Theatre in 2003. About *The Swanne: Princess Charlotte*, she observes that "sometimes race was dramatically significant" and at others it was not.
5. On Taymor's *Titus* and Luhrmann's *Shakespeare's Romeo + Juliet* see Lehmann 2001 and 2002. On *Romeo Must Die* see Beltrán and Kim.
6. From the moment Lavinia's hands are severed, we are assaulted with visual reminders of the importance of hands throughout the film.
7. When the Goth captives are brought into Rome, Aaron is covered by a muddied fur man- tle or cloak. At the film's conclusion, when he is about to be killed, he is naked except for a loincloth.
8. Interestingly, the name "Romeo" is used only once in the film. It occurs near the end when Mac is about to shoot Han and says, "Sorry Romeo, you gotta die." For the effect of the film's attempt at "racelessness" see Beltrán's discussion, especially p. 57.

References

Arden, Annabel, Margo Hendricks, and Lynette Hunter. "Gesture, Language and the Body." In *Shakespeare, Language and the Stage*, edited by Lynette Hunter and Peter Lichtenfels. London: Arden Shakespeare, 2005.

Beltrán, Mary C. "The New Hollywood Racelessness: Only the Fast, Furious, (and Multiracial) Will Survive." *Cinema Journal* 44 (2005): 50–67.

Burt, Richard. "Slammin' Shakespeare in Acc(id)ents Yet Unknown: Liveness, Cinem(edi)a, and Racial dis-integration." *Shakespeare Quarterly* 53 (2002): 201–226.

Fleming, John. "Much Ado About Race." *St. Petersburg Times*, May 11, 2004.

Hendricks, Margo. "Visions of Color: Spectacle, Spectators, and the Performance of Race." In *A Blackwell Companion to Shakespeare and Performance*, edited by Barbara Hodgdon and William Worthen. London: Blackwell, 2006.

Kendon, Adam. *Gesture: Visible Action as Utterance*. Cambridge: Cambridge University Press, 2004.

Kidnie, Margaret Jane. "'What world is this?': *Pericles* at the Stratford Festival of Canada, 2003." *Shakespeare Quarterly* 55 (2004): 307–319.

Kim, James. "The Legend of the White-and-Yellow Black Man: Global Containment and Trian- gulated Racial Desire in *Romeo Must Die*." *Camera Obscura* 55 (2004): 151–179.

Lehmann, Courtney. "Crouching Tiger, Hidden Agenda: How Shakespeare and the Renaissance Are Taking the Rage Out of Feminism." *Shakespeare Quarterly* 53 (2002): 260–279.

Lehmann, Courtney. "Strictly Shakespeare? Dead Letters, Ghostly Fathers, and the Cultural Pathology of Authorship in Baz Luhrmann's *William Shakespeare's Romeo + Juliet*." *Shakespeare Quarterly* 52 (2001): 189–221.

Pao, Angela C. "False Accents: Embodied Dialects and the Characterization of Ethnicity and Nationality." *Theatre Topics* 14 (2004): 353–372.

Saltzman, Simon, and Nicole Plett. "August Wilson versus Robert Brustein." *U.S. 1 Newspaper*, January 22 and April 16, 1997.

Wick, Nancy. "Shakespeare in Reconstruction: Classic gets Civil War Setting." *University Week*, February 3, 2005.

Wilson, August. *The Ground on Which I Stand*. New York: Theatre Communications Group, 1996.

11

The Cleopatra Complex: White Actresses on the Interracial "Classic" Stage

CELIA R. DAILEADER

"There are certain roles that haunt you, teasing your imagination, daring you to play them again. Cleopatra is one." — Helen Mirren

"The genius of Shakespeare is that Cleopatra is a composite of all women and in all aspects." — Zoe Caldwell

"Cleopatra is a little bit loony." — Chantal Jean-Pierre

Who wouldn't be queen for a day if she could? The title of the Australian actress Zoe Caldwell's autobiography cites Shakespeare while also posing as the actress's own performative reinvention: *I Will Be Cleopatra*. In doing so, Caldwell unknowingly anticipates Francesca Royster's reading of the cultural icon we call "Cleopatra." Using the proper noun as a verb, Royster uses "to Cleopatra" as shorthand for performance itself.[1] One does not simply *play* Cleopatra; one *becomes* her, according to Royster and her title, *Becoming Cleopatra*. This process of becoming is central to the role as Shakespeare crafted it: the Egyptian queen's "infinite variety," her evanescence, her racial ambiguity, in a word the *slipperiness* of this "Serpent of old Nile" (1.5.25) constitutes her essence. Cleopatra is pure theatre. She is the queen of all divas. And yet, does this not pose a practical problem for performers cast in the role? In an English classical theatre grounded on Stanislavskian modern notions of psychological realism, where audiences wish to identify with "characters" on stage (a character being defined by consistency of motivation, by a recognizable and stable "identity," and so on), how does one embody a character whose essence is *change?*

In the case of Caldwell, the first step in developing the role she calls "the cornerstone of [her] career" is to go to the Bahamas and become "brown as a berry." She describes "a beautiful young ship's mate who was black" diving fearlessly into the aqua waters and bringing up "wonders for us to examine and sometimes to eat" (Caldwell, 216). In this exotic environment she describes almost literally *conceiving* the role of Cleopatra: "When you become pregnant you consciously take care of your body for the baby. Taking on a role is very similar. All through the Bahamas, I was making my body fit and my mind relaxed for Cleopatra" (198–99). The metaphor is perfect, given the text's harping on Cleopatra's fecundity and that of the land metonymized by her body. Of all Shakespeare's female characters, this one is the most carnal — she is earthy to the point of *clayeyness*. Yet also, the pregnancy trope hints at a relationship between performer and role troubled by all the ambivalences of the mother/daughter dyad. We shall soon see how this deeply gendered trope (can you imagine John Gielgud describing himself as "pregnant" with the role of Prospero?) sheds light on the dialectic of identification and Othering that interracial casting exploits.

Despite the tan Caldwell acquires in the Bahamas, she still chooses to black up — or rather, brown up — for the role. "I took the word *tawny* for the color of her skin and concocted a makeup for my whole body using oils and perfumes" (208). She also finds a substance like henna but more temporary (this being repertory) for staining her palms — adding gratuitously that she had real henna applied years later at a Moroccan wedding. The simultaneous fascination with and estrangement from her own body that the henna tattoos provoke fleetingly recalls Laurence Olivier's obsession with his own blackface Othello. She writes, "Three weeks later I cooked our Thanksgiving dinner with pale red hands that still smelled dusky and foreign" (208).

This kind of exoticism runs through the autobiography and makes for some surprising — and curiously unselfconscious — tangents. Caldwell spends a good three pages describing the live-in Jamaican nurse of her white landlady, and unabashedly describes her racial fascination: "I saw Aborigines in the outback from a train window and the Katherine Dunham dancers at the Princess theatre, when I was a little girl, but no other blacks. ... Everything about these performers was exotic and I ... longed to be able to be close and touch their hair" (144). Admitting that guilt over Australian racial apartheid accompanied this desire for tactile knowledge of the Other, she proceeds to the anecdote about the Jamaican nurse: "She let me touch her hair and skin, and examine the line where her dark skin stopped and the pink palm of her hand began. I think we both learned about each other until color disappeared and we were just two people who could like or dislike one another. I needed that" (145). We do not know, of course, whether the nurse, Joyce, also "needed" this contact; we do know that her job involved around-the-clock feeding, bathing, bedpan cleaning, and entertaining a bedridden Caucasian female — I would hazard to guess that this was contact enough with a white female body. Indeed, the narrator's "I think" signals the real social gulf that divides the white Cleopatra-to-be and the black nursemaid. The borderline eroticism of the actress's reflections is a measure not of her identification with, but of her distance from, the subject. The disingenuousness of her statement that "color disappeared" becomes clear some fifty pages later, when the color of her own hennaed hands (described as simultaneously "pale" and "red") continues to surprise her after three weeks, as she cooks the meal that purports to commemorate colonial interracial brotherhood.

Photographs of Caldwell in the role of Cleopatra do not register the "tawny" make-up the actress wore; in fact, Cleopatra looks paler than Antony. And in 1967, when she performed the role to critical acclaim for the Ontario Shakespeare Festival, the tradition of framing Cleopatra with black or blacked-up bodies in her entourage — defining her *as* white by way of contrast, and as white and *regal* (i.e., aristocratic) in contrast to black servitude — was well underway. Documenting this tradition of "annexing" black bodies for the purposes of white (female) self-definition, Carol Chillington Rutter observes, "By practicing annexation, white theatre ... is simply reproducing the practices of white culture at large. In paintings, drawings and etchings [from the eighteenth century onward] ... black figures crouch at Cleopatra's white feet; black figures pour her wine, hold her mirror, steer her barge, play her music and stare down at her from wall paintings" (Rutter, 61). That, in theatrical terms, this makes black bodies quite literally *props* for the white female is nowhere more visible than in the gargantuan cast of black "extras" used in the 1963 film starring Elizabeth Taylor — dark-skinned bodies whose sole purpose is to bow to and *carry* the bejeweled, blue-eyed, bob-haired heroine. (Here it is worth pointing out that the word "prop" is an abbreviation for "property.")

Caldwell's autobiography interests me because it delineates so nakedly the connection between a Caucasian woman's "Cleopatra complex" and her powerful responses to the bodies of people of color. It is perhaps a given that these bodies are — with the possible exception of the "Katherine Dunham dancers" — encountered in the act of physical *service*: like the Jamaican nurse who cares for her crippled white charge, the black ship's *mate* (the captain, she tells us, is Welsh) who dives into the Caribbean waters to bring her white cohorts offerings of "wonders" (like Othello) and food (like Caliban). Even the Moroccan "ladies" who henna the actress's hands flit through the book as faceless, servile figures. The narrator's pleasure is quite candidly expressed in these passages, nor can anyone blame her for enjoying the sensory pleasures bequeathed her by darker hands than her own. My point here is that the *entitlement* to these services — the access to these serviceable bodies — is part of the lure of the role she names in her title.

In this essay I will take the position that the debates over Cleopatra's racial status — as exciting and colorful as they have been — are missing an important point. There is no justification — practical, historical, or textual — for the white monopoly on the role. Cleopatra, though unique among Shakespeare's heroines for her regality and the relative dignity of her demise, embodies a stereotype that poses as many problems on feminist as on antiracist grounds. Both the role and its racially whitewashed counterpart in modern Western visual culture translate the *political* power of the historical Egyptian sovereign into sheer, passive sex appeal. When this erotic so-called power is cast as epitomizing white feminine privilege — that is, sustained by, even arguably *produced* by black subservience — the message is doubly damning. Productions wherein Cleopatra's attendants are people of color both eroticize white female aristocratic decadence and expose this decadence, this sensuality, as racially parasitic.

Black Cleopatra: What's All the Fuss?

Since the civil rights and Afrocentric movements began to affect Shakespeare studies in the 1970s, the racial identity of "Shakespeare's" and of the "real" Cleopatra has inspired much commentary and debate. This discussion has left traces in museum exhibits, like the one detailed in Royster's fascinating conclusion, in discussions backstage at the Royal Shakespeare Company, in editorial copy, and in recent websites. The question crops up everywhere: "Was Cleopatra Black?" (It is usually followed by "Was Cleopatra Beautiful?" — a discussion inevitably illustrated by the coins stamped with her surprisingly hook-nosed profile.) It is one of those debates that interests me more *as* a debate than does its solution, which strikes me as stupefyingly obvious: Shakespeare's Cleopatra calls herself "black," and the historical Cleopatra was queen of an African nation. Yet mainstream visual culture harps on her (fictional) whiteness, both in the theatre and beyond. Indeed, in a recent Google image search that produced 683 hits for "Shakespeare and Cleopatra," all but *two* of the faces of Cleopatra were lily-white, while the image that recurred most often was, ironically but predictably enough, that of Vanessa Redgrave as Cleopatra alongside a black *Antony* in a not-so-colorblind 1995 production. I have argued elsewhere at length that white culture is more comfortable contemplating white women alongside black men than the gendered inverse, and this is further evidence of that "Othellophilia" (see Daileader). Here, however, the more relevant point is the way classic Anglophone theatre will have Cleopatra white *at all costs*, even if it means reversing the explicit and emphatic interracialism of Shakespeare's play.

The insistence that "Cleopatra was not black; she was a Macedonian Greek" peppers the literature on the play in a way that begins to sound shrill after a while. Indeed, Rutter's interview with the black actress Claire Benedict, cast as Charmian and understudy to Cleopatra for a 1992 RSC production, beautifully exposes the racial paranoia on both sides of the debate.[2] Yet the iteration of "Cleopatra was not black" — along with the identification it denies — belies the difficulty of aligning the modern notion of racial whiteness with Mediterranean classical ethnic categories. As Mary Floyd-Wilson and Gary Taylor have compellingly argued, Shakespeare was conscious of the classical geo-humoural schema for racial difference that posited a "golden mean" in Mediterranean complexions, in contrast to which both the pallor of northern populations and the blackness of sub-Saharan Africans were seen as unattractive extremes.[3] Thus, even if Cleopatra's ancestors hailed entirely from the

Figure 11.1 Reading Cleopatra: Chantal Jean-Pierre. Photo: Tony Firriolo.

northern region of Greece (and there is room for Egyptian blood in her family tree), that would only mean she identified with a people whose portraits use a brownish-red ochre as a flesh tone.[4] And any casual observer of "The Treasures of Tutankhamun" knows the preferred medium of pharaonic portraiture: solid gold. Even that widely cited stone bust of the "Grecian" Cleopatra at one point was painted as "tawny" as Caldwell's stage make-up. That time bleached her is an ideologically useful accident, but an accident all the same.

According to Richard Madelaine, early modern audiences of *Antony and Cleopatra* would have seen a young male in brown make-up performing the role of Egypt's queen. This practice of browning-up fell out of fashion in the Restoration when women began playing the role, and it was not until William Charles Macready's production in 1833 that the leading lady, Louisa Anne Phillips, donned the "tawny front" referred to in the sixth line of the text. But the practice did not catch on in the major companies. As Madelaine observes, mainstream classical theatre into the twentieth century (and, I would add, beyond), by and large represented "Cleopatra in terms of highly anglicized notions of wantonness: pale-skinned, frequently red-haired and often clingingly or scantily clad" (Madelaine, 81–82). Considering the long list of great white Cleopatras — Vivien Leigh (1951), Peggy Ashcroft (1953), Margaret Whiting (1957), Elizabeth Sprigg (1961), Helen Mirren (1965), and Vanessa Redgrave (1973) — Zoe Caldwell in 1967 and Janet Suzman in 1972 were breaking with tradition when they browned up. It is noteworthy, too, that the latter productions took place outside of England, in Ontario and — appropriately enough — South Africa.[5] Indeed, the single instance in which a *real* actress of color performed the role for the RSC was a sheer accident: as understudy to Cleopatra, Claire Benedict (whom I mentioned above) was called upon to play the role one night in 1992.[6]

As Royster and others have noted, at the same time that mainstream Anglo-American theatre has insisted on Cleopatra's whiteness, in popular culture, particularly in the United States, her name has been associated with black femininity and even black female empowerment — hence Tamara Dobson's heroine in the 1974 blaxploitation film *Cleopatra Jones*. Nonetheless, it is Elizabeth Taylor's kohl-lined blue eyes and beaded headdress that dominate the popular iconography; indeed, Royster's own book jacket singles out this arresting image, and she discusses its racial coding: "Liz Taylor-in-*Cleopatra* is a version of Cleopatra that is unambiguously white and American" (Royster, 97). I would only add that the image — while in some ways still Taylor's signature — is also curiously anonymous. The pallor is flattening and the make-up mask-like; the blueness of her eyes and eye shadow no longer read against the "orientalizing" kohl as a racial anomaly. It is as though Cleopatra-post-Taylor has become an assortment of props: a kohl eye pencil and a beaded headdress, and (for the studious) the hook and flail, ancient Egypt's dual version of the scepter. Indeed, the Cleopatra website mentioned above contains a lengthy subsection entitled "Dress Up!" featuring home-style snapshots of Liz Taylor wannabes in costume. White girls and their accessories. Queens for the day.

Shakespeare's Cleopatra: Unpeopling Egypt

Despite her blue eyes and fair complexion, Elizabeth Taylor's cinematic Cleopatra recalls Shakespeare's in one important respect: her propensity for theatrical self-display in which subservient bodies act as ornamentation — even, as I mentioned above, as literal props. Enobarbus's description of her on her golden barge highlights this: the "pretty dimpled boys" (2.2.208) who fan her, and the "gentlewomen" who "made their bends adornings" (214) are the textual cues for Taylor's grand entry in her golden litter on the shoulders of a host of muscular black men. As a figure for conspicuous consumption, Shakespeare's heroine has no peer: in the same passage, she is a veritable vortex, forcing the city to "cast / Her people out on her" (219–20) — a vaguely disgusting, regurgitory image — and threatening to make "a gap in nature" (224). The scenes in which she mistreats her messengers render comic what might otherwise appear an odious habit of treating people as expendable raw material: she threatens to "unpeople Egypt" (1.5.77) by wearing out messengers in pointless pursuit of Antony. These uses of the term "people" underscore the destructive flip side of her hyperfertility, hinted at in what at first glance appears to be praise: "her person / ... beggared all description" (2.2.203–204) — "she makes hungry / Where most she satisfies" (242–243). Her body — her person — *beggars* and *makes hungry*; it starves and impoverishes. It consumes.

In fact, the more one ponders this language, the more sinister Cleopatra's relationship to her own people, and to her own nation, becomes. Despite Antony's repeatedly calling her "Egypt," Cleopatra's own rhetoric — particularly in her oath-making at times of crisis — reveals a frightening disregard for the well-being of the land, its inhabitants, and even her own son Cesarion: "Melt Egypt into Nile, and kindly creatures / Turn all to serpents"; "So half my Egypt were submerged and made / A cistern for scaled snakes" (2.5.78–79; 95–96); "The next Cesarion smite, / ... Till by degrees the memory of my womb, / Together with my brave Egyptians all, / By the discandying of this pelleted storm, / Lie graveless till the flies and gnats of Nile / Have buried them for prey!" (3.13.165–69). At her death she cries, "Come, come, and take a queen, / Worth many babes and beggars" (5.2.46–47).

This savage disregard for the ruled on the part of a ruler would go on to constitute a central theme in what Edward Said calls "Orientalism" — in the Western imagination, the figure of the "Oriental despot" figured largely as justification for colonialism (see Said). Ironically, productions that cast black actors as extras and servants and that reserve Cleopatra's role for a Caucasian inadvertently mitigate the play's anti-Egyptian bias by granting the role of the Orientalist despot to a white woman. The play thus becomes legible as an allegory for white (female) tyranny over people of color, as is more than obvious in Vivien Leigh's heinously racist use of the whip in the 1945 film *Caesar and Cleopatra* (see Royster, 121–143). This, of course, is the central lie of masculinist-racist power, wherein white women become scapegoats for a system of racial oppression that is almost entirely run for the benefit of white men.

Leigh's Cleopatra — who gets a sexual thrill out of whipping black men — is unusually sadistic. As in most characterizations of the female will to power, Cleopatra's despotism is generally cast not in terms of political ambition or even blood thirst, but in the more trivial "feminine" terms of narcissism and sexual jealousy. In the Shakespearean comic sequence mentioned above, Cleopatra frets more over the sexual consequences of Antony's marriage to Octavia than its far more threatening *political* impact, harassing the messenger with questions about the details of her rival's physique in a most unqueenly manner.[7] And even at her most "Roman" and heroic — preparing to die rather than face the shame of being displayed as a war trophy — the obsessive focus of her speech is that of death as reunion with her "husband" Antony.[8] She is also inordinately concerned with presenting the perfect *tab-*

leau in death — that is, with dressing her best — in a way that productions inevitably highlight. Readers take for granted her bossing about of her maid-servants, as they would a bossy plantation mistress preparing for a party.

> Now, Charmian!
> Show me, my women, like a queen. Go fetch
> My best attires. . . .
> ... Sirrah Iras, go
> Now, noble Charmian, we'll dispatch indeed,
> And when thou hast done this chore I'll give thee leave
> To play till doomsday. — Bring our crown and all. (5.2.222–28)
> Give me my robe. Put on my crown.
> ....
> Yare, yare, good Iras, quick — methinks I hear
> Antony call. (270–75)

These are good servants, too; they die alongside their mistress, adding their final "bends" as "adornings" in one of the most frequently depicted scenes, in pictorial arts and in production photographs, from any of Shakespeare's plays. Indeed, Charmian's adjusting the dead queen's crown ("Your crown's awry" [308]) inspired a famous pre-Raphaelite painting, an image that made it into the top seven of more than 260 on a current Cleopatra website. The shadowy figure behind this luminously white-skinned Cleopatra seems not to have been a person of color in the mind of the nineteenth-century painter, but the image harkens back to a tradition in Anglo-European portraiture older than Shakespeare's play wherein the white female aristocratic model is framed — and often bowed to — by an African servant, often a child.[9] In at least one case, this subservient African presents the white mistress with a crown.

Given this visual tradition, it would not be appropriate at all for me to term productions of *Antony and Cleopatra* that cast black actors in the roles of Iras, Charmian, Mardian, or Eros as "nontraditional," never mind "color-blind." Cleopatra's court, in the Orientalist tradition that infuses the play's performance history, on the contrary *requires* either blackface performers or performers of color, as both decorative objects in themselves and subservient figures whose role is to help decorate the queen. My point here, however, is not so much to decry the practice as racist (though it is) as to underscore the way in which the more patent racism might work to obscure the underlying anti-feminism, for *Cleopatra herself is a decorative object.* And here the star system of any theatrical tradition comes to resemble a kind of caste system wherein prima donnas (and I note the political valence to the term's translation as "first lady") get to boss around the other female bodies on stage.

Yet there is a way in which Cleopatra — as the queen of all divas — simply crystallizes a kind of effeminacy and decadence that Western culture tradi-tionally views as the essence of theatre. Early modern and modern English theatre, associated with sexual transgression at the same time that actors mimicked royalty, provided fuel for and targets of antifeminist attacks on the female ruling class. The actor's or actress's making up and dressing up called to mind the pampered and powdered body of the fair-skinned aristocratic female body. Arguably, it still does. At the same time, however, theatrical moments that call attention to these "feminine" rituals of adornment, grooming, and/or cosmetic disguise subtly expose the dependency and vulnerability of the object of these practices — all the more so when Cleopatra calls upon her attendants for help getting dressed.

Servants who dressed their masters, like those who cooked for them, had to be the most trusted. Women's attire in early modern England, particularly in regard to the aristocracy, constituted a series of complicated machines. To each lady, her professional "staff" of attendants. My metaphor of the plantation mistress was not casually chosen: as a metaphor for Shakespeare's heroine, it is no more anachronistic than was the plantation mistress herself. Antebellum Southern aristocrats wore pseudo-Elizabethan clothes, and the boy actor who played Cleopatra may very well have called upon the actor playing Charmian to lace up his corset backstage.[10] The first Oscar to go to a person of color went to Hattie McDaniel for her role as Mammy in *Gone with the Wind*; her performance against Vivien Leigh's Scarlett O'Hara acquired its force not only by presuming its audience's (racist) appreciation of the "good servant" stereotype but also by pitting Mammy's grumbling usefulness against Scarlett's unsympathetic, spoiled, "feminine" petulance, passive-aggression, and conniving. It is not enough to say that McDaniel played a racial stereotype; so did Leigh. Though Leigh's Scarlett did not get to whip her slaves, Leigh's Cleopatra, just six years later, did.

Disappearing Act: Cleopatra in History

Joyce Green MacDonald notes the curious frequency with which early modern "texts of empire" represent as fair-skinned "women historically understood" to be African by birth, such as Cleopatra, Dido, and Sophonisba (the latter two from Carthage, in Northern Africa). These moments — considered alongside the curious case of Aphra Behn's African princess Imoinda, who was racially whitewashed by Thomas Southerne in his 1688 revision of Behn's novel for the stage — are characteristic, according to MacDonald, of the "female racial disappearances and emergences" that characterize protocolonialist discourse (MacDonald, 9). Cleopatra in particular continues to disappear racially in ways that bear out MacDonald's parenthetical caveat against the term *postcolonial* — as though colonialism were "neatly over and all that is left" were its "discursive remains" (MacDonald, 16). Of course, using the intransitive verb "disappear" obscures agency in the performance. My question, thus, is: Who is *doing* this? Who is behind the disappearance of Cleopatra as a woman of color?

When Caldwell asserts that between her and the Jamaican nurse "color disappeared," she is claiming a kind of racial colorblindness like that gestured toward in this volume's title. But most claims of racial colorblindness are patently insincere, and, as I have argued elsewhere, no one involved in the visual aspect of theatre can afford to be "blind" to anything. In this respect, Caldwell's biography perfectly encapsulates — in its evasions and its awkwardness about racial difference — the problematics of interracial casting on the classic Western stage. At the same time, however, Caldwell's relative candor vis-à-vis other major performers of the role of Cleopatra allows a sympathetic (if somewhat embarrassed) reading of her response.[11] For in fact, Caldwell finds in Cleopatra the realization of her own sexuality: Cleopatra is, to Caldwell, that mysterious essence of femininity, "a composite of all women and in all aspects."[12] In a kind of imaginative racial drag, white women either "brown up" or "sex up" for the role (though preferably, according to Caldwell, both). They dissolve into an essentialist myth of female sexual arousal and availability that is contrary to all notions of white feminine propriety — in a word, "black." The role is *both* a racial *and* a gender stereotype.

Caldwell does, however, talk about the historical Cleopatra, touching on the aspects of her characterization by the classical sources that got lost in translation where the legacy of Shakespeare's play is concerned. Shakespeare's main source in Plutarch portrays Cleopatra as learned and multilingual and emphasizes the role of her intelligence, courtly graces, and charisma in her erotic appeal. It is a commonplace that history is told by the victors: the denigration of Cleopatra — the effacement of her individuality, her intellect, and her statesmanship — is one of the best examples of this. Ironically, the most accurate portrait of her may be her profile stamped in those coins. Gayle Rubin argues in a seminal work of feminist theory that women as commodities are conduits of, rather than parties to, social and economic power in patriarchal capitalist societies (see Rubin). Like currency, whose value is not intrinsic but realized in the exchange, women can never *own* their merit or exercise power or agency in the market that they lubricate. What happens to this paradigm, though, when the mark that authenticates the coin as currency is the image (or the name) of a woman? What is the current dollar value of the Cleopatra coin pictured in all those history texts? It is perhaps no wonder that racist, masculinist consumer culture in the twenty-first century prefers the "cheap," tabloid-friendly image of Liz Taylor in her blue eye shadow.

Why is Shakespeare's Cleopatra called "whore," "strumpet," and "nag"? Why did "queen" spelled with an "a" ("quean") mean "whore" in early modern slang? Why is a "drag queen" called a queen? Why is a "drama queen" called a queen? How did "mistress" (feminine for "master") come to mean "lover," or more precisely, "kept lover" (how is that for a contradiction in etymological terms?). Mistress, missus, miss, missy. Why do female titles devolve? Why can't a queen simply be a queen the same way a senator is a senator, or a doctor a doctor? Why did Cleopatra — ruler of the most powerful empire in the Mediterranean world, her image circulating on coins across several nations — eventually become, in the Western imagination, a faceless, fungible sex kitten? It seems history cannot stomach women in power. Their names must be razed from the monuments. They must be made to disappear.

Conclusion

Who would *really* "be Cleopatra"? I mean, the one Shakespeare dreamed up? Would it not get boring lolling about on leopard skin and waiting for Antony to sail in? Cleopatra herself calls for drugs, so that she "may sleep away this great gap of time" (1.5.5) until her lover comes back and the next orgy can begin. Nonetheless, for at least one Caucasian actress, this role was the be-all and end-all (to steal a phrase from *Macbeth*) of her career; it might even have been the be-all and end-all of her life-as-a-woman, her life in the flesh. In the last paragraph of her biography, Caldwell quotes the Shakespearean passage from which she has drawn her title. I find this the most puzzling part of the book, and only partly because the Shakespearean quote within the quote is itself puzzling:

> Cleopatra became for me the cornerstone of my career, because I knew that all the women I had played, all the women I had known and reacted to, and, for that matter, all the men went into my being able to answer Antony by saying:
>
> It is my birthday.
> I had thought to have held it poor; but since my lord
> Is Antony again, I will be Cleopatra.
> And I was. (Caldwell, 216)

Shakespeare's "Since my lord is Antony again / I will be Cleopatra" is a familiar move to Shakespeareans. Shakespeare's characters often are not themselves rhetorically when they act this way or that. Petruchio in *The Taming of the Shrew* is "unlike himself" (3.2.104) when he arrives badly dressed for his wedding; Henry V is "like himself" when he is "warlike" in the Prologue (*Henry V,* Pro. 5). (This has also been parodied by his contemporaries, as in Thomas Middleton's *A Mad World, My Masters*, when the buffoon Sir Bounteous is "like himself — gone.") I return to Caldwell's prose; she says the role is "the cornerstone of" her career because "every woman" (and I do not buy her "all the men") she had played or known in life "went into" it. What precisely does that mean? How could any role be so spacious, and even playable? How is it possible to enact and embody *every* woman? And how can Cleopatra be Everywoman and still be memorable — to post-Stanislavskian, post-Freudian audiences — as a tragic heroine and a queen? Or is the actress's point that it is her *talent* in performance that is all-encompassing, that is bigger than life?

This makes logical sense of the passage, but we are not yet done with it. Having said this (if that is indeed what she means to say), the actress then closes with the mysterious "And I was." Presumably, she means to say that she "was" "every woman" in performing Cleopatra, and at the same time, that she "was" Cleopatra herself. But ending the book with a bare "I was" — echoing the performative "I will be" of the title, but also freezing it, placing it in the past tense — rings a curiously suicidal note. It is as if she performatively *undoes* herself. She plays herself into oblivion in playing Cleopatra. It is a kind of rhetorical disappearing act. And as an autobiographical *last act*, what a performance this is!

So few women of color have performed the role that it is difficult to say whether there is anything specifically "white" about this almost orgasmic reaction to Cleopatra's eroticized death-in-life and, presumably, her eroticized suicide ("Husband I come!"). But I have been able to track down one actress of color, Chantal Jean-Pierre, who played Cleopatra in April 2004 for the Orlando/University of Central Florida Shakespeare Festival. "This was the most challenging role of my life," Jean-Pierre stated, point blank. "I mean, Antony is *everything* to her; Antony is *her life*. I could *never* love a man that way — it's totally alien to my personality, to my sense of myself. I mean, this woman *literally* dies for love. That was a difficult place to put myself, psychologically."[13]

Nonetheless, Jean-Pierre's Cleopatra pleased the mixed audiences that attended the 2004 Orlando production: reviewers spoke of her "magnificent, mercurial Cleopatra" and described her performance as "impressive."[14] Director Jim Helsinger, in explaining his choice of Jean-Pierre, said, "I was looking for exotic. But I was also looking for the best performer. I auditioned both African-American and European-American actresses, and she embodied the kind of exoticism I wanted." He also made a point of casting the other Egyptians as nonwhite or "ethnic" and the Romans as "very pale." "This is a multicultural play," he explained.[15] Another dimension of this non-colorblind production was Helsinger's use of color generally in underscoring the play's central cultural binary. Romans wore white, silver, and purple and Egyptians gold, blue, and red — the colors that feature on the cartouche or hieroglyphic signature. The Egyptians also exposed "lots of skin" and were generally more decorated and effeminized (the soothsayer, a dark-skinned African American, was heavily tattooed). Accordingly, Antony in his effeminate Egyptian mode wore long hair, earrings, and make-up; when called to Rome he donned blue and silver and cut his hair. I cannot imagine — and certainly have never seen — a production of *Antony and Cleopatra* more appropriately color-*conscious*, and I am not surprised that audiences were too dazzled by Helsinger's stagecraft and Jean-Pierre's acting to note the play's disturbing racial and gender politics.[16] Commenting on the latter, Jean-Pierre discussed her experience in a more clearly "nontraditional" Shakespearean role — that of Gertrude in *Hamlet*. "Shakespeare just doesn't give his female characters much personal-

Figure 11.2 "Cleopatra was": Chantal Jean-Pierre. Photo: Tony Firriolo.

ity. Gertrude is just loony. Her love for Hamlet is her life; it's what she's about."
Asked to compare the two roles, Jean-Pierre commented, "Well, at least with
Cleopatra there's something for an actress to work with. You feel like with
Cleopatra Shakespeare at least *tried*." I would call that damning with faint
praise. But then again, I am an iconoclast.

Shakespeare penned Cleopatra's lines for an adolescent, Anglo-Saxon male
in both racial and gender drag; unlike white actresses such as Caldwell and
Taylor, adolescent Anglo-Saxon males did not want to "be Cleopatra" for life.
In 1999 the RSC's first notable actor of color, Hugh Quarshie, declared that
the role of Othello might be the one classical role an actor of color should *not*

perform, as doing so reinforces racial stereotypes (see Quarshie). I believe the same to be true of Cleopatra on both antiracist and feminist grounds, and I would like to see a production that consciously exposes this. Virginia Mason Vaughan provocatively considers the possibility that a return to blackface performance in regard to *Othello* might elucidate early modern ideologies of racial difference rather than naturalizing them (Vaughan, 170–174). What if an actress of color — like Whoopi Goldberg in her appearance at the Oscars — were to "whiten up" for the Liz Taylor look and play the beat-the-messenger scenes with allusion to Vivien Leigh's Scarlett O'Hara? A white actor in black-face as the messenger could invoke Hattie McDaniel's eye-rolling Mammy (or even better, poor Prissy with her "I don't know nuthin' 'bout birthin' no babies!"). Then again, that would have little to do with either Shakespeare's play *or* the figure of Cleopatra in history.

And maybe that is the best we can do with either. I return, in closing, to the two questions that haunt the critical and popular literature on Cleopatra, whether Shakespeare's or even history's Cleopatra. Those questions are "Was Cleopatra black?" and "Was Cleopatra beautiful?" Those two questions would never be asked — have not been asked, to my knowledge — about any *male* figure from classical history. Research on any of the Ptolemys, our heroine's male ancestors, or even on Tuthankhamun, highlights the way these questions are *about gender*. No one asks whether Tuthankhamun was black, even though one of his portraits is in onyx and several others are painted dark brown. Was Cleopatra black? Was she beautiful? Cleopatra was queen of Egypt. And that is all we can safely say, given the fact that her history was written by the victors of the battle of Actium, and given the fact that her history was written entirely by men. Was Cleopatra black? Was she beautiful?

Cleopatra *was*.

Notes:

1. In invoking "performativity" I follow Judith Butler's paradigm as famously articulated in *Gender Trouble: Feminism and the Subversion of Identity*. Francesca Royster describes Cleopatra "as a means of performing and often deconstructing racial and gender subjectivity" (9).

2. As understudy to Clare Higgins's Cleopatra, Claire Benedict did go on to perform the leading role in one unprecedented (and never repeated) nontraditional RSC performance. Benedict relates an amusing backstage anecdote. The director, John Caird, meeting with the cast for the first read-through, "wanted to 'get something straight right from the beginning': 'Cleopatra wasn't black. She was a Macedonian Greek.'" The actress was startled by this "'rather hysterical' disclaimer." Here are her reflections, as quoted by Rutter: "'I was the only black actor in the rehearsal room. Clearly I wasn't meant to be playing Cleopatra. I was only her understudy.' Then Benedict exchanged looks with Clare Higgins, 'And I could see her thinking, "I'm not a Macedonian Greek. So who's John got to play Cleopatra?"'" (Rutter, 82).

3. On the history of the modern notion of racial whiteness see Floyd-Wilson and Taylor.

4. Let me here clarify my own racial lexicon in this essay. Following Taylor's caveat about the invention of racial whiteness at the end of the seventeenth century, I avoid using the term "white" in the racial sense for early modern Englishwomen. When speaking of contemporary women who self-identify as "white" or "black," I use those terms only as shorthand, bearing in mind the constructed nature of all racial taxonomies.

5. Deats's essay contains a whole subsection on "interracial casting" (66–70).
6. Not surprisingly, New World productions led the vanguard when it finally occurred to white directors that women of color might play Cleopatra. In 1986 Shakespeare & Company of Lenox, Massachusetts presented "black, sensual, bewitching Michelle Shay" as Cleopatra; in 1987 Rosalind Cash played the role for the Los Angeles Center, and in 1988 Francehelle Dorn played the role at the Folger Theatre in Washington, DC. When the Actors Touring Company followed suit in 1989 and gave Britain its first black Cleopatra, the production was panned. For a discussion of the 1986 Shakespeare & Company production see Ayanna Thompson's interview of Timothy Douglas in this volume.
7. I elsewhere argue that the omissions of this discussion — particularly considered alongside Enobarbus's speech — constitute further proof that Shakespeare imagined Cleopatra as a woman of color (Daileader, 28–31).
8. For a fascinating discussion of Cleopatra's suicide, see Kehler.
9. A portrait by Titian dated 1523 is the first of this genre of which I am aware.
10. Diane Roberts comments on her great-great-grandmother's journal entry upon the discovery that their slaves had, post-Emancipation Proclamation, fled: "The Bradfords didn't know how to do anything. There had always been a black hand on the bucket handle, on the skillet handle, on the button, on the plow. They could barely dress themselves: all those collar-tabs, all those laces and ties and hooks ... 'Not a servant, not a one,' Susan kept saying. 'And we unused to work'" (Roberts, 126).
11. By contrast, Vanessa Redgrave, who performed the role three times, seems puzzled by Cleopatra's ethnicity, choosing first a blond wig, then settling for a red, curly one, and wondering "why she is called a gypsy" (Redgrave, 288).
12. As a "composite of all women" there is a way in which Cleopatra's complexional de-racing is logical: photographic composites will automatically blanch, just as the face of a coin will wear with handling (and the metal will darken with time). But reproductive technologies never just "happen," and it is worth asking whose interests they serve. Southerne's blanching of Behn's Imoinda — like, more recently, Disney's reinvention of the New World's Cleopatra in the light-skinned ethnic composite of Pocahontas — was a calculated and profit-minded effort, and the profits went largely to (surprise!) Caucasian men (see Edwards).
13. All quotes from Chantal Jean-Pierre come from a personal interview and are cited with permission.
14. See Elizabeth Maupin's untitled review in the *Orlando Sentinel*, April 4, 2004; Mathew MacDermid's on TalkinBroadway.com; Al Kruknik's in the *Orlando Weekly*, April 4, 2004.
15. All quotes from Jim Helsinger come from a personal interview and are cited with permission.
16. The Orlando/UCF Shakespeare Festival produced *Othello* during the same season without drawing criticism for the play's racism.

References

Butler, Judith. *Gender Trouble: Feminism and the Subversion of Identity.* London and New York: Routledge, 1990.
Caldwell, Zoe. *I Will Be Cleopatra: An Actress's Journey.* London: Norton, 2001.
Daileader, Celia. *Racism, Misogyny, and the Othello Myth: Inter-racial Couples from Shakespeare to Spike Lee.* Cambridge: Cambridge University Press, 2005.
Deats, Sara Munsen. "Shakespeare's Anamorphic Drama: A Survey of *Antony and Cleopatra* in Criticism, on Stage, and on Screen." In *Antony and Cleopatra: New Critical Essays*, edited by Sara Munsen Deats. London and New York: Routledge, 2005.
Edwards, Leigh H. "The United Colors of Pocahontas: Synthetic Miscegenation and Disney's Multiculturalism." *Narrative* 7 (1999): 147–168.
Floyd-Wilson, Mary. *English Ethnicity and Race in Early Modern Drama.* Cambridge: Cambridge University Press, 2003.
Kehler, Dorothea. "Cleopatra's Sati: Old Ideologies and Modern Stagings." In *Antony and Cleopatra: New Critical Essays*, edited by Sara Munson Deats. London and New York: Routledge, 2005.
Kruknik, Al. Untitled review of *Antony and Cleopatra*. *Orlando Weekly*, April 4, 2004.

MacDermid, Mathew. Website. www.TalkinBroadway.com

MacDonald, Joyce Green. *Women and Race in Early Modern Texts*. Cambridge: Cambridge University Press, 2002.

Madelaine, Richard. "Introduction." In *Shakespeare in Production: Antony and Cleopatra*, edited by Richard Madelaine. Cambridge: Cambridge University Press, 1998.

Maupin, Elizabeth. Untitled review of *Antony and Cleopatra*. *Orlando Sentinel*, April 4, 2004.

Quarshie, Hugh. "Second Thoughts About Othello." *International Shakespeare Association Occasional Papers* 7 (1999): 1–25.

Redgrave, Vanessa. *Vanessa Redgrave: An Autobiography*. New York: Random House, 1991.

Roberts, Diane. *Dream State: Eight Generations of Swamp Lawyers, Conquistadors, Confederate Daughters, Banana Republicans, and Other Florida Wildlife*. New York: Free Press, 2004.

Royster, Francesca. *Becoming Cleopatra: The Shifting Image of an Icon*. New York: Palgrave, 2003.

Rubin, Gayle. "The Traffic in Women: Notes on the Political Economy of Sex." In *Toward an Anthropology of Women*, edited by Rayna Reiter. New York: Monthly Review Press, 1975.

Rutter, Carol Chillington. *Enter the Body: Women and Representation on Shakespeare's Stage*. London and New York: Routledge, 2001.

Said, Edward W. *Orientalism*. New York: Vintage, 1979.

Taylor, Gary. *Buying Whiteness: Race, Culture, and Identity from Columbus to Hip-Hop*. New York: Palgrave, 2005.

Thompson, Ayanna and Timothy Douglas, "In the Blood: William Shakespeare, August Wilson, and a Black Director." In *Colorblind Shakespeare: New Perspectives on Race and Performance*, edited by Ayanna Thompson. London and New York: Routledge, 2006.

Vaughan, Virginia Mason. *Performing Blackness on English Stages, 1500–1800*. Cambridge: Cambridge University Press, 2005.

12

The Chicago Shakespeare Theater's *Rose Rage*: Whiteness, Terror, and the Fleshwork of Theatre in a Post-Colorblind Age

FRANCESCA T. ROYSTER

In the Chicago Shakespeare Theater's 2003 production of *Rose Rage*, an almost five-hour condensation of Shakespeare's *Henry VI Parts 1, 2,* and *3*, directed and co-adapted by Edward Hall, the extreme physical violence of the War of the Roses is rendered via the actions of butcher-surrogates who torture pieces of meat, organs, and cabbage heads. This production culminates in a dinner theatre of sorts that reaches its audience palpably through sight, sound, and eventually smell. When combined with nontraditional casting practices, the production's stylized and violent treatment of flesh yields new insights about the lived and embodied experience of systems of white supremacy. Hall's *Rose Rage* is a condensed dramatization of nation building and racialized consensus that works on both critical and visceral levels.

Significantly, Hall's production asks us to think about whiteness in particular as an often unmarked privileged location of social belonging. By the end of the production, we are forced to think of multiple forms of social whiteness: the heroic whiteness of English history and its relationship to the (sometimes default) fictional whiteness of the theatrical space; the "honorary" whiteness that some bodies are imbued with when supporting the status quo of power; and the relational and unstable aspects of this honorary whiteness, when linked to other aspects of difference, such as gender and class.

We might think of one of the central functions of the history play as rehearsing mythic pasts to support national, racial, and gendered hierarchies.[1] Early modern English history plays, like Shakespeare's *Henry VI* plays, present mythic (white, male, English) heroes, ordering those "others" who might support the English cause (e.g., Kate or the Welsh Fluellen in *Henry V*, Lady Bona in *Henry VI*) and casting out those who threaten the stability of the nation (e.g., Jack Cade in *Henry VI*). This sorting of heroes and villains along racialized lines is constitutive of a white English identity still in flux during the early modern period. Yet *Rose Rage* turns this function on itself, by stripping down those identities to flesh and asking the audience to think about the theatrical elements of community building, cultural belonging, and scapegoating. By the end of the play, we are forced to think about the civilizing process that maintains bodies — even dead bodies, as "bodies" — and the processes of humiliation and/or violence necessary to convert those bodies into "flesh," without identity or history. I call this ritualized and theatrically heightened process "fleshwork."

This production's complex treatment of whiteness as a shifting form of meaning "in the flesh" might be best understood in the context of a recent theatrical milieu irrevocably shaped by August Wilson's challenges to traditional strategies of colorblind casting. For Wilson, productions that cast a "blind" eye to race only succeed in erasing African histories, subjectivity, and artistic production. In *The Ground on Which I Stand,* for example, Wilson writes, "To mount an all-black production of *Death of a Salesman* or any other play conceived for white actors as an investigation of the human condition through the specifics of white culture is to deny us of our own humanity, our own history, and the need to make our own investigations from the cultural ground on which we stand as black Americans" (Wilson, 31). Wilson has changed the terms of the racial politics of casting. Since his debates in the public sphere and in his writings, we cannot naïvely think of the theatre as a racially neutral space; neither can we be satisfied with the mere substitution of white bodies by black (or other racial identities) without a nuanced attention to history and the economics of cultural production.

I see Hall's production as both responding to these new terms and offering new ways to think about casting and the racial politics of theatrical canons. Though not a substitute for producing stories authored by playwrights of color, Hall's *Rose Rage* highlights an important aspect of the physical impact of racism that is underanalyzed. *Rose Rage* presents a version of history that accounts for the painful production of "making" and protecting whiteness. Casting black and brown actors in precariously "white" roles, this production implicitly links early modern English history to the history of making "other" bodies into flesh in other moments in history — from the blood laws of the Spanish Inquisition, to the trans-Atlantic slave trade, to the lynching of African American, Latino, Italian, and other "dangerous" bodies in the nineteenth- and early twentieth-century United States, to the torture of prisoners of war at the Abu Ghraib prison. The making and protection of whiteness has had an inescapable impact on our lived experience of history.[2] Moreover, Hall's production also asks us to think about the situational subtleties of this process of assimilation. How, for example, might becoming white be differently affected by race, class, and rank? How is the experience of whiteness by one nonwhite group necessarily linked to the experience of others? Especially in times of cultural change and crisis such as these, we cannot afford to think about the physical and cultural violence on some bodies in isolation from other bodies.

Lessons in Terror: *Rose Rage* at Navy Pier

Edward Hall's *Rose Rage* was first performed in London at the Watermill Theatre as a mostly male production in February 2001. It premiered at the Chicago Shakespeare Theater, Navy Pier, in 2003, this time with a multiracial all-male cast. Barbara Gaines and Criss Henderson were artistic directors and co-adaptors for the Chicago production. Calling on scenic and costume design by Michael Pavelka and lighting design by Ben Ormerod, the production reset England's bloody War of the Roses in a Victorian slaughterhouse. The slaughterhouse and its historical location during the rise of the Industrial Revolution is an ideal setting to let us think about systems of efficiency and profitability in the killing and selling of flesh. It is, by extension, an excellent place to think about wars and the planning of wars as machines of death with a similar eye to efficiency, profit, and civility.

Yet the costumes reference several other time periods, rendered by multiply raced male bodies. In this version of the early modern English history play, we see black, brown, and white male bodies wearing World War II gas masks, football pads, long leather trench coats, the long red robes of medieval Catholic bishops, shining army boots, chain mail aprons worn over white muscle t-shirts, satin-lapeled 1920s tuxedos, pin-striped zoot suits, pearl-handled switchblades, ivory cigarette holders, the pea coats and watch caps of newly immigrated Italians (as rendered by Robert De Niro in *Godfather II*), and spiffy Victorian frock coats and top hats. Over the course of the production is a kaleidoscopic array of masculine bodies wearing the costumes of "civility," beneath which are histories of violence and of war. The history of war and power is presented in mall-like fashion, eras juxtaposed and sometimes intermingled. (Perhaps it is fitting that the performance takes place in the Chicago Shakespeare Theater on Navy Pier, a location that was once a military port but that has been transposed into an amusement park and mall.) On this choice, Hall says, "I didn't want fake daggers and chain mail. ... I wanted to take the story outside its English history, and I wanted it to be modern" (quoted in Smith). The production *is* modern. Despite its Victorian setting and early modern source, it reflects the often fragmented politics of terror in a post-September 11 age. The production speaks to our own racialized struggles with leadership, masculinity, war, and terror. Commenting on the timeliness of the production's 2004 New York debut, which coincided with the Republican National Convention, Hall notes, "They're plays about civil war and the hypocrisy of politicians, and audiences take those issues very seriously, I've found. You get to see how duplicitous people become when they're trying to gain power. The last person you should trust is a politician" (quoted in Glanville). At the same time, the play raises difficult questions about usurpation and the divine right of kings voiced by early modern thinkers like John Ponet and Richard Hooker.

Hall's eye to contemporary politics parallels Shakespeare's own inclusion of contemporary political parallels and allusions in the *Henry VI* plays. In his book *Shakespeare and Violence*, R. A. Foakes points out that while the *Henry VI* plays take full advantage of the theatrical spectacle of violence, they also "expose the horrors of civil war, and make drama out of the self-interest of the nobles whose professions of loyalty barely mask their real concern, which is for their own selfish advantage" (Foakes, 50). The literary historian Chris Fitter sees *Henry VI Part 2* in particular as a play of protest. Shakespeare sought through *Henry VI Part 2* to "destabilize establishment ideology" (Fitter, 129). By alluding to Elizabeth's unsteady alliances with France and the public torture of priests, Fitter argues:

> On its surface, the work wears the appearance of a loyalist drama, fitting topical realities into a pattern of orthodox, if beleaguered, political loyalties, royalist and hierarchical. Such reassuring fidelities were the condition, however, of evading censorship's proscription: for the drama's public context was a period of (literally) racking anxiety for the Elizabethan authorities. "I am not so carelesse," Elizabeth coolly informed representatives of Parliament in 1587, "as not to weigh that my life dayly is in hazard." The 1587 execution of Mary, prompting attempted invasion by the Spanish Armada in 1588, made only more graphic the dynastic menace. In his speech at the opening of Parliament in 1589, Sir Christopher Hatton summed up the heightened fears of domestic and international Catholic threat, noting the campaign of Jesuit infiltration of England, several assassination attempts on the Queen, a second papal bull excommunicating Elizabeth, this one by Sixtus V in 1587, and the blessing of this Pope ("exceeding all that went before him in tyranny and cruelty") upon attempts to murder Elizabeth. Terrorist acts against national leaders were no mere speculation: William of Orange had been fatally wounded in his townhouse by a serving man in July 1584; the Duke and Cardinal of Guise were assassinated by agents of Henri III in December 1588; and Henry III of France was murdered, in August 1589, by a Capuchin monk. England's secret service was expanded, and its expenditure increased, throughout the decade. (Fitter, 129–130)

As Fitter very convincingly documents, Elizabethan England was involved in its own war on terror.

Fleshwork and Hierarchies of Whiteness

The production features a chorus of white-smocked butchers, who often wear face masks or gas masks. They are responsible for carrying out fleshly translations of tightly choreographed fight scenes between the other actors. The chorus warns of impending doom with the rhythmic sharpening of knives. They wait on the edges of the stage, or in a gallery among the meat hooks that swing from the ceiling, or they peer from the grated openings of meat lockers, watching the action. These butchers are both chorus and "labor": for every body stabbed, gutted, smothered, bled, or beheaded, the butchers reciprocate — transposing the stylized work of the principal actors into literal fleshwork. When a fight scene occurs, a butcher appears on stage beside them. They sit or stand at waist-high butcher blocks and slice organs, pieces of raw meat, or cabbage heads. The chopping is carefully choreographed to match the rhythms of the actors' movements. One critic describes these butcher sequences as "Kabuki style," perhaps alluding to their ritualized treatment of violence (Solomon). The butchers are then in charge of clearing away the debris: a decapitated cabbage is gathered in a purple velvet bag for "display" on a pole near the town borders, or guts are gathered in plastic baggies. As the play progresses, the butchers' involvement with the bodies of the actors becomes closer, their relationship to the other action on the stage heightened. The butchering now takes place just inches from the spot where the "real" bodies of actors lie. By the last hour of the play, the butchers are in charge of removing the actors' bodies from the stage; they are now more organically integrated into the principal action. The butchers orchestrate the process of making bodies into flesh, but the audience is also vital, as they either disidentify with or identify with the bodies on stage.

Both a part of and outside of the action of the play, the butchers' ritualized fleshwork creates spaces of liminality, moments of "neither this nor that," when audiences are forced to rethink their relationship to the bodies on stage and the construction of the violence taking place. The cabbage heads and pigs' guts are not human, they are not attached to the bodies of the actors on the stage, yet they are, to a certain extent alive — particularly in the ways that the violence done to them registers sensually: the smells from the meat and organs linger, the blood and juices remain on the hands and clothing on the actors, and bits of guts and flesh stick to the floor. For those of us raised on *Friday the 13th* movies, the hacking of the cabbage heads sounds strangely familiar — and human. Audiences might notice and take in these details, perhaps even creating an appetite of sorts for the sounds and smells of the flesh, to add to their investment in the aggression and violence, and the moments of release or cleansing or purity that they might produce. When asked about his decision to use this device, director Edward Hall explains, "If you smash a cabbage, you can really smash it loudly, to smithereens. You can really hack pork guts to bloody bits. That allows the actors to explore feelings of genuine raw aggression. ... It's not what we're doing is that violent. But it enables the audience to connect with what we do and to contribute to it with their own emotions and instincts. They become collaborators" (quoted in Smith).

It might be useful to think about the powerful effect that the butchers' violence produces in the audience as a kind of cultural magic that takes the form of effigy. Effigies are the very stuff of flesh: "rough fabrications made from distorted parts of a person, often excrements such as saliva, blood, hair, fingernail pairings, semen, fingerprints, footprints, which are then performatively deployed to put the real person in harm's way. An effigy is the fusion of image and body, symbol and source, the figurative and the physical" (Conquergood, 353). In his essay "Lethal Theatre: Performance, Punishment, and the Death Penalty," the performance studies critic Dwight Conquergood argues that effigies are important components of rituals that make and remake belief on a community level, by "transforming vague ideas, mixed feelings and shaky commitments into dramatic clarity and alignment" (342). We might think of the importance of the creation of effigies in times of war: bombs have been painted with the flags of the enemy on them (or conversely, with "Hi, Mom" or the name of a girlfriend, a symbol of what is being fought for); more recently, t-shirts with the face of Osama bin Laden in crosshairs were sold at Ground Zero; the likeness of George W. Bush has been burned in Afghanistan and elsewhere. In *Rose Rage*, the bodies turned flesh are held up, posted on sticks before the city gates, and otherwise displayed as a sign of the might of the enemy, either Lancaster or York. But this production in part seeks to interrupt the mystified function of these effigies, forcing the audience to think about the effigies' production through fleshwork.

Fleshwork is central to the process of community building in a time of war. The meat and organs in the production are linked to an economy of sorts: some bodies (e.g., animal bodies, the bodies of an enemy, bodies that are valued less because of race or class) are turned into flesh or meat — the heart, guts, liver become by-products, lesser in value, disposable, trash, offal. But when we think of the human body as it is invested with spiritual and/or patriotic meanings (as in the medieval notion of the "king's two bodies"), those very parts — the heart, especially, but also the liver — become symbols of the virtues that separate the human from the inanimate and that link body and spirit. One might link this tenuous economy of bodies to the tensions around war and starvation in the *Henry VI* plays. Early in the cycle, in *Henry VI Part 1*, Alencon refers to the English as "Lean raw-boned rascals," while Charles replies,

> Let's leave this town, for they are hare-brained slaves,
> And hunger will enforce them to be more eager.
> Of old I know them: rather with their teeth
> The walls they'll tear down, than forsake the siege. (1.3.16-19)

And Joan cockily calls out to the struggling English troops, "Go, Go! cheer up thy hungry-starved men" (1.7.16). These lines speak to both the hunger and brutality of revenge, and the real economic tensions around feeding and compensating soldiers for their labor. War brings out that tension and changes the economy of flesh and meat. By the time we reach the end of the cycle, in Part 3, a weary Henry VI refers to the War of the Roses as "butcherly" (a key moment for this production's vision):

> What stratagems, how fell, how butcherly,
> Erroneous, mutinous and unnatural
> This deadly quarrel daily doth beget! (2.5.89-91)

Flesh is the physical material of human existence at the very boundaries of the social and the human. If theatre involves a collaborative creative process of producing meaning between actor and audience, the play asks us to consider the political aspects of producing meaning both within the play and metatheatrically. And as we bring the performance of our lives on the outside into the theatrical space in the postmodern moment, this process of meaning production is all the more complex, precarious, and politicized. As Herbert Blau has written, "When we think of the scale of awareness required to live consciously in this world, we're not entirely sure, in the illusory passage of current events, whether we are spectators or participants" (Blau, 2).

Watching and Being Watched: Conspiratorial Whiteness

The play opens with a gathering of the butchers. They first busy themselves about the stage, wiping surfaces, sharpening their knives. They then stare at the audience, waiting for our attention. At first the audience does not notice. Couples whisper to each other, cell phones are turned off, candies unwrapped. But then one by one we notice that we are being watched. Once everyone in the audience is silent, and meets their eyes, the lights go down and the production begins. And throughout the play, the butchers remain, daring us to watch them as they prepare for the slaughter. We are torn between ignoring them — doesn't that mean that someone is about to be killed? — but then we cannot help but watch. With the shushing of their sharpening knives, they provide a death pulse, the rhythm underlying the violence that ensues on the rest of the stage.

It is significant that, with one exception, only white actors play the butchers. In the opening scene, the African American Bruce A. Young, who also plays Richard Plantagenet, Duke of York, and several other roles in the production, appears at first indistinguishable from the others, engulfed from head to toe in pristine whiteness, including a long white smock and gloves, white surgical-style face mask, and white cap with the bill pulled down low. The butchers represent, in some ways, the force of white history and community standards, arbitrating our definitions of bodies versus flesh. They are, in the typical role of the chorus, representatives of the community, and as such, they are our guides for how to read the bodies before us. We cannot — and perhaps should not — take our eyes off them. When the actual killings take place, we may choose to avert our eyes from the chopping of the meat but we still hear it, and — more subtly — we smell it. By the end of the five-hour production, the air is heavy with the smell of blood. The butchers' face masks, darkened with particles of blood and soot, remind us that we are not only watching the bloodletting taking place, but we are breathing it in. It is becoming a part of us, whether we want it to or not. The audience, then, is figured as both co-conspirators and victims (depending on one's point of view).

As I consider the force of conspiratorial whiteness in this play, I would like to locate myself as an African American in an audience that is, for the most part, white. Indeed, even though Navy Pier itself is used by an audience that reflects the vividly multicultural and multiclassed population of Chicago, going to the Chicago Shakespeare Theater is an activity that feels to me to be profoundly white and middle- to upper-class. (These impressions are based on my experience gathered from five years as a season ticket holder.) Compared to the crowded and sometimes gritty interiors of the rest of Navy Pier, the the-atre feels (and is) newer, more luxurious and leisurely, with tasteful couches and chrome lamps. There is a small store with Shakespeare goodies for brows-ing during intermission, still apart from the rest of the Navy Pier revelers, and a simulated English pub for quiet drinks and chatting before or after the show. Even right before show time, the lobby is hushed, compared to the rest of Navy Pier, with its Ferris wheel, outdoor amphitheater, boat rides, food court, face painting, lemonade, and Budweiser stands. The clothing of the par-ticipants also changes, from jeans and t-shirts — amusement park wear — to skirts and pantsuits, velvets and silks. The ushers are mostly white, as are the people working in the box office, bookstore, and pub. When I come, I often feel conspicuous, and I probably am. More than once, I have been mistaken for "someone else" — a different black professor, a member of a church group, a parent of a child's classmate. I get the sense that people are trying to place me; my body is also being read, along with those of the actors.

The business of what bodies mean, how they signify for the audience, white and nonwhite, is complicated by *Rose Rage*'s use of nontraditional casting. Initial theories of colorblind casting followed a rule of "best actor for the part, regardless of race," but the idea has evolved to include what might better be described as conceptual casting. That is, the race or ethnicity of the actor might deliberately cut against the grain of the role to make a sociopolitical or aesthetic statement about identity and history. Edward Hall's *Rose Rage* fits this conceptual rather than colorblind casting technique. Conceptual casting practices use ethnic and female actors cast in roles to give the play greater resonance. This technique heightens the space of the stage to create new worlds. There is a split between the theatrical and actual, though that split is not entirely clean. As the performance scholar Angela Pao defines concep-tual casting:

there is an insistence upon the status of theatrical performance as a unique semiotic process, engaging rather than being parasitical upon the world of lived experience. When their full potential for producing meaning is realized, however ... conceptual casting practices belong to a different order of signification [than does colorblind casting]: they move a production from the field of artistic representation to that of cultural criticism. This shift is indicated in the response of Libby Appel, artistic director of the Oregon Shakespeare Festival in Ashland, to the issues raised by August Wilson. She stated, "There is no such thing as colorblindness. When people look at the stage, they see the colors of the actors. When I cross-cast, I'm looking to punch the audience's sensibilities in some way." (Pao, 15)

Though most of the players in this production of *Rose Rage* are white, two key players are actors of color: the Duke of York (played by Young) and King Henry VI himself (played by Carman Lacivita, who won a 2004 Bayfield Award for the role). Hall also casts adults as children and men as women. Hall further creates a sense of alienation or tension by doubling and sometimes tripling the roles that actors play, so that actors play across gender, class, and earlier performances of race. Lacivita, for example, plays both Henry VI and Lady Bona. Scott Parkinson performs Queen Margaret of Anjou as well as a white-smocked butcher. Young plays York, Stafford, a nobleman sacrificed in Cade's Rebellion, an unnamed member of the butchers' chorus, and Dick the Butcher, a worker in the rebellion who, in this production at least, turns out to be York, spying incognito. We are forced, in the process, to suspend our familiarity with the body and voice of the actor, as we understand further the role that actor plays. At times the body remains in between, neither fictional character nor actor, or both. This multilayered strategy of watching theatre parallels the shifting nature of racial performance in the American and British context. As the performance critic Richard Schechner points out:

Clearly, American audiences are not color or gender blind anymore than they are body-type or age blind. Our theatre and dance companies reflect the values and attitudes of their audiences. Gender, race, age and body type signal specific sociopolitical meanings. The categories themselves are definable only within certain contexts. That is, what constitutes a "black" or a "white" person is not some fixed objectively measurable entity, but a shifting set of circumstances that have emerged in America over the centuries and are continuing to change. ... Nor are the definitions in use objective indices — they are powerful determinants of social privilege (and despisement). It is impossible for spectators to see performers cast "against the text" (a narrative text, a body text) without wondering what such casting means. (Schechner, 6)

I would argue that in this particular moment of "the war on terror," the desire to fix racial and ethnic meanings, to see and read the body as always transparent, is nonetheless at work, despite race's shifting and performative meanings. Certainly the examples of racial profiling that have proliferated since September 11, 2001 reveals the urge to "fix" race. This desire for racial fixture and its failure was tragically acted out in the shooting of a suspect of London's July 2005 subway bombings: a brown man, an innocent Brazilian, was watched, fingered, and eventually killed for "suspect behavior" — jumping a subway turnstile and dressing in an inappropriately warm winter coat. However, the codes of "suspect behavior" collapsed upon investigation.

Hall's casting choices, I would argue, are not meant to be "blind" to the issues of race and gender; indeed, we are meant to think about how the bodies on stage perform their identities and how these identities are linked to the project of writing history. Hall's conceptual casting works together with the use of meat and vegetables, to ask us to think more consciously not only about violence, but also about the transformation of raced bodies into characters, characters into flesh, and flesh into symbol. This self-consciousness is especially important to the ways that the play performs whiteness.

Richard Dyer has written that in Western cultural history, whiteness presents itself as amorphous, "everything and nothing" — an act that masks a steady diet for violence and which in and of itself is an act of violence (Dyer, 8). Likewise, theatrical space is often thought of as a de facto white space. Black, Asian, or Chicano theatre is marked as raced, while theatres that present plays primarily about white lives or white actors remain unmarked. The director Clinton Turner Davis, co-founder of the Nontraditional Casting Project, argues that this de facto whiteness is at the heart of the concept of "colorblindness" and translates into the politics of what theatre is produced and funded: "White artists are given the artistic freedom or take the artistic license to discover and present 'new' interpretations of ethnically based work without accepting the tremendous responsibility to 'tell it right' that such a task entails" and, he argues, rarely are they made to a critical eye to white patriarchal culture (Davis, 32). What I find quite powerful in Hall's use of nontraditional casting is his more nuanced look at whiteness: its techniques of assimilating other bodies, and its history of extreme violence. Moreover, the play's casting highlights, as part of our social history, the situational possibility for and the collapse of "honorary whiteness."

The register of whiteness on Hall's stage is not stable, but, like other racial codes, is shifting and situational. The play asks us to rethink the ways that "colorblindness" works as a default category of performing whiteness. We are made to think about how and why we read bodies as "white." And it asks us to rethink our assumption of early modern English history as a story of stable white identity. As Gary Taylor, Mary Floyd-Wilson, Sujata Iyengar, and I have recently argued, early modern England's investment in an identity of whiteness was a gradual and at times contradictory process, fostered by its assimilation of other cultures within it (including Irish, African, and Native American cultures), and informed by its own anxieties of racial and ethnic purity (see Taylor, Floyd-Wilson, Iyengar, and Royster). Important is Arthur Little's insistence that as we historicize the shifting codes of early modern whiteness, and its differences from our own racial moment, we do not use this to argue that race — or perhaps more pertinently, racism — did not exist:

> It is worth noting from the onset that 'race' in the early modern era ... works less as a stable identity category than as a semiotic field, one as infinitely varying as the cultural discourses constituting what we have come to identify as the early modern era or Renaissance. Even in a single text, depictions of race can draw from mythology, the Bible, the voices of classical authorities, the humors, the physiognomy, and one's cultural location and habits. None of this, however, should be taken to argue that race in Shakespeare's day is less stable or real, that is, any less a discursive device, than it is in our own cultural moment. We come up short, I would argue, when we fantasize that our contemporary constructions of race — through our well-honed technologies of racism — offer us proof of a real racial ontology more truly embedded in individual subjects than arbitrarily embodied in and across an infinite number of our cultural discourses. Race, then and now, is not a discrete subject. (Little, 1)

Shakespeare dramatizes the tensions and complexity of racialized nation building in his *Henry VI* plays, always underlined by acts of violence that are at times brutal and often defy morality and logic. We are faced with the reality of leadership that, while supposedly chosen by God, cannot perform the act of nation building and protection. The feuding houses of Lancaster and York show that English history is repeatedly informed by "treason of the blood," to use Brabantio's words.

Hall uses the instability of the meanings of the color of the actors' bodies here to emphasize the anxieties around bloodline, succession, and morality also at play in the *Henry VI* plays. In the rose-picking scene, the moral language of the red and white of the houses is then played out on the bodies of the actors. The color codes of balanced "red" and "white" connote rightful succession, bloodline, and morality, while at the same time the play exposes the brutality and violence masked behind these conventional meanings. It is notable that in Hall's production, the red and white roses are rendered in a tangle of razor wire, chains, and a meat hook, menacingly dangled from the ceiling for a good part of the play. As we watch Bruce A. Young performing a "white" York defending his right to the crown, his body and performance style create a tension between early modern codes of whiteness and American codes of race and racism, informed by nineteenth- and twentieth-century stereotypes. As the codes of color break down, we are forced to reconsider the blind or natural position of whiteness, acting white, performing whiteness, representing a white family line, and ultimately a white history. We are slowed down to a state of liminality, where we have to think about the process of Young becoming York. Young as York dramatizes the boundaries of white belonging. Over the course of the play, York's mantle of whiteness is stripped and he becomes "flesh" — marked here by his blackness, calling on the hierarchical aspects of white over black.

In Part I, scene 2 of *Rose Rage*, in the first half-hour of the performance, the representatives of the houses of Lancaster and York gather around the rose bush. The men are dressed nattily in Victorian gentleman's suits, but York's is perhaps the most accessorized. His costume includes a stylish lace handkerchief in his pocket, a scarf, a gold cane, and a satin top hat. He seems especially attached to his hat and often removes it in a gesture of amplified solicitousness, bowing. Young embodies the stereotype of the "Nigger Dandy," a stock figure on the minstrel stage.[3] In nineteenth-century America, this "Dandy" was often associated with pastimes once barred to men of color — such as the theatre — and was a symbol of laziness, grandiosity, boastfulness, and non-productivity. The Dandy is the black man who wants to assimilate in white culture, but who, caught up in its trappings, never quite fits. In contrast with the restrained voices of the other white actors, clipped with tension, Young's style is much bolder, brasher — in fact, at times he yells his lines. Unlike the others, his face betrays his emotions as he moves in the scene from pride to frustration, anger, and mockery. He uses his hands more than the others, takes up more space on the stage, and is the only actor to touch the other actors — pulling one actor aside here, putting an arm around another there. His outsider status adds a layer of defensiveness and poignancy to his rehearsal of lineage in this scene:

> I claim the crown of birth and parentage:
> For by my mother I derived am
> From Lionel Duke of Clarence, the third son
> To King Edward the Third, while Henry
> From John of Gaunt doth trace his pedigree,
> Being but forth of that heroic line. (Hall and Warren, 18)

This scene creates cognitive dissonance: early modern English issues of pedigree and bloodline combine with nineteenth-century anxieties about blacks' increasing presence in the white public sphere. York's difference from the other nobles marks a different approach to ambition and violence, as well. York's lines are the most passionate, the least masked in his willingness to use violence to get what he wants. In one line he passionately vows to force his enemies to "drink blood" (Hall and Warren, 19). If the scene presents one layer of the color coding of morality — Vernon associates his choice of "plain and maiden" white rose with "truth and plainness" (Hall and Warren, 17), while for Somerset, the red rose marks his righteous anger — York's not-quite-whiteness presents another moral message. York's difference brings out the contrast between explicit forms of brutality (here, for this moment, figured as "black") and the masking of brutal acts behind a show of civility and systematic violence (here, figured as "white").

As the play proceeds, the deep foundation of brutality throughout England's civility is exposed. In Part II, scene 16, a key moment in the climax of the play, the Duke of York is tortured as a traitor by Queen Margaret and his Lancaster enemies. As York was hoisted up by his hands on a meat hook, kicked, beaten, jeered at, and mocked by the white Margaret and Clifford (the kicking translating into the chopping up of meat by the white butcher stationed immediately to his right), I was left thinking about the unfortunate familiarity of the tableau of a black man hung above a violent white crowd. The visual echo of the history of lynching was inescapable for me. For that moment, I thought of York's body as flesh — flesh that, in that parallel instance of lynching, would be purposefully mangled beyond recognition of the man that he once was. The theatre of lynching, like this theatre, implicates the onlooker: we participate in that mangling of his body by continuing to look. As an African American woman, I was keenly aware of the loaded privilege of my distance and safety, bought with and included in the price of my ticket.

"Honorary" Whiteness and Social Location

The play's conceptual casting marks (by strangeness or opposition) the ways that English history as it is told in Shakespeare is "white," to our eyes, by calling attention to the multiplicity of whiteness, and the ways that whiteness was not a de facto or invisible category. Particularly compelling is Scott Parkinson's portrait of Queen Margaret, the spoil of war from France. Strikingly paler than any of the other actors, Margaret's difference is always marked by her French-accented speech (she always calls Henry VI "Henri"), her sensuality, and her feminine ambition, which is remarked upon by the other characters as being French. In his death scene, York calls Margaret "that false French-woman" and "she-wolf of France" (Hall and Warren, 88). Over the course of the play Margaret becomes a powerful political figure, but her ambition and stratagems cast her under suspicion. Edward Hall and Roger Warren, in their adaptation of the *Henry VI* plays for the *Rose Rage* script, cut Joan Du Pucelle; and I would argue that Margaret absorbs some of the fear connected with her. Parkinson's powerful performance asks us to think about the labor involved in creating this version of gender and national difference that is nonetheless marked in the body.[4] From the first moment that she is presented to Henry VI, in Part I, scene 6, Margaret demonstrates a marked performance of looked-at-ness. She averts her eyes demurely as Duke Humphrey reads the terms of the marriage. She rearranges her scarf flirtatiously, but also always seems to be listening intently to the terms of the pact. Her costume presents the barest bones of feminine accoutrement: Parkinson's short strawberry blonde hair is moussed and topped with a white headband. Like the other actors on stage, Margaret always wears tall army boots and pants, though these are sometimes accented with a scarf or boa to mark her gestures. Rather than choosing the bold strokes of broad drag (wigs, tight dresses, a high voice), Parkinson asks us to think about femininity through its more subtle aspects — the pursing of lips, the ways she touches the shoulder of her lover, the gathering of a stole of white ostrich feathers. This also allows for moments when masculinity can break through, via a rough-voiced command, a steely glare, or a fast stalking walk across the stage. Parkinson's particular performance of drag reveals the cracks in Margaret's idealized femininity, at the same time as it shows her failure to assimilate fully as English.[5]

The production's representation of Jack Cade, performed by Joe Forbrich, further complicates the play's presentation of white identity. In these scenes, Cade's outsider status is marked by costume — a longshoreman's coat and fisherman's cap — movement, utilization of space, and speech style. Jack Cade actually enters the stage "rapping," leading an improvised "Down with the government!" call and response between himself and the workers (as well as some of the audience): "There's a maggot in the apple, corruption at the top, it's rotten to the core, we've got to stop the rot! Reformation!" Forbrich plays Cade as a blue-collar voice of the people, swinging from the sets, swaggering and rolling on his toes for emphasis, jumping up on crates, and posing with hands on hips. His speech, anachronistically twentieth-century working-class New York, also stands out from the others: he tells the crowd "My fadder was a Mortimah," uses scare quotes, points, and lectures with his hands on his hips. When he delivers the famous line "First thing we do: Kill all the lawyers," he makes a little "badda bing" hand roll, takes off his cap, and winks. Like York, he is "bigger," less contained, less masked than the nobles. His performance of class codes him as both white and not-quite-white.

This scene presents a fascinating dynamic between Forbrich's Cade and Bruce A. Young's performances of Dick the Butcher, Stafford, and York. At the opening of the scene, Nick and Jack Cade are on par; both are commoners and outside the world of white nobility. But then Young transmogrifies into the nobleman Stafford, at the same time that Cade's quest for power grows. Cade stages the execution of Stafford as the first sign to his potential followers of his power. The Cade Rebellion's first act of extreme violence is to stab and bludgeon Stafford; this is done by repeatedly stabbing a plastic bag filled with meat and offal, while Young screams in agony on a dais to the side of the stage. What does it mean that transforming this body, at once the noble Stafford and the black body of Young, into flesh, proves Cade's taking on the mantle of power? I would like to suggest that this scene references the tensions between the white poor and blacks, even while it stages a clash between nobleman and commoner. But to make the scene even more complex, as the rebels turn against Cade, Young returns to the stage in his Nick the Butcher costume, and with Wyle E. Coyote's "sly civility" removes his smock to transform into York. Again, York's role as the duplicitous Black Dandy returns. In this case, the use of the black actor, juxtaposed with Cade's not-quite-whiteness, reveals the interconnection and sometimes tension between nonwhite racial identities.

Terror needs an Audience: *Rose Rage* in Post-September 11 America

As *Rose Rage* gets us to think about the nature of race and racism, it also has the power to get us to think more deeply about the spectacular nature of war, its aspects of theatricality. As the *Chicago Sun Times* theatre critic Hedy Weiss has commented, "Rarely has the sick and gruesome circus of civil war and human desecration been so vividly conjured in pure theatrical terms, as everything in the lexicon of horrors — from ritualistic decapitations and castrations, to the most visceral of disembowelings — is enacted with a meticulously calculated yet clearly insane relish" (Weiss). I would like to end by considering how we might understand this performance of *Rose Rage* in the context of the recent use of the spectacle of terror on both sides of the current "war on terror," post-9/11, from the initial World Trade Center bombing to the tortures at Abu Ghraib prison. The play gives us the opportunity to think about the specific historical markings of bodies as white and nonwhite in this discourse. How is whiteness implicated in the dynamics of terror and revenge (and the pleasures the perpetrators might take in them)? Might the temporary community of the theatre audience still be a resource for social change? How might we consider this possibility for social change in the context of commercial theatre?

Particularly in these times of economic panic and war, our functioning models of race often make violent changes under pressure. On the one hand, for many Americans (especially those on the right), we might seem to be in a place where a colorblind model seems the most appropriate, and where individualism also reigns. We might think of the precarious state of affirmative action policies under the Bush administration as an illustration of the growing national desire to see America and Americans as colorblind. Yet many communities of color continue to experience the effects of racial profiling, related both to the "war on terror" and to the "war on drugs" in American cities. While the bombing of the World Trade Center directly affected people of virtually every racial and ethnic group, the mantra "Why do they hate us?" that emerged in newspapers, magazines, and public dialogues often implicitly assumed that the representative "us" is white and Christian and the "not-us" nonwhite. While the U.S. armed forces employ disproportionate numbers of working-class and poor men and women, and men and women of color, white men and women soldiers have often been the most sensationally and heroically profiled fighters in the media. (Think of the current success of Anthony Swofford's Gulf War memoir *Jarhead*, made into a major film). The word "terror" has been increasingly connected to people of color, despite the efforts of Timothy McVeigh. We might best understand this implicit (and sometimes explicit) whiteness of the "war on terror" as being an outgrowth of older notions of U.S. empire. Perhaps it is an aspect of nostalgia for the days of colonial white supremacy, when Europe and later the United States dominated as war powers. Hall's *Rose Rage* reveals that despite the mantle of white supremacy, white history is also structured by acts of terrorism.

By using some of the very same dynamics as terrorism, *Rose Rage* makes for a complicated theatrical experience for its audience. While these gory reminders of war might repulse us, and the markings of whiteness might make some of us uncomfortable, we might also experience pleasure. On one level is the pleasure of the wittiness of the play's conceit: war is butchery. This is, perhaps, the play's most distanced pleasure. At the same time, the play brings together the highly orchestrated and aestheticized versions of war that we get in the *Henry VI* plays with its more primal elements: the ripple of muscles, the whacking of knives into flesh, the payoff of blood, the lust of revenge. We — especially the rarified audience of the Chicago Shakespeare Theater — might not like to think of ourselves as craving these things, but blood lust (and just plain lust) are the buried part of many of our entertainments, from *The Apprentice* to *Desperate Housewives* to Janet Jackson at the Super Bowl.

But perhaps more important to my argument is the pleasure of knowledge and historical recognition. When we watch this play, we are reminded of our place in the continuing history of war. There is an uncomfortable but perhaps confirming proximity between Jack Cade's humiliation of the lawyers in *Rose Rage* and the staging of the humiliated enemy in the Abu Ghraib prison photos, or between the effect of the butchers' blood-flecked masks on us and the anthrax scares, fears of dirty bombs, and other ways that terror has recently been linked to airborne contaminants. *Rose Rage* takes the distanced history of the War of the Roses and makes it immediate and intimate by linking it to our immediate fears. Indeed, Edward Hall has said of his production:

When you create an act of extreme violence on stage and accompany it with loud drums and violent lighting, there's no contradiction. But if you contradict it somehow, you have a very interesting paradox. You might share the wonderful feelings of taking revenge, expressed through the music and juxtaposed with the horrible reality of what we're seeing. Paradox challenges the audience to address their own attitudes. If we're allowed to have a kind of banal attitude about things — it's wrong, it's right — then we're slipping into dangerous territory. But if we understand the complexity and contradictions involved in extreme acts of brutality, then I believe we get closer to understanding why we do it and how to stop it. Art has the ability to ask those questions. That's why I've tried to explore those contradictions in drama, between extreme beauty and extreme ugliness. (quoted in Lewis and Halperin)

Although I would say that this is a very painful knowledge, it is an important experience in a time when the media's reportage of the war distances us from war and its repercussions. The Shakespearean critic Brian Walsh has argued: "The Elizabethan audiences attending performances of *1 Henry VI* watched enactments of an absent history that was itself infused with a nostalgia for an absent past" (Walsh, 124). I do not think that *Rose Rage*'s audiences experience this same kind of nostalgia, but I do think that we exist in a moment of a split present, especially when it comes to our connection to the wars taking place around the globe. Lately, we have been asked to see the war in Iraq as already being done. We are told that it is not a war in fact, but the "aftermath" of a war. And in the meantime, thousands of U.S. and Iraqi soldiers and citizens have died. *Rose Rage* gives us an entrée into war in terms of the individual foibles and idiosyncrasies of the actors involved, as well as the experience of violence, revenge, and loss on a more primal level, represented by the butchers. *Rose Rage* interrogates the cultural cachet of "going to Shakespeare" by betraying the ways that theatre — even highbrow theatre — can capture the gruesome graphic display of violence of real life.

Most important, though, is the pleasure of inclusion. Our witnessing is necessary for these acts to take place. We listen, we smell, we cry out. We feel for the heroes and the enemies because Shakespeare's version of war lets us see both as vulnerable. What *Rose Rage* reminds us of is the disconnect that we make between the social body and flesh that is necessary for us to take pleasure in violence. This is especially true when we seek revenge. (This disconnect was very much in effect when Rush Limbaugh commented that the soldiers who tortured prisoners in Abu Ghraib were "letting off steam.") And this dynamic of distance and pleasure is deeply connected to the U.S. history of racist spectacle: lynching and slave markets, for example, are what Anatol Lieven has called the "demons in America's cellar" (Carby, 1). In *Precarious Life*, Judith Butler writes of the vulnerability that many Americans felt after 9/11. A key window of opportunity comes after such an event, she writes, if we can experience for a moment the precariousness of our own safety — and our interdependence on others in the world. Part of this process, she argues, is to realize that protecting the safety of some bodies in a time of war has required the dehumanization of others: "Violence against those who are already not quite living, that is, living in a state of suspension between life and death, leaves a mark that is no mark. There will be no public act of grieving" (Butler, 36).

Conclusion: Naked Lunch

How strange it was to break after the first two hours of this jolting play, and blinking with the brightened house lights, file along with the rest of the audience into a room with checkered tablecloths, box dinners, and open bar. Wall-to-ceiling windows gave us an excellent view of Lake Michigan, tourists, and the neon-lit Ferris wheel. At first, the audience seemed shaken, and couples mostly talked to each other. But eventually we spoke shyly across the table, in quiet voices. Many noted with relief that the menu seemed to be carefully chosen to avoid any echoes of the red meat of the performance. There also was comfort to be taken in the process of the spreading napkins on laps, opening up dressing containers, spearing lettuce, maneuvering chopsticks, and passing salt and pepper between neighbors. Not quite a community, still, together we fortified our bodies for the second half. The dinner functioned not only to sustain us through a difficult show, but also to ask us to think about the contradictions between our civilized state of theatre watching and the extreme drama that we were paying to watch. The food in our boxes and the food on stage forced us to think of ourselves as flesh-reliant (human or grilled chicken) for our pleasure, comfort, and eventually for our survival.

Grilled Chicken Strips
Wild Brown Rice
Mustard Seed Salmon
(Butter pat)
Finger-Sweet.[6]

Notes

1. Michael Neill points to tropes of Irish denigration and wildness in *Henry V,* and in *1 and 2 Henry VI,* as one of the means by which England rehearsed its ideals of nation, gender, and race that would fuel later colonial enterprises in the New World. He states, "As the site of England's first true war of colonial conquest, Ireland became both a proving ground for methods of 'plantation' that would later be applied in Virginia and elsewhere, and a forcing house for the enabling discourses of racial and cultural difference on which successful colonization would depend" (Neill, 4). Neill reads Burgundy's lament for France in *Henry V,* and its image of land turning in on itself, as a thinly veiled allusion to the ongoing Irish Wars: "Burgundy's lament for France — the 'best garden in the world.' Which now lies 'Corrupting in its own fertility' and so choked with 'hateful docks, rough thistles, kecksies, burs" that it turns to 'wildness,' savagery, 'And every thing that seems unnatural' (5.2.40–62) — echoes numerous descriptions of Ireland as fertile earthly paradise turned to wilderness by the barbarity of its own inhabitants; and Henry's function as the correcting 'scythe' (l.50) or 'the coulter ... That should deracinate such savagery' (ll.46–47), mirrors the civilizing mission attributed to Elizabeth's generals by contemporary propagandists" (Neill, 12).
2. The black feminist critic Hazel Carby makes a powerful connection between the spectacle of the lynching of African American bodies and the torture of prisoners at Abu Ghraib prison (see Carby).
3. For more on the "Nigger Dandy" and other minstrel roles, see Lott. For a fascinating example of the ways that the "Nigger Dandy" stereotype traveled across international contexts, see Magubane's analysis of the popularity of American minstrel shows in South Africa.
4. For a powerful discussion of the scapegoating of Joan and Margaret in the first tetralogy, see Howard and Rackin (43–99).

5. Like Margaret, Lady Bona (played by Carman Lacivita), sister to the French King Louis (played by Bruce A. Young) has few choices in the face of the machine of war. She becomes "englished" in order to survive. In this case, Lacivita's brownness serves to ask us to think about the performance of whiteness and national loyalty under the threat of violence. The white nation depends upon its might, deal making, and opportunism, as well as force, to create a state of unified community. Yet the casting of the French king as black complicates her trade.

6. Excerpts from "Menu for *Rose Rage* Dinner," provided by Jewell Events Catering, 424 North Wood Street, Chicago, IL 60622. I would like to give many thanks to Marilyn Halperin and the staff of the Chicago Shakespeare Theater's education department for their generous help in the writing of this chapter.

References

Blau, Herbert. *The Audience*. Baltimore: Johns Hopkins University Press, 1990.

Butler, Judith. *Precarious Life: The Powers of Mourning and Violence*. London: Verso, 2004.

Carby, Hazel. "A Strange and Bitter Crop: The Spectacle of Torture." *openDemocracy: Free Thinking for the World*, October 11, 2004. www.openDemocracy.net.

Conquergood, Dwight. "Lethal Theatre: Performance, Punishment, and the Death Penalty." *Theatre Journal* 54 (2002): 339–367.

Davis, Clinton Turner. "To Whom It May Concern." *Theater* 27 (1997): 30–34.

Dyer, Richard. *White*. London and New York: Routledge, 1993.

Fitter, Chris. "Emergent Shakespeare and the Politics of Protest: *2 Henry VI* in Historical Contexts." *ELH* 72 (2005): 129–158.

Floyd-Wilson, Mary. *English Ethnicity and Race in Early Modern Drama*. Cambridge: Cambridge University Press, 2003.

Foakes, R. A. *Shakespeare and Violence*. Cambridge: Cambridge University Press, 2003.

Glanville, Justin. "Instead of Butchering the Bard, Marathon *Rose Rage* Provides Meaty Material, Roles." *Columbia Daily Tribune*, October 3, 2005.

Hall, Edward and Roger Warren. *Shakespeare's* Rose Rage: *An Adaptation of* Henry VI *Plays in Two Parts*. London: Oberon, 2002.

Howard, Jean and Phyllis Rackin. *Engendering a Nation: A Feminist Account of Shakespeare's English Histories*. London and New York: Routledge, 1997.

Iyengar, Sujata. *Shades of Difference: Mythologies of Skin Color in Early Modern England*. Philadelphia: University of Pennsylvania Press, 2005.

Lewis, Kelly A. and Marilyn Halperin. "Interview with Edward Hall." *bill*, Autumn 2003.

Little, Arthur. *Shakespeare Jungle Fever: National-Imperial Re-Visions of Race, Rape, and Sacrifice*. Stanford: Stanford University Press, 2005.

Lott, Eric. *Love and Theft: Blackface Minstrelsy and the American Working Class*. Oxford: Oxford University Press, 1995.

Magubane, Zine. *Bringing the Empire Home: Race, Class and Gender in Britain and Colonial South Africa*. Chicago: University of Chicago Press, 2004.

Neill, Michael. "Broken English and Broken Irish: Nation, Language, and the Optic of Power in Shakespeare's Histories." *Shakespeare Quarterly* 45 (1994): 1–32.

Pao, Angela. "Recasting Race: Casting Practices and Racial Formations." *Theatre Survey* 41 (2000): 1–21.

Royster, Francesca. "'White Limed Walls': Whiteness and Gothic Extremism in *Titus Andronicus*." *Shakespeare Quarterly* 51 (2000): 432–455.

Schechner, Richard. "Race Free, Gender Free, Body-Type Free, Age Free Casting." *TDR* 33 (1989): 4–12.

Smith, Sid. "*Henry VI* Best Seen on an Empty Stomach." *Chicago Tribune*, October 12, 2003.

Solomon, Alisa. "Their Majesties' Butchers." *Village Voice*, September 21, 2004.

Taylor, Gary. *Buying Whiteness: Race, Culture, and Identity from Columbus to Hip-Hop*. New York: Palgrave Macmillan, 2005.

Walsh, Brian. "'Unkind Division': The Double Absence of Performing History in *1 Henry VI*." *Shakespeare Quarterly* 55 (2004): 119–147.

Weiss, Hedy. "Slaughter on Grand Ave: *Henry VI* Gets Chopped into Prime, Bloody Cuts." *Chicago Sun Times*, September 23, 2003.

Wilson, August. *The Ground on Which I Stand*. New York: Theatre Communications Group, 1996.

Afterword: The Blind Side in Colorblind Casting

PETER ERICKSON

The dazzling complexity and multiple directions of this collection open up exciting new points of departure for the study of race in Shakespearean texts and performances. My goal is not to offer a comprehensive summary but to continue the conversation by pursuing and extending one central strand in the overall discussion.

Seeing through the Word

The word "colorblind" has two distinct levels of meaning. In the narrow theatrical sense, it means placing actors of color in the roles of white characters and thus disrupting the strict racial alignment of actor with character. In the larger cultural sense, it raises the question of what outcomes, including unintended effects, are produced by cross-racial casting in particular cases. Here a sharp divide emerges. The first approach conceives colorblind casting as an exclusively positive opportunity for black actors' artistic growth and career advancement; this stance assumes a blind faith in Shakespeare's inherent value and goes no further. The second approach understands colorblind casting as an experiment that calls for analysis and evaluation, and thus allows for the need to explore, acknowledge, and confront Shakespearean blind spots regarding race.[1]

I do not wish to reject or prohibit colorblind casting, nor do I take it for granted.[2] Yet, equally, I feel the promotion of colorblind casting that limits itself to celebration blocks rigorous critical consideration of all the meanings generated by colorblind practices in the theatre.[3] To begin with, both components of the term "colorblind" are problematic. The word "color" means nonwhite, and thus implicitly excludes and protects racial whiteness. In one technical definition, color is produced when white light is broken into separate parts — a formulation that allows whiteness to stand apart as a category of its own.[4] More important, in current social usage, the phrase "people of color" refers to those who are not white. If white is not a color, then calling attention to the racial color spectrum leaves white privilege undisturbed as the tacit default setting, and hence gives license to remain white-blind.

The result is to make racial whiteness, not color, the truly invisible element — a paradox that is compounded by the addition of the word "blind."

In a theatrical context, blindness activates the concept of "willing suspension of disbelief" — that is, the idea that spectators accept certain conventions as necessary conditions of dramatic fiction. In the celebratory mode, the conventions of blackface and colorblind casting are accorded a suspension of disbelief that is not just willing but eager. The escapist impulse behind this eagerness deserves critical scrutiny.

We no longer adopt the posture of cultivated ignorance with respect to the boy actor motif on Shakespeare's stage. Rather, we respond to cross-dressing as an explicit metadramatic theme whose interpretation is crucial to a play's overall meaning. With regard to race, recent work shows that racial cosmetics are also thematically available.[5] This accessibility means that we are not restricted to a reductive selective perception but are encouraged to see and to interpret early modern blackface and whiteface. Similarly, instead of pretending we do not notice, we can register the full, varied range of colorblind effects. We may legitimately cast ourselves as an audience that is not colorblind but color-sighted, and may thereby give ourselves permission to see the maximum rather than artificially restrict ourselves to the minimum. This awareness includes alertness to the skewed structure built into the term "colorblind."

Situating the Theatrical Compact in the Social Contract

In assessing colorblind casting, a critically attuned scholarship must bring to bear the wider implications of colorblindness outside the area of Shakespeare performance. The Shakespearean field can too easily construct itself as a special, transcendent realm immune to the pressures and difficulties of meanings that pertain elsewhere. But Shakespearean theatre cannot be a pristine space hermetically sealed off from ordinary social discourses. The border between theatre and society, culture and politics, is porous, and the meanings cross back and forth. Theatre can aspire to renegotiate the terms, but it must first recognize rather than evade the problems.

The legal scholar Patricia Williams notes that the concept of colorblindness runs the risk of "a prematurely imagined community" created by "a short-circuiting of the process of resolution" when she eloquently warns "against the facile innocence of those three notorious monkeys, Hear No Evil, See No Evil, and Speak No Evil. Theirs is a purity achieved through ignorance. ... It is a dangerous if comprehensible temptation to imagine inclusiveness by imagining away any obstacles" (Williams, 4–6). Particularly relevant for colorblindness in Shakespearean performance are Williams's emphasis on the visual — "How, or whether, blacks are seen depends upon a dynamic of display that ricochets between hypervisibility and oblivion" — and her use of the theatre metaphor: the white "fantasy of black life as a theatrical enterprise is an almost obsessive indulgence" (17). When Williams's cautionary approach is combined with the formal sociological skepticism of *Whitewashing Race: The Myth of a Color-Blind Society* (Brown et al.) and the engaged cultural criticism of "Suturing Over Racial Differences: Problems for a Colorblind Approach in a Visual Culture" (Burns), we begin to build a sufficiently broad and resonant external frame of reference applicable to the interpretation of colorblind casting within the Shakespeare sphere.

Putting the Argument on Stage

No one can come away from the eye-opening commentaries by the two theatre people in this volume thinking that staging colorblindness is simple and easy. Antonio Ocampo-Guzman and Timothy Douglas have a dual perspective as both actor and director of Shakespeare that enables them to tell behind-the-scenes stories that are fascinating, candid, and moving — especially in addressing the complications involved in colorblind casting at the practical level of making it work in the theatre.

Ocampo-Guzman is a Colombian immigrant for whom Shakespeare becomes an empowering point of entry into American society, his "adoptive culture."[6] Success with Shakespeare in the United States offers both literal access in the form of employment and symbolic access in the form of a "fragile sense of belonging" in the face of being "picked on, insulted, and generally being discriminated against." His "rich Colombian accent" finds acceptance in Shakespeare performance. However, the reception of his direction of a bilingual *Romeo and Juliet* is less satisfying and unleashes the flurry of unanswered questions that take us to the brink at the essay's conclusion. The inquiry is the more anguished and poignant for being left open-ended.

Timothy Douglas is an African American whose range and versatility in the theatre lead to major backstage insights. Douglas gives two detailed versions of the interracial dilemmas of colorblind casting — one from his perspective as a black actor in tension with a white director, the other from his perspective as a black director discussing the racial implications of the performance relationship between a white and a black actress. In addition, Douglas's work as a whole places us in the potential minefield between Shakespeare and August Wilson, whose final play, *Radio Golf* (2005), Douglas directed at the Yale Repertory Theater in April 2005. Unwilling to give up either, Douglas manages to bridge the gap. Though the process is cut short by Wilson's death on October 2, 2005,[7] Douglas's achievement of breadth involves an implicit negotiation of difference with August Wilson:

> He and I have had very different journeys, and I have seen things and experienced things that either he hadn't or he simply wasn't interested in: things that I have found great value in, including this idea of people of color moving through a Eurocentric playwright and finding valuable lessons in it and being able to illuminate it. ... But I never felt that I was in opposition to August Wilson, and he knew my work. Unbeknownst to me, he had been traveling around seeing productions of my shows.

... My feeling was that if he knew my history then he didn't feel that my beliefs were going to get in the way of being able to interpret his work. (Douglas, this volume)

For me, Timothy Douglas's discussion of August Wilson is the emotional nexus in the present volume. Given the standard perception of Wilson's rigidity with respect to colorblind casting, Douglas's testimony about Wilson's willingness to collaborate with someone who did not share his views on the matter suggests flexibility.

Despite coming from different directions, Ocampo-Guzman and Douglas have an extraordinary point of convergence in Shakespeare & Company, the small regional theatre in Lenox, Massachusetts, in the Berkshires at the western end of the state, in a county whose economy depends on a network of cultural institutions.[8] Both launched their careers at Shakespeare & Company, with Douglas having spent the five years 1986–1990 there and Ocampo-Guzman the three years 1993–1995.[9] In terms of the company's overall history to date, these years fall in the middle segment.

Shakespeare & Company was founded in 1978; in 2001, it began the move from the original site at Edith Wharton's home, The Mount, with its outdoor stage, to a new location with an indoor theatre.[10] With reference to Douglas's account, the relocation means that the rain problem has been eliminated! Also, though at times uneven and attenuated, the commitment to multiracial casting is ongoing. In its twenty-eighth season, 2005, the mainstage production of *King John* included three black actors in the roles of Philip Faulconbridge the Bastard, Hubert de Burgh, and Blanche of Spain; the actor playing the first of these came close to stealing the show.[11] However limited, Shakespeare & Company's effort is important in part because it is intertwined with Joseph Papp's multiracial goals in New York City; Helen Epstein documents significant points of contact and overlap between Papp and Tina Packer (11, 34–35, 97–99).[12]

Renewing the Debate

Despite the 1997 forum "Beyond the Wilson–Brustein Debate," we are not beyond August Wilson.[13] As the number of contributors to this volume who refer to Wilson indicates, it is still necessary to revisit Wilson's forceful rejection of colorblind casting, as well as the larger discussion that provides a context for this specific stance. Without retracting his statement on colorblind casting, Wilson subsequently noted that the colorblind issue distracted from the more general argument he was making: "That became the lightening rod that everyone focused on as if that was the only thing I was saying. I think it muddled the speech. So leaving that aside would force people to focus on what I was really saying" (quoted in Shannon and Williams, 195).

August Wilson's position is mischaracterized as separatist. Apart from Wilson's explicit denial during the debate, his deep, abiding commitment to Romare Bearden's art for his collagist dramatic technique places him squarely in the tradition of Ralph Ellison's and Albert Murray's approach to African American culture as a vital part of American culture as a whole.[14] Bearden is a constant presence at the center of Wilson's work, from his discovery of Bearden in 1977 to his final interview.[15] When explaining what he means by "universal," Wilson cites Bearden as his touchstone: "The life I know best is black American life and through Bearden I realized that you could arrive at the universal through the specific" (Wilson 1994, 75).

Wilson negotiates the narrow gap between separatism and conventional universalism by distinguishing two kinds of universalism: one monolithic, the other genuinely plural. Wilson finds that the standard version is effectively a white universalism that cannot serve as "common ground." Instead, Wilson insists on an alternate definition that draws on multiple cultural strands — "a value system that is inclusive of all Americans and recognizes their unique and valuable contributions" (Wilson 1996, 28).[16] From the idea of multiplicity, Wilson's rejection of colorblind casting follows. I think it is possible to disagree with the absoluteness of this rejection, yet still wholeheartedly accept Wilson's searing indictment of colorblindness as erasure, negation, and insult. Wilson's assertions are right on the mark in emphasizing the value of seeing as a form of human recognition: "We want you to see us" (Wilson 1996, 32); and again, "*See* my color. Look at me. I'm not ashamed of who I am and what I am" (quoted in Lahr, 51).

The director Lloyd Richards explains the disagreement between Robert Brustein and August Wilson over colorblind casting as a historical difference: "I called Brustein a 1930's liberal. August was a 1960's liberal" (quoted in Nesmith, 293). But, from our current perspective, Brustein might more accurately be described as a 1980s neoconservative. For example, Brustein's use of Martin Luther King against Wilson — "I am among those who long for a time when, as King so majestically said, African-Americans — indeed all Americans — will be judged by the content of their character rather than the color of their skin" — is shaped by Shelby Steele's *Content of Our Character*, which decontextualizes King's language by removing King's accompanying sense of ongoing political struggle against entrenched institutional forces (Brustein 1996a, 82).[17]

Brustein's "longing" for the desired future is shifted to the immediate present in his peremptory rhetorical question, "Isn't there some kind of statute of limitations on white guilt and white reparations?" (Brustein 1996b, 100). The question amounts to an announcement that he wants the issue of white privilege magically to vanish, but the subject of whiteness is ruled out of bounds on a technicality. As the legalistic metaphor indicates, Brustein expects the clean slate of immunity and absolution to be granted automatically, without doing the work. The term "white guilt" generates its opposite, "white innocence." Yet both terms are unhelpful: the guilt basks in self-pity, the innocence is manifestly unearned, and together they block investigation, analysis, and assessment.

In addition to revisiting August Wilson, we must also reformulate the debate because the other side, as represented by Robert Brustein, is unproductive. More promising, I think, is to imagine a hypothetical dialogue between August Wilson and Joseph Papp, who, given the limited number of black characters in Shakespeare, promoted colorblind casting in an effort to extend the opening for black actors achieved by Paul Robeson. Putting Papp in conversation with Wilson provides a different historical perspective. When we consider the painfully long history from the original white actor in blackface who played Othello in 1604 to Paul Robeson's breakthrough performance as the first black Othello to appear in a mainstream venue in the United States on October 19, 1943, the two subsequent steps from Robeson to Papp and from Papp to Wilson involve extremely short time spans.[18]

Listen to this: "I don't like 'integration' on the stage because what you get is tokenism. Real integration comes from power, when there is equal justice, equal opportunity, not 'token' opportunity. ... If you form a fine company that has its own excellence ... that, to me, is integration." It sounds almost like August Wilson, but the speaker is Joe Papp. Identifying himself "as a white person," Papp expresses dissatisfaction with token gestures such as colorblind casting and proposes the formation of an all-black company (quoted in Epstein 1994, 355–358). As a practical reality, the venture quickly collapsed, but the take-home message about the difference between tokenism and substantive power still stands and places Papp in proximity to August Wilson.

Doing the Double Take

The reformatted image of Denzel Washington in the frontispiece of this volume prompts a smile of recognition that we can't put on blinders: we take notice of his color. The optical humor continues with the realization that Washington the actor occupies the author position. The Droeshout pose makes us expect the familiar sight from the title page of the 1623 First Folio, yet also registers its disruption by exposing and challenging Shakespeare's implied whiteness. By going all the way to the top, this revised image serves as a visual emblem of the expanded scope for ownership that goes beyond the minor adjustments of small-scale colorblind casting.[19]

The Washington/Shakespeare double take leads to the Washington/Wilson double take, for the black man who has literally taken over authorship is August Wilson. His challenge has a point: colorblind casting can be a token gesture if disconnected from the larger picture of the ways in which institutional power remains structured in white dominance. What makes us take Wilson's point seriously is that he backs it up by creating a new center of cultural power through his own plays. Wilson's dramatic work demonstrates that Shakespeare is not the only game in town; we have alternatives, multiple options. This larger playing field changes the stakes: it is no longer necessary to be satisfied with circumscribed forms of colorblind Shakespeare. We can instead aim for a wider critical rethinking in the context of a larger vision of what is possible.

Notes

1. A case in point concerns divergent accounts of racism in *Othello*. The consensus view confines the source of racism to Iago, who is singled out and punished as an isolated scapegoat in the conclusion, and credits Shakespeare with exposing it. An alternate version sees racism as more widely distributed in the play's society because it takes more subtle forms than the blatant stance expressed by Iago; through its multiple points of origin, this broad-based racism exceeds the play's unequivocal critical control, thereby introducing the blind spot. For a detailed discussion, see Erickson (2002).

2. The controversial nature of colorblind casting is brought home by opposition to the racial reversal in which Huck Finn is played by a black and Jim by a white, as reported in Mui.

3. In addition to the essays in this volume, complex assessments of colorblind casting include Albanese, Worthen, and MacDonald.

4. Colour, color, *n.*, definition I.2.a., *Oxford English Dictionary*, 2nd ed. (Oxford: Clarendon, 1989), vol. 3, p. 499. The chief point is that the question of whether white is a color remains thoroughly ambiguous and hence elusive.

5. Key accounts are Callaghan, Royster, and Parker. Parker's contribution is important because it shows how racial images are lodged in the deep structures of language and hence reside at a level that is independent of the specific racial status of individual characters.

6. *Latin American Shakespeares*, edited by Kliman and Santos provides useful background.

7. See Isherwood for an obituary. Luminous responses to Wilson's death include those of Lloyd Richards in Nesmith, Parks, and Alexander (2006). In an odd way, Wilson's opposition to colorblind casting has the effect of linking him more closely to Shakespeare: as Elizabeth Alexander puts it, "he chiseled something that will stand like Shakespeare" (125).

8. The most prominent cultural institutions in Berkshire County are, by category: music, Tanglewood; dance, Jacob's Pillow; theatre cluster, Barrington Stage Company, Berkshire Theatre Festival, Shakespeare & Company, Williamstown Theatre Festival; art cluster, Williams College Museum of Art, Clark Art Institute, MASS MoCA (Massachusetts Museum of Contemporary Art). The problem of racial representation and inclusiveness runs across all these institutions, which have addressed the issue in their program content with varying degrees of success.

9. The plays to which Douglas and Ocampo-Guzman refer can be located in the year-by-year timeline of "Performance History," the last item in the left-hand column on the front page of the website www.shakespeare.org.

10. The two principal sources on Shakespeare & Company are Epstein (1985) and the company's website. Epstein's book is badly out of date. It effectively stops in 1980 with the third season, whose *Tempest* is reviewed in Erickson (1981), and it lacks the depth and substance of Epstein's later *Joe Papp: An American Life* (1994).

11. The three parts in *King John* were played, respectively, by Peter Macon, Kenajuan Bentley, and Ashley Bryant. However, since all three were in their first season at Shakespeare & Company, their participation also reflects the absence of black actors in the core group of long-term members of the company.

12. Epstein (1994, 486–487) notes Papp's failure and Packer's success in seeking Ford Foundation support.

13. "Beyond the Wilson-Brustein Debate" (1997), including the introduction by Erika Munk, consists of seven pieces. To revisit August Wilson is not to exempt him from the serious criticism articulated by Margo Jefferson, Stanley Crouch, Eugene Nesmith, and Clinton Turner Davis in this special section.

14. The Wilson–Brustein debate played out over four issues of *American Theatre* 13, nos. 7–10 (September–December 1996), which allowed for additional responses by Wilson and Brustein, as well as for responses by others. A second important speech by Wilson (1997) was published in *Callaloo*.
15. The discovery is recorded in Wilson's Foreword to Schwartzman, *Romare Bearden* (Wilson 1990, 8–9). For the evocation of Bearden see Wilson's comments in the final interview with Suzan-Lori Parks after the announcement of his terminal illness (Parks, 25). Additional commentary on Wilson's response to Bearden includes Rocha and Fishman.
16. Similar terms are used in Wilson's second speech: "We are not willing to talk about a single value system that posits European Americans at the center of the universe. ... We can talk about a single value system that recognizes and encompasses the contribution that all of the various ethnic groups in America have made toward the material and spiritual health of an 'American' culture" (1997, 490).
17. Brustein not only quotes King but also echoes Steele.
18. See the chapter "The Broadway *Othello* (1942–1943)" in Duberman (263–279). Two brief references in Epstein (1994, 49, 69) link Papp's early career to the context of the Robeson phenomenon.
19. Elizabeth Alexander's remarkable essay "Denzel" in her book *The Black Interior* (2004, 151–174) shows how difficult it is for Denzel Washington to control the meanings of the cinematic positioning of his black body. A specific Shakespearean instance is the Kenneth Branagh racial scenario in the film of *Much Ado About Nothing* by which Washington, locked in the Don Pedro role, is so visually bracketed — as the isolated black man — in the final camera shot rising upward. How could we be colorblind if the camera fixes on the coincidence that the character excluded from the marital festivity is played by the actor who just happens to be black?

References

Albanese, Denise. "Black and White, and Dread All Over: The Shakespeare Theatre's 'Photo-negative' *Othello* and the Body of Desdemona." In *A Feminist Companion to Shakespeare*, edited by Dympna Callaghan. Malden, MA: Blackwell, 2000.

Alexander, Elizabeth. *The Black Interior*. Saint Paul: Greywolf, 2004.

Alexander, Elizabeth. "The One Who Went Before: Remembering the Playwright August Wilson, 1945–2005." *American Scholar* 75 (2006): 122–125.

"Beyond the Wilson-Brustein Debate." *Theater* 27, nos. 2–3 (1997): 9–41.

Brown, Michael K., et al. *Whitewashing Race: The Myth of a Color-Blind Society*. Berkeley: University of California Press, 2003.

Brustein, Robert. "Forum." *American Theatre* 13 (1996a): 62–63, 81–82.

Brustein, Robert. "Subsidized Separatism." *American Theatre* 39 (1996b): 26–27, 100–101.

Burns, Christy. "Suturing over Racial Difference: Problems for a Colorblind Approach in a Visual Culture." *Discourse: Journal for Theoretical Studies in Media and Culture* 22 (2000): 70–91.

Callaghan, Dympna. "'Othello Was a White Man': Properties of Race on Shakespeare's Stage." In *Alternative Shakespeares, Volume 2*, edited by Terence Hawkes. London and New York: Routledge, 1996.

Duberman, Martin. *Paul Robeson*. New York: Knopf, 1988.

Epstein, Helen. *The Company She Keeps: Tina Packer Builds a Theater*. Cambridge: Plunkett Lake, 1985.

Epstein, Helen. *Joe Papp: An American Life*. Boston: Little, Brown, 1994.

Erickson, Peter. "Images of White Identity in *Othello*." In *Othello: New Critical Essays*, edited by Philip C. Kolin. London and New York: Routledge, 2002.

Erickson, Peter. "A *Tempest* at The Mount." *Shakespeare Quarterly* 32 (1981): 188–190.

Fishman, Joan. "Romare Bearden, August Wilson, and the Traditions of African Performance." In *May All Your Gates Have Fences: Essays on the Drama of August Wilson*, edited by Alan Nadel. Iowa City: University of Iowa Press, 1994.

Isherwood, Charles. "August Wilson, Theater's Poet of Black America, Is Dead at 60." *New York Times*, October 3, 2005.

Kliman, Bernice W., and Rick J. Santos, eds. *Latin American Shakespeares*. Madison, NJ: Fairleigh Dickinson University Press, 2005.

Lahr, John. "Been Here and Gone." *New Yorker*, April 16, 2001, 50–65.

MacDonald, Joyce Green. "Bodies, Race, and Performance in Derek Walcott's *A Branch of the Blue Nile*." *Theatre Journal* 57 (2005): 191–203.

Mui, Ylan Q. "Colorblind Casting Roils 'Big River': Licensing Group Objects to Md. School's Musical." *Washington Post*, May 21, 2005.

Nesmith, N. Graham. "Lloyd Richards: Reminiscence of a Theatre Life and Beyond." *African American Review* 39 (2005): 281–298.

Parker, Patricia. "Black *Hamlet*: Battening on the Moor." *Shakespeare Studies* 31 (2003): 127–164.

Parks, Suzan-Lori. "The Light in August: An Interview." *American Theatre* 29 (2005): 22–25, 74–78.

Rocha, Mark Williams. "August Wilson and the Four B's." In *August Wilson: A Casebook*, edited by Marilyn Elkins. New York: Garland, 2000.

Royster, Francesca. "'White-Limed Walls': Whiteness and Gothic Extremism in *Titus Andronicus*." *Shakespeare Quarterly* 51 (2000): 432–455.

Shannon, Sandra G., and Dana A. Williams. "A Conversation with August Wilson." In *August Wilson and Black Aesthetics*, edited by Dana A. Williams and Sandra G. Shannon. New York: Palgrave, 2004.

Steele, Shelby. *Content of Our Character: A New Vision of Race in America*. New York: St. Martin's, 1990.

Williams, Patricia J. *Seeing a Color-Blind Future: The Paradox of Race*. New York: Farrar, Straus and Giroux, 1998.

Wilson, August. "The Art of Theater XIV." *Paris Review* 41 (1994): 66–94.

Wilson, August. "Foreword." In Myron Schwartzman, *Romare Bearden: His Life and Art*. New York: Abrams, 1990.

Wilson, August. *The Ground on Which I Stand*. New York: Theatre Communications Group, 1996.

Wilson, August. "National Black Theater Festival, 1997." *Callaloo* 20 (1997): 483–492.

Wilson, August. "Radio Golf." *American Theatre* 22 (2005): 87–108.

Worthen, W. B. *Shakespeare and the Force of Modern Performance*. Cambridge: Cambridge University Press, 2003.

Notes on Contributors

Lisa M. Anderson is Associate Professor in Women and Gender Studies at Arizona State University, with a part-time appointment in Theatre. She has published articles on African American Theatre in *Theatre Research International* and *Journal of Dramatic Theory and Criticism*, and her first book, *Mammies No More: The Changing Image of Black Women on Stage and Screen*, was published in 1997. She is currently completing *Black Feminism in Contemporary Drama*, to be published by the University of Illinois Press.

Richard Burt is Professor of English and Film and Media Studies at the University of Florida. He is the author of *Unspeakable ShaXXXspeares: Queer Theory and American Kiddie Culture* (1999) and of numerous articles and book chapters on Shakespeare, film, and mass media. He most recently edited *Shakespeares after Shakespeare: An Encyclopedia of the Bard in Mass Media and Popular Culture* (2006) and co-edited *Shakespeare, the Movie, II* (2003). Burt is presently finishing two books, *The Remains of the Play: Alluding to Shakespeare in Transnational Cinema and Television* and *Movie Medievalism*.

Krystyna Kujawinska Courtney is currently the Head of the British and Commonwealth Studies Department at the University of Lodz and Professor of British Literature at the Warsaw University. She is the author of two monographs, *"The Interpretation of the Time": The Dramaturgy of Shakespeare's Roman Plays* (1993) and *Shakespeare's English History Plays in English and Polish Theatrical Renditions* (1997); a dictionary of critical and literary terms (Russia, 1998); and several articles published in Poland and abroad (e.g., *Shakespeare Jahrbuch, Shakespeare Worldwide*, and *Shakespeare Bulletin*). In 2004 she became the co-editor of *Multicultural Shakespeare: Translation, Appropriation and Performance* (formerly: *Worldwide Shakespeare*), an annual international publication.

Celia R. Daileader is Associate Professor of English at Florida State University. She is author of *Racism, Misogyny, and the Othello Myth: Inter-racial Couples from Shakespeare to Spike Lee* (2005) and *Eroticism on the Renaissance Stage: Transcendence, Desire, and the Limits of the Visible* (1998), and is co-editor with Gary Taylor of John Fletcher's *The Tamer Tamed, or the Woman's Prize* (forthcoming). She has also published numerous articles on feminism, critical race studies, and Renaissance literature.

Timothy Douglas is a freelance theatre director, actor, and educator who has directed more than seventy productions for the theatre. He has held faculty positions at the University of Southern California, DePaul University, the American Conservatory Theater, and the New Zealand Drama School, among others. He has also served as the Associate Artistic Director for the Actors Theatre of Louisville. He directed the world premiere of August Wilson's *Radio Golf.*

Peter Erickson is the author of *Patriarchal Structures in Shakespeare's Drama* (1985) and *Rewriting Shakespeare, Rewriting Ourselves* (1991), and the co-editor of *Shakespeare's "Rough Magic"* (1985), *Early Modern Visual Culture: Representation, Race, and Empire in Renaissance England* (2000), and *Approaches to Teaching Shakespeare's* Othello (2005). His book *Citing Shakespeare: The Reinterpretation of Race in Contemporary Literature and Art* will be published by Palgrave Macmillan.

Margo Hendricks is Associate Professor of Literature at the University of California at Santa Cruz. She is co-editor of *Women, Race, and Writing in the Early Modern Period* (1994). She has published on Marlowe, Shakespeare, race and Renaissance culture, and Aphra Behn. She has completed a study of race, color passing, and early modern English literature. Her current research explores race, performance, and Shakespeare. A future project will examine women of African ancestry in Renaissance English culture.

Sujata Iyengar is Associate Professor of English at the University of Georgia. Her book *Shades of Difference: Mythologies of Skin Color in Early Modern England* (2005) explores the cultural mythologies of skin color in early modern Britain. She is currently writing a dictionary of Shakespeare's medical language for Continuum Press, and she is co-founder and co-editor of the online journal *Borrowers and Lenders: The Journal of Shakespeare and Appropriation.*

Courtney Lehmann is Associate Professor of English and Director of the Pacific Humanities Center at the University of the Pacific. She is the author of *Shakespeare Remains: Theater to Film, Early Modern to Postmodern* (2002), as well as co-editor, with Lisa S. Starks, of *Spectacular Shakespeare: Critical Theory and Popular Cinema* (2002) and *The Reel Shakespeare: Alternative Cinema and Theory* (2002). Her recent work focuses on the intersection of Shakespeare, film, and globalization.

Ania Loomba is the Catherine Bryson Professor of English at the University of Pennsylvania. She researches and teaches the histories and literatures of race, gender, colonialism, and nation formation from the sixteenth century to the present. Her publications include *Colonialism/Postcolonialism* (1998) and

Shakespeare, Race and Colonialism (2002). She co-edited *Postcolonial Shakespeares* (1998) and is co-editing a documentary companion to the study of race in early modern England.

Antonio Ocampo-Guzman is an actor, director, and teacher from Bogotá, Colombia. He currently serves as the Head of MFA Performance for the School of Theatre and Film at Arizona State University. He is also a Designated Linklater Voice teacher and a member of Shakespeare & Company in Lenox, Massachusetts.

Angela C. Pao is Associate Professor of Comparative Literature at Indiana University-Bloomington. She is the author of *The Orient of the Boulevards: Exoticism, Empire and 19th-Century French Theater* (1998). Her articles on race and ethnicity in twentieth-century American theatre have appeared in *Theatre Survey, Theatre Journal, Theatre Topics, Text and Performance Quarterly,* and *Amerasia Journal.* She is currently completing a book on nontraditional casting practices, provisionally titled *No Safe Spaces: Re-casting Race, Ethnicity and Nationality,* and she is serving on the MLA Drama Division executive committee.

Francesca T. Royster is Associate Professor of English at DePaul University in Chicago. Her areas of expertise include Shakespeare studies, women's studies, African American performance, and popular culture. She is the author of *Becoming Cleopatra: The Shifting Image of an Icon* (2003), and her numerous essays and reviews have appeared in *Shakespeare Quarterly, Shakespeare Studies, Approaches to Teaching Shakespeare's* Othello, *American Sexuality,* and *Talking Back/Acting Out: Women Negotiate the Media.* Her latest book project focuses on eccentric sexualities in contemporary black popular performance, including Michael Jackson and Grace Jones.

Ayanna Thompson is Assistant Professor of English and Women's Studies at Arizona State University. She specializes in early modern drama and focuses on depictions of race in the Renaissance. Her essays and reviews have appeared in *Shakespeare Quarterly, Renaissance Quarterly, Textus,* and *Arthuriana.* She has recently completed a book that analyzes how explicit theatrical depictions of torture reveal contradictory constructions of race. She has begun another book that examines the way popular culture addresses issues of race through Shakespearean texts, appropriations, and adaptations.

Index